Portland City Walks

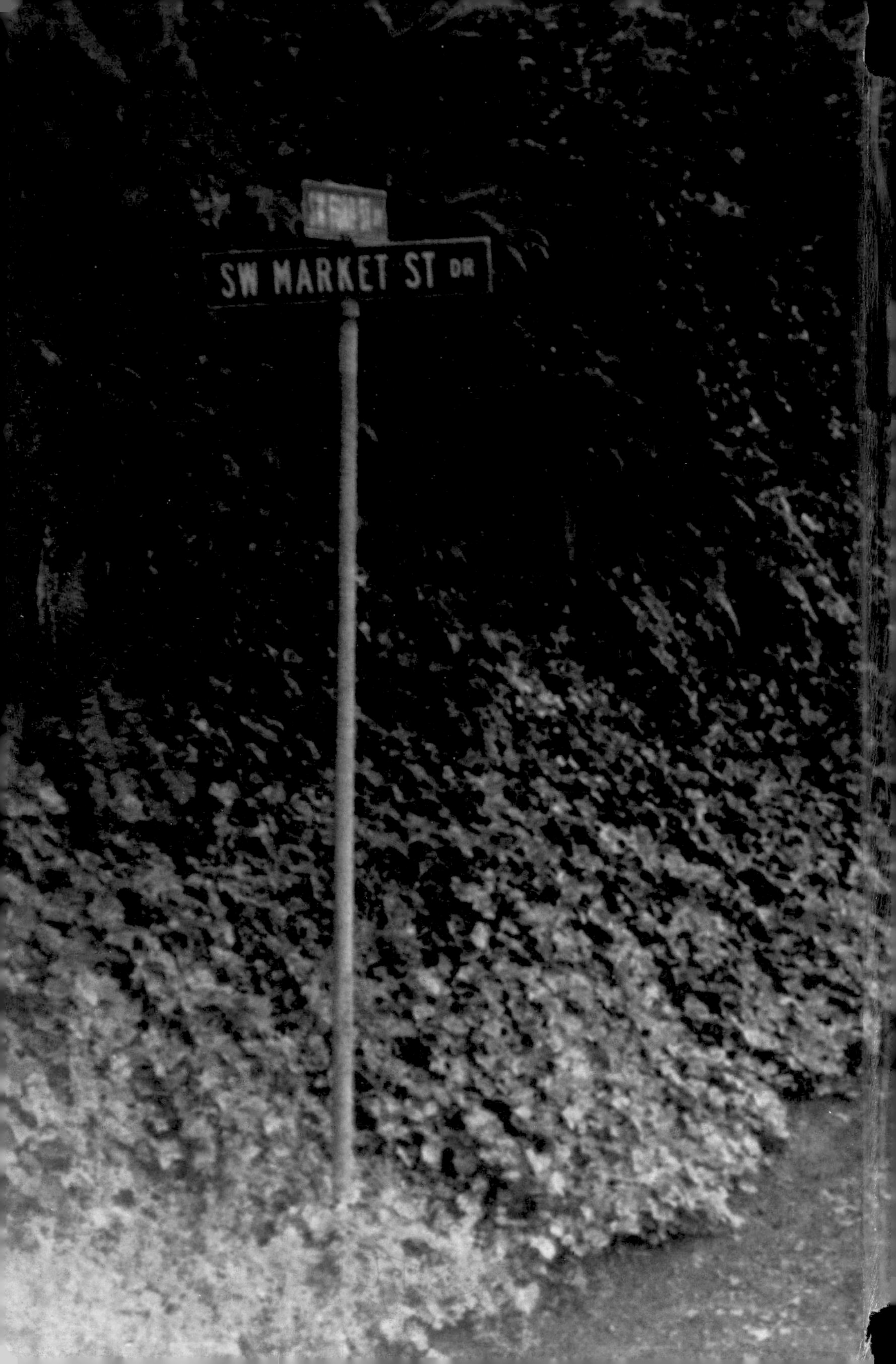
SW MARKET ST DR

Portland
CITY
WALKS

TWENTY EXPLORATIONS
IN AND AROUND TOWN

LAURA O. FOSTER

TIMBER PRESS
Portland * London

REGIONAL
ARTS & CULTURE
COUNCIL

This book is funded in part by the Regional Arts and Culture Council.

Frontispiece: Looking down Ford Street Drive, the last bit of unpaved road in Portland's Goose Hollow neighborhood. Photo by Zeb Andrews.

Published in 2008 by Timber Press, Inc.

The Haseltine Building
133 S.W. Second Avenue, Suite 450
Portland, Oregon 97204-3527
www.timberpress.com

2 The Quadrant
135 Salusbury Road
London NW6 6RJ
www.timberpress.co.uk

ISBN-13: 978-0-88192-885-3

Printed in China

Library of Congress Cataloging-in-Publication Data

Foster, Laura O.
  Portland city walks : twenty explorations in and around town / Laura O. Foster.
    p. cm.
  Includes bibliographical references and index.
  ISBN-13: 978-0-88192-885-3
  1. Portland (Or.)--Tours. 2. Walking--Oregon--Portland--Guidebooks. 3. Architecture--Oregon--Portland--Guidebooks. 4. Portland (Or.)--Buildings, structures, etc.--Guidebooks. I. Title.
  F884.P83F67 2008
  917.95'49--dc22   2008009644

To citizen activists who work to make the cities in this book walkable, beautiful, and less reliant on automobiles—thank you! We all benefit from your efforts.

CONTENTS

Foreword by Sam Adams   9
Preface   10
Overview Map   13

North Portland
   WALK 1   Kenton to Swan Island Beach Loop   14
   WALK 2   Piedmont and Overlook Loops   28

Northeast and Southeast Portland
   WALK 3   Fernhill Park to Alberta Street Loop   42
   WALK 4   Irvington to Sullivan's Gulch Loop   52
   WALK 5   Rose City Park, Beaumont, and Hollywood Loop   70
   WALK 6   Buckman to Kerns Loop   84
   WALK 7   Laurelhurst to Belmont Street Loop   98
   WALK 8   Ladd's Addition to Hawthorne Boulevard Loop   112
   WALK 9   Grand Avenue Historic District to Eastbank Esplanade Loop   126
   WALK 10   Brooklyn to Sellwood Loop   140

Southwest and Northwest Portland
   WALK 11   South Portland to South Waterfront Park Loop   152
   WALK 12   Goose Hollow to King's Hill Loop   170
   WALK 13   Nob Hill Loop   184
   WALK 14   Pearl District to Slabtown Loop   200

Beyond Portland

WALK 15   Garden Home to Raleigh Hills Loop   214
WALK 16   Beaverton Loop   224
WALK 17   Forest Grove Loop   236
WALK 18   Lake Oswego Loop   248
WALK 19   Oregon City Loop   262
WALK 20   Vancouver Loop   276

Acknowledgments   291
Glossary of Architectural Terms   293
Bibliography   302
Index   310

FOREWORD by Sam Adams

Many people come to Portland because you can hike, ski, and bike with at most a short drive from this distinctly livable city. But leaving Portland isn't necessary to experience the treasures of the Pacific Northwest. Within ten minutes of walking out your own door, you can lose yourself in beautiful tree-lined neighborhoods of historic houses and friendly homegrown shops and restaurants.

In my years in city hall, it has been an honor to support, help preserve, and build Portland's many communities. Meandering through each of Portland's fifty unique neighborhoods by bike or on foot sets a good pace for getting to know how each one makes a distinct contribution to the texture of our city.

Laura Foster's *Portland City Walks* is more than a good walking guide: it tells the stories of Portland's neighborhoods and surrounding towns. Let this book and her earlier *Portland Hill Walks* help you explore and learn more about our beautiful city. *Portland City Walks* covers diverse neighborhoods—on one walk, you learn about stately houses owned by early wealthy residents; on another you explore an eclectic mix of churches, synagogues, rose gardens, and community centers; and on yet another you follow the tracks of rail spur lines that once carried hemp, wool, and hops to local industries. My favorite walk takes you through industrial areas and a company town that has since been incorporated into Portland. Walk, eat, and shop along old streetcar lines, stroll where the Mount Hood Freeway isn't, and discover which companies originated in Portland, who immigrated here, and why.

I enjoy that *Portland City Walks* starts off in my neighborhood, Kenton. Kenton has a long and rich history, and I'm happy to share both Kenton and Portland with you.

Sam Adams was the Portland city commissioner in charge of transportation and environmental services from 2004 through 2008. Starting in 2009, he will serve as mayor of Portland.

PREFACE

When I moved to Portland, sight unseen, in the late 1980s, I couldn't believe I had found such a place—where natural beauty wasn't at the end of a four-hour drive. Why wasn't it crowded? Why were homes so affordable? Never mind there were already 400,000 people here, I felt like I'd discovered a secret Shangri-la of perfect weather (I love clouds), neighborhoods with personalities, and people who love books and nature and don't ask, "What do you do?" in the first five minutes of conversation.

A few things have changed: since 1990, 125,000 people have moved to Portland, homes are no longer affordable, and while we have a marvelous system of parks and greenspaces, infill means fewer open places in the close-in neighborhoods. And in the next twenty years another 75,000 people are expected to move to Multnomah County, and an even greater number are likely to move to the faster-growing Washington County. What will they find?

They'll find an urban geography made better by the people who inhabit it, and neighborhoods and towns where people recognize the gifts of nature and the responsibilities of citizenship. That's what I found when I began writing *Portland City Walks* in 2005. As with my first book, *Portland Hill Walks*, I would come home after exploring an outlying town such as Forest Grove or a Portland neighborhood like Piedmont and be ready to sell my house and move. So many great places! I'm excited to share my explorations with you, and hope you'll enjoy making your own discoveries. I avoid places other people tell me I must see, and usually am rewarded with the dead end that leads to a magical path through the woods, or the tucked-away commercial area where you can get a plate of hummus prepared by an emigrant from Bethlehem, or the historic district that I had never even heard of, among other wonderful experiences.

The walks cover neighborhoods throughout the city and five outlying towns. The disparity between the number of walks on Portland's west and east sides reflects the fact that the hilly west side was the star of *Portland Hill Walks*. In this book the walks are generally flat, but a few have significant elevation gain. Nine walks explore districts on the National Register of Historic Places, and two feature Portland conservation districts, intact areas of architectural and historical significance to the city. Because of the architecturally rich nature of many of the walks, an appendix of architectural terms is included. I am not an architect, just a fan. Descriptions of building styles are a bit subjective, but with the help of Portland historian William Willingham, and Virginia and Lee McAlester's *A Field Guide to American Houses*, I think this book achieves one of my goals, fostering a greater understanding and appreciation of our built environment. As in *Portland Hill Walks*, the basics for each walk are outlined at the start: restrooms, commercial districts where you can find food and shopping, distance, and other necessary information. Public transit information of a general nature is also given for each route. For personalized trip-planning assistance, call TriMet at 503-238-7433, or for information on bus and MAX (light-rail) routes, visit www.trimet.org. One vital bit of information: restrooms in parks are often closed in winter.

I'm a fan of immersion in a place, of spending enough time to soak up the local zeitgeist, so I've included at the start of each walk information about the best times to visit—so that you can combine your walk with Last Thursday on NE Alberta Street, for example—plus details of nearby historical or cultural attractions, such as the Stevens-Crawford Heritage House in Oregon City. Devote a day to a walk and you'll feel, as I often did, that you have just treated yourself to a small vacation.

Many of the walks are longer than those in *Portland Hill Walks* but can be shortened by using the map to return to the starting point. A handful are less than 4 miles; most are between 4 and 6 miles; and the longest, Walk 8, is 6.6 miles. After a bit of gentle prodding from my brother-in-law, Mike Foster, I tried to ensure that the walks are generally accessible. For stairs, unpaved trails, busy roads without sidewalks, or other obviously inaccessible portions, I've provided alternatives. However, I have not watched for missing curb cuts, uneven sidewalks, or other impediments to complete accessibility, so please use caution.

When I lead walks or give a presentation about a city neighborhood, people often ask how I got the idea to write my books. I credit a few sources: *Stairway Walks in San Francisco* by Adah Bakalinsky, *Portland's Little Red Book of Stairs* by Stefana Young, and *Romewalks* by Anya Shetterly. I took *Romewalks* on a solo trip to Rome in 1998, and it took me away from other tourists onto backstreets and into neighborhood parks where I sat and watched Romans do what Romans do. Later, after working as an editor for a local publisher for a few years, and seeing other books get published (some of which needed a serious amount of work), I thought, "If they can do it, so can I." I wrote a sample chapter, researched potential markets for a book of Portland neighborhood walks, and found a wonderful partner in Timber Press, who agreed that a book exploring Portland was probably a good bet.

Not surprisingly, a lot of other Portlanders love the city as much as I do, and the first book's success spawned this book. I hope you'll enjoy exploring Portland and surrounding towns as much as I have. I'd love to hear what you discover, and also of any updates to information in the text. Reach me at www.timberpress.com or www.portlandhillwalks.com.

See you out there!

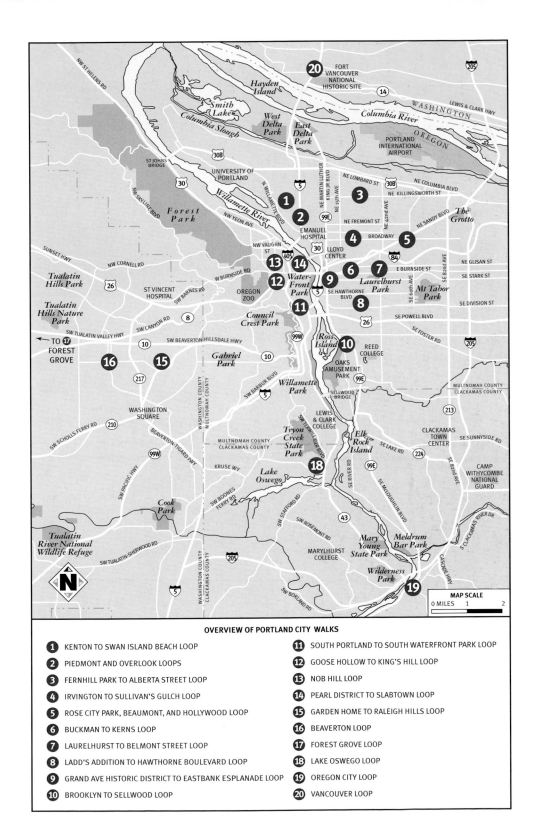

OVERVIEW OF PORTLAND CITY WALKS

1 KENTON TO SWAN ISLAND BEACH LOOP

2 PIEDMONT AND OVERLOOK LOOPS

3 FERNHILL PARK TO ALBERTA STREET LOOP

4 IRVINGTON TO SULLIVAN'S GULCH LOOP

5 ROSE CITY PARK, BEAUMONT, AND HOLLYWOOD LOOP

6 BUCKMAN TO KERNS LOOP

7 LAURELHURST TO BELMONT STREET LOOP

8 LADD'S ADDITION TO HAWTHORNE BOULEVARD LOOP

9 GRAND AVE HISTORIC DISTRICT TO EASTBANK ESPLANADE LOOP

10 BROOKLYN TO SELLWOOD LOOP

11 SOUTH PORTLAND TO SOUTH WATERFRONT PARK LOOP

12 GOOSE HOLLOW TO KING'S HILL LOOP

13 NOB HILL LOOP

14 PEARL DISTRICT TO SLABTOWN LOOP

15 GARDEN HOME TO RALEIGH HILLS LOOP

16 BEAVERTON LOOP

17 FOREST GROVE LOOP

18 LAKE OSWEGO LOOP

19 OREGON CITY LOOP

20 VANCOUVER LOOP

WALK 1

KENTON TO SWAN ISLAND BEACH LOOP

DISTANCE Variable, depending on the route. The walk as laid out is 6.1 miles. If only bluff-top areas are walked (see "Accessibility"), the walk is 3.1 miles to **9**, plus about 2 miles back to the starting point, for a total of 5.1 miles. If Swan Island alone is walked, the distance, one way, from **10** to **16**, is 3 miles, though this can be shortened by a bus ride up N Going Street.

STARTING POINT North Lombard Transit Center (MAX station), northbound platform: N Interstate Avenue and Lombard Street

GETTING THERE AND PARKING From downtown Portland, drive north on Interstate 5 to N Lombard Street westbound (Exit 305B). Take the first right onto N Montana Avenue, which parallels the west side of the freeway, and then a left onto N Russet Street. Park on Russet.

TriMet: Take the MAX Yellow Line to the North Lombard Transit Center.

RESTROOMS AND DRINKING FOUNTAINS Restrooms are at cafés in downtown Kenton (for customers), in Kenton Park (on the west side, near the playground), Columbia Annex Park, and at the Swan Island Lagoon boat dock (a portable toilet). Drinking fountains are at Columbia Annex Park and in restaurants on Swan Island (for customers).

FOOD AND DRINK Downtown Kenton offers various options, as does Swan Island, along N Anchor Street and N Channel Avenue.

BEST TIMES TO VISIT Take this walk on a weekend. Swan Island is industrial; along Basin Avenue and Going Street, traffic is nasty, noisy, and unceasing. On Sundays, however, island streets are much more enjoyable—so deserted, they'd

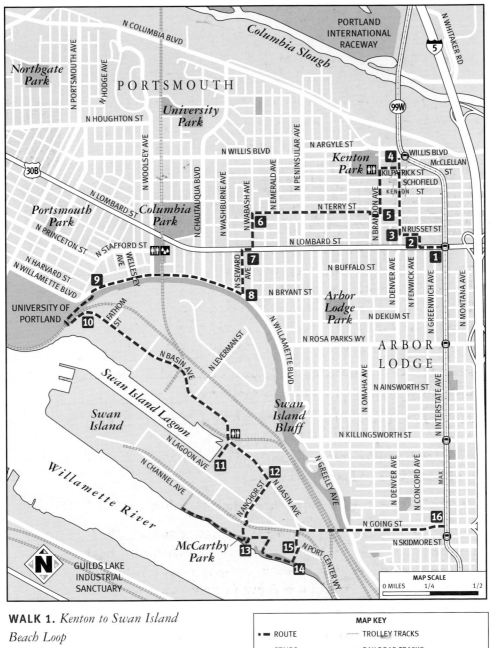

WALK 1. *Kenton to Swan Island Beach Loop*

MAP KEY

- ▪▪ ROUTE
- ▪▪▪▪ STAIRS
- ▪ ▪ TRAIL
- ⋯⋯ MAX TRACKS
- ⊜ MAX STATION
- ⋯⋯ STREETCAR TRACKS
- ⋯⋯⋯ TROLLEY TRACKS
- ⊞⊞⊞ RAILROAD TRACKS
- ▨ PARK/GREENSPACE
- ▨ HISTORIC/CONSERVATION DISTRICT
- 🛉 PUBLIC RESTROOM
- ⚲ WATER

make a great place to bring a novice bike rider for practice. In fact, the Oregon Bicycle Racing Association holds an annual criterium on Swan Island.

Also consider timing your walk with a barge launch. Visit River Renaissance (www.portlandonline.com/river) for times of launches from Gunderson, a barge manufacturer on the west bank of the Willamette, across from Swan Island's McCarthy Park. This site also lists other river-related events.

ACCESSIBILITY This long walk has one inaccessible portion, a steep trail at **9**, which makes for a natural point at which to split the walk into two separate, shorter walks: one above the bluff, the other below. To walk only in areas above Waud Bluff, at **9**, return via a route of your choosing to the start, or to the N Rosa Parks Way stop on the MAX line, and take the train north back to the starting point.

To visit only Swan Island, take MAX to the Prescott station at **16** and walk the route backward, up to **10**, returning to the MAX station via bus 85 (Swan Island), which stops at **10** (Monday through Friday only), or via the bus stop at **15**, bus 72 (Killingsworth/82nd Avenue), which runs daily.

CAUTION Construction of the Waud Bluff Trail (at **9**) is to begin in 2008; check with npGREENWAY (www.npgreenway.org) to ensure construction is complete. Until it is, the informal trail on Waud Bluff has an unprotected crossing of an active railroad track. Use extreme caution when crossing the track, and never cross next to a stationary train. If a long train is blocking the tracks, go back up the bluff and return at another time, after the pedestrian overpass above the tracks is completed.

THIS URBAN FIELD TRIP starts in Kenton, the only company town in Portland's city limits, and travels south to magnificent Willamette Boulevard, which runs along the top of an oak-and-madrona-forested bluff overlooking Mocks Bottom. The walk follows the bluff for about a mile before descending the Waud Bluff Trail to historic Swan Island. Although the swans fled as industry encroached, Swan Island still holds a surprising amount of interest, with close-up views of Portland's working waterfront.

Bring water and food, since opportunities to snack are limited. The walk is long, with two unremarkable stretches, but the lack of turns in those places provides an opportunity to put the book in a pack and walk fast. Bring binoculars; from the river bluff along Willamette Boulevard are far-reaching views of the city, the waterfront, and Forest Park, and at the waterfront you may want to get a closer look at the shipping activity in the lagoon and on the west side of the river.

1 From the northbound platform of the North Lombard Transit Center, cross N Interstate Avenue's southbound lane and walk west on N Lombard Street one block. The fields on the right belonged to Kenton School, a Portland public school that closed in 2005. In 2006 the school building was leased to De La Salle North Catholic High School for twenty years. The easternmost fields, with their proximity to the redeveloping Interstate Corridor, have been the target of development speculation.

From Lombard, turn right on N Fenwick Avenue to walk along the front of the school. This school was built in 1913 to serve children in the growing company town of the same name. As with most old school buildings in town, the decorative scrollwork, icons, and symbols are worth a close look.

The history of this area is connected to the history of Chicago-based Swift and Company, which came to Portland in 1906 when it bought the Union Meat Company, a group of five local butchers who had consolidated in 1892. Swift's subsidiary, the Kenwood Land Company, purchased 3400 acres along the Columbia River for a meatpacking plant, stockyards (the Union Stockyards), and planned residential area. (Swift's holdings spanned the area along Marine Drive, west of Interstate 5 and east of the railroad bridge; they included the Expo Center, which sits on land donated by Swift to be the Pacific International Livestock Exposition Center.)

On a rise to the south of the Columbia Slough, the Kenwood Land Company platted out Kenton (originally named Kenwood until it was discovered that the name was already in use in Oregon). Workers commuted to the riverside packing plant via a streetcar elevated on a trestle above the slough.

In 1908 the railroad bridges across the Willamette and Columbia Rivers went up, and Swift, through a subsidiary, platted out its industrial holdings and marketed them as ideal for manufacturing: close to rail, for transportation; and close to the river, for waste disposal. By 1911, Portland was livestock central for the Pacific Northwest, with fifteen hundred employed at Swift and ancillary companies such as Portland Cattle Loan and the Columbia Wool Basin Warehouse. By 1917, twelve industrial firms, including lumber mills, a safe and lock manufacturer, and a wood pipe manufacturer, operated in the slough. The Kenton commercial area became the business district for these industries and their employees.

In the 1950s the meatpacking industry changed with the introduction of refrigerated trucking and the decline of the railroads for meat distribution, and

Swift became less of a presence in Kenton. The automobile brought mobility, spelling doom for Kenton's small retailers in the old streetcar district along N Denver Avenue. In residential areas, short-term renters moved in where property owners once tended their homes. When Interstate 5 was built in 1964, Interstate and Denver Avenues became backwaters, and store owners were forced to close up shop. In 1966 Swift closed its plant, and the ten other slaughterhouses in the area soon followed. Downtown Kenton became known as a seamy place of taverns and transients, a place many Portlanders had only vaguely heard of.

In the 1970s, as elsewhere in Portland, Kenton residents acted to restore and protect their neighborhood, starting with the rehabilitation of its old firehouse. The derelict Kenton Hotel was refurbished and given National Register status in 1990. In starts and stalls, Kenton has worked to revitalize itself. In the early 2000s, with Portland's old neighborhoods almost universally on the ascendance, Kenton's turn came, with average home prices doubling between 2003 and 2008.

2 From Fenwick, turn left onto N Russet Street. At this intersection, stop to look at the many fine homes. At 1811 and 1835 Russet are beautiful Dutch Colonials, built in 1923 and 1917, respectively. They likely belonged to executives at Swift or other industries, who primarily settled on streets east of Denver Avenue, or on Denver itself.

Walk one block west on Russet. Ahead, at 7577 Denver, is a fine example of one of Kenton's claims to local fame: cast-stone buildings. This 1910 house uses a concrete mixture poured into forms to simulate hand-cut, rusticated ashlar (a square block of building stone). The effect is muted a bit on this home, as it has been painted. With advancements in the concrete industry at the end of the nineteenth century, cast stone grew in popularity. While it was often used as ornamentation, in the early 1900s it enjoyed a brief surge of popularity in Portland as an exterior siding material. Kenton has the city's largest concentration of buildings sided with cast stone.

3 From Russet, turn right onto Denver Avenue. Denver was Kenton's main street, with Kenton Traction Company's tracks connecting the company town to downtown Portland. At 7807 is a 1909 cast-stone home on the National Register, the Thomas and Alla Paterson property.

Particularly impressive is the large 1909 cast-stone home at 7830 Denver, restored in 2006, and with an enormous beech in the yard. At 8007 to 8015 is the eight-unit Kelburn Apartments, also of cast stone, developed in 1910 with Swift money and advertised as up-to-the-minute modern: "tiled baths in every apartment . . . make the building one of the best apartments on the peninsula."

In the northeast corner of Denver and Schofield (8104 to 8108) is the Mission-style Chaldean Theatre, built in 1925. Storefronts along its Schofield side included a jeweler, a wine shop, and a cigar store. Across from it, at 8119, is a classic streetcar-era commercial building from 1924. This was originally a butcher shop and grocery.

This stretch is in the Downtown Kenton Redevelopment Project, begun in 2005 by the Portland Development Commission (PDC). Kenton is part of the Interstate Corridor Urban Renewal Area; the goal here is to craft a new streetscape and stimulate redevelopment of the commercial core, as has been done on N Killingsworth Street. This part of Denver is on the National Register of Historic Places as the Kenton Commercial Historic District.

Next to the old theater, at 8112, is a 1911 streetcar-era building, originally the Kenton Grocery and Market, hiding behind a 1960s façade. At 8120 to 8128 is a 1923 Art Deco store that held various meat and grocery businesses between 1910 and 1950. Its style derives from the stucco façade and stepped parapet.

Next to it, at 8130 to 8134, the Kenton Lodge is in the always-fun-to-see Egyptian Revival style. It dates from 1923. King Tut's tomb had been discovered one year earlier, launching an Egyptian craze in this country. The building's parapet has a cavetto cornice, a characteristic cornice of Egyptian buildings, consisting of a concave molding that continues for at least a quarter circle. The window head over the three-bay section also has a cavetto cornice. The cornice's shape, vertical lines with rounded tops, derives from the original form of the cornice, which may have been a group of sticks or rods placed over a door frame, perhaps to shade out the sun.

In the northeast corner of Kilpatrick and Denver, at 8202 to 8208, is the 1909 Dupey Block, one of Kenton's first commercial buildings. Note the half wagon wheel frieze, a nod to the many eastern Oregon cattlemen coming to Kenton to do business. The Kenton Publishing Company put out a newspaper from this cast-stone building in its early years; later, from 1930 to 1950, it was home to grocers and taverns. The back of the building, facing Kilpatrick, was home to the Kenton Billiard Hall; later it housed a Prohibition-era bootlegging operation.

In the northwest corner, at 8203 to 8207, is the 1910 Kenton Bank Building, owned and operated by Swift to fund development in Kenton. It closed in 1926. In it, physicians treated the many workplace injuries suffered by workers at the stockyards and nearby factories. The Kenwood Land Company also had its offices here. Today, its first floor is unrecognizable as a bank, and its cast stone has been covered with stucco.

Cross N McClellan Street. In the northwest corner is the Kenton Hotel, built in 1910 by Swift for visiting cattlemen. On the main floor were storefronts: a café, grocery, beauty shop, and furniture store. It is on the National Register and has been converted to twenty-one apartments, with a restaurant on the main floor.

(Here, I recommend a side trip one block east on McClellan. It ends at Fenwick Avenue, where a small plaza holds architectural remnants removed from the Portland Union Stockyards. The stockyards building, on Marine Drive west of today's Expo Center, was demolished in 1998.)

4 At McClellan and Denver, you're nearing the north end of Kenton. Walk one block beyond this intersection to N Willis Boulevard. Beyond it, and visible north of N Argyle Street, is the 1928 concrete viaduct that carried workers across the slough to the packing plant and other industries. It replaced a wooden trestle. If it were the 1940s, you would be standing at the main access to Vanport, a city on the Columbia River built hastily during the war to house workers at the Kaiser shipyards in Portland and Vancouver. Vanport was destroyed in one day during a 1948 flood. Alongside the old concrete viaduct, the MAX line runs on a sleek viaduct from the early 2000s. Also at Willis is Kenton's Paul Bunyan statue, a relic of the neighborhood's contribution to Oregon's 1959 centennial celebration.

From Willis, retrace your steps back along Denver to McClellan. Turn right (west) on McClellan, and then left onto N Brandon Avenue. On the right is Kenton Park. At Schofield is the 1913 Kenton Fire Station, used until 1959. South of Watts, small homes housed the meat packers and machinists who provided Kenton's muscle. From 7835 to 7803 is a good lineup of homes from 1911 typical of those built by Swift's stockyard laborers. Unlike most company towns, Swift did not own its workers' homes; instead it sold to its workers lots on which to build.

5 From Brandon, turn right on N Terry Street. Follow it west as it jogs right at Omaha. Homes on the right side of this block, from 1910, are tiny, classic, early-twentieth-century laborers' cottages of less than 600 square feet, on lots just 45 feet deep.

Walk another 0.5 mile on Terry. Past Emerald Avenue, Terry becomes narrow and alleylike.

A 633-square-foot 1910 Kenton cottage from Kenton's industrial heyday, likely home to a laborer in the stockyards or other nearby industries.

6 From Terry, turn left onto N Wabash Avenue. At Baldwin is Open Meadow, an alternative school in a bungalow-type commercial building, operating since 2004 in what was the S. B. Klahn Company, a small, family-run manufacturer of cloth money bags used by banks and their commercial customers.

From Wabash, cross Lombard Street at the stoplight and walk one block west. The Mock Crest Grocery is another block west, at Chase and Lombard. In 1853 Henry Mock took a donation land claim along the Willamette bluff here. This area, Mocks Crest, is the upland portion of his claim; Mocks Bottom was a swampy lowland along the east channel of the Willamette, where he lived with his family.

7 From Lombard, turn left onto Seward Avenue. This is the northern edge of the Arbor Lodge neighborhood. Residences on the north end of the block date generally from the early 1940s; closer to the bluff, they date mostly from the 1920s and 1930s.

8 From Seward, turn right onto N Willamette Boulevard, for a 0.9-mile tour of this scenic street. Walk on the sidewalk fronting beautiful homes. Past Fowler

Street, carefully cross the boulevard to walk along the uneven (but usually mown) grass on the bluff side, where views down into the steep and heavily forested bluff face are too good to miss, with dense stands of massive Oregon white oak and madrona. This combination of oak savanna and woodland is native to much of the Willamette Valley, but little of it remains in Portland. In the 2000s the city's Bureau of Environmental Services began tending this treasure—removing nonnative blackberry, which had grown head-high, and generally opening up the forest floor. The wild aspect of the bluff is a wonderful counterpoint to the refined homes above it and the concrete and steel industrial area below.

At 4333 Willamette is the elaborate John Mock home. He was Henry Mock's son, and this was his third home, built in 1894 on the family's land claim. John Mock was active in real estate and donated the land for what is now the University of Portland. Adjacent to Mock's home is the Columbia Annex, once part of the family's farm, now a park connected to the larger (and worth seeing) Columbia Park.

Continue walking along Willamette; at this point you've been in the University Park neighborhood for a few blocks. At N Wellesley Avenue the bluff becomes too steep to walk along, so cross to the north side again.

9 At N Harvard Street, cross back to the south side of Willamette to access the Waud Bluff Trail. (Note that the trailhead may be in a slightly different location due to ongoing improvements, including a bridge over the rail tracks and a bike slot along the trail's stairs, to encourage bike commuting to the island.)

Before descending the trail, stop a minute to survey the island and Mocks Bottom. Swan Island was once a true island to the right (southwest) of the current lagoon (the narrow, slotlike waterway) viewable from here. The lagoon, in which oceangoing vessels are often moored, was the original river channel that ran between the island and the swampy wetlands of Mocks Bottom, the wide, semicircular area below the bluff, which has been filled and is now an industrial park.

The original channel was a navigation hazard: swift and narrow, with a sharp curve on its downstream end where the water hit the bluff. In 1921 the Port of Portland purchased the island and began dredging the wider west side channel, originally so shallow that at low water a person could walk from the west bank of the Willamette River to Swan Island.

In its original state, Swan Island was one-fourth its current size, and low enough that it was completely inundated during high water. Dredge spoils quadrupled its size and raised its entire elevation. A link to the mainland was created by fill. North Going Street runs along this filled causeway.

Swan Island, circa 1926. The view is looking north, or downriver. The east channel is still open for shipping, and Mocks Bottom (to the east of the island) is still a wetland. To the west of Swan Island is Guilds Lake, partially filled by this point in time. Photo courtesy of the Oregon Historical Society.

Look along the forested bluff. The treeless green space in the distance is at the foot of N Killingsworth Street. It was once a ravine incised in the bluff face by springs. Decades ago the ravine was filled with asphalt by the Portland Department of Transportation; in the same way, fill has evened out several other ravines in that part of the bluff. (See Walk 2 for more on the bluff.)

In the 1920s the Port of Portland built its first airport on Swan Island, with graveled runways, rows of Japanese cherry trees, and an Art Deco terminal that reportedly made it one of the prettiest airports in the nation. In 1927 Charles Lindbergh landed on the island to dedicate its opening. The glory days were short, however. By 1935, faster and larger planes made the tiny airport under the bluff obsolete.

In 1942 most of the cherry trees were bulldozed, and Henry J. Kaiser built the Portland Shipyard on Swan Island. It was one of three government-contracted yards building warships for World War II in the Portland area. After the war, the infrastructure left behind became the basis of today's Swan Island Industrial Park. The Kaiser ships, incidentally, were not the first ships built on the island. In 1841 entrepreneurs built the first ship in the state here, calling it the *Star of Oregon.* They sailed it to San Francisco, sold it, and used the proceeds to buy cattle, which they drove back to the Willamette Valley.

By the first decade of the twenty-first century, 10,000 people worked on the island in 170 different businesses, making trucks, shipping packages and freight, wholesaling flowers, distributing beer and wine, repairing ships, building barges, making yogurt, and bottling milk.

Leave Mocks Crest by turning downhill on the Waud Bluff Trail, which takes you down 140 feet of gravels and cobbles laid here by the Missoula Floods of the last Ice Age. As you proceed along the trail, beware the lovely head-high bushes with the shiny leaves. They are some extremely healthy specimens of poison oak.

10 At the bottom of the trail, if the bridge across the tracks has not yet been built, carefully cross the train tracks (caution: do not cross in front of or behind a parked train!), and walk toward the perimeter fence of the U.S. Coast Guard base. Turn left at the fence, taking a made trail to N Basin Avenue, one of Swan Island's main thoroughfares. Basin runs on fill laid over Mocks Bottom. A bus stop here makes a good place to sit, rest, and view the bluff from a different vantage point.

Walk along Basin past the Coast Guard base and the Navy and Marine Corps Reserve Center. Past N Fathom Street, you will see UPS on the right. With about seventeen hundred employees at peak shipping season, it is one of the island's largest employers.

Cross N Leverman Street. South of it, the sidewalk ends, but you can continue walking along a grassy strip. About 0.25 mile past Leverman, and just beyond Northwest Paper Box (look for a sign facing south, on the right) and a railroad track, turn right into a parking lot that leads to a boat ramp.

11 Walk into the lot, and take the paved path on the left that leads to the foot of the Swan Island Lagoon. An interpretive display provides information on Swan Island's evolution from a navigational hazard to an industrial hub. From here, views are great: large ships, tugboats, and piers, with the forested West Hills as backdrop. From the display, you can wander down to the beach. All of this area is fill, but it has its charms, enough that it would be a great place to develop as a park. It is owned by the city's Bureau of Environmental Services, the same entity that has cleaned up the bluff. During World War II, this area at the foot of the lagoon held a daycare for the children of government shipyard workers. The building has been razed.

On the west side of the lagoon is an enormous square maw. It is a wind tunnel owned by Freightliner (a division of Daimler Trucks), which since 1929 has designed, built, and marketed heavy-duty trucks, first on NW Quimby Street, and soon after from its Swan Island headquarters and manufacturing plant. In 2007, 754 jobs went to the company's North Carolina and Mexico plants as Freightliner stopped producing on-highway trucks here. Still manufactured on Swan Island are the specialty Western Star rigs and military trucks. The tunnel accelerates air to 60 miles per hour to test the wind resistance of truck body designs.

12 After visiting the lagoon, come back to Basin and turn right. Walk 0.25 mile further and turn right on N Anchor Street. (At this intersection is a Vietnamese restaurant I can recommend.) From Anchor, come to the intersection of N Lagoon Avenue. Look to the right. On the north side of Lagoon are a few remaining flowering cherry trees.

Continue walking on Anchor to N Channel Avenue. Cross it. Beyond the intersection you're in a parking lot. Follow the sidewalk past Freightliner offices to the riverside McCarthy Park, owned by the Port of Portland. A few more cherries grow here.

13 From McCarthy Park, I recommend turning right to walk north along the river, either along the beach or on a sidewalk. This quarter-mile linear park is beautifully landscaped and makes a great place to picnic and watch the river scene.

Near the end of the park is an informational display about Portland ship-building. Across the river from the display, barges are often under construction at Gunderson, with launches occurring about every three months. This stretch of park is part of the Willamette Greenway Trail. The citizens group npGRE-ENWAY is working to promote access to the river and to build a continuous system of trails along the Willamette from Cathedral Park in Saint Johns to the Vera Katz Eastbank Esplanade across from downtown. This section was built in the 1970s as a discrete bit of greenery but is now part of the evolving greenway system.

Retrace your steps to McCarthy Park. To continue the walk, from McCarthy Park come back from the river a few feet, turn right, and walk on a sidewalk in front of a brown, two-story complex designed in a neo–Arts and Crafts style. Now occupied by Freightliner, this Ports O' Call facility was built as a shopping center in the 1970s. When retail failed, it became office space.

Follow the sidewalk to the end of the brown building, and turn right on a sidewalk that leads to the river. At the river, turn left and walk along a sidewalk, another portion of the Willamette Greenway Trail. During the 1996 floods, this section of trail was under 2 feet of water.

River traffic as seen from a log-strewn Swan Island beach in midsummer. Forest Park is in the background.

The brick and glass building on the left is also Freightliner offices. Across the river is the Port's Terminal 2. Near it is the mouth of Balch Creek, a beautiful, free-flowing West Hills creek that once flowed into Guilds Lake, a large, shallow lake filled in the early 1900s; it is now the industrial area seen here. When Guilds Lake was filled, the last mile of Balch Creek was shunted into a culvert. The last neighborhood seen in the hills across the river, before the wilds of Forest Park begin, is Willamette Heights.

Beyond the Freightliner building is a segment of the Willamette Greenway Trail that opened in 2006. The sidewalk consists of permeable concrete, designed to allow water to percolate into the soil below instead of flowing into drains where it would require treatment.

On the bluff to the left is the colorful campus of the athletic wear manufacturer adidas (not a company confined by the conventions of capitalization), seen in Walk 2. Further south on the riverbank are large white tanks at the Ash Grove cement plant, where the Willamette Greenway Trail dead-ends (though the route doesn't go there). It is hoped the trail can eventually continue south to the Steel Bridge.

14 From the Willamette Greenway Trail, turn left at a sidewalk that runs along the fence of the 8-acre Swan Island Pump Station. The pump station, completed in 2006, is designed to keep untreated runoff, known as combined sewer overflows (CSOs), out of the Willamette River, a common occurrence after rain events (that is, until the pump became operational). In 2006 the pump station began receiving sewage and storm water collected from the new west side CSO Tunnel. West side sewage and water flow through a 14-foot pipe under the Willamette to the station. From there the sewage is pumped to the Columbia Boulevard Wastewater Treatment Plant. When the east side CSO Tunnel is finished in 2011, the Swan Island Pump Station will serve both tunnels, with a total capacity of 220 million gallons of water per day. The pump is below the surface in a shaft 150 feet deep and 124 feet in diameter.

15 The sidewalk ends at N Port Center Way. Turn left and walk on a sidewalk to the traffic light at Port Center Way and Going Street, next to a McDonald's.

Cross Going at the light, turn right, and walk east on its north side. The reward for walking along noisy Going is a bird's-eye view of the rail yards. Stay on Going to the first traffic light, Interstate Avenue. To skip this noisy, uphill walk, catch bus 72 (Killingsworth/82nd Avenue) in front of McDonald's. It runs daily and travels to the MAX stop at Interstate and Killingsworth. Or, Monday through Friday, bus 85 (Swan Island) runs from Port Center Way and Going to the MAX stop at the Rose Quarter Transit Center. Use your bus ticket to get on the MAX Yellow Line and head back to the starting point.

16 From Going, turn right onto Interstate and walk one block to Prescott. Cross the southbound lane of Interstate to get to the MAX station. To return to the starting point, take a northbound train (marked "to Expo Center") to Interstate and Lombard.

PIEDMONT AND OVERLOOK LOOPS

DISTANCE Excluding the 1.5-mile MAX ride between **7** and **8**, the walking distance is 5.9 miles: 2 miles for the Piedmont Loop, **1** through **6**; 0.3 mile to the MAX stop at **7**; 3.3 miles for the Overlook Loop, **8** to **14**; and 0.3 mile back to the starting point from the MAX stop at Rosa Parks Way.

STARTING POINT Northwest corner of Peninsula Park: N Albina Avenue and Rosa Parks Way

GETTING THERE AND PARKING From downtown Portland, drive north on Interstate 5 to the N Rosa Parks Way exit (Exit 304). Travel east on Rosa Parks three blocks to the intersection with N Albina Avenue. Park along the street adjacent Peninsula Park.

TriMet: Take the MAX Yellow Line to the N Rosa Parks Way station. Walk about seven blocks east on Rosa Parks to the starting point. Or take bus 4 (Fessenden) or bus 44 (Mocks Crest) to stops adjacent the starting point.

RESTROOMS AND DRINKING FOUNTAINS Restrooms are inside the Peninsula Park Community Center during center hours and near the children's playground; at the Portland Community College (PCC) Cascade Campus, in Terrell Hall and the Student Center; at the North Portland Library during library hours; and in coffee houses, restaurants, and a grocery store along the route (for customers). Drinking fountains are inside the Peninsula Park Community Center and at PCC Cascade south of the parking lot and in Terrell Hall and the Student Center.

FOOD AND DRINK Coffee shops and restaurants cluster along N Killingsworth Street near the PCC Cascade Campus. Other options are at the intersection of

WALK 2. *Piedmont and Overlook Loops*

N Rosa Parks Way and Interstate Avenue; and along Killingsworth between Greeley and Burrage, Gay and Denver, and at the intersection with Concord.

BEST TIMES TO VISIT   Take this walk in late spring to summer, when residential gardens show off their colors and the rose garden in Peninsula Park is at its peak (June). Plan to see the carved ceiling inside the North Portland Library (for hours, visit www.multcolib.org or call 503-988-5402). You may also want to time the walk with the Interstate Farmers Market in Overlook Park, Wednesdays, May through September (www.interstatefarmersmarket.com). Tuesday evenings are open houses at Overlook House (www.historicoverlookhouse.org).

ACCESSIBILITY   The walk is virtually flat. In Peninsula Park the rose garden is not accessible, though paths run around its perimeter. Other short inaccessible stretches are addressed in the text, with alternate paths noted.

THIS CITY WALK consists of two separate loops connected by a 1.5-mile ride on the Interstate MAX Yellow Line. It is possible to walk from one loop to the other, but the MAX line's station art and key role in reinvigorating adjacent neighborhoods make it an intriguing part of the journey.

1   Start at the northwest corner of Peninsula Park, a classic early-twentieth-century park from the City Beautiful movement, which influenced architecture and urban planning from about 1890 to 1910. The idea was to use beauty and grand monuments in the inner city as a means of promoting moral and civic virtue, especially among the poor, whom it was felt were particularly at risk for moral decay. The park's site was earlier a racetrack (as were Irving Park, Rose City Golf Course, and Sellwood Park). The city purchased its 17 acres in 1909, a time when the neighborhood was seeing a construction boom, as did much of the east side in the years after Portland's 1905 world's fair, also known as the Lewis and Clark Exposition.

Walk into the park on the diagonal sidewalk and stop at the city's oldest community center. In 1911 a local women's club asked the Park Board to build a recreation center here, suggesting it would lessen the need for jails and reformatories. This building was erected in 1913, designed in the spirit of an Italian villa by Ellis Lawrence. Step inside to see murals of athletes and dancers in the main room; a lot of thigh is showing, leading me to suspect the murals are of a slightly later vintage than the building itself, perhaps from the tradition-bending 1920s rather than the staid 1910s. The pool on the building's north

The sunken rose garden at Peninsula Park. Photo by Zeb Andrews.

side was entered from either of two symmetrical wings. Each wing also had its own gym, one for each sex.

After looking inside, step onto the front porch, where the emphasis on formal symmetry continues into the park. Walk down the right-hand path through a grove of tall, old firs. Stay on the path and continue south toward a picnic shelter, then across the grass to the octagonal bandstand. Also designed by Lawrence in 1913, it is on the National Register of Historic Places. Behind it are fine views of the tree-framed lawn and community center, and ahead is the city's first formal, public rose garden.

Instead of walking straight into the gardens, turn right out of the bandstand and follow a gravel path under an allée of massive linden trees, past a century-old thicket of rhododendrons and camellias. The concrete and brick balustrade also dates from 1913.

On the park's west side, descend a brick staircase into the gardens, which are sunken 6 feet below the road grade. In 1913 the Park Board enlisted religious leaders in its efforts to pass a bond measure. One local reverend, George Schooner, responded enthusiastically as he exhorted his congregation: "Learn children to love flowers, they will learn to know God in His secrets and mysteries of nature. We will have less socialists, less anarchists, less hobos, less criminals. We will have loving people with a working spirit. This is the mission of the rose for the social uplift for all that is good and beautiful."

The gardens were designed by Park Superintendent Emanuel T. Mische, who came to Portland after working as a horticulture expert for the world-famous Olmsted Brothers landscape architecture firm. His place in the Portland pantheon was earned by planning many beloved city parks, such as Laurelhurst. The fountain, which has been repaired, was also built in 1913. In 1917 this garden was superseded as the city's official rose garden by Washington Park's International Rose Test Garden.

Exit the park on its south side. Cross N Ainsworth Street at N Borthwick Avenue, and walk a few blocks south to Borthwick's dead end. Here you enter a parking lot for the PCC Cascade Campus. In the lot, look to the left at a remnant of this block's residential past: a hundred-year-old cherry tree whose life was spared as the parking lot was poured around it. Whoever decided to spend the extra money to save the tree deserves a hand.

2 Pass straight through the lot and walk to the first building on the left, Terrell Hall. PCC Cascade began as Cascade College, a Christian college, and was reborn in 1971 as the PCC Cascade Campus, purchased through the Model Cities Program, a federal urban aid program. PCC Cascade offers twenty-five one-year certificate programs, twenty associate degree programs, and the general college transfer degree. PCC Cascade is the smallest of the three PCC campuses. A $60 million overhaul, funded by a 2000 voter-approved bond measure and completed in 2005, has given the campus a second rebirth with several new buildings and renovations of older ones. In the 2004 to 2005 school year, enrollment was more than fifteen thousand.

Enter Terrell Hall at its west door and walk through it to the Cascade Art Gallery, which features student and faculty art. Exit Terrell Hall on its east side and turn right. Walk past the Student Center, which houses the cafeteria and library. On the left is the Technology Education Building; in it is the HVAC and Electrical Trades and Skill Center.

Exit the campus at N Kerby Avenue, and cross N Killingsworth Street at the crosswalk. Turn left (east) on Killingsworth. On the right is Jefferson High School, a Portland public school that has been tinkered with for years, as administrators seek to change declining enrollment and low scores. Undimmed through its troubles have been the school's Jefferson Dancers, an elite troupe of dance students that tours nationally and performs at the Portland Center for the Performing Arts. The 1909 building's classical lines and original twelve-over-one double-hung windows have been overlain by some postmodern attempts at improvement, making it look a bit like downtown's Portland Building.

Just east of Jefferson on Killingsworth is the North Portland Library, definitely worth a stop. Built in 1913, it is a Carnegie library, one of more than twenty-five hundred libraries funded between 1883 and 1929 by railroad and steel tycoon Andrew Carnegie, who ultimately gave away 90 percent of his fortune. One caveat that Carnegie stipulated in his library grants was that the local group requesting money had to provide a fund for ongoing maintenance; hence, most Carnegie libraries are made of stone, brick, or concrete. The North Portland Library was designed in the Jacobethan style by Joseph Jacobberger, who designed many Catholic churches and buildings in Portland, including Saint Mary's Cathedral of the Immaculate Conception. The exterior is Flemish bond brick, a style in which on each course, brick headers (the short side) and stretchers (the long side) are alternated. The entry features a crenellated parapet, Tudor arch, and the building's name in a cut-stone tympanum. The magnificent carved and vaulted wooden ceiling inside the reading room was covered following a 1960s update, an "improvement" finally undone during a 1999 renovation. Don't miss the faces of Dante, Plato, and others gazing down, and the wooden window seat against the back wall. The round tables in the children's and adult areas are original. The light fixtures, though they look it, are not.

Next on Killingsworth is the Little Chapel of the Chimes, a Portland funeral home designed in 1933 by Richard Sundeleaf in the Italian Renaissance style, with a façade of brick with cast-stone ornamentation, a tile roof, and Moorish accents. (Sundeleaf's 1928 Jantzen headquarters can be seen in Walk 6.)

The west side of the building was the entrance mourners used to enter the chapel. The loggia here has slender terra-cotta columns set between massive, rusticated, terra-cotta corner piers. A loggia by definition is a corridor on the façade of a building, open on one side, where it is supported either by columns or a wall with openings within its face.

This gem, after being closed in 2005 by the national mortuary firm that acquired it, was purchased by the McMenamin brothers, who have saved many Oregon treasures from decay. In August 2006 they moved their corporate headquarters to the top floor and opened the Chapel Pub on the main floor. Inside the pub is incredibly graceful ironwork by master craftsman O. B. Dawson; if you go inside to eat, don't miss the gates in the former chapel. Later in the 1930s, Dawson led the team that created the ironwork found throughout Timberline Lodge on Mount Hood.

3 Just past the Little Chapel, cross Killingsworth carefully at N Haight Avenue, and walk north on Haight. This is the Piedmont Conservation District, an area of beautiful Craftsman and Queen Anne homes. Like some other east side neighborhoods, Piedmont was platted in the 1880s but didn't see much action until the 1905 world's fair created a rush of newcomers. Of 920 listed properties in the district, only thirty-nine predate 1905; most are from 1905 to 1930. The name Piedmont comes from the topography: a plateau lying near the foot of a mountain range. In this case the flat ground was formed not by erosion of adjacent hills but by the Missoula Floods. During the last Ice Age a series of torrents rushing down the Columbia River laid down a vast plain of sand and silt here, in some places 30 to 40 feet thick. This sand and silt was scraped away from eastern Washington, creating that state's channeled scablands.

Walk one block north on Haight, and turn right on N Jessup Street. At Jessup's intersection with N Moore Avenue, notice the lack of utility lines overhead. When Piedmont was platted, all water, gas, and electric lines were relegated to alleys. This is generally still true, making for streets where trees can grow unmolested by Portland General Electric chainsaws, and giving the area a nice, old-fashioned feeling.

4   From Jessup, turn left on N Williams Avenue, quiet and residential in this part of its run, and home to some of the oldest houses in Piedmont. Williams is the dividing line between North and Northeast Portland. At 5755 is an 1894 Queen Anne; across from it is a 1907 foursquare with an unusual cast-stone front porch and porch pillars.

At N Jarrett Street, an optional one-block detour to the east leads to the Piedmont United Presbyterian Church, built in 1913 in the Italian Renaissance style. With clear windows set in the stonework, instead of stained glass, the church has a striking beauty.

Back on N Williams, the home at 5919 is another foursquare, this one from 1915. The intersection with Ainsworth is worth a few minutes of wandering around to look at the beautiful, large, restored old homes. At 10 Ainsworth is a 1906 Shingle-style home with a semicircular bay above the front porch. Across from it, at 9 Ainsworth, is a 1910 Arts and Crafts home with a bell-cast roofline. This home was a flophouse during World War II: any shipyard worker in need of a bed could stay for $1 per night. Across from it, at 6013 Williams, is an 1894 Dutch Colonial with a gambrel roof.

Further down the block at 6127 Williams is a Queen Anne from 1894 with a diamond motif. This house belonged to C. J. Crook, a Union Pacific engineer known for his work on the Steel Bridge. Neighborhood tennis courts were once located behind this house. The home at 6215 is a gorgeous, low-slung bungalow of the sort often seen in Laurelhurst.

From Williams, turn left on N Holman Street. Walk one block and turn right on N Moore Avenue. Walk two blocks to N Rosa Parks Way. In front of you is the Holy Redeemer Catholic Church, built in 1926 in the Byzantine style. The adjoining school was built in 1952.

5 From Moore, turn left onto N Rosa Parks Way; walk one block, and cross Rosa Parks at the light at N Vancouver Avenue. Walk another two blocks on Rosa Parks and turn right onto N Commercial Avenue, a street of homes from the 1920s to 1940s. Here the land begins sloping northward, down toward the Columbia River. Downtown Vancouver, Washington, can be seen in the distance.

On Commercial, walk one block, and turn left onto N Dekum Street. At Dekum and N Congress Avenue, follow Dekum as it jogs west. In front of you is a magnificent site listed on the National Register of Historic Places, the Villa Saint Rose. Like the North Portland Library, this convent and girls' school was designed by Joseph Jacobberger. Built in 1917 in the Georgian style, the school was closed in 1993. In 1998 the Portland Development Commission (PDC) purchased it and its 7 acres. The convent was turned into one hundred low-income senior rental units, called Rosemont Court, and the grounds were developed with homes built by Habitat for Humanity and other programs that help subsidize housing costs for first-time homeowners; other new homes were sold at market rates. In 2004 the City of Portland won a Community Development Excellence Award from the U.S. Department of Housing and Urban Development for redevelopment of this site.

The intersection art at Dekum and N Borthwick Avenue is a traffic-calming device painted in May 2006 by volunteers organized by City Repair.

6 From Dekum, turn left on N Albina Avenue and walk one block back to the starting point. From Rosa Parks and Albina, walk west on Rosa Parks 0.3 mile to N Interstate Avenue. On the left you will see the Gainsborough Subdivision, developed in the late 1920s and 1930s in the English Cottage and Norman Cottage styles. It was a street of dreams of its day, but in the early 1960s two and a half blocks of the neighborhood were destroyed to construct Interstate 5. This section of Interstate 5 was originally known as the Minnesota Freeway, named for the street whose alignment it follows.

7 At Interstate is a New Seasons Market, a locally owned grocery chain that stocks local produce, meats, and other products. An in-store deli, with a seating area, makes excellent made-to-order stir-fries.

Cross the northbound lane of Interstate to get to the Rosa Parks Way MAX station. Buy a two-zone ticket and take a train south toward Portland's city center. At the station, drawings cut into the steel column wraps were designed by local Native American artists with inspiration from Columbia Gorge petroglyphs; the platform pavers follow a traditional Klikitat basketweave pattern.

Ride the MAX about 1.5 miles. Before construction of Interstate 5, Interstate Avenue was part of the Northwest's interstate road system, which accounts for the many roadside motels. The atomic-age enthusiasm of their exuberant neon signs adds considerable charm to this road.

The train passes the Killingsworth and Prescott stations. After Prescott, look left. At the corner of Failing and Interstate is the 1907 Saint Stanislaus Church, seat of Portland's Polonia (Polish community). Beginning in the 1890s, Polish immigrants moved to this area and worked in the nearby Albina rail yards, port facilities, and warehouses. Though the Polish community has dispersed, Sunday Mass is still said in Polish as well as English and Croatian.

8 Get off the train at the Overlook Park station. The light towers here were inspired by roadside shrines in Poland. The Kaiser Town Hall at the corner of Interstate and N Overlook Boulevard was built in the early 1900s as a Finnish lodge and social center. It was moved here in the 1990s and is now an education and conference center. The campus of Kaiser Permanente's Northwest Region sprawls along Interstate. Henry J. Kaiser, the man who built the Grand Coulee and Hoover Dams, came to Portland in World War II to construct three shipyards. The "Permanente" in the name of Kaiser's health plan for his workers came from Permanente Creek, south of San Francisco. Early Spanish settlers had named the creek because of its year-round flow, unusual in the dry hills of the Bay Area. Near the creek, Kaiser had built a cement plant in the 1930s, and for Kaiser and his wife, Bess, the quiet mountain creek was a place of refuge. The first Kaiser hospital in the Northwest was built near Kaiser's Vancouver shipyard during the war. In 1959, Bess Kaiser Medical Center (which the route will pass at **12** opened a few blocks northwest of here. The Interstate campus began to be developed by Kaiser in 1971. Today it houses a variety of medical services, physicians' offices, and the Center for Health Research, which opens its library to the public by appointment.

From the station, exit at the painted crosswalk onto the west side of Interstate, walk south half a block to N Fremont Street, and turn right into Overlook Park. Here, on Wednesdays afternoons from May to September, Kaiser Permanente sponsors the Interstate Farmers Market.

Overlook Park in 1935, shortly after fill was placed in the steep ravine once located here, and the land acquired by the city for a park. Photo courtesy of the City of Portland Archives.

This park occupies landfill. From the flat, silty-sandy uplands you've just traversed, water drained to the Willamette here, incising a ravine deep into the 130-foot-high bluff. The ravine extended several blocks back from the bluff face to the northeast, and its springs and creeks filled the wetlands adjacent to the river (which themselves were filled in the 1880s to be occupied by the rail yards). One neighborhood gentleman told me that in the 1920s kids would poke sticks in the ground here. When a stick was pulled out, methane from the decomposing fill would escape. The kids would light the methane with a match and make a Roman candle. A stick and match: the tools of an unfettered childhood the likes of which no modern child is permitted. By 1930 the city had acquired the land as a park. In it grows my vote for the best tree in town, an enormous elm standing solo in a lawn. Its limbs swoop almost to the ground, creating a magical haven inside their circle. Also on the grounds are large English walnut trees and a stone picnic shelter.

Cut across the grass to the chain-link fence that separates the park from the bluff below. (To avoid the grassy walk through the park, retrace the route to Interstate, walk north on it to Overlook Boulevard, turn left, and walk west on Overlook along the park's boundary, rejoining the route at **9**.) Once at the fenceline, walk north. Through the trees are good views of the rail yards and the city's working waterfront below. Water-loving black cottonwoods growing on the bluffs attest to the springs that emerge from its face. Follow the fence to its end, where there's a great view of the Fremont Bridge and the towers of downtown, juxtaposed nicely against the heavily forested bluff face.

9 From the park, emerge onto N Melrose Drive and turn left. Melrose sits at the edge of the bluff, and the homes have stupendous views. The beautiful English Cottage–style home at 3769 is from 1925, reflecting an era when many such homes were built in Portland, after soldiers returned from World War I with a taste for vernacular European architecture. Across from it, at 3786, is a home from 1911; beside it is an old Oregon white oak, native to the Willamette Valley.

Across from 3804, an undeveloped lot gives more great views of the city. The Port of Portland owns the blue crane across the river. To its left are the homes of Willamette Heights, the last West Hills neighborhood before Forest Park takes over the hills. This lot also is a good place to watch trains, which began moving through here in the early 1880s.

Continue on Melrose to Overlook House, a facility of Portland Parks and Recreation. Built in 1928 by Herman and Elvira Raven, owners of the Raven Dairy, it was a community center even while the Ravens lived in it. Mrs. Raven gave it to the city in 1951. Today it is maintained by Friends of Overlook House. Walk behind the house into the lovely gardens and back onto Melrose.

Turn left out of Overlook House and come to the intersection of Melrose and Overlook Boulevard. Go left here. Across the street is a large pin oak. Walk past a few homes, and then turn left on N Overlook Terrace.

In the open space across from 3948 is a beautiful Oregon white oak and a good dandelion patch if you forgot to buy greens at the farmers market. This is a street of diverse architecture capped by a home fit for a small Southern plantation at 4036; it dates from 1910.

10 At the intersection of Overlook Terrace and Overlook Boulevard, turn right. At N Shaver Street, come to a triangular park filled with three large London plane trees. This park was the turnaround for a streetcar. Turn left onto Shaver, and then left onto N Castle Avenue, a quiet, leafy street where you can easily imagine a Model T emerging from someone's driveway.

On Castle, walk two blocks and turn right on N Skidmore Street.

11 From Skidmore, turn left onto N Concord Avenue, which starts running downhill to a gulch. Cross N Prescott Street, and climb the spiral ramp leading to a pedestrian walk over N Going Street, the only street that leads to Swan Island. Once over Going, turn left onto N Going Court, a gravel street that once had a nice rural view down into a ravine. (To avoid the gravel, stay on Concord to N Blandena Street; turn left and follow Blandena to N Denver Avenue.) Going Court, a charming bit of urban landscape that escaped complete citification, passes the Beach Community Garden. Turn right onto N Campbell Avenue.

From Campbell, turn left onto the paved Blandena. At Denver, turn right, and then immediately turn left onto N Wygant Street. If you want a scenic out-and-back detour, just past 2310 Wygant, turn left and walk down to a stub of Blandena that sits on the edge of the canyon that now holds Going Street.

Back on Wygant, walk west to its dead end.

12 From the end of Wygant, follow the concrete sidewalk into Madrona Park, whose namesake tree, ill with blight, strikes a sinuous pose ahead of you. This 8-acre park was given to the city in 1921 by Mr. and Mrs. Amos Benson, who lived in a house further down the bluff (see *Portland Hill Walks*, Walk 20). Benson was the son of timber baron and philanthropist Simon Benson.

Once past the madrona, emerge from the park into adidas Village. Based in Germany, adidas was founded in 1925 by Adi Dassler with a pair of spiked soccer boots. This campus, headquarters of adidas America, was formerly the Bess Kaiser Medical Center, named for Henry J. Kaiser's wife, who had died in 1951. It was she who named Kaiser Permanente, believing that the name of the creek she loved was well suited for a company whose mission is health maintenance. The hospital closed in 1996. In 2000, its three main buildings were recycled by adidas. Working with Portland-based Mercy Corps, the company filled shipping containers with the hospital's cabinets, doors, stainless steel sinks, and toilets, and sent them to hospitals in Honduras and one of the former Soviet republics. Three other buildings are new. Each building is accented with one of the colors of the Olympic rings and is named for an Olympic city.

Just past the basketball court, turn left up a ramped sidewalk, where you're surrounded by a playground, basketball and tennis courts, and a soccer field. Walk north, alongside the buildings. A café here is open Monday through Friday. Next to the café, climb twenty-six stairs to a parking lot. (To avoid the steps, turn right at the base of the stairs onto a sidewalk and then left on a sidewalk that follows the east perimeter of the campus. Take this north to N Sumner

The adidas campus, in the old Bess Kaiser Medical Center on N Greeley Avenue. Photo by Judy Blankenship.

Street and turn left. Avoid the south sidewalk on Sumner; there is no curb cut at its west end.) From the top of the steps, walk alongside the Rome building (yellow) sidewalk, which ends at the intersection of Greeley and Sumner.

Turn right onto Greeley. As you pass N Willamette Boulevard, you could turn right and walk its quiet residential way all the way to Interstate, where you can catch the MAX at the Killingsworth stop. But if you're ready for a grand view and opportunities to eat, continue along the route.

13 From Greeley, turn left onto the leafy peace of Willamette Boulevard; in one block it begins its several-miles-long traverse of the edge of the bluff. At Willamette and Killingsworth, step over to the bluff for fine views of Swan Island (not an island anymore), where Kaiser had a shipyard, and Waud Bluff, home of the University of Portland. (For more on these areas, see Walk 1.)

From Willamette, turn right turn right onto N Killingsworth Street. Food options begin at the intersection of Greeley, starting with Yorgo's Bar and Grill and Mio Sushi. Along Killingsworth, more restaurants and stores serve African, Creole, deli food, and old-timey cafeteria fare. Though a busy street, Killingsworth gives a walker plenty to look at, from vintage garden apartments to knit shops and pet washeries. It passes the lovely Omaha Parkway, Detroit Avenue (a street so wide you expect to see a triumphal arch at the other end), and the intriguing "Podkrepa Association 1939" building, home to a Bulgaro-Macedonian social club.

14 At Interstate Avenue, cross the southbound lane to get to the northbound Killingsworth Street MAX station. The station art here is influenced by the area's multicultural history. The shelter columns are decorated in mosaic patterns reminiscent of African Kente cloth, and geometric motifs found in South American textiles are cut into the guardrails.

Take the northbound train (Expo Center) to the next station, Rosa Parks Way. Once there, walk back to the starting point at Peninsula Park.

WALK 3

FERNHILL PARK TO ALBERTA STREET LOOP

DISTANCE 4.3 miles

STARTING POINT Northeast corner of Fernhill Park: NE 41st Avenue and Holman Street

GETTING THERE AND PARKING From downtown Portland, cross the Burnside Bridge. Before reaching SE 12th Avenue, get in the left lane to veer onto NE Sandy Boulevard. Drive sixteen blocks on Sandy to NE 28th Avenue; turn left, and then right onto NE Weidler Street. From Weidler, turn left on NE 33rd Avenue and follow it 1.4 miles to NE Prescott Street. Drive nine blocks to NE 42nd Avenue and turn left, following it up to NE Ainsworth Street (just past a running track on the left). Turn left on Ainsworth and right on NE 41st Avenue, adjacent to Fernhill Park. Park here.

TriMet: Take bus 75 (39th Avenue/Lombard) to the stop at NE 42nd Avenue and Holman Street. Walk one block west on Holman to 41st.

RESTROOMS AND DRINKING FOUNTAINS Restrooms are at Fernhill Park, Alberta Park, and in cafés and restaurants along NE Alberta Street (for customers). Drinking fountains are at Fernhill Park, Concordia University, and Alberta Park.

FOOD AND DRINK Restaurants, coffee houses, and bars offer a plethora of options along NE Alberta Street from NE 10th Avenue to 31st. McMenamins Kennedy School is near the end of the route at NE 33rd Avenue and Jarrett Street.

BEST TIMES TO VISIT Try to time this walk to coincide with the annual Alberta Street Fair or Alberta Art Hop, or with Last Thursday on Alberta, held each

BROADMOOR
GOLF COURSE

Columbia Slough

NE COLUMBIA BLVD

NE LOMBARD ST

W O O D L A W N

NE BRYANT ST

NE DEKUM ST

30B

NE LIBERTY ST

NE 22nd AVE
NE 23rd AVE
NE 24th AVE
NE 25th AVE

NE PORTLAND HWY

NE PORTLAND BLVD

NE 39th AVE

NE HIGHLAND ST

CONCORDIA
UNIVERSITY

NE 33rd AVE

NE 15th AVE

NE HOLMAN ST

1

4

NE AINSWORTH ST

2

*Fernhill
Park*

NE 16th AVE
NE 17th AVE

*Alberta
Park*

3

NE 26th AVE
NE 27th AVE
NE 28th AVE
NE 29th AVE

NE SIMPSON ST

5

NE JARRETT ST

8

NE JESSUP ST

C O N C O R D I A

VERNON
ELEMENTARY
SCHOOL

NE KILLINGSWORTH ST

NE 15th AVE

NE EMERSON ST

V E R N O N

NE SUMNER ST

NE 34th AVE
NE 35th AVE
NE 35th PL
NE 36th AVE
NE 37th AVE

NE 41st AVE
NE 42nd AVE

6

NE ALBERTA ST

7

NE 38th AVE

N

NE 18th AVE
NE 19th AVE
NE 20th AVE
NE 21st AVE

NE WYGANT ST

NE 30th AVE
NE 31st AVE
NE 32nd AVE
NE 32nd PL

NE GOING ST

MAP SCALE
0 MILES   1/8   1/4

WALK 3. *Fernhill Park to Alberta Street Loop*

MAP KEY

▪▬ ROUTE

⁞⁞⁞⁞⁞ STAIRS

– – TRAIL

──── MAX TRACKS

🅜 MAX STATION

········ STREETCAR TRACKS

········ TROLLEY TRACKS

╠╣╠╣ RAILROAD TRACKS

▪ PARK/GREENSPACE

▪ HISTORIC/CONSERVATION DISTRICT

🚻 PUBLIC RESTROOM

💧 WATER

month. Visit www.artonalberta.org for more information on any of these events, including details about artists and galleries.

Bring a swimsuit for a relaxing soak in the Kennedy School's soaking pool, near the end of the walk. For $5 the 35-by-12-foot tiled tub is yours to enjoy. Photo identification is required; no minors are allowed after 8:00 p.m., and the pool closes at 10:00 p.m.

Monday is not the best day to take this walk; many stores on Alberta are closed that day.

ACCESSIBILITY This route is relatively flat and on city sidewalks. Elevations range from 90 feet at the start to around 200 feet along NE Alberta Street. The last stretch, through Fernhill Park, is on grass, but the grass can be avoided by keeping to the park's perimeter.

THIS WALK EXPLORES the lovely and racially diverse Concordia neighborhood, home to Fernhill Park, Ainsworth Linear Arboretum, and Concordia University, and on into the adjoining Vernon neighborhood with its classic Alberta Park and hundred-year-old homes. The two neighborhoods share the wealth of a booming Alberta Street. It's fun to end the walk by meandering through Alberta's shops and choosing a restaurant to linger in. The exclamation point to this city walk is the Kennedy School, a decommissioned Portland public school on NE 33rd Avenue that is a wonder to behold, where what was once a girls' restroom now houses a brewery and you can take a post-walk soak in the former teachers' lounge.

1 Start at the northeast corner of Fernhill Park, a 24-acre park born in 1940. The wooded ravine along its northern edge and its grassy hills were once desecrated by car thieves, who according to Portland Parks and Recreation used this area to strip and dump stolen cars. Fernhill is in the northeast corner of the large Concordia neighborhood, which runs from NE 42nd Avenue to 22nd, and from Columbia Boulevard to Prescott Street. Most of Concordia was platted in the 1910s, with 40 percent of existing homes built before 1940, 30 percent built during the 1940s, and 20 percent built during the 1950s.

Walk west along NE Holman Street, a street of classic and well-tended midcentury brick homes sited on the last terrace before the land falls to the Columbia River bottomlands. At NE 37th Avenue, turn left.

2 From 37th, turn right onto NE Ainsworth Street, one of the few Portland streets with a parklike median along much of its length. Here starts the Ainsworth Linear Arboretum, a unique museum of street and yard trees planted primarily by Friends of Trees beginning in 2000. The arboretum, still in its infancy, includes offbeat exotics such as the Kentucky coffee tree (*Gymnocladus dioica*) and American hornbeam (*Carpinus caroliniana*). Friends of Trees' goal is to inspire Portland homeowners to plant these seldom-seen varieties to increase the city's species diversity. To identify the tree species, download a list of trees and their addresses at www.friendsoftrees.org.

In the parking strip at 3627 is a tricolor European beech (*Fagus sylvatica*) whose cultivar name, 'Roseomarginata', describes its unusual leaves. At 3676, a Natchez crapemyrtle (*Lagerstroemia* 'Natchez') blooms white in July.

Homes in this stretch of Ainsworth were built in the 1940s and 1950s, and those on the south side enjoy deep, quarter-acre lots. Cross 33rd and remain on Ainsworth, now lined with English Cottage homes developed earlier, in the 1920s and 1930s. An old Atlas cedar (*Cedrus atlantica*) towers in the yard at 3269. This is a true cedar, its cones much different from those of the common western redcedar (*Thuja plicata*), which isn't a cedar but a member of the cypress family. Look down. If you find a fresh cone, heavy and tightly wrapped, take it home to watch it dry and slowly open for a wonderful bit of nature's performance art. At 3231 is an especially nice English Cottage from 1929, nested in a grove of old Douglas firs.

At NE 30th Avenue is the Ainsworth United Church of Christ, built in the 1930s. The church resulted from the joining in 1984 of two United Church of Christ congregations who had shared the building, one predominantly white and the other predominantly African American and Nicaraguan. The church describes itself as "multiracial, multicultural, open, and affirming," welcoming gay, lesbian, bisexual, and transgendered people.

3 From Ainsworth, turn right on NE 29th Avenue. The homes from here until the route enters Alberta Park have alleys running behind them. Note the green roof at 6217.

At 29th and NE Holman Street, take the diagonal sidewalk into a quadrangle surrounded by buildings of Concordia University. The school, which is the source of the neighborhood's name, takes its own name from Concordia, the Roman goddess of peace and harmony. The school was established in 1905 and is affiliated with the Lutheran Church–Missouri Synod. Centennial Hall, the building to the right (along 29th), was a dormitory when the school boarded students from seventh grade on up. Boarding for junior high and high school students ended in the 1970s, and now the university is a liberal arts school with strong elementary and secondary education programs. Though the school was founded in 1905, none of the early buildings remain. About sixteen hundred students attend the school, most from the Pacific Northwest, and four hundred underclassmen live in four residence halls around the school. One notable graduate is U.S. Congressman Dave Reichert of Washington, who first as a detective, and then as King County sheriff, was instrumental in finding and prosecuting the man known as the Green River killer, responsible for forty-eight murders in Seattle in the 1980s.

Exit the west side of the quadrangle, which puts you into a small parking lot. Cross it to NE Highland Street. Walk one block west on Highland and turn left onto NE 26th Avenue, a street with beautiful homes from the late 1930s and early 1940s.

4 From 26th, turn right on Ainsworth. The 1938 English Cottage at 2234 has exotic-looking green stones embedded in its rockwork, and architectural stonework from an old building flanks its steps.

From Ainsworth, turn left onto NE 22nd, the western boundary of Concordia. As you take the diagonal path that leads into Alberta Park, you're entering the Vernon neighborhood. This 16-acre park is a classically beautiful Portland park, with stands of mature Douglas fir, a vintage playground where kids can still experience the thrill of speed and height, and a concrete wading pool for toddlers and their parents. The park was acquired by the city in 1921. Walk through the children's playground, and exit the park on its west side at NE Jarrett Street.

From Jarrett, walk two blocks west to NE 17th Avenue.

5 Turn left (south) onto 17th. As the walk draws closer to the Willamette River, the houses get older; here they date from the early 1900s.

From 17th, turn right onto NE Killingsworth Street, named for William Killingsworth, a real estate developer in the 1880s. Carefully cross this busy street, walk one block west, and turn left onto NE 16th Avenue.

The houses along 16th generally date from the early 1900s. At 5318, however, is a "snout house," a look much discussed in the 1990s as the city suffered the pains of infill. The home at 5225, from 1911, is a Portland foursquare with a twist: cast-stone classical columns and a cast-stone foundation. Several examples of cast stone can be found in the Vernon neighborhood. The concrete plant that manufactured the material was on N Killingsworth, near today's PCC Cascade Campus.

On a 100-degree July afternoon, neighborhood kids whoop it up in a parks-sponsored Slip 'n Slide in Alberta Park.

From 16th, turn right onto NE Sumner Street, walk one block, and turn left onto NE 15th Avenue, which features a lovely bunch of restored homes from the first decade of the twentieth century. The home at 5125 is a classic Portland foursquare from 1906, with an unusual bit of column-work on its second floor. The home at 5117 shows the Japanese influence on the bungalow form, with its bell-cast roofline. The bungalow at 5037, from 1908, has a flared bargeboard, one with slightly more attitude than most bargeboards in town. The home at 5026 has an entire first floor of cast stone. (For more houses built of this vintage material, see Walk 1.)

6 From 15th, turn left onto NE Alberta Street. Since 1903, when a streetcar line was installed, Alberta has been a neighborhood business hub, serving its original population of working-class German and Irish immigrants who came to Portland in the 1880s to work in the Albina rail yards. They were joined by immigrants from Russia, Scandinavia, and Poland. Later inhabitants included families who moved here from Vanport after it was destroyed by the 1948 flood. The Alberta business community thrived until the 1940s, but transportation changes and a trend away from small neighborhood retailers brought a decline. Redlining meant that by the 1950s the neighborhood was one of the few Portland neighborhoods to permit black homeowners, and white investment fled to less racially integrated parts of town and to the emerging suburbs. (For more on redlining, see Walk 4.) In the 1960s, national unrest over the Vietnam War and racial inequality didn't leave Alberta Street untouched: businesses were looted, burned, or vandalized, and the street entered a long period of decline. Alberta's deterioration was reversed in the early 1990s, when Portland housing prices began to soar. The street and its surrounding residential area caught the eye of homeowners and investors, and gentrification followed, with some decline in the neighborhood's racial diversity and a considerable decline in its affordability.

The street scene along Alberta is vibrant and always interesting. Many of its streetcar-era commercial buildings were rehabbed in the early twenty-first century and are home to businesses such as a food co-op, restaurants, clothing stores, and the hippest office supply store you'll ever find. Mixed with the newly rehabbed and just plain new construction are the long-lived pillars of the community, such as the New Rose City Cab Company, in an old home at 1533 Alberta, and Earl's Barbershop, in a 1909 building at 1726 Alberta. A surprising number of single-family homes still exist on the street.

The home at 1614 was built in 1908 and originally belonged to Joe S. Morak. It was probably the first home this immigrant from eastern Europe ever owned. I can imagine Joe's pleasure at watching the mason stamp his name and address in the concrete of his walkway. The address is from a prior street-numbering system; the present system was set in place in the early 1930s.

At NE 17th Avenue is the Community Cycling Center. In 1994 it began life in a boarded-up building on Alberta with a target clientele of children from the neighborhood's many low-income families, its goal to use bikes to teach life skills to young people. Within a decade it became the largest nonprofit of its sort in the nation. Kids in its programs learn bike maintenance and earn their own bikes, locks, and helmets. Among its programs is "Create a Commuter," which provides fully outfitted commuter bikes to low-income adults. The center's retail shop is open to the public.

At NE 22nd Avenue, a 1956 building with space-age streamlining is home to a hip office supply store. At 24th is a former Rexall Drug Store from 1909, now a coffee house. One hot summer day I noticed an old man across the street from the noisy latte crowd on the sidewalk here; with his back to the scene, he watered his lawn, seemingly unimpressed by the changes to his neighborhood.

In the northeast corner of NE 26th Avenue and Alberta is a historic structure so mundane it may go unnoticed: a Quonset hut. In 1941, as the Navy anticipated an imminent need for housing large quantities of people and matériel, it requisitioned a cheap and easy-to-construct shelter. Designed in New York, the shelters entered mass production near Quonset, Rhode Island. During World

A streetscape at NE 15th Avenue and Alberta Street, circa 1950. Photo courtesy of the City of Portland Archives.

A purveyor of wisdom and solace at a summertime Last Thursday on Alberta. She is one of the vendors who once a month turn the street into a combination carnival, county fair, and art show.

War II, 170,000 huts were produced and shipped virtually all over the planet to house people and supplies at airstrips, MASH units, and barracks. When the war ended, the huts were sold as surplus for $1000 each.

At 2703 Alberta is the distinctive Siam Society Bistro and Bar, housed in a 1910 electrical substation. Also intriguing at this point in the walk are the alleys that bisect each block. Unpaved and unmown, they remind me of country lanes. While the alleys are public property, they seem a bit too private to write about in a book.

At NE 30th Avenue is an old movie theater reborn as the Victory Outreach Church. This was the end of the streetcar line; from 30th, the streetcar turned north and ran to its terminus at Ainsworth. As a result, east of 30th, the commercial presence fades on Alberta. But don't miss the Vita Café, at 31st, which serves great vegetarian food and offers one of the city's best outdoor patios.

7 From Alberta, turn left onto NE 32nd Avenue. Most homes on this street are from the first two decades of the 1900s. At the intersection of NE Emerson Street is a 1911 home whose owner had a serious affection for river rock. The home at 5434 32nd, off Killingsworth, is a Dutch Colonial with a gambrel roof; it was built in 1909 at a time when the predominant style in Portland's east side was the bungalow.

From 32nd, turn right onto NE Jarrett Street and follow it to NE 33rd Avenue.

8 Across 33rd is the front entrance to the Kennedy School, named for John D. Kennedy, an early landowner in town. The school was built in 1915 on 4 acres just south of Kennedy's 1888 home (which the walk will pass). It operated until 1975 when it was closed due to declining enrollment. In 1997 the bell rang again when the building reopened as one of the McMenamin brothers' chain of restaurants housed in historic structures.

The school's rambling, single-story design was unique during the era in which it was built. An Ohio school fire was on the mind of the architect, Floyd Naramore, of Portland Public Schools, and the result was this gorgeous Mediterranean villa–like building. While the grounds alone are worth an hour's attention, go inside. Just within the door are bas-relief sculptures commissioned by Kennedy for the school, reproductions of fifteenth-century Florentine art. The art-filled halls are fun to explore; look for ornate ironwork from the Portland Hotel, located at the site of Pioneer Courthouse Square downtown until 1951, when it was turned into a parking lot—a loss still lamented by

Portland preservationists. The ladies' bathroom on the school's north side has a "view stall" you might not want to miss.

Exit the school at its main entrance on 33rd, turn right, and walk half a block to NE Simpson Street. Turn right. At 3327, behind a holly hedge, is Kennedy's 1888 homestead. From it he directed the operations of his gentleman's farm, which ran from 33rd to 42nd; the original barn is where the school is now located. He subdivided his land in 1890, but Kennedy's Addition, as it was called, saw little action for several decades.

Walk east on Simpson. At 35th you may want to detour half a block to the south to visit the Kennedy Community Garden, one of Portland Parks and Recreation's many neighborhood gardens. This one is especially nice, and historic as well. During World War I, this space was a Victory Garden tended by students at the school.

Back on Simpson, the 1940s homes continue east to 37th. Turn left and pass more homes from the 1940s. At 5954 is a ranch from 1949, in never-painted concrete block, with metal windows. It's an odd look for a ranch, but intriguing.

At Fernhill Park, cut a diagonal northeast through the park back to the starting point. To stay on sidewalks, remain on 37th to Holman; then turn right and walk four blocks to the starting point.

7/21/10 – PR

WALK 4

IRVINGTON TO SULLIVAN'S GULCH LOOP

DISTANCE   4.6 miles

STARTING POINT   NE 10th Avenue and Tillamook Street

GETTING THERE AND PARKING   From downtown Portland, cross the Burnside Bridge. Turn right on Martin Luther King Jr. Boulevard, then left at the first block, SE Ankeny Street, and left onto Grand Avenue, a one-way street going north. Drive north on Grand about seventeen blocks to NE Weidler Street. Remain on Grand three more blocks, staying in the far right lane. At NE Hancock Street, turn right rather than curving left (where Grand rejoins MLK as the one-way couplet ends). From Hancock, turn left on NE 10th Avenue and drive one block to the starting point at 10th and Tillamook Street. Park along the street.

TriMet: Take the MAX Blue Line to the NE 7th Avenue stop at Holladay Street. Walk east on Holladay to NE 9th Avenue, turn left, and walk north on 9th to Tillamook Street. Turn right and walk one block to the starting point. Bus 9 (Broadway) and bus 6 (Martin Luther King Jr. Boulevard) have stops near the starting point.

RESTROOMS AND DRINKING FOUNTAINS   Restrooms at Irving Park (NE 9th Avenue and Klickitat Street) operate seasonally, spring through autumn. Restrooms are inside the Fred Meyer Hollywood West store (NE 30th Avenue and Weidler Street), Lloyd Center Mall (entrance at NE 12th Avenue and Halsey Street), and commercial establishments along the way (for customers). Drinking fountains are at the Irvington School playground (southeast corner of the school building) and Irving Park (west of NE 11th Avenue, at Klickitat).

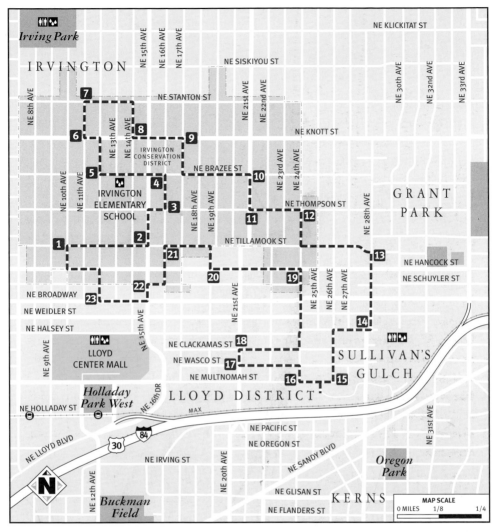

Irving Park

IRVINGTON

NE KLICKITAT ST

NE SISKIYOU ST

NE 15th AVE
NE 16th AVE
NE 17th AVE

NE STANTON ST

NE 21st AVE
NE 22nd AVE

NE 30th AVE
NE 32nd AVE
NE 33rd AVE

7

NE 8th AVE

6

8

NE 13th AVE
NE 14th AVE

IRVINGTON
CONSERVATION
DISTRICT

9

NE KNOTT ST

5

NE 10th AVE
NE 11th AVE

4

IRVINGTON
ELEMENTARY
SCHOOL

3

NE BRAZEE ST

NE 23rd AVE
NE 24th AVE

10

GRANT
PARK

NE 18th AVE
NE 19th AVE

NE THOMPSON ST

11

12

NE 28th AVE

1

2

NE TILLAMOOK ST

13

NE HANCOCK ST

NE SCHUYLER ST

21

20

19

NE 25th AVE
NE 26th AVE
NE 27th AVE

22

NE 21st AVE

23

NE BROADWAY

NE WEIDLER ST

NE HALSEY ST

NE 15th AVE

14

SULLIVAN'S
GULCH

NE 9th AVE

LLOYD
CENTER MALL

NE CLACKAMAS ST

NE WASCO ST

18

17

NE MULTNOMAH ST

16

15

*Holladay
Park West*

NE 16th DR

LLOYD DISTRICT

NE 31st AVE

NE HOLLADAY ST

MAX

*Oregon
Park*

30   84

NE LLOYD BLVD

NE PACIFIC ST

NE OREGON ST

NE 20th AVE

NE IRVING ST

NE SANDY BLVD

NE 12th AVE

N

*Buckman
Field*

NE GLISAN ST

KERNS

NE FLANDERS ST

MAP SCALE
0 MILES   1/8   1/4

WALK 4. *Irvington to Sullivan's Gulch Loop*

MAP KEY

▪▬ ROUTE

┈┈ STAIRS

─ ─ TRAIL

─⋯─ MAX TRACKS

🚈 MAX STATION

STREETCAR TRACKS

TROLLEY TRACKS

RAILROAD TRACKS

PARK/GREENSPACE

HISTORIC/CONSERVATION DISTRICT

PUBLIC RESTROOM

WATER

FOOD AND DRINK This city walk provides abundant choices for food and drink, beginning with a small charcuterie and a gelato store at NE 15th Avenue and Brazee Street. Later in the walk, restaurants populate NE Broadway from 28th Avenue west, with a concentration between 10th and 18th.

BEST TIMES TO VISIT Combine this walk with a movie at nearby Lloyd Center Mall or with dinner and window-shopping at NE Broadway's stretch of local shops and restaurants. Take the walk when Irvington School is open to see its historic Works Progress Administration (WPA) murals; call 503-916-6386 for information.

ACCESSIBILITY This walk is flat and on city sidewalks.

IRVINGTON IS ONE OF PORTLAND'S most architecturally interesting neighborhoods. When I was creating a route for this walk, my goal was to show-case as many neighborhood treasures as possible. It turns out, however, that just about every block in Irvington is worth seeing, and to include them all would have involved a zipperlike march up one street and down the next. You may want to return to explore more of this beautiful neighborhood.

The starting point at NE 10th Avenue and Tillamook Street was once part of the donation land claim taken by William and Elizabeth Irving in 1851. Their 635 acres ran from 7th to 24th, Fremont to Tillamook, with a southern panhandle that extended to the river. Being a riverboat captain, William was primarily interested in the claim's narrow bit of river frontage (at about the location of today's Broadway Bridge), so the couple built their house there, and ventured into the forest that is now Irvington only to harvest timber for William's steamboats.

The Irvings left Portland for Victoria in 1859, but Elizabeth came back after William died in 1872. She moved with her daughter and son-in-law into a home they built in 1884, also near the river. That home, seen during this walk, was moved out of the path of the Broadway Bridge in 1913 and is today said to be the oldest home in the Irvington neighborhood.

In 1887 three investors bought 288 acres of the claim and platted it out, naming it Irvington to honor William and Elizabeth. It was planned to be an upper-class suburb and was marketed to professionals and mid- to high-level executives. Garages and barns were not allowed, and indeed were unneeded, as the neighborhood was served by a streetcar line starting in 1890, the year home construction began. To keep a high tone to the neighborhood, developers took the then-unusual step of incorporating other deed restrictions: homes must cost at least $2500, and no commercial establishments were allowed. Later, similar covenants were used to control development in Laurelhurst and other new sub-divisions.

This walk begins with a look at homes from Irvington's first phase of growth, the early 1890s.

1 At the corner of NE 10th Avenue and Tillamook Street, notice the iron band-ing along the curbs. These protective strips, common all over town, kept the wheels of horse-drawn delivery trucks from scouring the edges of the pavement. Rings on curbs can also be found throughout the city, once used to tether horses while their driver made deliveries. The street name "E. 10. St. N." is imprinted on the pavement here; the city changed its street nomenclature in 1933 to the current system (see Walk 13 for more information).

Walk east on Tillamook. At 1016 is a cottage from 1891, one of the first two built in the West Irvington subdivision, the portion of the land claim west of NE 15th Avenue, retained by Elizabeth Irving when she sold part of her claim to developers. The builder of this cottage, Neils Paulsen, lived next door at 1020.

The home across the street at 1033 was built in 1908 by Henry Reimers, a brick contractor who borrowed techniques he'd used on the construction of Portland's Union Station in the early 1890s. The two buildings share a unique pattern of brick and gravel-faced stucco.

At 1123 is an 1893 Queen Anne, and at 1137 is another from that year. According to neighborhood historian Roy Roos, the latter home was "prob-ably the first home built by the Portland Cottage Building Association" and is "strongly believed to have been a demonstration model, due to its small size."

The 1200 block is full of massive Craftsman homes. Especially notable is 1216: big and plain, it has a self-assured dignity that derives not from ornament but from functionality. At 1211 is a good example of a garage added to a 1913 home, an addition from the 1920s, perhaps, when cars came within the reach of more Americans. As you stroll the streets, notice these later garage additions, some tucked into the backyard of homes, others carved into the foundation, and some set like bulky shoeboxes in the front yard.

As you cross 13th, look to the right to see five row houses—two of them new, three others beautifully restored—lined up and showing off their differences while achieving a lovely unity.

At 1302 to 1306 Tillamook is an 1892 home built by Phillip Barndorf. As his family grew, Barndorf added on, and in 1909 transformed this Queen Anne, with its ornate touches and vertical aspect, into a Craftsman foursquare. The stained glass and tall narrow windows at the front hint at the home's first incarnation. It has been a duplex at least since 1933; the old addresses are still in place about the two front doors.

Next door is the home of one of the Povey Brothers, whose company produced art glass that enhances homes and churches all over the Portland area. John Povey built this home in 1891; his name and the old street address are inscribed in the steps.

At 14th in the northeast corner is a bigleaf maple, a tree known in Irvington as a Plummer maple. This tree and many others seen in parking strips on this route were planted along Irvington streets in the 1890s by the son of Oakes Plummer, a local resident. Many have reached the end of their life: rot has set in, and the trees have been topped or removed to prevent damage to nearby homes. Licorice fern (*Polypodium glycyrrhiza*) is often found on bigleaf maples in Northwest forests; it flutters here from the crotches of the old mossy branches. The rhizomes of the fern were used by local native peoples as a remedy for sore gums or throats; they were also chewed to curb the appetite, or for the pleasant licorice-like taste.

2 From Tillamook, turn left on NE 15th Avenue. Beginning in 1890, the streetcar ran up 15th from NE Multnomah Street, connecting Irvington to downtown and points beyond. The northwest corner of 15th and Tillamook once held one of the neighborhood's most spectacular homes. Here the Queen of Romania slept on a visit to the Northwest. The house was demolished in 1965, and apartments—the Regal Terrace—went up, a not-unusual occurrence at that time. (More later on how the 1960s treated Irvington.)

At 2026 15th is the Blue Plum Inn, built in 1906 and now one of Irvington's several bed-and-breakfast inns.

At 2225 is a much-altered home built in 1893 by Oakes Plummer. He started as a stock clerk at the Portland Union Stockyards (see Walk 1). Within a decade Plummer had worked his way into the executive suite and established the Pacific International Livestock Exposition. For forty years he rode the Irvington streetcar to work. In 1906 the Plummers moved into the large home next door at 2233.

From 15th, turn right at NE Thompson Street. As with the rest of Portland, Irvington's growth exploded after the 1905 Lewis and Clark Exposition, which showcased the region to the nation. For a decade, Portland carpenters, plumbers, and electricians had as much work as they could handle, and this neighborhood thrived. By 1908, the first homes had gone up north of Knott Street, and the streetcar ran up 15th to Klickitat Street.

At 1508 Thompson is a 1909 Arts and Crafts home designed for W. L. Fleidner, a druggist for the Blumauer-Frank Drug Company, a drug wholesaler that operated from 1890 to 1937. The developer was Marcus Delahunt, who from 1898 through the 1920s built many of Irvington's Arts and Crafts homes, from near-mansions to bungalows.

3 Walk one block on Thompson and turn left at NE 16th Avenue, a gorgeous street. In the northeast corner is a spectacular Prairie home, with its characteristic low, hipped roof, banks of windows, and horizontal aspect. It was designed in 1909 by John Bennes, architect of many Prairie homes in Portland. (More of his homes will be seen later in the walk.) At 2332 16th is a great Arts and Crafts home with beautiful stained glass. The home at 2405 is a brick bungalow of the sort seen in old Chicago neighborhoods but rarely in Portland.

At the northeast corner of 16th and NE Brazee Street is a neoclassical four-square built in 1908 for Charles Painto, the manager for Coconut Products Company in Portland. Kitty-corner, at 2439 16th, is a 1910 Dutch Colonial; the owner of Allen Shingle Company (of Kent, Washington) lived here.

Cross Brazee for a look at a remarkable home, at 2531, sited beautifully under towering firs: a large Craftsman foursquare with classical elements and a unique third-floor balcony.

4 Come back to the intersection of 16th and Brazee and turn west on Brazee to 15th. Here is an opportunity to sit down and soak up the Irvington ambience. Beginning in 1916, when the neighborhood's no-commerce covenant expired, a grocery store occupied this corner. The original store was torn down, and most recently a charcuterie and gelato shop continue to take advantage of the excellent location—an island of commerce in a sea of fine homes.

Across the street at 1510 Brazee is a 1924 duplex by Wade Pipes, a prolific and long-lived Portland architect who never bothered to open his mail, it is said, unless he suspected there was a check inside. Multiplexes such as this were allowed in Irvington only after the restrictive covenants expired.

Cross 15th at the light. After World War II, a 1948 flood displaced all the residents of the wartime city of Vanport, many of whom were African American. Portland was not known for its racial inclusiveness, so the question after the flood was where these now-displaced families could move without upsetting the white status quo. The answer was redlining, an informal practice of allowing blacks or other minorities to buy homes only in certain areas. Irvington, west of 15th, was one of those areas, as were Albina and Piedmont.

At NE 14th Avenue and Brazee you encounter the Irvington School. During the school's construction in the Depression, the contractor hired 350 men, using them on a rotating basis in order to maximize employment. This Mediterranean building, with its terra-cotta and cast-stone accents, replaced an earlier wooden structure at this site. One result of the heinous redlining practice is that Irvington School is well integrated, with 45 percent black and 45 percent white students.

Inside the school is a grand example of WPA art. Check in at the school office, get a name badge, and enjoy *The Settling of the West*, murals by Edward Quigley, who went on to fame as a western-genre painter. An underemployed artist in 1936, he earned $160 for the four months it took him to paint the murals, working while school was in session.

5 From Brazee, turn right on NE 12th Avenue and climb the only hill on this walk. The oldest home in the neighborhood sits at 2611. In 1884 it was built on Broadway, near the river, by Elizabeth Irving's son-in-law. When it was moved in 1913 to this site, the highest ground in Irvington, an Italianate porch was removed and the Craftsman wraparound porch added. Elizabeth Irving lived here until her death in 1922.

From 12th, turn left onto NE Knott Street.

6 From Knott, turn right onto NE 11th Avenue. This block has a personality all its own, thanks in part to Parker Sanderson and Sean Hogan, owners of Sauvie Island's Cistus Nursery, who moved here in the 1990s and spread their gospel of "zonal denial" to their neighbors. Here you'll find plants growing that other experts have claimed won't grow in our climate zone, but that in fact thrive in our wet, mild winters and summer droughts. With cypress and eucalyptus leaning over sidewalks and the boundaries between houses ignored by happy palms and grasses, this block is an outdoor conservatory. Sanderson and Hogan were also the planting designers of the Portland Classical Chinese Garden.

This part of Irvington once shuddered under the pounding of horses' hooves: from 1892 to 1907 it was home to the Irvington Racetrack. Its limits were from 7th to 14th, and from just north of Siskiyou to a bit south of Knott. When platted in 1907, the area was called Prospect Park, due to its slightly higher elevation.

7 From 11th, turn right on NE Stanton Street. At 1135 is a relatively rare home from the Depression. In 1938 Henry and Esther Schwartz, owners of H. H. Schwartz Fixture Company, built this English Cottage bungalow.

From Stanton, turn right on NE 14th Avenue. The Mediterranean bungalow at 2842 dates from the mid 1920s when Hollywood's growing influence began to be felt across the nation, as new homes reflected the Spanish Colonial Revival style common in California. Most of the other houses on the block were built around 1910. The effect of a garage added later is quite apparent at the bungalow at 2738. Especially nice is a bungalow at 2726 with an original cast-stone retaining wall that matches the cast-stone porch columns. This home's gardens were featured in one of Paul Duchscherer's books on the bungalow aesthetic.

8 On 14th, as you approach Knott, the 1950 Augustana Lutheran Church is on the left. It was originally a church for immigrant Swedes, located in Albina. At Knott, turn left.

Homes on Knott, from here east, are of the executive sort. In the first decade of the twentieth century, the bungalow form was wildly popular, but for those of a certain social stature, the Colonial Revival style was seen as more fitting—mature, dignified, and bespeaking success. In Irvington, many such homes were built for owners of retail concerns, mill owners, and timber and grain tycoons, among others. In this era, Irvington was advertised to potential homeowners as "the home of our governor and other decent people."

At 1408 is a 1913 English manor–style home with its original glass canopy, which protects guests from the rain while still letting in light. This home was designed by Joseph Jacobberger. (More of his homes are seen later in the walk, on NE Thompson Street.)

Cross 15th. The 1912 Colonial Revival at 1511 Knott was built and occupied by Edmund Mautz, who constructed approximately fifty such homes in Irvington. He lived here for two years, then moved to a smaller Colonial Revival that he built at 2008 NE Siskiyou Street.

At 1529 Knott is a large Craftsman from 1910. It retains Colonial Revival influences with the Doric columns, while its Craftsman style shows itself in the deep, bracketed eaves and flared roofline.

Between 15th and 17th, Knott is lined with Caucasian wingnut trees (*Pterocarya fraxinifolia*). Native to the Caucasus and northern Iran, this tree, according to plant expert Michael A. Dirr, is "a handsome specimen plant; much superior to ashes and honeylocusts, but little known." These specimens have been topped—a nasty arboreal practice that scars a tree for life.

At 1609 is another huge Colonial Revival, built in 1912 for $28,000 on spec. A Tudor sits at 1628; it was built in 1914 for the owner of the Majestic Theater in downtown Portland. Across from it, at 1633, is a three-story Craftsman with great leaded glass from 1910.

A regal home in Irvington.

The walk turns south on 17th, but before making the turn, look across Knott. At 1719 is a 1915 Colonial Revival that commands the entire block face. Designed by Ellis Lawrence, it was owned by John L. Bowman, who made a fortune in the woolen mills business. The home cost $35,000 to build in 1915 and is made of reinforced concrete block, a popular material at the time. In the front yard is an enormous purple beech, a Portland Heritage Tree.

9 From Knott, turn right onto NE 17th Avenue. In the southeast corner is a 1912 Colonial Revival owned by the Lutheran Church. A tree swallowing a pipe in the parking strip here is a sight to ponder. Seventeenth is a street of more beautiful Craftsman homes from the boom years before World War I. One exception is the Mediterranean at 2627; it's from 1928. This style was virtually nonexistent in Portland prior to the First World War.

From 17th, turn left on NE Brazee Street. Walk one block. At the northwest corner of NE 18th Avenue and Brazee is a 1910 Craftsman with a wildly unconventional chimney of clinker brick and river rock, the best example I've seen. It was designed by Raymond Hockenberry, architect of the Crater Lake Lodge. Another of his distinctive homes is seen in a few blocks. According to neighborhood historians Jim Heuer and Robert Mercer, during World War I the federal government seized control of Douglas fir lumber products for use in the war effort. With the resultant collapse in housing construction, Hockenberry moved to New York, where he became a plumbing engineer and never designed another home.

At NE 19th Avenue and Brazee is a bungalow making use of a classic Craftsman material: river rock, one of the many organic or naturalistic materials favored by this style for chimneys and porch columns. The original river-rock retaining wall further anchors this house to the land it occupies.

10 From Brazee, come to NE 21st Avenue. Before turning right, look at the two homes on the north corners. In the northwest corner at 2509 is a home once owned by Mary Ward See, who with her husband started See's Candies in Los Angeles in 1921. Across the street at 2512 is an example of what happened in Irvington after World War II, a once-elegant home carved into ten apartments. After the removal of ten kitchens and many partitions, the home was restored in 2001 to its original Craftsman glory.

Turn right onto 21st. The home at the southwest corner, 2439 21st, is among Irvington's grandest, designed in 1911 by Ellis Lawrence for Henry Miller, a diplomat for the American Consulate to China. It combines Tudor, Arts and Crafts, and Craftsman styles. The original front porch canopy and second-story balcony were removed at one time, but both were restored in 2000.

Across from it are houses from a less prosperous era. In 1938 the Irvington Club (the green building on the south end of the block) was in a bind caused by its members' dwindling fortunes during the Depression. To raise money, the north end of its property was sold and seven homes were built, their smaller size reflecting that era of deprivation. Four are visible here.

11 From 21st, turn left on NE Thompson Street. In the southeast corner is a 1907 Craftsman built by the owner of a timberland investment firm. It was reportedly a brothel in the 1930s.

Walking east on Thompson, you will pass the front of the Irvington Club, one of the nation's oldest tennis clubs, from 1898. The structure midway through the block was the first clubhouse, built in 1905. Ellis Lawrence designed the 1912 addition at the east end of the block.

At 2210 is an executive home from 1912, designed by Joseph Jacobberger and Alfred Smith in the Jacobethan style for the owner of a railroad equipment manufacturing company. Across from it at 2211 is another Jacobberger home, built for the chief building engineer of the Oregon Railroad and Navigation Company.

Concrete block imitates stone at 2230 in a 1910 Craftsman designed by Raymond Hockenberry. This home was built for William Kennard, owner of Kennard and Adams Department Store at 2601 N Williams Avenue.

John Bennes, who favored the Prairie style after working for a time in Chicago, designed the home at 2330 in 1911. With its tiled roof and stucco exterior, this home has a strong Mediterranean accent. It resembles Bennes's own home on SW Marconi. The glass canopy, which replaces the original canopy that had been removed, was copied from Bennes's residence.

12 From Thompson, turn right on NE 24th Avenue. In 1912, homeowners on this block were not pleased by plans for a fire station in their midst. To appease them, the station at 2200 was made to look like a bungalow, complete with flower boxes and a frontyard fountain. The firehouse was retired in 1964 and now houses Project Linkage, a program in which employees and volunteers help older adults remain independent by providing assistance with driving, shopping, yard work, and home repairs.

At the northwest corner of 24th and NE Tillamook Street (2323 Tillamook) sits a residence on five lots. It was designed by Joseph Jacobberger and built in 1903 by Frank Doernbecher, whose furniture manufacturing plant began operating in Sullivan's Gulch in 1900. The route later passes some of the old factory buildings, where Doernbecher pioneered mass production in the manufacture of bedroom and dining room furniture. In the 1920s his fortune endowed the Doernbecher Children's Hospital at Oregon Health and Science University. Some of the architectural detailing on this home was reputedly manufactured at the Doernbecher Furniture Factory. For three generations, until 1976, Doernbechers lived here.

From 24th, turn left on Tillamook. At 2407 is a grand old Queen Anne from 1891. At NE 26th Avenue, you leave Irvington and enter the Grant Park neighborhood. The home at 2615 has a chimney made of basalt mined from Marquam Gulch, once the site of the city dump. Its neighbor at 2621 must have gone to the same quarry; it also has a feature unusual for 1910: a built-in garage. By today's bloated standards, this one looks no bigger than a closet.

An unexpected curve on Tillamook at NE 27th Avenue allows for romantic home sites unhindered by the prosaic nature of 50-by-100-foot lots. Especially nice is 2748.

The city's first bungalow fire station, on 24th Avenue in Irvington, designed to blend with the neighborhood aesthetic. Photo courtesy of Portland Fire and Rescue and the Historic Belmont Firehouse.

13 From Tillamook, turn right on NE 28th Avenue. At NE Schuyler Street, the land slopes slightly downhill to its natural drainage in the gulch a few blocks south. Cross Broadway to enter the Sullivan's Gulch neighborhood. In one block, at NE Weidler Street, is the Fred Meyer Hollywood West store, built in 1990 on an old industrial site. During its construction, neighbors worried that their untrafficked streets would turn into conduits for shoppers; their activism led to the blocking off of all streets between Broadway and the gulch, at 28th.

14 After Weidler, 28th curves; turn right at the first road after the curve, NE Halsey Street, and the charms of the gulch are immediately apparent. Despite its proximity to the roaring freeway, this neighborhood has thrived. Within walking distance of Lloyd Center shops and MAX, it is urban and noisy, but visually retains a quiet, serene aspect with streets intentionally cut off from commuters. Small bungalows along Halsey date from the early 1900s.

From Halsey, turn left at NE 26th Avenue. At 1420 to 1422 is a rarely seen tree in Portland: *Cunninghamia lanceolata*, commonly known as China fir (though it is not a fir). This member of the cypress family looks like a friendlier

63

cousin of the monkey puzzle tree. It is a native of China, Taiwan, and northern Vietnam. Because of its fragrance, it is used in temple buildings.

15 From 26th, turn right onto NE Multnomah Street. At NE 25th Avenue, a stub of a street that looks like a parking lot, walk south to look over the bottom-land now thoroughly occupied by a freight-rail line, the freeway, and MAX. The proposed multi-use Sullivan's Gulch Trail will follow alongside the freight line. Across the gulch is the Kerns neighborhood.

The gulch was formed in the wake of the Missoula Floods thirteen to twenty thousand years ago. After bursting out of the Columbia River Gorge, floodwaters surged down the Willamette Valley as far south as Eugene, depositing sand, gravels, and cobbles. As the water began to drain out of the Willamette Valley, it scoured channels out of the material that had been deposited. Sullivan's Gulch is such a channel. The floodwaters also carved into the underlying bedrock at sites such as Lacamas and Oswego Lakes.

Timothy Sullivan's donation land claim ran from Broadway to Stark Street, straddling the gulch. He farmed both sides of it. In 1883 the Union Pacific Railroad laid the first tracks through the gulch. In the early 1900s the gulch was a picnic spot, with a waterfall at 19th Avenue ending in a pool. During the Depression, as many as three hundred homeless men built shacks here. A 1941 fire destroyed most of the shacks; the last was torn down when the Banfield Freeway (Interstate 84) was built in the mid 1950s. MAX came in the 1980s. Many of the old industrial buildings still lining the north side of the gulch in this area were part of the Doernbecher Furniture Factory.

16 From Multnomah, turn right onto NE 24th Avenue, then left onto NE Wasco Street, here a lovely block of homes from the first five years of the 1900s. Many homes in this block are a mix of styles typical of that transition time between classically derived styles and styles inspired by vernacular English architecture. Especially nice, a few blocks further west, is the home at 2152, with its unpainted shingles and Stick-style overlay that suggests the house's underlying framework.

17 From Wasco, turn right onto NE 21st Avenue. West of 21st, the land is now increasingly commercial and high-density housing. It once, however, looked much like the neighborhood you're now passing through, with blocks of single-family homes. Some streets were grand (such as 15th Avenue, called Senator's Row), others more humble.

As construction of high-rises and commercial structures moved eastward from Lloyd Center, Sullivan's Gulch residents successfully fought off a total demolition of their neighborhood with its single-family homes. The result is visible here.

From 1923 to 1953, Ralph Lloyd, who had become wealthy from California oil, started buying blocks of these homes with a vision of a large town center, with a retail core, civic center, hotels, apartments, and recreational facilities. By the time of his death in 1953, he had purchased one hundred blocks and had built a golf course (now buried under the Banfield Freeway). According to Jim Heuer and Robert Mercer, the lessons of Lloyd Center are bitterly remembered by east siders. Lloyd's agents would buy homes and leave them to moulder, thereby bringing down the values of adjacent properties, which the Lloyds could then purchase at a depressed price.

Lloyd's daughter finished Lloyd's plans after his death; homes were razed, and in 1960, Lloyd Center opened as the largest shopping mall in the world. (It sits between Halsey and Multnomah, 9th and 15th.) The mass of the mall drew other commerce to its fringes. With the flight to the suburbs in the 1960s, the neighborhood now called Sullivan's Gulch (originally Holladay Park Addition) deteriorated. By the late 1970s it was seen as expendable: too urban and close to the freeway to attract homeowners. The city planned high-rise apartments and more commercial development. In 1979, however, neighbors organized, calling themselves the Sullivan's Gulch Neighborhood Association, and countered the city's plan with one of their own. They won, and the result is a three-zone development plan, with a gradual step-down of building heights east of Lloyd Center. High-rises are allowed closest to the mall, with lower heights permitted up to 21st, and single-family or row housing permitted east of 21st. At 1309 21st is a 1925 home, built just when Ralph Lloyd was beginning his acquisitions.

18 From 21st, turn right onto NE Clackamas Street, another especially beautiful street. At 2173 is a Craftsman with elements of a Swiss chalet, a not-uncommon variant of the Craftsman theme. It was designed by Henry Hefty. In 1895, then a prominent architect in town, Hefty won a contract to design Portland's new City Hall. After construction began, it became clear that his grandiose design was both financially and aesthetically over the top. Construction ceased, the city fired him, and Whidden and Lewis were given the contract. Their design stands today. A humbled Hefty saw no more large public commissions. He spent the rest of his life designing middle-class homes. His exuberance is apparent, even today, in the artful details of this home.

The Prairie style, with its horizontal aspect, is represented at 2216 and 2234. Compare these homes with the more vertical orientation of the Queen Anne across the street at 2305. The home at 2320 was built circa 1885; it was occupied by farmhands who worked the fields along the gulch.

From Clackamas, come to NE 24th Avenue. In the southeast corner is a spectacular Arts and Crafts home with an unusual two-story, half-round bay on its west side.

From Clackamas, turn left at 24th, and walk one block to NE Halsey Street. In 1870, when East Portland was incorporated, this intersection was the end of town: east of 24th and north of Halsey, you stepped into unplatted forests.

At Broadway and 24th is the beautiful Arts and Crafts–style Metropolitan Community Church, here since 1977. The church building went up in 1909 as the Universalist Church of Good Tidings. A decade later it changed hands, becoming Grace Lutheran, and the Broadway streetcar brought German immigrants to worship here. When Broadway was widened in 1930 to accommodate auto traffic, the church lost a chunk of property, and a fire in 1988 destroyed the west face of the building. The large stained glass window was installed after the fire, in memory of church members who have died of AIDS.

19 From 24th, turn left at Hancock Street. On the right, as you approach NE 22nd Avenue, is the Robert and Ida Lytle mansion, reputedly the most expensive home in Irvington at the time it was built ($46,000 in 1911). Robert Lytle was a lumberman who founded Hoquiam Lumber and Shingle Company in Washington. In 1920 the home was purchased by Willard Hawley, who founded Hawley Pulp and Paper in Oregon City (now the Blue Heron Paper Company, seen in Walk 19). Hawley was a member of the Hoot Owls, a musical group that played in the home's basement ballroom. In the 1920s the Hoot Owls were broadcast over KGY radio, a station founded in a studio inside the mansion by Hawley's son. At the time it was the most powerful station in the city. Reputedly, the first radio commercial (for a local ice cream store) was broadcast from KGY's studio here.

Kitty-corner from the Lytle mansion are the Silver Court Apartments from 1919. Continue walking west on Hancock. At the southeast corner of 21st and Hancock is the Central Lutheran Church, designed in 1948 by internationally known Portland architect Pietro Belluschi. The style is International but with a Northwest nod to local materials, and subtle Nordic and Japanese elements.

West of 21st, Hancock shows the effects of Irvington's low point in the 1960s, when homeowners fled in the face of integration, and developers snapped up properties at depressed prices to build low-rise apartments. In the face of these incursions into the neighborhood's historic character, the Irvington Community Association formed in 1965 to revitalize Irvington and preserve its homes. In 1967 it held the city's first historic home tour, a tradition that continues each May. Further west in this block, fine homes from the early 1900s remain. At 1903 is a home built by Harry Nicolai of Nicolai Door, one of Portland's largest employers. It was designed by Emil Schacht in 1905, architect of many Arts and Crafts homes in Willamette Heights. In the 1960s, Minnie Olson lived here; she resisted developers who wanted to tear her house down to build apartments.

20 From Hancock, turn right on NE 19th Avenue. Walk one block, passing an enormous blue Atlas cedar (*Cedrus atlantica* 'Glauca') planted in a long-gone front yard. Stop a moment at Tillamook Street. The home in the northeast corner, where 19th jogs, belonged to Governor George Chamberlain (also a U.S. senator) from 1904 to 1928. Built in 1891, it was an early design of Whidden and Lewis, but some of their signature elements, such as curved bays, were altered.

From 19th, walk west on Tillamook. In the northeast corner of NE 18th Avenue is a large Craftsman from 1907 built for banker Walter Cook and designed by John Bennes. Since 1986 the house has been the 18th Avenue Peace House, home to the Metanoia Peace Community United Methodist Church, a cooperative Christian living society. Metanoia is Greek, meaning "a change of mind." Members, some of whom live in the Peace House, renounce the culture of individualism and commit to a community in which they share their incomes, possessions, time, and faith with each other. This pooling of resources allows them to share their talents and resources with the larger community.

At 1748 Tillamook begins a set of three gorgeous homes. At 1748 is a 1910 Arts and Crafts house built for Loyal Kern, owner of a brickyard at NE 33rd Avenue and Tillamook (today the site of Fernwood Middle School). At 1734 and 1724 are two Arts and Crafts homes, both built in 1914 by prolific developer Marcus Delahunt.

At 1729 Tillamook is a 1907 foursquare, home for years to Clifton Easeley, who gardened the large, farmlike lot until he was ninety-nine years old. In the 1990s, Mooshe, the neighborhood's beloved potbellied pig, obligingly consumed kibble given him by visitors—sometimes, as in the case of my two-year-old daughter, mistaking their fingers for treats.

The F. E. Bowman Apartments at 1636 to 1624 were built in 1913 and are listed on the National Register of Historic Places.

At NE 16th Avenue in the northeast corner (2110 16th) is the Coleman Scott House, which has been in the same family since it was built in 1915. Mr. Coleman, an insurance executive, passed the home on to his daughter, Elizabeth, and her husband, Lesley Scott (son of Harvey Scott and nephew of suffragist Abigail Scott Duniway). Inside are original pieces of furniture and other items exhibited at the 1905 Lewis and Clark Exposition.

21 From 16th and Tillamook, walk south on 16th. At 1927 is a Queen Anne built in 1894. At 1905 are Craftsman apartments from 1912, also designed by F. E. Bowman. Across from them on Hancock is another set of Bowman apartments, from 1912, with a clinker-brick façade. Density increases on the streets nearest the old streetcar line on Broadway. To the left is the basalt Westminster Presbyterian Church, designed in 1912 by Ellis Lawrence, who lived in Irvington. In this church in 1965, three hundred Irvington residents gathered to oppose the city's plan to demolish everything west of NE 15th Avenue in order to build an industrial park.

From 16th, turn right on NE Schuyler Street. At the end of the block, at 1810 NE 15th Avenue, looms the spectacular Freiwald House, built in 1905 for Gustav Freiwald, a German immigrant who owned the Star Brewery and other breweries from Hood River to Astoria. The home looks like a happy extrovert, blending Queen Anne, Craftsman, and Colonial Revival elements in a big, showy way. In the mid-twentieth century this home was a boarding house. It was restored in 1993 as a bed-and-breakfast, The Lion and the Rose.

22 From Schuyler, turn left on 15th, and walk one block to a beautiful commercial intersection of streetcar-era buildings. Fifteenth and Broadway was the intersection of two streetcars and is the heart of NE Broadway's commercial district. Good places to eat and shop are centered between 18th and 10th Avenues, with one of Portland's signature attractions, an independent bookstore, Broadway Books, at 1714, and our homegrown version of Crate and Barrel, Kitchen Kaboodle, at 16th. Virtually all the shops and restaurants here are locally owned and make for a nice hour or two of shopping and sightseeing.

If you turn left, at 1700 NE Broadway you'll see a 1920s Mediterranean streetcar-era commercial building. Its front had to be cut back in 1930 when Broadway was widened. Other brick structures between 17th and 14th are also from the 1920s. At 14th is the 1924 Irvington Theatre building. A few years after the Lloyd Center multiplex opened in 1986, this theater closed its doors.

At 13th, a Goodwill inhabits a former Barnes and Noble, which moved from this locals-only street into the mall with the other chain stores.

23 Continue on Broadway to 12th Avenue. To explore Lloyd Center, turn left at 12th and walk a few blocks south to the mall entrance. Inside are retail shops, a food court, an ice rink, and a multiplex theater.

The walk turns right at 12th, leaving the commercial district. Walk two blocks to Hancock Street and turn left, passing multiplexes that span the last century. Walk two blocks on Hancock to 10th Avenue. The tower at the corner is Dahlke Manor, low-income housing operated by the Housing Authority of Portland. It was built in 1971.

From Hancock, turn right onto 10th and walk one block to the starting point.

ROSE CITY PARK, BEAUMONT, AND HOLLYWOOD LOOP

DISTANCE 5.8 miles

STARTING POINT Frazer Park: NE 52nd Avenue and Hassalo Street

GETTING THERE AND PARKING From downtown Portland, cross the Burnside Bridge. Before reaching SE 12th Avenue, get in the left lane to veer onto NE Sandy Boulevard. After the light at NE 20th Avenue, watch for NE Glisan Street; it will veer off to the right at NE 22nd Avenue. Drive east on Glisan through Laurelhurst to a stoplight at NE 53rd Avenue. Turn left and cross Interstate 84. Turn left on NE Hassalo Street. Park along the street and walk to the starting point.

TriMet: Take the MAX Blue Line to the stop at NE 60th Avenue. Walk north on 60th to Hassalo Street, and then west on Hassalo eight blocks to the starting point. Alternatively, take bus 77 (Broadway/Halsey) to the stop at NE 53rd and Halsey Street; walk one block west to 52nd, and then four blocks south to the starting point.

RESTROOMS AND DRINKING FOUNTAINS Seasonal restrooms and a portable toilet are at Normandale Park, and restrooms are available during daylight hours at the Rose City Golf Clubhouse. A drinking fountain is at the northwest corner of NE 57th, Sandy, and Alameda.

FOOD AND DRINK An Asian market, bakery, and restaurant are at NE 67th Avenue and Broadway. Along NE Fremont Street, food options range from a bagel to upscale Northwest cuisine, and along NE Sandy Boulevard are more cafés.

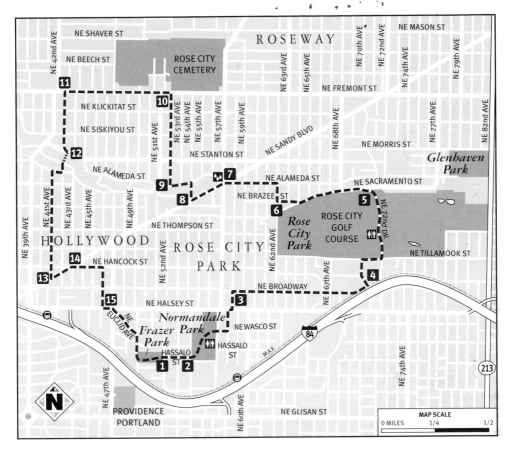

NE SHAVER ST
NE BEECH ST
NE 42nd AVE
ROSEWAY
ROSE CITY CEMETERY
NE 63rd AVE
NE 65th AVE
NE 70th AVE
NE 72nd AVE
NE MASON ST
NE 74th AVE
NE 79th AVE
NE FREMONT ST
11
NE KLICKITAT ST
10
NE SISKIYOU ST
NE 51st AVE
NE 53rd AVE
NE 54th AVE
NE 55th AVE
NE 57th AVE
NE 59th AVE
NE SANDY BLVD
NE 68th AVE
NE MORRIS ST
NE 77th AVE
NE 82nd AVE
Glenhaven Park
12
NE STANTON ST
NE ALAMEDA ST
9
NE 41st AVE
NE 43rd AVE
NE 45th AVE
NE 49th AVE
NE 39th AVE
8
NE BRAZEE ST
7
NE ALAMEDA ST
NE SACRAMENTO ST
6
5
NE 72nd DR
Rose City Park
ROSE CITY GOLF COURSE
NE THOMPSON ST
HOLLYWOOD
ROSE CITY
PARK
NE 52nd AVE
NE 62nd AVE
NE TILLAMOOK ST
14
NE HANCOCK ST
13
NE BROADWAY
4
NE 67th AVE
15
NE HALSEY ST
3
NE EUCLID AVE
Normandale Frazer Park Park
NE WASCO ST
84
NE 74th AVE
213
HASSALO ST
1 **2**
HASSALO ST
MAX
NE 47th AVE
NE 60th AVE
NE GLISAN ST
PROVIDENCE PORTLAND
N

MAP SCALE
0 MILES   1/4   1/2

WALK 5. *Rose City Park, Beaumont, and Hollywood Loop*

MAP KEY

- ▪ ▬ ROUTE
- ▪▪▪▪▪ STAIRS
- ▬ ▬ TRAIL
- ‑‑‑‑ MAX TRACKS
- 🚇 MAX STATION
- ‑‑‑‑‑ STREETCAR TRACKS
- ‑‑‑‑‑ TROLLEY TRACKS
- ▦▦▦ RAILROAD TRACKS
- PARK/GREENSPACE
- HISTORIC/CONSERVATION DISTRICT
- 🚻 PUBLIC RESTROOM
- 💧 WATER

BEST TIMES TO VISIT   The Hollywood Farmers Market is held at NE 44th Avenue and Hancock Street, near **14**. One of the city's largest farmers markets, it is open Saturdays from May through October. See hollywoodfarmersmarket. org for times and dates.

ACCESSIBILITY   This walk climbs and descends Alameda Ridge, with about 70 feet of elevation gain from its lowest to highest point. Alternate routes to paths and staircases are noted in the text.

THIS CITY WALK EXPLORES Rose City Park, a neighborhood born of the boom in Portland that followed the 1905 Lewis and Clark Exposition. This world's fair, a successful showcase of the city's attributes, triggered a bout of civic bragging by the Chamber of Commerce: "Portland is at present the mecca for tourists and large investors." Jobs were created, and immigrants came west to fill them.

To meet the demand for housing, new real estate developments sprung up on Portland's east side, where land was abundant and easy to develop. One new neighborhood was Rose City Park, from 45th Avenue to 62nd Avenue, along Sandy Boulevard. (Today its boundaries are 47th and 65th, Fremont and Interstate 84.) Promoted by Theodore B. Wilcox and others, it was planned as a community of homes affordable to the average skilled craftsman. No home could cost less than $1500 (in Irvington the minimum was $2500 at that time). Rose City Park was a stunning success. Wilcox made an 800 percent profit; one lasting result of his financial success is the Wilcox Maternity Hospital, now part of Legacy Good Samaritan Hospital and Medical Center (seen in Walk 13). Wilcox's home is seen in Walk 12.

The walk also travels through parts of the Beaumont, Grant Park, Hollywood, Madison South, and Roseway neighborhoods. You may want to bring binoculars to better view sites visible from Alameda Ridge.

1   The building in Frazer Park, where this walk begins, was a Portland public school built in 1961 to relieve baby boom congestion at Laurelhurst and Rose City Park Schools. In 1962, Portland Public Schools reached its all-time enrollment high of eighty-two thousand students, climbing from forty-nine thousand in 1947, just after World War II. Later, when this school was no longer needed as the number of school-age children declined, the building was sold to Child Development, Inc. (CDI) Early Head Start. (More on the intriguing history of this park at the end of the walk.)

Walk east on NE Hassalo Street. The home at 5242 dates from 1900, before the Rose City Park subdivision was platted, when the area was agricultural. Across from it at 5241 is a 1910 foursquare with a beautiful arched porch. At NE 55th Avenue the residential neighborhood abruptly ends. The streets south of Hassalo are adjacent to the rail line that since 1883 has run through Sullivan's Gulch. (That line is now adjacent to Interstate 84.) Until the 1930s, Pacific Car and Foundry built rail cars south of Hassalo, between 55th and 60th Avenues. In general, farms between the gulch and Halsey, and from 39th to 64th, gave way in the early 1900s to industry.

2 From 55th and Hassalo, cut diagonally northeast through Normandale Park, walking toward an asphalt path that runs north of the dog area. (To avoid the grass, turn left at 55th, and turn right onto a paved path leading into the park at NE Wasco Street.) The park was once the site of competing dairies. In 1923, in an earlier postwar baby boom, the Rose City Park neighborhood was bursting with children. To relieve crowding at Rose City Park School (NE 57th Avenue and Sacramento Street), Normandale School was built here. It closed in 1931, and the grounds became a city park in the 1940s.

Walk along the asphalt path to the eastern edge of the park at 57th and Wasco. The commercial building at the southeast corner of this intersection was the Hall Dairy, from 1911.

Walk one block east on Wasco and turn left on NE 58th Avenue. Cross NE Halsey Street carefully, and jog slightly to the right, staying on 58th. Up on the hill a few blocks north is the red brick Rose City Park School, closed in 2007 when Portland Public Schools had an enrollment of about forty-six thousand students, a decline of ten thousand students in ten years. The decline in enrollment seems likely to continue as Portland's real estate values climb beyond what many young families can afford.

3 From 58th, turn right onto NE Broadway, a street loaded with small homes from the late 1930s (5824) and early 1940s (5837). At NE 59th Avenue, the curb reads "E 59th St. N," a street name system that disappeared in 1931 when the city adopted the current system (see Walk 13 for more information).

At NE 61st Avenue are homes in the English Cottage style, with leaded glass front picture windows, steep roof pitches, and stonework on the front façade. These homes (6134 and 6125, for example) date from the late 1930s, when not a lot of houses were being built. At 6330 and 6411 are homes built circa 1940, when styles were transitioning to a modern aesthetic with few historical references and a clean, linear orientation.

At NE 65th Avenue, apartments begin. This area saw radical change in the 1970s as refugees from Southeast Asia found homes in this apartment complex, with the help of the Catholic Resettlement Agency. Fleeing economic and political chaos, they may have thought they'd landed well, with the leafy, peaceful Rose City Park nearby.

Continue on Broadway. The small strip mall at NE 67th Avenue and Broadway reflects the area's heritage, with an Asian market and restaurant, and a bakery that specializes in Vietnamese and French sandwiches. Beyond it, Broadway is hard up against Interstate 84. The roar of traffic is muffled by a barrier wall with an uneven surface that grabs sound waves more effectively than a smooth wall.

4 At NE 70th Avenue, turn left and walk through the vine-covered and shady Binford Garden Townhomes. Built from the late 1940s to early 1950s by the Binford family, these townhomes are a beautiful example of a large, midcentury garden apartment complex. The Binfords themselves lived in various units for years. Of the 274 units, most are midrange apartments, though some were converted to condominiums in the 1980s.

Turn right at NE Tillamook Street and then left at NE 72nd Drive to enter the Rose City Golf Course, situated in a depression formed by the Missoula Floods, a series of Ice Age flood events of the Columbia River caused by repeated failures of ice dams at glacial Lake Missoula (in today's Montana). With each dam's collapse, walls of debris-laden water hundreds of feet high blasted through the Columbia River Gorge. Rocky Butte, about twenty blocks due east, was a huge obstacle in the path of the floods as they emerged from the gorge. Churning furiously around it, flood waters scoured out this "plunge pool," a depression whose violent past is now peacefully at rest under the green links of the golf course. Above it, to the north and west, is Gravelly Hill, now called Alameda Ridge, a deposit of Rocky Mountain and eastern Washington gravels, sand, and cobbles ferried here by the floods.

With the development of the adjacent neighborhood, the depression became home to the Portland Country Club and Livestock Association. Horse racing was the primary attraction; ten horse barns were built in the infield, and a grandstand was built on the hill you are about to climb.

In 1912 history was made at this site with the first airmail service in the Pacific Northwest. A bamboo Curtis biplane took off from the racetrack infield loaded with fifteen hundred letters. Thirteen minutes later its destination was reached: the parade grounds of Vancouver Barracks (seen in Walk 20).

One building in the Binford Garden Townhomes.

In the 1910s the course was used for motorcycle racing, and later for auto racing, but with increasing urbanization, racecar engines became less tolerable to neighbors. The track was removed in 1923, and the property sold to the city for the quieter sounds of a golf course. In 1931 a Depression-era work relief project built the Tudor clubhouse, and if you look carefully along 72nd Drive, you can see hand-hewn basalt blocks from that period lining the road as it winds through the golf course. They are nearly obliterated by asphalt and turf but would be a lovely feature if they were maintained, the kind of simple, artful touch that money rarely buys anymore.

Follow 72nd Drive as it climbs uphill.

5 From 72nd Drive, turn left onto NE Sacramento Street. Its views are less heralded but even better than those on NE Alameda Street, where enormous homes block the view from pedestrians. Walk along the mulched path on the golf course side for magnificent, wide-angle vistas of Mount Tabor, Mount Hood, and the rising landscape between them. Views get better the further west you walk.

One early resident of the neighborhood, Maria Moe, recalled taking the trolley in 1910 to her new home on 68th Avenue near here. From the trolley stop at

63rd and Hillcrest (now Sacramento), she carried her baby girl on trails through hazel and fir groves to her house. Moe and her husband had a cow, chickens, and a vegetable garden. On one memorable day, circus elephants wintering at the racetrack escaped from their pens, clambered up the hillside, and rampaged along the bluff here, breaking clotheslines and trampling fences.

The homes along Sacramento are a nice lot, from the 1910s (6707), 1920s (6877, 6631, 6609), 1940s (6915), and 1950s (6535).

At NE 64th Avenue, turn right, and then immediately left onto NE Brazee Street. Homes here are older, as the route gets closer to NE Sandy Boulevard, the route of the streetcar.

6 From Brazee, turn right on NE 62nd Avenue. As you're walking the one block to NE Alameda Street, notice the house on the left, in the southwest corner of Alameda and 62nd. It was built in 1907 as a club for jockeys working at the racetrack. The clubhouse grounds occupied four lots. A barn still remains at the back of the house.

Turn left onto Alameda, and at the front of the house, notice the full wrap-around porch and recessed second-story balcony. It's easy to imagine clouds of cigar and cigarette smoke billowing from the porches as jockeys unwound after a day at the races. Across the street, at 6131, is a Craftsman bungalow from that same year. Pass more homes built circa 1910, and cross NE 59th Avenue. The 1925 Rose City United Methodist Church is on the left.

7 At NE 57th Avenue the route encounters Sandy Boulevard, one of Portland's oldest streets, having been laid out in 1855 as a route to the Sandy River. Sandy cuts a diagonal through Northeast Portland. Cross Sandy, 57th, and Alameda at the stoplight to get positioned to walk downhill on the north side of Sandy. This intersection of three streets atop Gravelly Hill (Alameda Ridge) was the social heart of the Rose City Park neighborhood. On the right, between Alameda and Sandy, is the 1913 Rose City Park Club. It offered neighborhood residents a place to bowl, play tennis, and hold meetings and banquets. Unlike the Laurelhurst and Irvington clubs, however, this neighborhood club failed soon after it was built. In 1921 the building became the Friendship Masonic Lodge. In front is a statue of George Washington given to the city in 1927 by Dr. Henry Waldo Coe (who also donated the spectacular statue of Joan of Arc at NE 39th Avenue and Glisan Street, seen in Walk 7). A water fountain from 1916 shares the space.

Across Sandy from the old club is a 1913 firehouse, of a style often seen in Portland firehouses. When built, it housed horse-drawn trucks, but it was designed for future conversion to "automobile apparatus." The grooved cement

The sculpture at Fire Station 28 (Rose City).

that provided traction for the horses is still visible beneath the doors. In 1985 the city gave this building to the Office of Neighborhood Involvement; in 2006, with a renovation, it became an active fire station again.

Walk downhill on Sandy and enjoy the view of downtown Portland ahead. Streetcar service was essential to the success of Rose City Park when it was plat-

77

ted. Starting in 1907, with the sales of the first lots, the main line ran up Sandy to its terminus at 68th. The section of Sandy from 45th to 57th Avenues was the area's first commercial district, predating the Hollywood Business District. A public market, theater, grocery store, bakery, and pharmacy thrived here alongside homes. Most of the homes are gone now, but various businesses remain.

8 You'll leave Sandy at NE 54th Avenue, but before you do, look across the boulevard to the red brick Sandy Crest Terraces, townhomes built at the site of a quarry, where the gravels and cobbles from the Missoula Floods were put to economic use. Another gravel pit was at NE 33rd Avenue and Fremont Street, atop Alameda Ridge.

Turn right on 54th and walk uphill, past the grounds of Our Lady of Lavang, Southeast Asian Vicariate. The vicariate was born of the 1975 boat lifts of refugees from Cambodia, Laos, and Vietnam. Since 1981 the Catholic Archdiocese has operated a church and resettlement agencies here to serve immigrants and refugees from Ethiopia, Haiti, San Salvador, the former Soviet Union, the former Yugoslavia, eastern Europe, and Africa. Along with the usual church activities, immigrants can take part in traditional celebrations and festivals, martial arts classes, and workshops on the political, judicial, and social systems of the United States. Other transitions to America are facilitated here, with links to schools, public agencies, housing, tutoring, medical services, transportation, and counseling.

Before it was the Southeast Asian Vicariate, the Gothic Revival building on 52nd was the Holy Child Academy. Beginning in 1913, the Sisters of the Holy Child Jesus lived and taught here. The last class graduated in 1973.

At Alameda, turn left. On the right is the 1911 Spanish Colonial Revival–style Saint Rose of Lima Catholic Church and its adjacent school. Walk past a group of deep-porched bungalows. The house at 5212, built in 1912, is a bit unusual in that the bungalow form is not known for its perfect symmetry.

9 Turn right on NE 52nd Avenue, a quiet street of small and varied bungalows. Over the last century, home improvement fads have washed over this neighborhood. Today most of the homes have seen the renovator's claw hammer, returning them to their original lines, but even the few remaining 1960s architectural apostasies have historical interest at this point.

The house at 3202 has a sweetly simple addition of river rock to its chimney, which makes me wonder if the builder's child wasn't invited to help dad out that day. The home at 3215, built in 1922, is tiny—just 750 square feet—and very attractive. At 3315 and 3314, evidence suggests that a traveling wrought-iron salesman once came a-calling and convinced a fair number of homeowners to replace their aging Craftsman wooden porch columns with New Orleans–style ironwork.

As you walk toward NE Fremont Street, ahead is the Rose City Cemetery, which contains the graves of many gypsies, including Frank Ellis (1906 to 1966), "King of the Gypsies in eight western states." Contained within the larger cemetery is the Japanese Cemetery, here since the 1890s. During World War II, some of its graves were vandalized when patriotism ran amok.

10 At Fremont, turn left and enjoy ten blocks of shops, food, coffee, and bars. In the last decades of the twentieth century, as the neighborhood turned over to young families, older taverns such as Stanich's and McPeet's have welcomed sellers of yoga, pizza, and bagels to the street, as well as more offbeat products such as wallbeds.

Cross NE 47th Avenue. On the left is a majestic bungalow from 1910 that once occupied the entire block face. In 2002 the townhomes adjacent to it sprouted where the yard used to be, with architecture that is somewhat sympathetic to the mother house. The ancient hedge that used to encircle the entire property still exists in places.

The route turns left on NE 42nd Avenue, but if you want a great bagel, walk a few steps further on Fremont to Bagel Land. It's the only place in town, they say, where they boil bagels the old-world way. If you time your walk to arrive here after 2:30 and before 3:00, the day's bagels will be going on sale, half price. It's a bargain worth shuffling a schedule for.

11 From Fremont, turn left at NE 42nd Avenue onto a block full of large Craftsman homes. The house at 3325, from 1912, has a roofline reminiscent of the Flying Nun's habit, and the 1912 home at 3311 evokes the quiet countryside with its large double lot. At 42nd and NE Klickitat Street, notice the iron rails set in the curbs to protect the concrete from the wheels of passing horse-drawn delivery trucks.

The home at 3205 has a secret: it used to be a one-story bungalow. Now a two-story home, it is not atypical in this neighborhood, where the amenities, neighborliness, and proximity to downtown make it hard for some folks to leave, even when they've outgrown their home.

Across NE Siskiyou Street, 42nd ends; you're now on Alameda. At NE Beaumont Street, veer left to stay on Alameda. Walk by grand homes built to maximize Alameda's fine hilltop views. (To avoid the stairs in the next section, turn right onto Beaumont, then left onto NE 41st Avenue, and take it downhill.

As 41st curves around, it becomes 42nd. Follow 42nd to NE Stanton Street and rejoin the route.)

12 Just past 4196 Alameda, 123 steps take you off Alameda Ridge and down to the flats. From the steps, views of the West Hills are superb, from the red and white tower at Healy Heights, to Council Crest to its north, and beyond that to Forest Park above Willamette Heights.

The steps end at NE Wistaria Drive and 42nd Avenue. Carefully cross 42nd, a busy street, walk one block south (left) on 42nd, and then turn right onto Stanton, a quiet street whose curves beckon. Resist them, and turn left onto 41st. You won't be disappointed. Northeast 41st Avenue is one of the rare streets in the Hollywood area to sport a canopy of mature elms. This combined with the variety of old and well-loved homes along its length makes 41st a walker's treat.

Cross NE Brazee Street. All marriages have conflicts, and the house at 2415 has what seems to me a nice architectural feature: identical porches on either corner, each offering a retreat for feuding spouses.

At NE Tillamook Street, enter the Hollywood Business District. The public library branch at the corner was built by Multnomah County in 2002 with condominiums above it, a successful mixed-use project that has attracted national attention. With more than two million items in circulation each year, the Hollywood Library is the busiest in the Multnomah County library system, itself one of the busiest library systems in the nation.

Beyond the library, at 1905 NE 41st, is Dania, a furniture store located in a 1940 Art Moderne building originally built for Paul Schatz Furniture. Walk south toward the spires of the Hollywood Theatre.

At 41st and NE Hancock Street is a block that was used in the 1920s as a public garage. During that time, cars were becoming popular, yet few homes had garages, so car commuters would stash their cars here and walk or take the streetcar the rest of the way home.

Also in this block is a bit of retail history. Fred Meyer was born in Brooklyn in 1886. As a twenty-three-year-old, he moved to Portland and began peddling coffee, tea, and spices from a horse-drawn wagon. Eventually he entered the grocery business and pioneered the concept of a self-service store. In 1931 he opened the first self-service drugstore in the world in downtown Portland. Later, in 1950, he turned this block into his first "suburban" store. Customers chased their carts on the store's sloping floors until 1990, when the Fred Meyer Hollywood West store was built in Sullivan's Gulch (seen in Walk 4). This store closed a few years later; small retailers now occupy the building. When Meyer died in 1978, he left his estate in trust; today, the Meyer Memorial Trust awards

The street scene in 1934 at NE 41st and Sandy Boulevard. This is the south side of the street, looking east from 41st. Photo courtesy of the City of Portland Archives.

grants in just about every conceivable field to nonprofits in Oregon and Clark County, Washington.

At Sandy, study for a moment the rococo glory of the Hollywood Theatre, with its maidens modestly covering their chests and cherubs immodestly romping above the marquee. It was designed by John Bennes, known for his Prairie homes in Portland. Bring a pair of binoculars and see if you can find the terracotta caryatids (columns shaped like women), mermaids, bearded warrior, ram's head, lyre-playing angel, theatrical masks, putti (cherubic infants), shell, and acanthus leaves. The theater was built in 1925, a time when the Hollywood and Grant Park neighborhoods were booming (nearby Grant High was also built that year). It is still a focal point of the Hollywood community—which, incidentally, was named for it, not the other way around.

13   From 41st, turn left onto Sandy. At 42nd is a fine brick and terra-cotta building that was built in 1926 as the Oregon State Bank. It didn't survive the Depression. The door at the southwest corner of 43rd and Sandy is a portal to another era. Take a few minutes for a drugstore milkshake at the counter of Paulsen's Pharmacy, here since 1918. It's open every day except Sunday.

14   From Paulsen's, cross 43rd and veer off Sandy to walk east on Hancock. Northeast 44th Avenue and Hancock is the site of the splendid Hollywood Farmers Market.

At 45th and 46th Avenues along Hancock are several classic low-slung Craftsman bungalows, with deep eaves and a rich use of diverse organic materials. The porch at the northwest corner of 46th and Hancock, like a Jackson Pollock painting, looks at first glance like something anyone could pull off, but in the chaotic jumble of bricks is a coherence that could only be created by a master.

From Hancock, turn right on 46th, where bungalows on one side escaped the 1960s wrecking ball long enough to become economically viable again. Across the street, a 1969 apartment complex sits at the site of some less fortunate homes.

15   From 46th, turn left onto Halsey. In one block, cross Halsey and 47th Avenue at the light to walk southeast on NE Euclid Avenue, a surprising little hill with fine views to the southwest.

Turn right on 49th and walk to its end, at the back side of Frazer Park. (For an accessible route, from 49th, turn left on Multnomah, right on 52nd, and return to the start.) The grounds here were occupied from 1910 to around 1950 by the Frazer Detention Home, a three-story Multnomah County home for juvenile delinquents. It held up to seventeen girls and thirty-one boys. The home was demolished when the Donald E. Long Center at 1408 NE 68th Avenue opened. Large cherry and chestnut trees are the only vestiges of the home, remnants of the garden that provided meaningful work for the occupants.

Walk through the park back to the starting point at 52nd and Hassalo.

The Hollywood Theatre, designed by John Bennes and built in 1925.

3/3/10 Phyllis

WALK 6

BUCKMAN TO KERNS LOOP

DISTANCE 4.4 miles

STARTING POINT SE 19th Avenue and Washington Street

GETTING THERE AND PARKING From downtown Portland, cross the Burnside Bridge. Turn right onto SE 20th Avenue and drive five blocks to the stoplight at SE Stark Street. Drive one more block on 20th and turn right onto SE Washington Street. Drive one block to SE 19th. Park on the street.

TriMet: Take bus 15 (Belmont) east toward the Parkrose/Sumner Transit Center. Get off at SE Belmont Street and 20th Avenue, walk three blocks north on 20th to Washington Street, turn left, and walk one block to the starting point.

RESTROOMS AND DRINKING FOUNTAINS Restrooms and drinking fountains at Colonel Summers Park (SE 18th Avenue and Yamhill Street) operate seasonally. Restrooms can also be found at various restaurants and coffee shops along the route (for customers).

FOOD AND DRINK Food and drink are well spaced along this walk, with cafés on SE Morrison Street between 13th and 14th Avenues, a coffee shop at NE 22nd

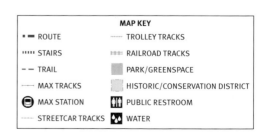

MAP KEY	
▪ ▬ ROUTE	⋯⋯ TROLLEY TRACKS
⁙⁙⁙⁙ STAIRS	⊢⊢⊢ RAILROAD TRACKS
– – TRAIL	▩ PARK/GREENSPACE
――― MAX TRACKS	▨ HISTORIC/CONSERVATION DISTRICT
🚌 MAX STATION	🚻 PUBLIC RESTROOM
⋯⋯ STREETCAR TRACKS	🌊 WATER

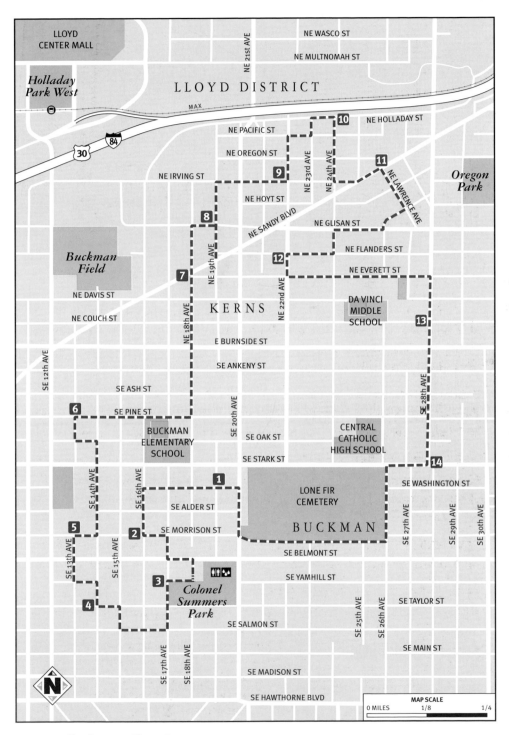

WALK 6. *Buckman to Kerns Loop*

Avenue and Pacific Street, and various options on 28th Avenue from NE Everett Street to SE Stark Street.

BEST TIMES TO VISIT Buckman Art Show and Sell, at Buckman Arts Magnet Elementary School, is an annual two-day spring fundraiser with one hundred Northwest artists selling their art, plus student art from the arts magnet program. Call 503-916-3506 or see www.buckmanelementary.org/artsale for information.

The da Vinci Arts Fair is an annual two-day winter fundraiser for da Vinci Arts Middle School that features local visual and performing artists. Call 503-916-5356 or see www.davinci.pps.k12.or.us for information.

ACCESSIBILITY The walk is relatively flat, with about 90 feet of elevation gain in a gentle grade. It is on city sidewalks, with one staircase; directions to avoid the staircase are given in the text.

THIS CITY WALK is a wonderful mix of nineteenth-century homes, opulent 1920s apartment houses, cafés and coffee houses, and architecturally historic commercial buildings. Buckman is among the city's older neighborhoods. Like most close-in east side neighborhoods, its growth was directly tied to the opening of the city's bridges in the 1880s and 1890s. Kerns, a neighborhood largely unchanged for a century, is heavy on apartments and light industry. It lies north of Buckman, running up to the edge of Sullivan's Gulch. Squeezed between the gulch and NE Sandy Boulevard, the triangular north end of Kerns offers some terrain little visited by most Portlanders.

1 The corner of SE 19th Avenue and Washington Street is the heart of Buckman, which was originally bounded by 12th to 28th, Burnside to Hawthorne. (Today its western border extends to the Willamette River.) In the southwest corner of the intersection is a 1908 multiplex with a beautiful stone foundation. In the northeast corner, at 534, is an Italianate home from 1888. At that time, though this was the city limits of East Portland, homes were contiguous only to about SE 12th Avenue; this far out, homes were widely spaced, with vacant land often used for gardens. Infill came over the next forty years.

On Washington, begin walking west. At SE 18th Avenue in the southwest corner is a home built around 1890 that has been turned into a warren of apartments. During World War II, the neighborhood, like many in town, accommodated some of the influx of shipyard workers by housing them in old, spacious homes. Many of these apartments still exist. Since the late 1990s the run-up in the neighborhood's property values, as elsewhere in old city neighborhoods, has meant that many timeworn buildings have been restored.

In 1959 zoning changed in Buckman to allow forty apartments per city block; one consequence is that almost every residential block east of 12th has a 1950s- or 1960s-era apartment building. Sometimes called "barracks in asphalt," these apartments were often built to minimum standards at a time, in 1965, when Buckman was deemed one of the city's poverty pockets. By the mid 1970s it was not atypical for a single-family residence in Buckman to have a land value four times its building value, due to the zoning that allowed multifamily housing. To avoid further incursions into the neighborhood's historic character, activists later convinced the city to downzone parts of the neighborhood that held the best single-family homes.

From Washington, turn left on SE 16th Avenue, a block of beautiful homes. The house at 602 dates from 1897, and the house at 603 from 1902; both are foursquares with classical elements such as Tuscan columns and dentil moldings. The home at 626 is the oldest on the block, a grand Queen Anne with Stick-style ornamentation from 1892, home of Judge William Fenton. Fenton Hall on the University of Oregon campus was named for him. At 16th and SE Alder Street are more homes built as multiplexes from the first decade of the 1900s, when the city's population more than doubled.

2 Still on 16th, come to SE Morrison Street. A much-altered 1875 home sits in the southwest corner. Cross Morrison and turn left. Two Queen Anne homes from the mid 1890s sit at 1630 and 1636, each an ebullient riot of shinglework, turned columns, spindlework, porches, and dormers. Note the zipperlike shingle pattern on the east dormers.

From Morrison, turn right on SE 17th Avenue, and then left on SE Belmont Street. On the right is a lineup of great homes. Those at 1704 and 1710 date from 1895. One of the oldest homes in town sits at 1728; it dates from 1870, when it sat on a small hill out in the country beyond East Portland's city limits. (To avoid the stairs in the next paragraph, keep straight on 17th and rejoin the route at **3**.)

From Belmont, turn right on SE 18th Avenue. In one block 18th dead-ends into a staircase leading down into Colonel Summers Park, which opened for play in 1921. If you're a fan of community gardens, check out the one at the east

A multiplex in Buckman complements the dramatic birches that front it.

end. From the stairs, walk west on the paved path behind the old park building. Ahead is a giant sequoia; its odd curving trunk appears caught in a moment of umbrage at some long-ago insult.

3 Exit the park at 17th and turn left. Turn right on SE Salmon Street. In the southwest corner are four Victorian-era workers' cottages, all built in 1890. The men of these houses likely climbed aboard the streetcar each day to ride down Belmont to jobs at riverside sawmills, foundries, or warehouses.

From Salmon, turn right on SE 15th Avenue, a lovely block of homes with a northern catalpa, a Portland Heritage Tree.

From 15th, turn left on SE Taylor Street, another beautiful block. These streets, though close to the city center, are quiet, with car traffic largely leaving them alone. The house at 1428 is a 1900 Dutch Colonial with a gambrel roof. The home at 1415 dates from 1895, a combination of Queen Anne and Stick styles. At 1405 is another home with a gambrel roof, this one with an Asian flair, from 1905.

4 From Taylor, turn right on SE 14th Avenue to see more great homes. At 1005 is a 1911 Colonial Revival apartment house with massive three-story-high columns.

From 14th, turn left on SE Yamhill Street and walk by a remarkable bit of landscaping. This ancient laurel hedge has grown beyond its rank adolescence stage, in which it needs thrice-yearly trimmings, into an exotic, sinuous sculpture that turns an ordinary city sidewalk into a dramatic passage.

From Yamhill, turn right on SE 13th Avenue. At 923 is an 1890 Queen Anne on the National Register of Historic Places. Across the street at 916 is an Italianate cottage from 1880.

On 13th, cross Belmont. As you approach SE Morrison Street, on the left is the beautiful 1913 Rex Arms apartment building with a lushly ornate cornice. It was renovated by REACH Community Development in 1986 and 1997. Formed in 1980, REACH refurbishes and builds affordable housing in the Buckman area.

On the southeast corner of Morrison and 13th, in a classic streetcar-era commercial building, is Zells, one of my favorites for breakfast. When I first moved to Portland, a white-haired Adelle Zell would stroll the streets of my Hollywood neighborhood, cutting flowers from yards (by prior arrangement with the homeowners, as she assured me one day when my curiosity turned into nosiness). She brought the flowers here, to place on tables at her son's restaurant.

5 From 13th, turn right on Morrison, which leads past homes from the 1890s. At SE 14th Avenue, cross Morrison after checking for cars. If traffic permits, look up and down this street. It provides good perspective on the morphology of East Portland: a series of relatively flat terraces separated by gentle grades, the result of materials laid down by thousands of years of floods, and subsequent erosion of the flood deposits. In the northeast corner of the intersection, upmarket retail and restaurant establishments inhabit the spot where Subees Discount Foods once served a less wealthy clientele.

From Morrison, turn left on 14th. On the left is the 7-acre Washington High School, erected in 1923 but unused as a high school since 1981. Linus Pauling attended school here in an earlier building. He never graduated, having failed to take a required history course, but in 1962 the school awarded the two-time Nobel Prize winner an honorary diploma. After Hurricane Katrina in 2005, this building was readied for hundreds of evacuees, though none ultimately came. Five acres of the school's grounds, including the gym, were sold to Portland Parks and Recreation in 2005 with plans for a community center. Future plans are to convert the other acreage and the school building into housing with retail on the main floor.

On 14th, cross SE Stark Street. In its northeast corner is a streetcar-era commercial building that is much altered but still worth restoring, with ornate cast-stone capitals on pilasters between storefronts.

From 14th, turn left on SE Oak Street. On the right are the Oak Street Rowhouses. In 1980 this then-vacant block was developed by members of the Buckman Community Association to be sympathetic to the neighborhood's architecture. The homes were recognized by President Carter in 1980 as an example of good urban design.

From Oak, turn right on SE 13th Avenue and walk through a miniature bamboo forest. At 13th and SE Pine Street is a set of 1926 apartments in the southeast corner. An imaginatively restored home sits at the northwest corner; a blend of several styles, its Craftsman columns and Stick-style details harmonize with a twenty-first-century garage and porch addition.

6 From 13th, turn right on Pine. The houses at 1324 and 1336 date from 1883. The home at 1324 has a classic bit of Italianate styling: a flat roof with a projecting cornice supported by prominent brackets. Cross 14th; at 1437 is a home from 1885.

At SE 16th Avenue is the 1921 Buckman School, now the Buckman Arts Magnet Elementary School. It was named for Cyrus Buckman, an early public school proponent. His home was on the grounds of Buckman Field, adjacent to Benson High School in Kerns.

From Pine, turn left on SE 18th Avenue, a mix of homes transitioning to businesses. In three blocks you will come to E Burnside. Cross this busy street carefully; there is no marked crosswalk here. (To cross at a stoplight, walk to SE 20th Avenue.)

Continue along 18th to NE Sandy Boulevard.

7 From 18th, cross Sandy at the stoplight. The unusual Art Deco Salvation Army building at the corner was designed in 1947 for Farmers Insurance Group by Charles Ertz. The Salvation Army Divisional Headquarters moved here in 1971. Don't miss the metalwork above the entry.

From Sandy, walk north on 18th. On the right is the back of the Jantzen Apparel administration building, designed in 1928 by Richard Sundeleaf. Even this hind end is ornamented with seahorse medallions, fish and lion gargoyles, and other whimsical elements. From 1929 to 2002 this was Jantzen's world headquarters.

Continue north on 18th to NE Glisan Street. In the northwest corner is a 4.5-acre garden apartment complex from 1941. Turn right on Glisan and walk one block to NE 19th Avenue. Turn right and walk a block south to view the front of the Jantzen building with its melange of ornament: winged horses at the capitals of the engaged columns, the diving girl medallion that is Jantzen's logo, Romanesque arches, and a travertine surround of the entrance.

In 1910 Carl Jantzen, a native of Denmark, joined John and Roy Zehntbauer to found the Portland Knitting Company, making heavy sweaters and wool hose to sell at their downtown store. A few years later, in 1913, a men's rowing club asked Jantzen if his company could knit a suit for winter rowing; in return Jantzen invented a ribbed-stitch suit, which was later patented. He then invented an automated circular knitting machine, derived from hosiery-knitting machines, which could work a lightweight material with an elastic knit stitch. This machine had the added benefit of producing suits more cheaply. In 1918, as swimsuits began to dominate sales, the company changed its name to Jantzen Knitting Mills. One of its early slogans was "The suit that changed bathing to swimming," reflecting the alternative it provided to the prevailing wool suits, whose heavy weight did not encourage exertion. By 1930 Jantzen had factories in Canada, England, South America, and Australia and was actively promoting swimming as a healthful sport. Portland's Jantzen Beach was born from this marketing scheme, created as a recreational swim center and amusement park. In 2002 Jantzen Apparel, LLC, was purchased by Perry Ellis International. However, Jantzen swimsuits are still designed in this building, some of which are sold under the Nike label. The building also contains Jantzen's sample sew department, which makes production samples and suits for early line releases. Jantzen's Island on Oswego Lake (see Walk 18) is where Carl Jantzen built a home in the 1930s. Sundeleaf was to have designed the home, but Mrs. Jantzen reportedly didn't want a factory architect to design her residence. She chose Charles Ertz, who designed the Salvation Army building seen earlier in the walk.

At 19th and Sandy, opposite Jantzen, is Everyday Music. This building is where Jantzen operated prior to 1928.

Retrace your steps to the corner of 19th and Glisan. In the northeast corner is the Jantzen warehouse building from 1935, also by Sundeleaf. It features great Art Deco elements such as lotus flowers, a blue wave motif, and more of the diving girl (whose physical attributes really should promote her to womanhood status).

8 From Glisan, continue north on 19th, which gets more residential, with 1925 apartments at 625 to 639 and a 1926 duplex at 632 to 638.

From 19th, turn right on NE Irving Street. Cross NE 20th Avenue; on the right are old garages belonging to a set of courtyard apartments from 1925. At the northwest corner of Irving and NE 21st Avenue are the Bennett Court apartments, with a great Moorish design. In the northeast corner at 710 21st is the 1928 Superior Service Laundry building.

9 From Irving, stop a minute at NE 22nd Avenue. In the intersection's northeast corner is the brick Davidson Baking Company building, home of Davidson Sunbeam Bread, for many years Portland's largest bakery. The company was started in 1914 at NE 24th Avenue and Broadway by Eugene Davidson, a descendant of Linus Dexter, who invented angel food cake in 1839. In 1918, Davidson built part of the existing structure at 22nd and Irving, adding on as the company grew. He ran the show from his second-floor corner office until 1967. Five years later the doors closed due to competition from grocery stores' new in-store bakeries. Beneath Irving Street in front of the bakery, tanks that held liquid sugar moulder in disuse, a relic for future archeologists to ponder.

Turn left on 22nd. Urban Grind Coffeehouse, at the north end of the bakery building, is housed where an 80-foot-long traveling oven used to be. Bread traveled through the oven to a wrapping machine, and then was transported through a tunnel under the street and upward into a garage where delivery trucks carried it to stores in Oregon and southwest Washington.

From 22nd, turn right on NE Pacific Street and then left on NE 23rd Avenue. Ahead is Interstate 84, and this portion of the walk reveals what's behind those implacably bland freeway walls. At 915 23rd is a tiny cottage from 1910, built when the clatter of horses and occasional whistle of a train in the gulch were the only traffic sounds to be heard.

Twenty-third ends at NE Holladay Street; turn right. On the right at 2400 Holladay is a great-looking building, a 1912 stable, now housing an auto body shop. Earlier versions of the shop can be decoded from layers of advertisements painted on the side of the building. Across from the old stable, Interstate 84 is visible as it runs through Sullivan's Gulch. (For more on the gulch, see Walk 4.)

10 From Holladay, turn right on NE 24th Avenue and walk three blocks to NE Irving Street. At Irving and 24th is the Castle Rose, an exuberantly stylish, multistory apartment building from the optimistic 1920s. Many more of these

Davidson Baking Company, circa 1930, prior to the building's expansion. Photo courtesy of Nancy Davidson Shaw.

architectural gems come up later in the walk, all of them hinting at a carefree California life.

From 24th, turn left on Irving to walk along the front of the Castle Rose. At 25th, where Irving intersects NE Sandy Boulevard, walk along Sandy.

11 From 26th and Sandy, cross Sandy at a crosswalk and walk straight onto NE Lawrence Avenue, part of an oddly angled bit of streets. On the left, at 630, are the Santa Monica Court apartments from 1925. With their palm trees, Mexican-tiled courtyard, and tile roof, they evoke vacation memories.

From Lawrence, turn right onto tiny NE Buxton Street, which offers another great apartment house, the Del Rey from 1926. Turn right off Buxton onto NE Glisan Street, where the 1929 Rasmussen Apartments building lines the block; it was designed by the prolific Elmer Feig. (See Walk 13 for more of Feig's stylish buildings.)

From Glisan, turn left on NE 24th Avenue, and then right on NE Flanders Street, which features good-looking apartment buildings on both sides. On the right, the 1928 Salerno Apartments have been turned into condominiums.

The 1928 Salerno Apartments at NE 24th Avenue and Flanders Street. Note the little wooden door on the main floor for the dairyman to deposit deliveries of milk, cream, and butter.

At 2250 are gorgeous townhomes from 1929 in the Spanish Colonial Revival style. Across from them is the Albertina Kerr Nursery Home, built in 1921 as an orphanage and adoption agency. In 1928, 306 babies filled the halls with their cries. By 1967, foster care was replacing the use of orphanages, and the Kerr Nursery closed. In 1980 the building was restored. Today, volunteers run a variety of businesses inside: a restaurant, second-hand store, and consignment antique shop to benefit the nonprofit Albertina Kerr Centers; its dozen or so programs assist children with emotional or mental health challenges and adults with disabilities.

12 From Flanders, turn left on NE 22nd Avenue. In the northwest corner are the Moorish San Da Roda apartments from 1925. From 22nd, turn left on NE Everett Street, which has more single-family homes and attractive 1920s duplexes.

At NE 25th Avenue and Everett is da Vinci Arts Middle School, a special-focus Portland public school formed in 1996. It was built as the Girls Polytechnic High School in the 1920s and designed by Portland Public Schools' architect George Jones. Girls learned practical skills here in a sister school to the all-boy Benson Polytechnic High School (which still exists but became coed in 1973). In 1968, Girls Polytechnic went coed and became Monroe High School, which later merged with Washington High School (seen earlier at SE 13th Avenue and Stark Street).

From Everett, turn right on NE 28th Avenue. For the next eight blocks, restaurants, shops, coffee houses, and a movie theater offer a perfect way to end this tour of the city.

At NE Couch Street and 28th is one of the neighborhood's snazziest buildings, the 1941 Art Moderne Coca-Cola plant, which is still mostly used for its original purpose. When built, it was both a bottling plant and a syrup facility. The bottling operation moved to Wilsonville in 1977. Today the building is one of Coca-Cola's seven U.S. syrup plants, producing Coke syrup used in soda fountains everywhere in the Northwest. It employs thirty-five people.

13 At Couch, turn right and walk half a block. On the left is the 1911 trolley barn used in the Ankeny streetcar line, two blocks from here. It is now office space. Come back to 28th and continue south. The building on the right is the Laurelhurst Theater; its entrance is on Burnside. Work your way through the shops and food options on 28th down to Stark, where you'll find a few more places to eat in the block east of 28th.

14 From 28th, turn right on Stark. Walk two blocks and turn left on SE 26th Avenue, at Lone Fir Cemetery. Midway down the block, the cemetery gate is locked unless a service or grave-digging is taking place. The cemetery has been in use since 1846, when James Stephens buried his father here; the area was part of Stephens's donation land claim. (Stephens's home is seen in Walk 8.) In 1855 it became an official cemetery. Well-known Portlanders such as Asa Lovejoy and Dr. James C. Hawthorne are buried here. Other prominent residents were buried here, but their bodies were exhumed and moved to the more upscale Riverview Cemetery after it opened in 1882.

If the gate is open, enter the cemetery and walk west on its path, exiting at SE 20th Avenue and Morrison Street (please note, however, that dogs are not allowed). From there, turn right on 20th and left on Washington to return to the walk's starting point. Metro, which runs Lone Fir, says that this gate will be opened daily only if money can be found to pay for security, contending that vandalism takes place when the gate is open. It restricts access to one gate, at the southwest corner of the cemetery. I hope some day the cemetery can be open to strollers to use as part of a loop, or for bike and foot commuters, whose presence would add an element of community policing.

If the gate is closed, come back another time for a visit to this pioneer cemetery to enjoy the stone monuments, arboretum-quality trees, and the respite this oasis provides from the city that surrounds it. From the gate, walk south on 26th to Morrison. At this intersection, streetcar tracks disappear into a yard. They were part of the Belmont line, which ran east on SE Belmont Street, diverting northward onto Morrison at about 20th and then dipping back to Belmont at about 27th.

Turn right on Morrison. At SE 21st Avenue is the former Tice Electric, home for more than fifty years to an electrical contracting firm. In 2006 the firm moved to Swan Island, and in 2007 apartments were built on the site.

On Morrison, come to SE 20th Avenue and turn right. Walk two blocks to SE Washington Street and turn left. Walk one block to the starting point.

The Jantzen Apparel building, a happy blend of travertine, brick, iron, and terra cotta, at NE Sandy Boulevard and 19th Avenue.

WALK 7

LAURELHURST TO
BELMONT STREET LOOP

DISTANCE 5.2 miles

STARTING POINT NE 42nd Avenue and Senate Street

GETTING THERE AND PARKING From downtown Portland, cross the Burnside Bridge and stay on E Burnside Street. Turn left on NE 39th Avenue and drive north twelve blocks. Just before the Interstate 84 overpass, turn right on NE Senate Street. Drive three blocks and park along the street, near NE 42nd Avenue.

TriMet: Take the MAX Red Line to the Hollywood stop. From the tracks, take the stairs or elevator to the pedestrian overpass over the freeway. At the top of the stairs, turn right; walk to the end of the overpass, and descend the steps or ramp to the intersection of NE 42nd Avenue and Senate Street.

RESTROOMS AND DRINKING FOUNTAINS Restrooms and drinking fountains are at two locations in Laurelhurst Park, SE Ankeny Street and Laurelhurst Place, and SE Oak and 37th Avenue. Midway through the walk, restaurants and coffee houses along SE Belmont Street between 35th and 30th Avenues offer restrooms for customers.

FOOD AND DRINK Time your hunger for lunch or dinner along SE Belmont Street. Options abound.

BEST TIMES TO VISIT The annual Belmont Street Fair takes place in September. See www.belmontbusiness.org for information.

To arrange a tour of the Historic Belmont Firehouse at 900 SE 35th Avenue, call 503-823-3615. Inside, drop down a fire pole, sit in a real fire truck to experience

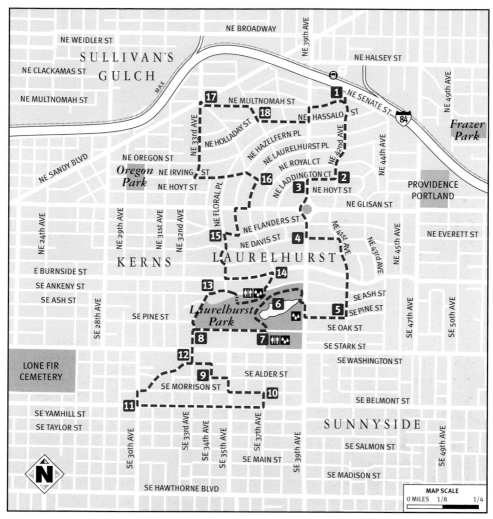

NE WEIDLER ST
NE CLACKAMAS ST
SULLIVAN'S
GULCH
NE MULTNOMAH ST
NE BROADWAY
NE HALSEY ST
NE SENATE ST
Frazer
Park
NE MULTNOMAH ST
17
NE HASSALO ST
18
1
84
NE 49th AVE
NE 39th AVE
NE 33rd AVE
NE HOLLADAY ST
NE HAZELFERN PL
NE LAURELHURST PL
NE 42nd AVE
NE 44th AVE
PROVIDENCE
PORTLAND
NE SANDY BLVD
Oregon
Park
NE OREGON ST
NE IRVING ST
NE HOYT ST
NE ROYAL CT
16
NE LADDINGTON CT
3
2
NE HOYT ST
NE GLISAN ST
NE FLORAL PL
NE 24th AVE
NE 29th AVE
NE 31st AVE
NE 32nd AVE
15
NE FLANDERS ST
NE DAVIS ST
4
NE 41st AVE
NE 43rd AVE
NE 45th AVE
NE EVERETT ST
KERNS
LAURELHURST
E BURNSIDE ST
SE ANKENY ST
SE ASH ST
14
13
Laurelhurst
Park
6
SE ASH ST
5
SE PINE ST
SE 47th AVE
SE 50th AVE
SE 28th AVE
SE PINE ST
8
7
SE OAK ST
SE STARK ST
SE WASHINGTON ST
SE 49th AVE
LONE FIR
CEMETERY
12
9
SE ALDER ST
SE MORRISON ST
10
SE BELMONT ST
11
SE YAMHILL ST
SE TAYLOR ST
SE 30th AVE
SE 33rd AVE
SE 34th AVE
SE 35th AVE
SE 37th AVE
SE 39th AVE
SUNNYSIDE
SE SALMON ST
SE MAIN ST
SE MADISON ST
SE HAWTHORNE BLVD

MAP SCALE
0 MILES   1/8   1/4

WALK 7. *Laurelhurst to Belmont Street Loop*

MAP KEY	
▪■▪	ROUTE
׀׀׀׀׀	STAIRS
‒ ‒	TRAIL
⋯	MAX TRACKS
🚇	MAX STATION
⋯	STREETCAR TRACKS
⋯	TROLLEY TRACKS
┝┿┥	RAILROAD TRACKS
	PARK/GREENSPACE
	HISTORIC/CONSERVATION DISTRICT
🚻	PUBLIC RESTROOM
🌊	WATER

a dizzying (or nauseating, depending on your age) ride through city streets in an audiovisual re-creation of a real emergency response, and learn the history of a city bureau that responds to sixty-two thousand calls each year.

ACCESSIBILITY This walk is mostly flat, with a few hills, and follows city sidewalks or paved park paths. Elevations range from 130 feet at SE Belmont Street to around 200 feet in the Laurelhurst neighborhood. Staircases can be easily avoided.

THE LAURELHURST NEIGHBORHOOD was born in 1909. From the first, it was a restricted "high-class residential district that will, for all time to come, maintain its character as such," as promised in a 1916 promotional book. The restrictions, common to the newly popular "residential parks" such as Laurelhurst, were in response to the fate befalling posh Portland neighborhoods like Nob Hill, where, the book notes, "apartment houses, flats, industrial plants, business houses, garages, moving picture theatres and everything else that isn't a home" had changed the character of the neighborhood, causing residents to "dispose of their costly and beautiful homes on almost any terms."

A century later the result remains intact: a homogenous and beautiful group of homes. After touring this residential enclave and its park (now on the National Register of Historic Places), the walk leads into the funkier and less regulated Sunnyside neighborhood, and to the shops and restaurants along SE Belmont Street, before returning to the quiet confines of Laurelhurst. As in Irvington or Eastmoreland, every street in Laurelhurst rewards an explorer; come back another time to explore streets not featured on this walk.

1 Northeast Senate Street, where this walk begins, originally had homes along both sides. Behind it, where Interstate 84 and the MAX line now run, were tracks of the Oregon-Washington Railroad and Navigation Company. Beyond them, the streets of Laurelhurst continued on the other side of the tracks, up to Halsey, an area now commercialized.

From the corner of Senate and NE 42nd Avenue, walk south on 42nd under a canopy of maples that, despite having once suffered the indignity of topping, are once again presentable. The homes here date from the 1920s, a decade when Laurelhurst began to fill to capacity. By 1935 only 10 percent of the neighborhood's lots were unbuilt, and it held more than a thousand bungalows. At 1142 is an especially nice bungalow, with unusual clustered columns and its original garage.

The pedestrian overpass at NE 42nd Avenue adjacent to Laurelhurst is much changed. Today it crosses over a freight-rail line, light-rail line, and multilane interstate highway. This earlier version, built in 1933, shows a simple wood structure over railroad tracks, built so children living north of Sullivan's Gulch and attending Laurelhurst School wouldn't have to cross the tracks, as they had been doing. Photo courtesy of the City of Portland Archives.

Cross NE Hassalo Street. In the 1870s this land was first developed as a gentleman's farm by Portland merchant, banker, and entrepreneur William Sargent Ladd, who called it Hazel Fern Farm. Guernsey and Jersey cattle grazed here, and by 1880 the farm had become known for breeding high-quality draft and light-harness horses. By the time Ladd died in 1893, East Portland, once a separate town, had been annexed and linked to Portland via the Morrison Bridge, and land surrounding the farm was being platted into neighborhoods. After sixteen years settling challenges to their ownership, Ladd's heirs began developing the farm in 1909. They consulted with New York's Olmsted Brothers landscape architecture firm. The Olmsteds' signature elements are present: streets that follow contours of the land, picturesque vistas that unfold as a pedestrian walks along, and a naturalistic effect, as if the homes have been set in existing groves of trees. The philosophy of the Olmsted Brothers' father, Frederick Law Olmsted, is evident in Laurelhurst. Rather than creating a completely man-crafted landscape that was independent of the underlying land, Olmsted sought to heighten the "genius of a place," to remain true to the character of the natural surroundings but also to enhance them with added architectural and horticultural elements.

Laurelhurst's boundaries today are Interstate 84 on the north, 44th Avenue on the east, Stark Street on the south, and 32nd and 33rd Avenues on the west. It is divided into four quadrants split by Glisan Street and 39th Avenue. The northeast and southeast quadrants, which this walk first explores, are a bungalow city. In general, the larger homes are on the west side of 39th, and those will be seen in the last portion of the walk.

At NE Hazelfern Place, the route climbs a bit to Laurelhurst's highest elevation, about 200 feet, high enough to reward early homeowners with fine views of Mount Hood. At NE Laurelhurst Place is the neighborhood school. I have always been amused by the "keep off grass" sign here, from an era when adults were not afraid to be stern with kids.

Between Laurelhurst Place and NE Royal Court, 42nd turns into NE 41st Avenue.

2 From 41st, turn right onto NE Laddington Court, named to honor the Ladds. At 3941 is a 1913 bungalow with unusual brick columns and a fantastic clear fir porch ceiling.

Laurelhurst, according to a mailman walking his route on a warm April Tuesday, is a great place to deliver mail: people don't move often (he gets to know them and doesn't have to keep dealing with address changes), and it's a beautiful setting, with few apartments (he likes chatting with residents as they garden or wash their windows). The downside is that many homes are reached only by climbing steep stairways. While new neighborhoods don't get front-door mail service anymore, the postal service honors tradition: any house that has had mail delivered to its door slot or porch box, even if the porch is at the top of twenty steps, will continue to be so served. A mixed blessing for the mail carrier is the large number of periodicals and catalogs Laurelhurst residents receive: they make for a heavy pack but mean fewer stops, as there are only so many Pottery Barn catalogs and *Atlantic Monthly*s one person can deliver in a day. Chatting with a mailman walking his route is one of life's small joys, one I'm thankful hasn't been erased by technology.

3 From Laddington, turn left onto NE 39th Avenue. West of 39th is All Saints School, a Catholic school and church. A large home and gardens owned by the widow of Harvey Scott occupied the land where the church now sits.

Within a block the walk enters the heart of Laurelhurst, a parklike traffic circle at 39th and NE Glisan Street. In 1909 the Ladds deeded a right-of-way along Glisan to a streetcar line (later known as the Montavilla line) to bring folks into the new area; also a factor in the Ladds' largesse is that they owned the rail line. At 39th and Glisan the Laurelhurst sales office handily intercepted folks as they stepped off the car.

With most lots developed by the 1920s, the office closed, and the circle turned into a park: Coe Circle, named for Dr. Henry Waldo Coe. He donated the Joan of Arc statue to the City of Portland in 1925 in remembrance of American soldiers who fought in France during World War I. Coe, a friend of Theodore Roosevelt, owned an insane asylum at SE 100th Avenue and Stark Street, the Morningside Hospital. He lived at 412 NE Royal Court in Laurelhurst.

The statue is worth a closer look. It is one of eight cast from the mold of an 1874 Emmanuel Frémiet sculpture located in the Place des Pyramides in Paris. Carefully cross at the painted crosswalk to a bus stop marooned in the middle of traffic lanes. From here, very carefully cross over to the grassy circle. (Coe Circle is not accessible but has sidewalks surrounding it.)

After looking Joan over, exit the circle in front of her, first walking to the bus stop on the south side of the circle and then crossing back to the east side of 39th.

4 From 39th, turn left at NE Davis Street, lined with Dutch Colonials, four-squares, and English Cottage–style homes. At NE 41st Avenue is a home with a rolled roof, the shingles curving around the roof's edges to simulate the thatched roof of an English cottage.

From Davis, turn right on 41st. In two blocks, cross Burnside. In the southeast corner of 41st and Burnside is a delightful Craftsman bungalow with many classic elements: a low-pitched roof, pagoda-like rafter tails, and a brick-and-river-rock chimney that appears to be smiling. This house is part of a specially named section of Laurelhurst: Fernhaven Court. A promotional book describes it as a "bungalow fairyland," developed with "high-class California bungalows." Fernhaven Court, from Burnside to Ash and 41st to 44th, has its own alley so that garages can face a central court and avoid "cutting up and ruining the lawn with runways." Homes are small and low. Despite their size, however, none would be called affordable anymore. That era ended in the 1990s.

At the northeast and southwest corners of 41st and SE Ash Street are "airplane bungalows," so named because the single-room second story perched on the apex of the first story's roofline looks like the cockpit of an early-day airplane. To see some low-slung bungalows, walk a few steps east on Ash; the first few houses on the left have low-pitched roofs and massive columns that seem to pull them to the earth. After looking them over, continue walking south on 41st.

5 From 41st, turn right onto SE Pine Street. At 4035 is a 1917 home with a porte cochere. At 4015 sits a grand Colonial Revival with a porticoed second-story porch. The home at 3964, built during the waning years of the Arts and Crafts movement, is a neat mix of Craftsman columns and eaves with Tudor half-timbering and windows, a popular effect in the 1920s. The house at 3935 is a 1913 Craftsman with classic river-rock columns and chimney, and a pergola on which a vine such as a wisteria can be trained, as is the case here. When I moved to Portland in the 1980s, it was common to see this architectural feature roundly disrespected, with a sheet of corrugated fiberglass slapped over a pergola to turn it into an ugly bit of roof. Thankfully the charms of Craftsman bungalows have been rediscovered, and pergolas throughout the city are again doing their job of bridging the ground between the manmade and natural worlds.

Carefully cross 39th and walk one block north to an entrance into Laurelhurst Park, opposite Ash. Once inside the park hedge, keep to the right to walk around the park perimeter path. Laurelhurst Park, on the National Register of Historic Places, was purchased by the city in 1909 as the neighborhood was developing. Before then its spring-fed pond was a swimming hole for locals. When the park was developed, the pond was deepened and extended. The park was designed by Emanuel T. Mische, Portland's park superintendent. Using Olmsted Brothers designs, he created several distinct sections, much like the sections of Central Park: a concert grove, Firwood Lake, a children's lawn, a plateau and broad meadows, a picnic grove, and a children's play park.

Walk past massive Douglas firs. The path curves to parallel SE Ankeny Street. At 3721 Ankeny, visible through the trees, is the 1912 Laurelhurst Club. Originally a private club for neighborhood residents, with tennis courts and a pool, today it is a private ballroom dancing club popular for wedding rentals.

Picnic tables in this serene park beg us busy people to sit down, soak in the dappled light, and let the landscape rejuvenate us. The view from the tables is a crafted, naturalistic work of art. Frederick Law Olmsted's philosophy was to avoid dominance of any single landscape element and to create compositions of natural and cultivated plantings and hardscape that produce a sense of the peacefulness of nature. In such a setting, he felt, the spirit could be restored. Classic Olmsted design is evident here in the broad greenswards broken by groves of trees, with reflections of trees in water providing another layer of scenery.

Along the Ankeny path is a lineup of lindens, a quintessential city tree of lopsided heart-shaped leaves that is known for its spring perfume. *Unter den Linden* (Under the Lindens) is a street in Berlin planted in 1647 with these graceful trees. Their only fault is to cover cars parked below with sticky honeydew (the excrement of aphids who feed off their leaves).

A group of moms multitask in Laurelhurst Park, entertaining their babies while exercising, a park activity not likely foreseen by the Olmsted Brothers.

6 Along the park perimeter path is a maintenance building with restrooms and water. Turn left here onto a path that leads into the heart of the park, and then keep left where the path forks. The trees ahead with the symmetrical pointy silhouette are giant sequoias, native to just seventy-five groves scattered along the west slopes of the Sierra Nevada in California. Stay left as the path touches the west end of the pond. Once past the pond, the path climbs out of its natural hollow. Cross the park perimeter path and exit the park at SE 37th Avenue and Oak Street. In the southeast corner is a section of the park that holds basketball courts, a concrete wading pool, a playground, tennis courts, a restroom, and the beautiful Laurelhurst Studio, where Portland Parks and Recreation offers dance classes.

7 From 37th and Oak, turn right and walk west on Oak, one of the nicest streets in town, lined with big homes set back on deep lawns. My only kvetch about Oak is that the hedge along the park is too high, making it impossible to see into the park. If I lived here, I would be tempted to do a bit of bootleg pruning to enhance my view.

At 3636 is a home designed by Herman Brookman in 1946 in the Northwest Regional style. He also designed the similarly styled "Menucha," Oregon

Governor Julius Meier's country estate in the Columbia River Gorge, now a retreat center. This home has wide, deep eaves and a hipped roof.

Most of the other homes along this stretch are from the early 1920s. The view into the park opens up and is sublime at about 3542: London plane trees, tulip poplars, beeches, elms, and firs in the foreground with rolling lawns and flowering shrubs artfully placed beyond their towering trunks. The home at 3400 was late to the block, a modern take on the Arts and Crafts style from 1937.

8 From Oak, turn left at SE 33rd Avenue. Cross SE Stark Street and you're out of Laurelhurst and into the Sunnyside neighborhood, which predates Laurelhurst by about two decades. In 1887 the Morrison Bridge across the Willamette went up, opening up a whole new cookie jar for real estate developers. Within months, ground for the Belmont streetcar line was broken and lots for the newly platted Sunnyside neighborhood, adjoining the streetcar, went on sale. Sunnyside's boundaries run from Stark to Hawthorne and from about 30th to 37th.

From 33rd, turn left onto SE Washington Street. The feel of this neighborhood is quite different from Laurelhurst. The home at 3324 is from 1908. Built before cars were common, this home is a tasteful example of a garage being added after the home was built. In this case the garage was excavated from below the house, and the lawn cut away for a driveway, with the cut retained behind high concrete walls.

From Washington, turn right on SE 34th Avenue and pass several gorgeous Queen Anne cottages. There are numerous old homes along this street: the home at 615 was built in 1893, 624 dates from 1891 (and features channel siding and Queen Anne scrollwork), 629 is from 1890, and 630 was built in 1888.

At the southwest corner of 34th and Alder is a sign that times have changed for modest, affordable Sunnyside: upscale townhomes, more and more of which are peppering the neighborhood.

9 From 34th, turn left at SE Alder Street, right onto SE 35th Avenue, and then left onto SE Morrison Street, a nice block of homes from the 1890s and early 1900s. The house at 3519 dates from 1896, 3546 dates from 1902, and 3558 (which listed for $500,000 in 2006) was built in 1899. While walking this route, I met a woman who told me that when she moved to Sunnyside in the 1960s as a single mother, just about every home on her street was a rental. With home prices at half a million dollars, this neighborhood's rental days are soon to be behind it.

10 From Morrison, turn right onto SE 37th Avenue and then right onto SE Belmont Street. Despite being a neighborhood retail hub since its streetcar days began in the 1880s, Belmont is still home to many single-family residences. The house at 3649 dates from 1904, the house at 3641 from 1906. In front of the duplex at 3527 to 3529 is a good-size eucalyptus. Also known as gum trees, eucalyptus are native to Australia but have become so common in California as to have reached "noxious weed" status. With its cooler winters, Oregon is about the northern limit for this tree.

On the left is a two-story brick fire station that now serves as the Historic Belmont Firehouse and Safety Learning Center. The stub of a tower in the northeast corner is all that remains of the once-taller hose tower, where hoses were hung to dry after a fire; it was also used as a watchtower to look for columns of smoke. The station was built in the horse-drawn era, which lasted from 1883 to 1920. Look through the front doors, where up to eight horses were stabled. The rings in the ceiling along the walls were harnessing rings; a horse's harness would always hang ready for action from the ceiling, which is why stations from that era have such tall interiors. When the alarm bell rang, each horse knew to move under the harnessing, which would drop on him and be buckled. The whole operation took just fifteen seconds. Also visible inside is antique firefighting equipment such as an 1879 steam pumper and an 1860 hose cart, from the pre-horse days, when men pulled firefighting apparatus themselves. The firefighters slept above the horses, on the second floor at the west end of the building. This station saw its last emergency response in 2003.

Kitty-corner from it is the 1912 Avalon Theatre, with apartments above. The streetcar initially terminated at NE 34th Avenue and Belmont, and here, as was typical, was the greatest concentration of stores and services—a fact still true today, with lots of great food and shopping options. At 33rd, on the south side of Belmont, the sidewalk says "Works Projects Administration 1940." Street improvements were a typical make-work project during the Depression.

At 3244 is the Pied Cow, a Queen Anne beauty from 1893 turned into a coffee house. This building was once owned by Jerry Bosco and his partner Ben Milligan. In the 1950s, when the machine age had Americans in thrall, Bosco was among the first to begin rescuing handcrafted architectural features such as doors, molding, stained glass, and windows from soon-to-be-razed homes and buildings. As a teen he hauled the bits home on his bike. Later he and Milligan owned a business, Victorian Façades, located in this building. Their 1892 Queen Anne home was behind it at 913 to 915 SE 33rd Avenue. It is on the National Register and is well worth a look for its Povey stained glass, rectangular tower, and shinglework. By the 1980s the men's collection filled 40,000 square feet of warehouse space. After both were diagnosed with AIDS, they formed the Bosco-Milligan Foundation to preserve their collection and expand awareness of the craftsmanship of Portland's architecture. Their trove of cast-off architectural ornamentation from demolished buildings has become the foundation of Portland's Architectural Heritage Center (701 SE Grand, seen in Walk 9), which offers great classes and tours about the city's architectural treasures. Fronting the Pied Cow is a fine old granite wall.

11 From Belmont, turn right onto SE 30th Avenue and then right onto SE Morrison Street. Veer left onto SE Alder Court, a street with curves that buck the linear grid. Because of its less favorable topography (its location in a slight hollow), it was developed later than the surrounding streets. Homes date from the 1920s (3100 and the triplex at 3124 to 3128) to the 1950s (3025 and 3033). At SE Alder Street, keep right onto Alder Court. East of 32nd, it begins climbing out of the hollow.

12 From Alder Court, turn left onto NE 33rd Avenue. The area at 33rd and Stark was a community garden until 2006, when a skilled nursing facility was constructed. Continue walking north on 33rd to the west side of Laurelhurst Park. The bowl at this end of the park was envisioned for concerts, which are still performed here. A spring emerged in 2006, turning the bowl—always a wet lowland—into a quagmire. Thirty-third climbs steeply to SE Ankeny Street.

13 From 33rd, turn right onto Ankeny. Besides being fabulous, the two mansions located here are wonderfully viewable, not sequestered behind tall hedges or recessed far off the road. At 3316 is the 10,000-square-foot Harry Green house. The architect was Herman Brookman, whose Northwest Regional home was seen on SE Oak Street. Brookman came to Portland in 1923 to design the M. Lloyd Frank estate (well worth visiting—it forms the nucleus of Lewis and Clark College). He was also architect of the Northwest Portland landmark Temple Beth Israel. This 1928 Mediterranean mansion, which looks like it belongs on Sunset Boulevard in Los Angeles, was built for $410,000 at the apex of 1920s exuberance. In 2006 this house went on the market for the first time in fifty-five years. Robert Bitar, who had bought it with his wife, Mabel, in 1951, told his daughters that, as a young boy delivering groceries on his bike, he vowed he would own this home one day. Bitar, a grocery store owner, real estate investor, and honorary consulate to Lebanon, lived in the house until his death in 2000.

Next to it is the H. Russell Albee mansion, designed by the illustrious A. E. Doyle in 1912 in the Colonial Revival style. Albee was mayor, and Doyle received many of the plummiest commissions of the day, including Reed College's Eliot Hall and Old Dorm Block, and the Central Library downtown.

After the Albee mansion, take a brick staircase down to the right to dip back into the park. (Avoid the stairs by staying on Ankeny to SE Laurelhurst Place, and rejoin the route there.) Pass a landing where the paved path intersects the stairs. At the third landing, turn left at a gravel path for a woodsy stroll under a sheltering canopy. Where the path forks, veer left to join the paved path and emerge at the same maintenance building seen earlier.

Turn left at the maintenance building, cross Ankeny, and climb the steep Laurelhurst Place. At the top of the hill, at Burnside, is a large 1922 home with a half-acre lot, a rare commodity in a city of 5000-square-foot lots.

14 From Laurelhurst Place, turn left onto Burnside to walk by a lineup of large, beautiful homes you can barely appreciate on a drive down this busy road. At 3574 is the Paul Murphy house, designed in 1916 by Ellis Lawrence in the Arts and Crafts style. Originally from Seattle, Murphy was the principal sales agent for the neighborhood. He named the area after the Laurelhurst subdivision in Seattle that he had earlier promoted. Murphy was later instrumental in designing and promoting similar "residence parks" in Oswego (now Lake Oswego); see Walk 18 for those areas.

Most of the homes along here were built during the 1910s. The house at 3517, however, dates from 1933, and the house at 3448 dates from 1921. Palms grow in front of the home at 3506, perhaps an increasingly viable landscape option as Portland's temperatures rise due to global warming.

From Burnside, turn right at NE Floral Place.

15 From Floral, turn right at NE Flanders Street and left at NE Hazelfern Place. Here you get a feel for the "serpentine drives" designed to preserve the natural beauty of the land. At 412 Hazelfern is an American ash (or white ash), a Portland Heritage Tree prized for its straight-grained, lightweight, strong wood that has long been used to make Major League Baseball bats.

Notable at 424 is a 1915 Dutch Colonial with beefy porch columns, a nod to the Craftsman influence. North of it is a 1912 bungalow with many Craftsman elements to admire: an exaggerated clinker-brick chimney, truncated obelisk porch columns, an unusual wrought-iron porch rail, and a roofline with a Japanesque flair.

From Hazelfern, turn right at NE Glisan Street and left at NE Laurelhurst Place, a very nice block to follow as the streets begin dropping down to Sullivan's Gulch.

A classic Laurelhurst Craftsman home, with an American ash, a Portland Heritage Tree, in the foreground.

16 From Laurelhurst Place, turn left on NE Peerless Place. Walk a block and come to a confusing intersection of several streets. Turn left on NE Irving Street. With so many lovely homes in this neighborhood, realtors must have to get out their thesauruses to find fresh superlatives. The home at 3309 is a 1915 Prairie-influenced Craftsman, with deep eaves and banks of windows.

From Irving, turn right at NE 32nd Avenue, which quickly turns into 33rd. North of the Presbyterian Church of Laurelhurst, on the left is the Nityananda Institute, a center for spiritual practice that offers yoga and meditation programs. Inside are an ashram and the Rudra Press, a publishing house. It occupies the 1910 Anna Lewis Mann Old People's Home, which was built as an upscale retirement home for "elderly people of a certain class—teachers, ministers, physicians," according to one former board member. The Mann Home was an outgrowth of the Old Ladies' Home Society founded in 1893 by the wealthy Mrs. H. W. Corbett and her friends. Prior to the building of the Mann Home, the society paid for room and board for elderly women at places such as the Patton Home in North Portland. The Mann Home operated as a retirement home until the 1950s and underwent several different uses until 1992 when it was bought by the Nityananda Institute.

17 At the intersection of NE 33rd Avenue, Sandy Boulevard, Multnomah Street, and Peerless Place, use the marked crosswalks to end up at the corner of Peerless and Multnomah. On Peerless is one of the four formal entrances to Laurelhurst.

At Peerless and Multnomah, turn left on Multnomah. At 3391 is a Craftsman bungalow with intersecting gables, a kicky bargeboard, and a porte cochere anchored by two massive, tapered columns. In half a block, come to NE Imperial Avenue. On the left is the 1926 Eighth Church of Christ Scientist. Its many rooflines stacked atop each other look like an extension of the hilly landscape on which it sits.

18 From Multnomah, turn right on Imperial, and then left on Hassalo, a street of more classy homes. Notice the enormous elms in the parking strips east of 37th.

Cross 39th at the stoplight and then turn left. Walk one block and turn right onto Multnomah. Walk to 42nd and turn left to return to the starting point.

WALK 8

LADD'S ADDITION TO HAWTHORNE BOULEVARD LOOP

DISTANCE 6.6 miles

STARTING POINT SE 12th Avenue and Harrison Street

GETTING THERE AND PARKING From downtown Portland, cross the Hawthorne Bridge. Turn right onto SE 11th Avenue, a one-way street heading south. Turn left onto SE Harrison Street. Drive one block to SE 12th Avenue, a one-way street heading north. Turn left. Park along 12th or adjacent streets to the west, where parking is unrestricted.

TriMet: Take bus 70 (12th Avenue) to the stop at SE 12th and Harrison (northbound) or SE 11th and Stephens (southbound).

RESTROOMS AND DRINKING FOUNTAINS Find restrooms for customers at restaurants and coffee shops on SE Hawthorne Boulevard (between 16th and 23rd Avenues, and between 33rd and 39th Avenues), New Seasons Market (SE 20th Avenue and Division Street), restaurants and coffee shops around SE 26th Avenue and Clinton Street, and Fred Meyer (SE 39th Avenue and Hawthorne). There are drinking fountains at New Seasons and Fred Meyer.

FOOD AND DRINK Southeast Hawthorne Boulevard is a foodie's paradise, with concentrations of eateries between 16th and 23rd Avenues, and between 33rd and 39th. The area around SE 26th Avenue and Clinton Street also offers options to sit down and enjoy local foods prepared well.

BEST TIMES TO VISIT Try to take this walk between June and October when the roses are out in Ladd's Addition's four rose gardens.

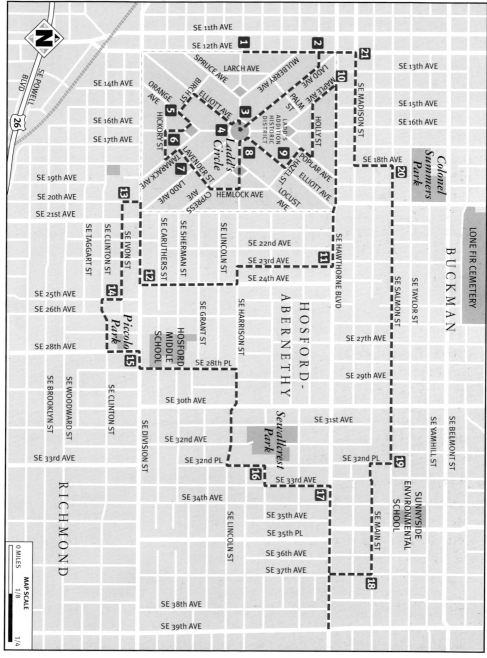

N

SE POWELL BLVD

SE 26

SE 11th AVE
1
SE 12th AVE
2
21
SE 13th AVE

SPRUCE AVE
LARCH AVE
MULBERRY AVE
LADD AVE
MAPLE AVE
10
SE MADISON ST
SE 14th AVE
SE 15th AVE

ORANGE AVE
BIRCH ST
ELLIOTT AVE
PALM ST
PALM
LADD'S ADDITION HISTORIC DISTRICT
SE 16th AVE
5
3
HOLLY ST
SE 16th AVE

HICKORY ST
SE 17th AVE
6
4
Ladd's Circle
8
9
POPLAR AVE
HAZEL ST
SE 18th AVE
20
Colonel Summers Park

TAMARACK AVE
LAVENDER ST
7
ELLIOTT AVE
LOCUST AVE

LADD AVE
CYPRESS AVE
HEMLOCK AVE

LONE FIR CEMETERY

13
SE 19th AVE
SE 20th AVE
SE 21st AVE

SE TAGGART ST
SE CLINTON ST
SE IVON ST
SE CARUTHERS ST
SE SHERMAN ST
SE LINCOLN ST
SE 22nd AVE
SE 23rd AVE
11
SE 24th AVE
12
SE HAWTHORNE BLVD

BUCKMAN

SE 25th AVE
14
SE 26th AVE
Piccolo Park
15
SE 28th AVE

SE GRANT ST
SE HARRISON ST
HOSFORD-ABERNETHY
SE 27th AVE
SE SALMON ST
SE TAYLOR ST

HOSFORD MIDDLE SCHOOL
SE 28th PL
SE 29th AVE

SE BROOKLYN ST
SE WOODWARD ST
SE CLINTON ST
SE 30th AVE
SE 31st AVE
SE YAMHILL ST
SE BELMONT ST

SE DIVISION ST
SE 32nd AVE
Sewallcrest Park
SE 32nd PL
19
SUNNYSIDE ENVIRONMENTAL SCHOOL

SE 33rd AVE
16
SE 33rd AVE

RICHMOND
SE 34th AVE
17
SE MAIN ST

SE LINCOLN ST
SE 35th AVE
SE 35th PL
SE 36th AVE
SE 37th AVE
18

0 MILES
MAP SCALE
1/8

SE 38th AVE
SE 39th AVE
1/4

WALK 8. *Ladd's Addition to Hawthorne Boulevard Loop*

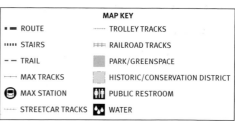

MAP KEY

▪ ▪ ROUTE ⋯⋯ TROLLEY TRACKS

⋮⋮⋮⋮ STAIRS ╫╫╫ RAILROAD TRACKS

– – TRAIL ■ PARK/GREENSPACE

—— MAX TRACKS ▨ HISTORIC/CONSERVATION DISTRICT

🚍 MAX STATION 🚻 PUBLIC RESTROOM

⋯⋯ STREETCAR TRACKS 💧 WATER

ACCESSIBILITY This walk is relatively flat, on city sidewalks. There is about 110 feet of elevation gain in a gradual ascent from Ladd's Addition to SE 30th Avenue.

YOU COULD EASILY MAKE A DAY of exploring this corner of Southeast Portland. This long walk starts in one of the city's most unique neighborhoods, Ladd's Addition, which is on the National Register of Historic Places, and passes through four thriving business districts, several other picturesque neighborhoods, and a quiet stretch of cityscape that was almost obliterated by a freeway.

From used clothes to high-end shoes, and from pizza by the slice to white-tablecloth restaurants, this trek is loaded with excuses to slow your pace and savor the local scene. Let serendipity guide you, or visit www.thinkhawthorne. com and www.divisionclinton.com, two merchant association Web sites where you can zero in on targets for shopping and eating. One treat on this walk is the surprising variety of houses of worship, from Mennonite to Maronite, Buddhist to Baptist, and a few others.

1 In 1957, 11th and 12th Avenues became a one-way couplet. Southeast 11th is the old wagon road linking Portland to Milwaukie, once a prominent river town. South of Clinton Street, the two join to become SE Milwaukie Avenue. Southeast 12th is the edge of Ladd's Addition, the first neighborhood explored on the walk. It is part of the larger Hosford-Abernethy neighborhood, which runs from the river to 30th, between Hawthorne and Powell Boulevards.

You're standing on what in 1850 was land owned by James Stephens. Then, and for several decades afterward, the east side was rural; farmers' claim boundaries became roads, which then often became streetcar routes, and later, major arterials for auto traffic. In 1869, Stephens platted out part of his land, calling it Stephens Addition, the east side's first residential district.

From Harrison, walk north on 12th one block. Just past SE Stephens Street, at 1825 SE 12th, is Stephens's home. He built it in 1862 along the river, where he operated a ferry. It was moved here in 1901, and in 1941 was divided into apartments to house wartime shipyard workers. It remains a multiplex today.

At 12th and SE Mill Street, look to the left to a scene of industry and warehouses that was once the residential Stephens Addition. Twelfth is seldom viewed leisurely, but it has wonderful Craftsman apartment houses and homes, and streetcar-era commercial structures to enjoy.

2   From 12th, turn right on SE Clay Street, walk one block, and turn right on SE Ladd Avenue, a street lined with Ladd's Addition's century-old elms. Save Our Elms, a citizens group that works with the city, helps safeguard these treasures from Dutch elm disease. They ask pedestrians for help: in spring and summer, as you walk along under old elms, look upward into the canopy. If you see wilted foliage, often just on a single branch, call the Urban Forestry Division at 503-823-4489. Diseased leaves on infected limbs can be gray-green, brown, or prematurely yellow. When diseased trees are removed, new disease-resistant elm varieties are planted. Each year, Save Our Elms holds home tours in Ladd's Addition, with proceeds going to pay for fungicides to fight the disease.

Ladd's Addition has a one-of-a-kind layout that looks like the sort of angular doodling you might create while on hold on the telephone. The layout, thirty-two polygonal blocks organized around a circular park, with four secondary diamond-shaped parks, is attributed to William Sargent Ladd.

Ladd was one of Portland's biggest nineteenth-century movers and shakers. He was born in Vermont in 1826 and came to Oregon in 1851 to set up business as a liquor importer and dealer. Successful he was; by the late 1850s, he began expanding into ventures ranging from a steamship company to a flour mill, telegraph company, bank, and real estate. It was the last two undertakings that formed the genesis for Ladd's Addition. Ladd acquired the land in 1877 in foreclosure against James Stephens, who had borrowed against it five years earlier. By the 1880s, Ladd controlled 1700 acres on the east side of the Willamette, land that would later become neighborhoods such as Laurelhurst and Eastmoreland.

The neighborhood was platted in 1891 during the east side's first boom, brought about by the opening of bridges across the Willamette and the annexing of East Portland and Albina to the city. When Ladd died in 1893, however, a recession had slowed the economy, and the land lay undeveloped for a decade, used by a local farmer to pasture livestock. It wasn't until after the 1905 Lewis and Clark Exposition that development sparked, and then primarily in the northern half of the neighborhood. Early residents were mostly middle class, with a sprinkling of executive sorts.

At 1819 Ladd is a home with the steeply pitched roof of the Arts and Crafts style and an unusual double gable on the north side. The home at 1846, built in 1910, has a wonderful side yard and stone columns that extend through the roof. Side yards were common in the neighborhood through the 1920s.

3   Come to Ladd's Circle, the park at the heart of the neighborhood. On the left is the Chinese Baptist Church, here since 1946, an era when Asian Americans

An Arts and Crafts home on SE Ladd Avenue with spectacular cast-stone elements.

were not welcomed in some city neighborhoods. The plantings inside Ladd's Circle were designed by Portland Park Superintendent Emanuel T. Mische. It and the four other parks in Ladd's were planted between 1909 and 1912.

Walk into the circle, where lawn—a bit mucky but worth the effort—weaves through mature rhododendron and camellia. (To avoid the grass, stay on the sidewalks around the circle.) This circle has at times been seen as a nuisance but has somehow survived various plans to eliminate it. In 1917, automobiles were growing in popularity, and with no test required for drivers to prove their competence, Ladd's Circle became the site of weekly accidents as novice drivers misunderestimated, as George Bush might say, how to handle the curving street. Some residents petitioned to have it removed. In later decades, Ladd Avenue's diagonal alignment tempted city planners: with the park eliminated, it would make an efficient conduit to bring traffic from outer Southeast neighborhoods to the Hawthorne and Morrison Bridges.

The circle was a bit neglected until the 1990s, when the tangle of bushes was pruned and grassy patches were planted to create a "village green" effect.

Veer to the right and emerge from the circle at SE Harrison Street, where you'll see three photogenic 1920s California-style bungalows. Walk southeast around the circle.

4 From the circle, turn right onto SE Elliott Avenue, named for Ladd's wife, Caroline Elliott Ladd. Typical lot dimensions in Ladd's Addition are 40 by 128 feet, and the neighborhood is also characterized by its alleys. As one walks along the sidewalk, the absence of curb cuts and driveways gives the impression that homes are set in a park.

From Elliott, turn left on SE Birch Street. On the right is Abernethy Elementary School. On this site, from 1914 to 1924, a rail line ran to Clackamas, Oregon. When it ceased operating, the school was built, in 1925. On the grounds is the Garden of Wonders, a nationally recognized project to improve the quality of school lunch food. With grants from national foundations and help from local chefs, restaurants, and groups such as Ecotrust, kids and parents grow food crops, study food and food-related topics in class, and cook and serve their homegrown food in the school cafeteria.

Most houses along the school grounds were built between 1919 and 1939, at which time bungalows in the Colonial style and romantic English or French Cottage styles and were popular. Many of the houses were built on spec by developers.

5 From Birch, turn left at SE Orange Avenue, and then right at SE 16th Avenue. Here is the south rose garden, one of the four gardens on the compass points. It is surrounded by small homes, many of which were first purchased by Italian Americans in the 1920s, who emigrated out of their "stopover" immigrant neighborhood in South Portland. (See Walk 11 for more on Portland's Italian immigrants.)

Follow 16th as it bends to the right. At the intersection of SE Hickory Street is a magnificent Arts and Crafts building, the 1913 Saint Philip Neri Catholic Church, founded to serve Portland's Italian American community. A parish school operated until 1972 south of this building, and other church buildings, including this building's successor, occupy the entire block.

6 From 16th, turn left at Hickory. At 1636 is Carvlin Hall, built in 1943. It was the school cafeteria. Just beyond it, on the corner of SE Tamarack Avenue, is the 1916 church rectory. A Portland Heritage Tree, California myrtle (*Umbellularia californica*), grows there. Known in this state as Oregon myrtle (or myrtlewood), this tree's wood leaves the state each year in the form of thousands of souvenirs carved by craftspeople on the Oregon coast. Its leaves are extremely fragrant, though their sap is an irritant to the eyes. It is native only to California and the southern Oregon coast.

The walk turns left off Hickory onto Tamarack, but if you want to see one of Pietro Belluschi's churches, turn right on Tamarack. He designed the modern basilica-like church in 1950, replacing the first Saint Philip Neri house of worship. Across from it at 2456 Tamarack is the 1891 Mizpah Presbyterian Church, now a fourplex.

7 From Tamarack, turn right on SE Lavender Street; after crossing SE Cypress Avenue, veer a bit left onto SE Hemlock Avenue, another street with old elms. From Hemlock, turn left at SE Harrison Street and come to the east rose garden. Stay on Harrison, walking through or around the garden, and you'll end up again at Ladd's Circle, where you can sit and enjoy the neighborhood scene. In 1923, after the expiration of protective covenants prohibiting commercial establishments, a grocery went in on Ladd's Circle. It closed in 2002. Today, other commercial ventures enjoy their neighborhood monopoly, a situation similar to Irvington's market site–turned-café at NE 15th Avenue and Brazee Street.

8 From Harrison, turn right to walk counterclockwise around the circle, passing by cute Mission-style duplexes from the 1920s. Exit Ladd's Circle by turning right onto SE Elliott Avenue. At 1927 is one of the newest homes in the neighborhood. The site was the last remaining lot visible from the neighborhood's central feature, Ladd's Circle. Since by 1996, when the home went up, the neighborhood had been named a National Historic District, construction had to meet certain guidelines; it did, and the updated version of the Arts and Crafts style fits in nicely.

Behind the home at 1909, Saint Sharbel Catholic Church can be seen. This church is part of the Maronite Rite, a community of Eastern Catholics founded in the fifth century around Saint Maroun, a monk who spent his life as a hermit on a mountain in Syria. Eastern Catholics differ from Roman Catholics in matters of liturgy and other ways, but remain in communion with the Pope.

At 1838 is a splendid 1908 Craftsman with a unique porch railing. Its side yard was swallowed by a second round of postwar infill in 1950. The home at 1818, built in 1913, provides a great example of the rare result when infill is resisted.

9 From Elliott, turn left on SE Hazel Street, then right on SE Poplar Avenue, both of which were the earliest streets to develop in Ladd's Addition.

From Poplar, turn left on SE Holly Street. The next few streets hold beautiful, large homes, such as the one at 1640. As the route crosses SE 16th Avenue, you may want to wander down it to look at the front of Saint Sharbel, built in 1909 of cast stone. At 1530 Holly is a grand 1910 home in the Mission style, with a sweeping stepped parapet.

From Holly, turn right on SE Maple Avenue. At 1517 is a spectacular Arts and Crafts home from 1910 with columns and a balustrade so beautiful it is hard to believe they are made of concrete. Roof brackets don't get much more elaborate than these.

10 From Maple, leave Ladd's and turn right onto SE Hawthorne Boulevard. The next nine blocks are a gradual uphill climb, with opportunities to eat. Many of these businesses occupy streetcar-era buildings. The first streetcar ran down Hawthorne to Mount Tabor in 1889, two years before the Madison Street Bridge connected Hawthorne to the west side. At that time Hawthorne was a country road flanked by berry fields and small orchards. Typical of streets on which streetcars ran, Hawthorne features many 1920s-era apartment buildings, though it still holds a number of single-family homes from the early 1900s.

11 From Hawthorne, turn right on SE 23rd Avenue. Instantly the streetscape changes to upscale residential, with beautiful homes mostly from the 1920s. This is the Colonial Heights neighborhood; many large homes were built here to take advantage of the nice views from the slight rise in elevation. The large Colonial Revival at 1824 was, according to its owner, the first home in Colonial Heights; built in 1915, it boasted modern electrical conveniences such as a built-in vacuum system. Its architect was Morris Whitehouse, who about that time designed Lincoln High School (now Lincoln Hall on the campus of Portland State University).

Follow 23rd to SE Harrison Street, turn left, and then turn right onto SE 24th Avenue. At SE Lincoln Street, in the southeast corner is the convent of the Sisters of Reparation of the Sacred Wounds of Jesus. Home to just a few nuns who constitute the entire order, the building began life in 1912 as the home of a judge, who built it with many windows, hoping to brighten the days of his invalid wife.

12 From 24th, turn right on SE Division Street. Division's commercial existence began not with the streetcar but with the automobile. At 22nd a commercial scene begins that makes a good place for a break. Continue west to 20th. At 20th is a New Seasons Market, one in a homegrown chain featuring local and organic products. It sits at the former site of the Antonio Graziano home, where in 1913, priests at the new Saint Philip Neri Catholic Church celebrated the parish's first Mass. The Grazianos, like many Italian immigrants, raised vegetables on the land to the west of their home. They later donated part of the land to the church for a convent.

From Division, turn left on SE 20th Avenue.

13 From 20th, turn left on SE Ivon Street. Walk east on this quiet street, something that would be quite impossible if citizens hadn't started fighting the conventional wisdom. In the early 1960s the Mount Hood Freeway was planned to connect Portland to its eastern suburbs; it would have run directly over Ivon's alignment through this area. The area south of Division Street was deemed a "poverty pocket" and seen as a relatively easy place to displace hundreds of citizens for a roadway. In 1969 the city started buying properties to clear the way for the eight-lane freeway, with plans that Division would be a frontage road.

About that time, neighborhood activists found an ally in Neil Goldschmidt, who was running for city council. Arguing that the freeways benefited the suburbs more than Portlanders, and with an Environmental Impact Statement that argued the freeway would be obsolete when it was built, Goldschmidt was able to win support for his campaign as well as for his plan to take the $500 million in federal funding pledged to the freeway project and spread it out all over the metropolitan area. By 1974 the freeway plan was dead, and the federal money went instead to projects recognizable today: the downtown transit mall (revamped from 2007 to 2008), the city's first light-rail line (Eastside MAX Blue Line), Eastman Parkway in Gresham, and Cornell Road in Hillsboro.

A vestige remains of the vanquished freeway: the odd crossover one must make while driving south on Interstate 5 near downtown Portland. To get to Highway 26 West, you must cross over two lanes to get in the left lanes, which is counterintuitive. This is because the ramps of the Mount Hood Freeway (which would have been part of Highway 26) were to enter the bridge via these same left lanes, making lane changes for those on that freeway unneeded if they wanted to continue west on Highway 26.

At 2324 Ivon is the Grace Olivier Peck home from 1891. This beautiful brick Queen Anne is on the National Register of Historic Places. Peck was an Oregon state legislator from 1948 to 1950 and again from 1956 to 1977. Her passion was for improving conditions for the disabled, poor, and imprisoned.

14 From Ivon, turn right on SE 25th Avenue, and then left on SE Clinton Street, a pleasant scene of coffee houses and cafés. Clinton had a streetcar line on it at one time. Walk three blocks on Clinton and turn left onto SE 28th Avenue. On the left is Piccolo Park, a half acre of ground acquired by the city for the freeway, and turned into a park in 1989. Next to it, at 2523 28th, is an 1895 farmhouse.

The 1891 Grace Olivier Peck home would have been destroyed if the Mount Hood Freeway had been built, and this tree and squirrel would not be here for a walker to enjoy.

15 From 28th, turn right on SE Division Street. Walk half a block to a stoplight and turn left onto SE 28th Place. As you pass the fields south of Hosford Middle School, look over your shoulder to the view of the West Hills and the radio tower on Healy Heights. A student-built labyrinth is in the courtyard behind the school. Climb 28th Place to SE Harrison Street, where you can see the old street name, Kenilworth, inscribed in the pavement.

From 28th Place, turn right on Harrison. At SE 30th Avenue, where a beautiful basalt Mormon church occupies the highest land in the neighborhood, Harrison jogs and becomes SE Lincoln Street. Stay on Lincoln, and then turn left onto SE 32nd Place, where the homes are now a bit older than those just passed.

16 From 32nd Place, turn right on SE Stephens Street. Notice at 3265 a Craftsman with an unusual balcony and stepped porch railing.

From Stephens, turn left onto SE 33rd Avenue, a great street of century-old bungalows and foursquares. Especially nice is the intersection of SE Market Street, occupied by old homes and elms.

17 Thirty-third runs into Hawthorne, and here you may want to linger for hours. I recommend turning right and walking at least to 39th, and then meandering back. In old streetcar-era commercial buildings, funky local shops have thrived for decades. Though some national stores have moved in, the area still has a good local vibe, so hip you may wonder if maybe you're just a little too mainstream to be walking around here (or at least I do). Highlights include the Perfume House at 33rd, Bread and Ink Café at 36th, and Powell's Books on Hawthorne and Pastaworks, both at 37th. Also at 37th stands the 1927 Mediterranean-style Bagdad Theater, designed by Thomas and Mercier, now a McMenamins theater and pub.

As you begin to walk east on Hawthorne, notice the wonderful clinker-brick apartment house at 3334. Clinker bricks are created when bricks too close to the fire in a brick kiln become misshapen and transformed by the heat into molten globules and chunks, not unlike the 'a'a lava so aptly named by native Hawaiians. Clinkers (named for the sound they make when chunked together) were discarded until around 1900, when architects in the Craftsman tradition, intrigued by the bricks' organic shapes, began using them.

18 When you're ready to leave Hawthorne, walk north on SE 37th Avenue, and then turn left in two blocks onto SE Main Street. This is the Sunnyside neighborhood, named by nineteenth-century real estate developers who understood the reality (if not the science) of microclimates and rain shadows caused by the West Hills.

At SE 36th Avenue is an anomalous home built in 1992 in the Art Deco style by Paul Wenner, who founded Gardenburger in 1985. This meatless burger derived from a recipe Wenner invented while running a health food restaurant in Gresham. One day, with too much leftover rice pilaf on his hands, he added oats, lowfat cheese, and mushrooms, put it all in a pan, and baked it. The next day, "garden loaf" sandwiches were on the menu.

At SE 35th Avenue and Main is the Portland Mennonite Church, a denomination named after Menno Simons, a sixteenth-century former Catholic priest. Like the Quakers, Mennonites are committed to nonviolence and pacifism, with an international reputation for disaster relief and service to others.

Walk west on Main past Queen Anne homes from the late 1890s. Don't miss the Edward Dupont house at 3326. This Craftsman was built in 1905 and is on the National Register for its fine architectural details.

From Main, turn right on SE 32nd Place.

19 From 32nd Place, turn left onto SE Salmon Street. No more turns for fifteen blocks unless you want to see a spectacular basalt church built in 1909 (at 32nd Avenue and Taylor). Its architect was Willard Tobey. (Another of his beautiful churches is seen in Walk 19.) This was for years the Staub Memorial Congregational Church, later the Sunnyside Congregational Church. It was sold in 2003 for $750,000 and is now a private residence.

At SE 29th Avenue, on the right is the sixty-two-unit Hawthorne Gardens Assisted Living Community, built in 2006. The Belleville Sanatorium was formerly on this site. At 2712 Salmon is an enormous brick house from 1911, built on the same high rise of land occupied by the Mormon church passed earlier. West of here, Salmon begins to drop downhill toward the river, with many lovely homes built to enjoy the West Hills view. At 28th Avenue the walk enters the Buckman neighborhood.

At SE 20th Avenue is yet another church, the East Side Baptist Church from 1910, now the Hinson Memorial Baptist Church. It was built of Tenino sandstone, a sedimentary rock from Tenino, Washington. In 1888 two quarrymen from Minnesota came west, hearing of the need for building stone to supply a growing Seattle. After scouting out sites north of Tenino, they found no good stone. Before heading back to Olympia, they spent the night at a farmer's home, which happened to have a stone fireplace. After scraping away the soot, the two men found that the fireplace was built out of a fine-grained sandstone. The farmer informed the men that he had used an axe to hack the fireplace's stone blocks out of boulders located south of town. The quarrymen bought the land where the stone was found and began operating the Tenino Sandstone Quarry. Until 1926 the quarry supplied material for many commercial structures and homes in the Northwest, including Pittock Mansion and Vista House in the

A steam car passes Hans Hanson's house and farm (60 acres from SE 27th Avenue to 30th Avenue, between Stark and Main Streets), circa 1890. Photo courtesy of the Oregon Historical Society.

Columbia River Gorge. Tenino sandstone is a fine-grained, easily worked stone and has the valuable property of hardening after being quarried. The Tenino quarry eventually filled with spring water and is now the town's swimming hole.

20 From Salmon, turn left onto SE 18th Avenue, walk two blocks, and turn right onto SE Madison Street. On the left at 17th and Madison is the Miao Fa Chan Temple, previously the World Buddhist Preaching Association. At 16th is Hawthorne East, a high-rise of subsidized apartments built in 1982. Further on Madison are some nice old homes from the early 1900s, an intact neighborhood that ends abruptly at 12th, where industry takes over.

21 From Madison, turn left on SE 12th Avenue. From 1862 to 1883 this area was part of the Oregon Insane Hospital grounds, which stretched from Hawthorne north to Belmont and from 12th west to 9th. It was operated by Dr. James C. Hawthorne, Oregon's first psychiatrist. Until 1888, Hawthorne Avenue (now Boulevard) was known as Asylum Avenue.

One of the oldest houses in Portland: the James Stephens Home, built in 1862.

Nearby are several food options. Walk one block on 12th, cross Hawthorne at the light, and then cross Ladd at the light to continue south on 12th to the starting point.

WALK 9

GRAND AVENUE HISTORIC DISTRICT TO EASTBANK ESPLANADE LOOP

DISTANCE 2.7 miles

STARTING POINT SE 11th Avenue and Pine Street

GETTING THERE AND PARKING From downtown Portland, cross the Burnside Bridge. Turn right at SE 13th Avenue, drive three blocks, and turn right on SE Pine Street. Drive two blocks west to SE 11th Avenue. Park between 11th and 10th on Pine, where parking is unrestricted.

TriMet: Take bus 19 (Glisan) or bus 20 (Burnside/Stark) to the stop at E Burnside and 13th Avenue. Walk south on 13th three blocks to Pine. Turn right and walk two blocks to the starting point. Use caution when crossing 12th and 11th; both are one-way streets with fast-moving traffic.

RESTROOMS AND DRINKING FOUNTAINS A portable toilet and drinking fountain are located on the Eastbank Esplanade at SE Madison Street. Restrooms for customers are inside restaurants along SE Grand Avenue and SE Morrison Street.

FOOD AND DRINK Restaurants, bars, and coffee shops are located along SE Grand Avenue, along SE Morrison Street, at SE Martin Luther King Jr. Boulevard and Stark Street (one block off the route), and along E Burnside between 7th and 10th Avenues.

BEST TIMES TO VISIT Walk this part of Portland during the week, when trains are running, loading docks are busy, and the city's vibrance is on full display.

ACCESSIBILITY This walk is accessible, virtually flat, with less than 100 feet of elevation gain. The route follows city sidewalks and streets, with some unregu-

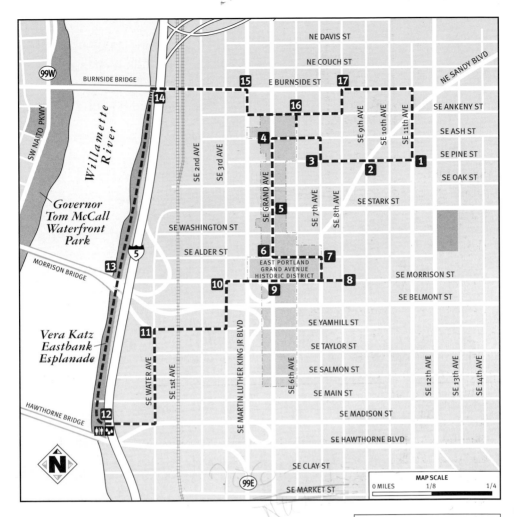

NE DAVIS ST
NE COUCH ST
99W
BURNSIDE BRIDGE
14
15 E BURNSIDE ST 17
16
NE SANDY BLVD
SE ANKENY ST
SE ASH ST
SE PINE ST
SE OAK ST
4
3
2
1
SW NAITO PKWY

Willamette River

Governor Tom McCall Waterfront Park

SE 2nd AVE
SE 3rd AVE
SE GRAND AVE
SE 7th AVE
SE 8th AVE
SE 9th AVE
SE 10th AVE
SE 11th AVE

SE STARK ST

5
SE WASHINGTON ST
SE ALDER ST

MORRISON BRIDGE
13
5

6
EAST PORTLAND GRAND AVENUE HISTORIC DISTRICT
7
8
SE MORRISON ST
SE BELMONT ST

10
9

Vera Katz Eastbank Esplanade

11

SE WATER AVE
SE 1st AVE
SE MARTIN LUTHER KING JR BLVD
SE 6th AVE

SE YAMHILL ST
SE TAYLOR ST
SE SALMON ST
SE MAIN ST
SE MADISON ST
SE HAWTHORNE BLVD

SE 12th AVE
SE 13th AVE
SE 14th AVE

HAWTHORNE BRIDGE
12

N

SE CLAY ST
99E
SE MARKET ST

MAP SCALE
0 MILES   1/8   1/4

WALK 9. *Grand Avenue Historic District to Eastbank Esplanade Loop*

MAP KEY
■ ▪ ROUTE
⋯⋯ STAIRS
– – TRAIL
—— MAX TRACKS
🚌 MAX STATION
⋯⋯ STREETCAR TRACKS
⋯⋯ TROLLEY TRACKS
┼┼┼ RAILROAD TRACKS
▒ PARK/GREENSPACE
▒ HISTORIC/CONSERVATION DISTRICT
🚻 PUBLIC RESTROOM
💧 WATER

lated street crossings. A staircase elevator bridges the vertical distance between the Eastbank Esplanade and E Burnside Street at **14**. It is operable with a universal key, which can be obtained from Portland Parks and Recreation by calling 503-823-2223. If the elevator does not work, backtrack on the Esplanade to SE Morrison Street and take the ramp up to it. From there, follow city streets back to Burnside and MLK, rejoining the route at **15**.

THIS WALK EXPLORES the core of East Portland, a once-separate town on the swampy east bank of the Willamette that developed into the city's largest concentration of warehouse and industrial employment. Unlike the Pearl, this district still retains its industry, though of a lighter sort. Gone are the pipe foundry, sawmill, and wharves. In their place are companies such as Ann Sacks Tile, Tazo Tea, and microdistillery House Spirits, as well as institutions like Portland Community College and the Oregon Ballet Theater. Retail shops and restaurants fill old streetcar-era storefronts along SE Grand Avenue, a street whose many buildings from the 1880s to the 1920s are preserved in the East Portland Grand Avenue Historic District.

After leaving the historic district, the walk follows the Vera Katz Eastbank Esplanade, a splendid bit of urban reclamation of an abused waterfront. It offers a panoramic view of downtown Portland and a window into the Willamette's past lives.

1 On SE Pine Street between 11th and 10th Avenues is the Troy Laundry building. The prolific Ellis Lawrence designed it in 1913. Among his more than five hundred projects, he developed a master plan for the University of Oregon campus and designed Mahonia Hall, since 1988 the official residence of Oregon's governor. Troy Laundry Machinery Company, based in Troy, New York, manufactured laundry equipment for power laundries (as they were then known) worldwide that bore its name. These laundries, employing mostly women, would take in work from industry and neighborhood laundries. Portland's Troy Laundry also offered a home pickup and delivery service through the 1950s.

Here, ten blocks from the river, is land acquired by James Stephens in 1845. He platted his holdings in 1850 and called it East Portland, which at that time extended from Glisan Street to Hawthorne Boulevard and from the river to 1st Avenue. Eleven years later, East Portland was extended to 12th. But few others were interested in settling here; by 1870, when Portland had eight thousand residents, East Portland had just two hundred.

Stephens's hopes for development were hampered because East Portland was on the wrong side of the river for farmers of the Tualatin Valley who brought produce to riverside docks. And unlike Portland's natural deepwater port, much of East Portland was a marshy, shallow slough, its lowlands incised with ravines, creeks, and ephemeral lakes. Before wharfs, warehouses, and roads could be built, an extensive network of trestles had to be constructed. Around 1900, when the lowlands were filled, the east side's topographical handicaps were surmounted, and it became the Northwest's largest wholesale distribution center. By 1914 the east side warehouse district had become the city's primary source of industrial jobs.

The Depression halted the district's further growth, and after World War II, changing transportation and distribution practices began sapping its vitality. In the 1980s, however, the Central Eastside began attracting entrepreneurs and investment, and by the early 2000s the area had evolved into an industrial, commercial, and retail center, and successfully avoided the dreaded preciousness that sometimes accompanies urban reincarnations.

Walk west on Pine and stop at SE Sandy Boulevard. Before crossing, look to the right. In the ochre stucco building at SE 9th Avenue and Ash Street, Portland's Gay Liberation Front had its first meeting in March 1970.

2 Staying on Pine, carefully cross Sandy (which has no crosswalk but good visibility), and then cross 9th. At SE 8th Avenue are a few remnants of the area's residential past: 303 8th is an 1899 home. Just north of Pine, at 217 8th, is Lloyd Cottage, a facility of Volunteers of America (VOA). This old home sheltered under ancient maples now houses offices of the VOA-run state parenting program. Other VOA programs include parent-to-parent mentoring; free childcare at the Multnomah County Courthouse for parents appearing in court; and support and treatment for addiction, homelessness, and other needs. The cottage was named for Lloyd Forsyth, a veteran homebuilder who retired from Neil Kelly in 1987 and spent the next twelve years being the all-purpose handyman and carpenter for the VOA.

New condominiums across the street from the Lloyd Cottage suggest that this early residential area has come full circle.

3 From Pine, turn right on SE 7th Avenue, and then left on SE Ash Street. Walk one block to SE 6th Avenue. At the northwest corner is the East Bank Lofts, built in 1912 as the warehouse for Lipman-Wolfe, one of Portland's major department stores from the late 1880s on. The warehouse was built the same year the company built its third and largest downtown store, at SW 5th Avenue and

Washington Street. Lipman-Wolfe was sold in the 1950s. In the 1980s Marshall Fields turned the downtown store into a Frederick and Nelson; it closed in 1986. In 1996 the former store became the 5th Avenue Suites Hotel, now the Hotel Monaco Portland.

4 From Ash, turn left onto SE Grand Avenue. After East Portland's slow start, things began to pick up in 1870 when the rail line from California's Sacramento Valley was laid along the east bank of the Willamette. This led to a construction boom for factories, steel and flour mills, lumberyards, and warehouses. The tracks still run along the alignment of SE 1st Avenue. A bigger impetus to east side development came with the construction of Willamette River bridges: the Morrison in 1887, the Steel in 1888, the Hawthorne in 1891, and the Burnside in 1894. Once the river was breached, the east side rapidly populated, soon surpassing the west side.

At the southwest corner of Ash and Grand is the Osborn Hotel from 1890. Such hotels were rooming houses for single men working on the railroad or in riverside docks.

Cross SE Pine Street. On the right is Miller Paint, at this location since 1926. The company began making and selling paints in 1890 when Ernest Miller, a German-born artist and house painter, discovered that the East Coast paints he was using did not hold up in the Northwest climate. He began grinding pigments and manufacturing his own paints at a shop on NE San Rafael Street. Miller paints are now made at a plant near the Portland International Airport.

Southeast Grand Avenue is part of the Central Eastside Urban Renewal Area formed in 1986 by the Portland Development Commission (PDC). In 2006 the Central Eastside Urban Renewal Area was extended until 2018. On Grand, improvements include street trees, period street lights, and funding to upgrade individual buildings. At SE Oak Street in the southeast corner is the 1911 Grand Oak Apartments building from 1911; it originally housed a home furnishings store on its main floor, with apartments above. PDC money helped refurbish it in 1996. Upstairs are forty-two apartments, twenty-two of which are classified as affordable. In front of it, vault lights in the sidewalk—once a source of light for the basement below—have been paved over.

Oak, west of Grand and to the river, was originally East Portland's primary commercial street, with the rail depot on 1st and Oak, and a ferry landing at its foot. (There was also a ferry landing at Washington Street.) When the Morrison Bridge opened in 1887, Morrison Street and Grand Avenue became the area's thoroughfares.

The ornate Barber Block, a standout in the East Portland Grand Avenue Historic District.

5 At Grand and SE Stark Street, in the southwest corner, is the Chamberlain Hotel from 1897, now Shleifer Furniture. It was designed in the Second Empire style, with a mansard roof, dormers, and elaborate window surrounds. Next to Shleifer, at 529 Grand, is the spectacular Logus Block from 1893. It has been called one of the finest examples in the state of Richardsonian Romanesque, a style popular for commercial buildings of that decade. Characteristics of the style are a massive presence and use of stone to accent brickwork, seen here in the rough-faced Tenino sandstone columns and lintels. The building is a celebration of forms, with carved sandstone capitals on the main-floor columns, groups of brick colonettes with terra-cotta capitals (third floor), and a wildly exuberant cornice that looks like the work of dueling bricklayers, each layer something different and intriguing. This building received PDC funds in 2000; inside are seventeen affordable apartments.

Across from the Logus Block, at 532 Grand, is the Barber Block from 1889, one of the earliest commercial buildings in East Portland. The style is eclectic, with elements of Queen Anne (the two-story bay windows, multi-height sky-line, and polychrome paint scheme), Romanesque (the arched entrance and rus-tic stonework, which is actually cast iron) and Gothic Revival (the verticality of the building), with Eastlake detailing (intricate, geometric decorative elements repeated throughout the façade). The original cast-iron thresholds are intact: peer into the doorway at 534 to see the hallway and staircase inside, which appear unchanged from the building's early days. On the corner of this building was the Barber and Hill Mortuary, which operated here until 1919.

At Washington's southeast corner is a bank, actually two buildings, one from 1915 and one from 1919 hiding behind an International façade. This style is a 180-degree contrast to the excessive ornamentation of much late-Victorian architecture. The International style emphasizes a radically simple form and rejects ornamentation. Celebrating mass-produced materials, it makes use of glass, steel, and concrete.

Come to SE Alder Street and stop at this corner of many significant old buildings. In the southeast corner is the 1907 Lambert Building with Craftsman elements. Originally it had a theater on the main floor. Sidewalk vault lights are intact on its west side. (For more on vault lights, see Walk 14.)

Across from the Lambert Building, in the southwest corner, is the N. K. West block, from 1883. This two-story Italianate building is the oldest com-mercial building in the district. Nathaniel West lived upstairs and sold dry goods (textiles and clothing) downstairs. This is the building where preserva-tionists Jerry Bosco and Ben Milligan (see Walk 7) stored the treasures they gleaned from soon-to-be-demolished buildings. Their trove formed the basis for the Architectural Heritage Center, which has its offices here. Next to it are other buildings built by West. (More on them a bit later, when the walk crosses Grand.) When West built his block, his back windows looked out over a swampy lake where MLK now runs.

6 From Grand, turn left on Alder. On the left, at 537 Alder, is the 1930 East Side Mortuary, designed by Thomas and Mercier; the landmark Bagdad Theater on Hawthorne is another of their creations. The mortuary building is an Art Deco gem with wide vertical bands of cast concrete in floral and vine motifs. VOA programs are operated inside, such as a vehicle donation program and Community Partners Reinvestment, which helps people emerging from corrections facilities to reengage with society.

Kitty-corner from this building, on SE 6th Avenue, is the 1907 Orient Lodge of the Independent Order of Odd Fellows (IOOF), a fraternal organization. The IOOF began in seventeenth-century England as a group of people organized to aid others in need and to pursue projects for the common good. This was evidently considered odd behavior, hence the name. The Odd Fellows came to the United States in 1819, beginning in Maryland. The lodge is in the Arts and Crafts style, with vertical stanchions extending above the roofline, and elliptical arched bays on the second floor, linked by a continuous lintel.

Across from it, at the northeast corner of 6th and Alder, was another fraternal organization lodge, the Woodmen of the World. Founded in 1890, Woodmen of the World began by providing assistance to the widows and children of its members, later building itself into a fraternal benefit organization. Inside this 1925 Colonial Revival building was meeting space for east side organizations such as labor unions, the Moose Lodge, and the American Legion. Today it is the Melody Ballroom; its two ballrooms are a popular place for quinceañeras and school fundraising auctions. On its frieze, the building offers some aphorisms for interested passersby to ponder, such as "The hand that gives gathers."

Continue east to SE 7th Avenue. At the southwest corner of Alder and 7th is the 1909 Jacobethan-style City Water Office. This building has seen better days; with its Tudor windows, ornamental gable at the parapet, lion gargoyles, and elaborate cast-stone door and window surrounds, it looks like it might belong to a slightly down-on-his-luck baronet. Joseph Jacobberger was the architect.

7 From Alder, turn right on 7th and walk one block to SE Morrison Street. For a look at a bit of the city's early-day produce markets, turn left on Morrison. In one block, at SE 8th Avenue, is the Grand Central Public Market. By the turn of the last century, Italians had settled in Southeast Portland, and in 1906 their truck farms evolved into a city market. The 1920s were the east side's golden era; farmers markets were well attended, and this block-size market building went up in 1929. Produce and meat were sold here until the 1950s. The only surviving neighborhood grocer from Southeast Portland's produce-marketing heyday is Sheridan Fruit Company at SE Oak Street and MLK. The Grand Central Public

Market became the Grand Central Bowl in the 1950s, and sheet metal was slapped up over its Italian façade. In 2006 the metal came off, and the building later reopened as the new Grand Central Bowl, where bowling has become a multimedia experience and the word *alley* is no longer welcome.

8 From 8th and Morrison, walk west on Morrison. At the northwest corner of 7th and Morrison is a 1909 apartment building, typical of those constructed along streetcar lines. On the left, between 7th and 6th Avenues, is the Oregon Ballet Theater, at home in a former bank building. In the bank's vault is the office of what the ballet likes to call its "most valuable asset," its artistic director. The building, renovated in 2000 with the help of the PDC, holds the ballet's administrative and ticket offices, dance studios, and school. One significant renovation was the installation of a L'AIR suspended floor to provide the best working surface for the dancers, too late to bring relief to the bank tellers of the building's past life. The ballet is part of an emerging cultural district on Portland's east side, with Miracle Theatre, KBOO, Do Jump, and Imago all nearby.

As you approach SE Grand Avenue, the skyline is dominated by a twelve-story skyscraper, the Weatherly Building. Built in 1928, it represents the pinnacle of twentieth-century east side aspirations. George Weatherly was the east side's leading citizen during the 1920s and 1930s, and this building was part of his effort to develop the area as an uptown district. It originally housed doctors and dentists. Attached to it was the eighteen-hundred-seat Oriental Theater, now demolished. The building has Romanesque brick and terra-cotta embellishments such as the arcade of arches near the roof. Above the arches are two rooftop penthouses.

9 Still on Morrison, cross Grand at the light. In the northwest corner, at 721 Grand, is the Eastbank Saloon, in the 1896 Nathaniel West Building No. 2. The main floor was originally a drugstore. North of it, in the middle of the block, is another Nathaniel West building, built in 1896 in an Italianate style. West was president of the East Portland city council before the city merged with Portland in 1891.

Continue straight on Morrison, jogging to the right to walk downhill next to the Morrison Bridge ramp. This slight downhill was the original break in the landscape between dry ground and the slough. At MLK, wait for traffic, cross the street, and enter the Central Eastside's old warehouse district, a former wetland filled in the early 1900s with garbage, sawdust from nearby mills, river dredge spoils, and building materials. At 326 is a building from 1930, likely a thriving location before the new Morrison Bridge approaches soared right over it in 1958.

At 301, in a 1905 building, is Montage, a restaurant that has turned a dubious location under the bridge into cachet. On the right, at SE 3rd Avenue and Alder Street, is Rinella Produce. In the early 1900s this was part of Produce Row, which stretched from MLK (then Union Avenue) to Water Avenue and from Washington Street to Clay Street. Produce Row was home to nine major produce wholesalers. Ancillary businesses were agricultural implement companies and seed companies.

10 From Morrison, turn left on 3rd. City Liquidators is on the right. Shop there and you can crow, "I got it at City Liquidators!" when your friends admire the deal you got on your leather sofa, vintage American Airlines china coffee mugs, or the bank of old U.S. postal boxes you use to stash your bills in. It's not all treasure, but finding a bargain or the odd fixture among the mass-produced bits of plastic is part of the fun.

From 3rd, turn right on SE Yamhill Street. At 81 Yamhill is a 1908 brick warehouse with a hoist adjacent to its rail siding along SE 1st Avenue.

11 From Yamhill, turn left onto SE Water Avenue. In the 1870s this was a plank road set atop 16-foot-high pilings. Walk four blocks south on Water, passing some smartly renovated warehouses. Inside are cafés and restaurants.

12 From Water, turn right on SE Madison Street toward the Willamette River and the Vera Katz Eastbank Esplanade. Pass beneath Interstate 5. Just beyond it, carefully cross a path for bicyclists and pedestrians, and walk to the pier. The Hawthorne Bridge is in front of you. Here, from Madison south one block to Hawthorne Boulevard, was Wolfe and Zwicker Iron Works, a pipe foundry. Also along the river near here was the H. A. Hogan Sawmill and Power Company, Markle's Wharfs, and Standard Box.

Today the Portland Fire Bureau's Emergency Medical Services (EMS) unit is located along the Esplanade at the foot of Madison. Below the EMS facility on the water is a boat dock and gangway with a one-hour free moorage, so paddlers and other boaters can get off to sample the Esplanade and its adjoining attractions.

During the early 1990s, old weeping willows were the sole object of beauty on the abandoned waterfront. In 1998, construction began on the 1.5-mile Esplanade, and these trees began to get the audience they deserve. Today they're accented by a pile of artfully placed columnar basalt. Sit on the basalt and watch

Mayor Vera Katz watches the parade of early-morning walkers, runners, and bikers on a hot July day.

the river scene through the swaying willow branches; despite the racket of the freeway, from here it is clear that Portland's spirit of innovation is alive and well. Finished in 2001, the Esplanade was later named for Vera Katz, who championed its construction during her time as Portland mayor (1993 to 2005).

Come off the pier, look for bikers, and turn left (north) onto the Esplanade. It is hard to imagine that in the 1880s a sawmill operated on the river here, between Madison and SE Salmon Street. Just past SE Main Street, a statue of Mayor Katz provides a great photo op. Beyond Salmon, the Esplanade widens a bit, and plantings of native alder, snowberry, and roses show off their beauty.

Across the river is the downtown seawall, erected in 1929 after numerous floods inundated downtown Portland. In February 1996, with experts warning of a one-hundred-year flood event, hundreds of Portland's citizens jumped at the chance to stand in drenching rains to fill sandbags and line the rail of the seawall with plywood. The river came within inches of the top of the wall.

North of SE Taylor Street, the freeway noise gets fairly unpleasant. The roaring traffic is on Interstate 5, part of a loop around the city's core made by Interstate 405 and Interstate 5. This east side section was planned to be in a trench (as it is on the west side) eight blocks off the river's edge. Cost containment in the 1950s brought the freeway to the then-decaying waterfront, a decision deeply lamented by current Portlanders, as it puts one of the ugliest of modern necessities right in the city's front yard, like putting a toilet in a living room. Movements to put the freeway in a tunnel surface occasionally, not just for aesthetic purposes but to alleviate the loop's congestion and tight turns.

Starting at the Morrison Bridge, watch for four public art installations, the work of RIGGA, a group of local artists. The copper-plate *Echo Gate*, beneath the bridge, echoes vanished pier buildings and Portland's Shanghai tunnels.

13 North of SE Morrison Street along the east bank are cliffs that look like sedimentary rock such as limestone. A riverside overlook here provides a good spot to investigate them. They consist of layers of concrete, what was once the sludge left in cement trucks after delivering loads of cement to the new Morrison Bridge foundations being poured in 1958. In those environmentally naïve days, trucks would back up to the river here and hose out their tanks. Other remnants of the river's industrial past are visible from the pier: iron mooring cleats, iron cables, and concrete slabs accented by a grassy thatch, just like a Roman ruin.

Cross SE Washington Street. Here was the Stark Street Ferry landing. Three hotels at the foot of SE Oak Street near here accommodated travelers and dock workers.

North of Washington, stay left to walk on a steel ramp cantilevered out from an old concrete wall. This wall was the foundation for Municipal Terminal 2, located between Washington and Oak in the early 1900s. Cargo handled here included hemp, paper, and machinery. South of the terminal, the shore had seven major slips dredged out of it to provide berths. Most of the docks in this vicinity were demolished by 1940, and the Port of Portland moved its facilities further downriver.

After a November downpour, seagulls in the river were enjoying the fruits of an overtaxed municipal sewer system, courtesy of Outfall Pipe 37, which emerges from the old concrete wall. This pipe lays along the route of a stream that originally drained the slough. (See Walk 1 for information on Portland's decades-long work to prevent untreated sewage from reaching the Willamette.)

Two pieces of art on the Terminal 2 wall remnant hark back to early river commerce. *Ghost Ship*, on the south end of the wall, is a lantern of copper and hundreds of pieces of prismatic art glass. *Stackstalk*, at the north end, is part masthead, part wheat stem, part smokestack.

Further north on the Esplanade is *Alluvial Wall*, installed on a concrete retaining wall. Referring to interwoven layers of the river's pre-industrial geol-

Front Street
Intercepting Sewer
4/23/27
Dredge working on fill at
foot of Salmon street

The west bank of the Willamette, visible from today's Esplanade, is markedly different from this 1928 photo in which warehouses dominate the waterfront. The seawall was built in 1929, warehouses torn down, and a freeway built on the west bank in 1940. It was torn out in 1974, and Waterfront Park replaced it. The bridge in the background is the old Morrison Bridge, which was replaced in 1958. Photo courtesy of the City of Portland Archives.

ogy and human artifacts, the sculpture's cold-forged steel plate is layered with bronze castings.

At SE Ash Street, the Esplanade's 1200-foot-long floating walkway begins, the longest in the United States. White caps on the pylons discourage birds from landing and leaving their droppings below. The walkway's sixty-five pylons are embedded 30 feet in the riverbed and allow it to rise and fall 30 feet, the potential annual range between high and low water. However, don't take the walkway; this tour of the Esplanade ends here.

14 Leave the Esplanade by taking the staircase up to the Burnside Bridge. Turn right. Walk over twelve lanes of traffic and two railroad tracks. The scent of tea may surprise you. Below are the offices of Tazo Tea, founded in Portland by Steven Smith, who also founded Stash Tea here. Both were later sold, Tazo to Starbucks in 1999. Inside warehouses under the bridge, millions of pounds of tea leaves, herbs, roots, and berries are blended and packaged.

As you cross SE 2nd Avenue (the first street east of the river), the famous Burnside Skatepark is underneath. It was built on public land by entrepreneurial skateboarders in the early 1990s without permission, using unwanted cement left over from Ross Island Sand and Gravel trucks at the end of each working day. By 1992 the city gave the official nod to the park, in large part due to its positive impact on the street scene below the bridge. Today it is arguably the best-known skatepark in the world.

15 From Burnside, cross MLK at the light, turn right, and in one block, turn left on SE Ankeny Street, the route of an old streetcar line. (If you want to see the skatepark, turn right at Ankeny and walk two blocks to 2nd; the skatepark is at 2nd, under the bridge.) On Ankeny, walk one block east and cross SE Grand Avenue at the light. In one more block, at the southwest corner of SE 6th Avenue and Ankeny, is the unusual 1903 Pacific States Building, a telephone and telegraph company.

16 From Ankeny, turn right on 6th for a look at what is most likely the oldest building in the district, an 1871 home tucked behind the Pacific States Building, built when the nearest neighbor was likely out of earshot, and the home's backyard was just feet away from creeks and forest.

Come back to the intersection of 6th and Ankeny, and turn right (east). Walk two blocks and turn left onto SE 8th Avenue. On the right, at 20, is KBOO, Portland's listener-supported radio station. It went on the air in 1968; its call letters were based on a popular strain of marijuana called "Berkeley Boo." Across from KBOO, at 17, is the Imago Theatre, with a beautiful brick façade. Especially nice is the Greek key motif along the top.

17 Eighth brings you to Burnside. On both sides of Burnside between 7th and 8th are buildings that provide a bit of coffee, food, shopping, and dance (Viscount Ballroom). The odd sidewalk colonnades of these 1909 buildings were created in the 1920s when Burnside was widened and a sidewalk had to be carved right through the buildings' main floors.

From 8th and Burnside, walk east (right). At 1020 Burnside is the 1921 Cromwell Tailors building, manufacturer of clothes for department stores. In 1990 Hippo Hardware moved in, a combination lighting, plumbing, and hardware store, and repository for architectural house parts old, offbeat, or just plain beat.

From Burnside, turn right on SE 11th Avenue. At the intersection of 11th, Ankeny, and Sandy, cross Sandy at a painted crosswalk and then cross Ankeny. Continue south on 11th, a one-way street heading south. For a great neighborhood coffee house, turn left at Ash and walk one block to the corner of Ash and 12th. Otherwise, stay on 11th to reach the starting point at Pine.

BROOKLYN TO SELLWOOD LOOP

DISTANCE   About 6 miles

STARTING POINT   SE 7th Avenue and Franklin Street

GETTING THERE AND PARKING   From downtown Portland, cross the Burnside Bridge. Turn right at the first light, Martin Luther King Jr. Boulevard. Get in the left lane; drive south ten blocks to the light at SE Belmont Street and turn left. Drive seven blocks to SE 11th Avenue and turn right. At SE Clinton Street, 11th becomes SE Milwaukie Avenue. Stay on Milwaukie through the light at SE Powell Boulevard. Drive two blocks beyond Powell, turn right onto SE Franklin Street, and go four blocks to the intersection of SE 7th Avenue and Franklin. Park along the street.

TriMet: Take bus 9 (Powell) to the stop at SE 9th Avenue and Powell Boulevard. Walk one block south on 9th and two blocks west on SE Franklin Street to the start.

RESTROOMS AND DRINKING FOUNTAINS   Restrooms and drinking fountains are at the north and south ends of the walk, at Brooklyn Park (seasonally, March through November) and Westmoreland Park. Restaurants and coffee shops along SE Bybee Boulevard and SE Milwaukie Avenue have facilities for customers. There is a drinking fountain at Milwaukie and SE Mitchell Street, in the parking lot for Oaks Bottom Wildlife Refuge.

FOOD AND DRINK   Bring an appetite for the many good restaurants at SE Bybee Boulevard and Milwaukie Avenue, midway through the walk. True Brew Coffeehouse, at Milwaukie and SE Pershing Street, is near the end of the walk.

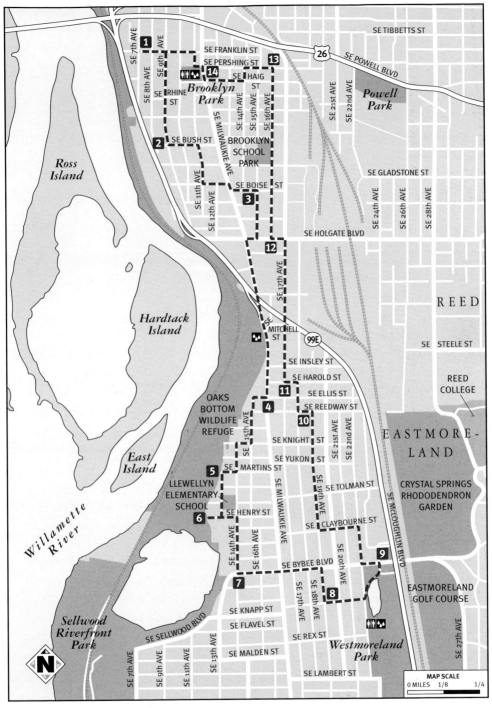

WALK 10. *Brooklyn to Sellwood Loop*

MAP KEY

▪▪ ROUTE	⋯⋯ TROLLEY TRACKS
⋮⋮⋮ STAIRS	⊢⊢⊢ RAILROAD TRACKS
‐ ‐ TRAIL	▒ PARK/GREENSPACE
┼ MAX TRACKS	▨ HISTORIC/CONSERVATION DISTRICT
Ⓜ MAX STATION	🚻 PUBLIC RESTROOM
⋯ STREETCAR TRACKS	◆◆ WATER

BEST TIMES TO VISIT   If you want to stop in at the mausoleum at Portland Memorial, time your visit to arrive before it closes for the evening; otherwise it is open seven days a week.

ACCESSIBILITY   This long walk can be easily divided into two shorter walks: first, the Brooklyn neighborhood north of SE Holgate Boulevard; and second, the Sellwood and Westmoreland neighborhoods, starting at SE Mitchell Street and Milwaukie Avenue (at the Oaks Bottom parking lot) and following the route from there. It is virtually flat, on city sidewalks, with only 50 feet of elevation gain throughout.

BROOKLYN AND SELLWOOD, which anchor the two ends of this walk, are among the oldest neighborhoods on the east side, from the 1860s and 1880s, respectively. Between them, the route travels through Westmoreland, a quiet neighborhood of bungalows and foursquares platted out in 1909 from some of William Sargent Ladd's immense landholdings, during a decade in which Portland was experiencing a large influx of new residents. The route also visits SE Milwaukie Avenue, whose streetcar days live on in charming shops and restaurants that thrive in old commercial buildings, especially around SE Bybee Boulevard. On this city walk the old homes, bluff-top views of the river, and thriving retail scene along Milwaukie make for a pleasant day of walking, eating, and window-shopping.

When the Brooklyn neighborhood was platted in the 1860s by Gideon Tibbetts, it was centered on about SE 12th Avenue and Division Street, now an industrial area. Before settlement, parts of Brooklyn were a slough fed by springs emerging from terraces that run approximately along the alignment of 28th Avenue. This sloughy area of springs and creeks extended south to the town of Milwaukie and included the springs in Reed Canyon and the Crystal Springs Rhododendron Garden (two areas where the wetlands remain unfilled). Around Brooklyn, the springs and creeks were in the lowland between 17th and 26th Avenues, an area long since drained, filled, and given over to rail lines and commercial uses; Fred Meyer headquarters is located there, for example, as is Bullseye Glass Company, a manufacturer of art and architectural glass.

Tibbetts sold his swampland in 1868 to the Oregon Central Railroad. At the north end of the neighborhood, another large employer, the Inman-Poulsen sawmill, began operations in 1890. Located at the foot of Clinton Street, the mill, along with the rail yards, attracted immigrants from northern Europe, and they in turn attracted the Catholic Church. In 1893 the Benedictine Fathers of Mount Angel founded Sacred Heart Parish in Brooklyn. As the economy waxed and waned over the following two decades, so did the neighborhood, with residents, many of them single men, coming and going with the jobs.

In 1926 Multnomah County built the Ross Island Bridge as a major link in a new highway system, transforming Powell into a wide boulevard that cut the neighborhood in two and destroyed the Brooklyn town center at Powell and Milwaukie (though some businesses from that era remain, notably the Aladdin Theater). Also in 1926, the neighborhood lost its prime recreation land when Ross Island was closed to the public and gravel mining began. Before then, the island had been a place for boating, picnicking, fishing, and swimming. The final blow came in 1937 when McLoughlin Boulevard, a work relief project, was built on Brooklyn's western edge, separating it from the river. In the 1960s, as new, low-cost apartment buildings were changing the neighborhood, the Brooklyn Action Corps formed to give residents a voice in their neighborhood's future. It was among the first Portland neighborhood associations to fend off freeways, force developers to create homes sensitive to existing properties, and foster the "livable" aspect for which the city is now renowned.

1 This walk begins atop a terrace formed by the Missoula Floods, a series of Ice Age floods that deposited loads of cobbles, pebbles, sand, and silt throughout the Willamette Valley. Franklin Street lines up with the downstream tip of Ross Island and the aerial tram to Oregon Health and Science University. Train whistles will likely serenade you at the beginning of the walk, a fitting sound for a neighborhood joined from birth to the railroad.

From SE 7th Avenue and Franklin, walk two blocks east on Franklin and turn right on SE 9th Avenue, where you'll see a medley of homes from different eras, from old workingman cottages to 1960s apartments to classic foursquares and Craftsman bungalows built between 1905 and 1910. In the northwest corner of 9th and Franklin is an 1890 Queen Anne.

During the first few decades of Brooklyn's existence, this land was vacant, owned by the railroad. It wasn't until Sacred Heart Church moved to the heights in 1911 (from Cora Street and Milwaukie) that this section of Brooklyn began to develop, with homes built by its parishioners, who sent their kids to the adjoining school. This area, on higher ground than land to the east, became known as Benedictine Heights.

2 From 9th, turn left onto SE Bush Street. The 1961 duplex at 909 to 911 is an example of the plain, functional design of 1960s homes. Next to it, at 931, is a 1942 home, a streamlined look with a touch of Art Moderne in the curved brickwork at the entry, a style that faded with World War II.

From Bush, turn right at SE 11th Avenue, a block dominated by Sacred Heart and its buildings. In the southeast corner is the 1914 convent, home to the nuns who taught at the school next door. The school operated until 1994 and has since been torn down. The convent is a relatively unadorned Arts and Crafts building with plain trim and a gothic window in the gable end. Contrast this simple building for the women of the church with the much grander rectory, built in the Classical Revival style in 1910 for the parish's priests. Its Ionic columns, decorated cornice, and pediment provide a few clues to the ecclesiastical hierarchy of the sexes. Across the courtyard from it is the 1901 Sacred Heart Church, combining Colonial Revival and Gothic Revival styles. Teams of horses pulled it from its original site in 1911.

From 11th, turn left onto SE Boise Street, turn right onto SE Milwaukie Avenue, and then cross Milwaukie to continue walking east on Boise, which has jogged a bit off its alignment. Here you begin to leave the heights and walk downhill toward the former slough. At 1410 Boise is the first convent for Sacred Heart's nuns; this was built in 1893, adjacent to the original church site. The convent was later called the Boise Apartments but is now Sellwood House, an appropriation of a neighborhood name that, at least in its owner's opinion, is more desirable. It is a clear case of what I call "chic creep," a phenomenon that occurs in Northwest Portland, where some businesses in adjoining areas claim to be part of the tony Pearl District.

3 From Boise, turn right on SE 15th Avenue. At 1511 SE Holgate Boulevard is the 1907 Pacific States Telephone Company building. Clark Gable once worked here.

From 15th, turn right onto Holgate, which used to be the Portland city limit, and walk one block to Milwaukie. Cross it and walk south. In the 1890s, when the streetcar ran from Brooklyn to Sellwood along Milwaukie, south of Holgate was open country until Sellwood. At the first intersection, SE Pardee Street, a nice view opens to the east, of the lowlands below the next higher river terrace.

While on Milwaukie, cross SE McLoughlin Boulevard on an overpass. Despite the clamor of cars, here are good views to the west of the red and white Healy Heights radio tower in the West Hills and of east side volcanic buttes.

A bluff-top home on a dead end in Sellwood enjoys West Hills views, old oaks, and an almost-rural tranquility.

Once off the overpass, look down the bluff into the city's first wildlife refuge, Oaks Bottom.

4 From Milwaukie, turn right onto SE Ellis Street to stroll along little-traf-ficked neighborhood streets, some of my favorite in town. This is the Sellwood neighborhood. Ellis ends at SE 15th Avenue at the top of the bluff, so turn left onto 15th. The 1930 home at 5715 15th has a fancy, hand-sculpted retaining wall, unusual for a fairly modest home; perhaps the original occupant was a stonemason.

Walk a few more blocks south on 15th, and then turn right onto quiet SE Knight Street, which has several old homes. Especially nice is a 1908 bungalow at 1414 with classical columns. The home at 1335 dates from 1907; its reuse of architectural remnants might earn a nod of approval from Jerry Bosco, one of Portland's first and most famous architectural salvagers. Next door at 5903 SE 14th Avenue is a Craftsman bungalow with a large addition situated to take full advantage of city and river views.

From Knight, turn left onto 14th. At 5916 is a charming 800-square-foot home from 1900, small enough to make a 1750-square-foot lot seem just right.

On 14th, cross SE Yukon Street, and turn right at SE Martins Street.

5 From Martins, come to SE 13th Avenue for a fantastic river and bottomland overlook. A bench here is a good place to rest and enjoy the view of the upstream end of Ross Island. The adjacent Hardtack Island is commonly referred to as Ross Island. The two were at one point joined by a berm of land by the Army Corps of Engineers. Across the river is the Willamette Park boat ramp, and traffic on Interstate 5 and SW Barbur Boulevard is visible as it crosses large trestles over canyons in the forested George Himes Park. The trail below the bluff, in Oaks Bottom, is part of the Springwater Corridor system of hiking and biking trails.

From Martins, walk south on 13th. A large Arts and Crafts home from 1912 sits at 6209. Thirteenth runs behind Llewellyn Elementary School, named for Henderson Llewellyn (sometimes spelled Luelling), who settled in the Sellwood area in 1847. He and his brother founded a community of nursery growers, specializing in fruit orchards.

6 From 13th, turn right onto SE Henry Street, which dead-ends into the bluff. The wide spot on the bluff just beyond Henry's end provides another great look into Oaks Bottom. After enjoying the view, come back from the dead end. On the right, at 1250 Henry, is a 2005 home likely built on the site of a smaller, older house—the fate of old view properties everywhere.

From 13th and Henry, head east, cutting through the school's field to SE 14th Avenue and Henry. Turn right on 14th. Just beyond the school grounds begins Portland Memorial, the largest mausoleum west of the Mississippi. Inside its eight floors of vaults lie the remains of 100,000 people; nevertheless, on one visit I noticed a cheery sign flapping from the wall, announcing, "Yes! We have space available!" Drawn in by the friendly banner, I passed under ominous-looking pyramids at the door and discovered that Portland Memorial is open to the public and well worth a visit. Inside the gate is a 1901 chapel with a wonderful stained glass ceiling and walls lined with ornate silver funerary urns. As the chapel filled, more space was needed; in 1910 the first part of the separate mausoleum building opened, and additions were made to it over the next seventy years. Enter its 7 miles of corridors at the fifth floor; the floors below follow the bluff face downward. Inside, halls are lined with marble squares; the large squares hold casketed remains. In hallways containing smaller squares are columbarium niches, for cremated remains. The word *columbarium* originally meant "pigeon house." And because you may want to know, the niches at eye level cost more than the ones higher up. A walk through the silent halls lined with crypts is not something you'd do every day, but something you should do once, if for no other reason than as a source for arresting dinner-table conversation. Notable sights are an original Tiffany stained glass window near the main entrance to the mausoleum; and, in the mausoleum's Devotion Corridor, an exact replica of Michelangelo's *Pietà*, commissioned through the Vatican and sculpted of marble from the same quarry used for the original. The Rose Room skylight was created by Portland's famed Povey Brothers.

7 From 14th, turn left onto SE Bybee Boulevard. In a few blocks, at Bybee and Milwaukie, you'll encounter a thriving commercial town center born during the streetcar era. It's a pleasant place to spend a few hours, shopping at antique stores, eating at great restaurants (including one run by Caprial and John Pence), or catching a movie at the 1926 Moreland Theatre, one of the few places around where you can enjoy first-run films in a single-screen theater. With the 1928 sidewalk clock at the William R. Johnson Jewelers, the Art Deco Moreland Hardware, and other shops straight from 1950s America, you may find yourself glancing around for Beaver, Wally, and Eddie, who were surely roller-skating down the sidewalk just a few moments before.

Continue east on Bybee to SE 19th Avenue, and turn right. This is the heart of Westmoreland, a street of beautiful bungalows and many trees. The numbered streets here are laid out with fewer cross streets, giving them a peaceful, less trafficked feel.

8 From 19th, turn left onto SE Knapp Street. East of 21st, the street was repaved in 2004 with the city's first use of permeable paving material on a public street. The interspaces in the concrete blocks allow rain to percolate downward into the soil, keeping water out of the sewage system and helping alleviate the city's ongoing problems with street run-off overwhelming sewage treatment facilities during heavy rains. Volunteer plants (don't call them weeds) in the interspaces, pounded by car tires into a bonsai state, add an element of subtle beauty to the pavers.

Ahead is Westmoreland Park's casting pond. Walk toward it. Hand-dug during the 1930s for a work relief project, the 3-foot-deep concrete-lined pond was designed for practicing fly casting and sailing toy boats, a popular practice in those days and perhaps a good pastime to revive. This casting pond is thought to be one of only a handful of such ponds in the United States. It is fed by Crystal Springs Creek, a clear and beautiful stream originating from springs in Reed Canyon and its surrounds. Westmoreland Park was originally a swampy lowland, similar to Crystal Springs Park and the industrial section of Brooklyn between 17th and 26th Avenues. Prior to becoming parkland in the late 1920s, the area had been filled and used as an airstrip.

At the pond, turn left on the gravel path; at the end of the pond, continue north, following the creek. Cross Bybee at the light at SE 23rd Avenue. Notice the Depression-era rockwork at the creek bridge here.

9 From the intersection of Bybee and 23rd, turn west (left) on Bybee, and walk one block before turning right onto SE 22nd Avenue. From 22nd, turn left on SE Claybourne Street. Notice the old elms between 21st and 19th Avenues. From Claybourne, turn right on 19th, another leafy street with plenty of homes to admire. The home at 5819, new in 2006, is a bold departure from the prevailing style.

10 From 19th, turn left on SE Reedway Street. At the northwest corner of SE 18th Avenue and Reedway is a 1923 Craftsman with interesting elbow brackets and exceedingly deep eaves; it predates its neighbors across the street by twenty years.

From Reedway, turn right onto 18th, which is unpaved. On the right, at the southeast corner of 18th and SE Ellis Street, is a 1902 farmhouse from the area's rural days. Cross Ellis, walk one more block, and turn left off 18th onto SE Harold Street, which is lined with attractive homes from the first decade of the 1900s.

11 From Harold, turn right on SE 17th Avenue. Cross McLoughlin and walk a fairly unpleasant 0.3 mile to Holgate. On the right, in the block north of Schiller, is Peco, Inc., which supplies products to the aerospace, computer, medical, agricultural, and commercial cooking markets.

12 From 17th, turn left on Holgate and then right on SE 16th Avenue to reenter the quiet residential streets of Brooklyn. At 16th and SE Center Street is Brooklyn School, built in 1930 and now occupied by Winterhaven School, a special-focus public school that emphasizes math, science, and technology for grades K through 8.

On 16th across from the school grounds are City Life homes, part of Portland General Electric's 1995 Urban Show of Homes. The U.S. Department of Housing and Urban Development gave the homes an award for affordable housing using innovative design and technology. They were also granted a Governor's Livability Award, given to projects that encourage Oregon's economic growth without expanding urban growth boundaries. A decade later one of the innovative technologies, the exterior Louisiana Pacific (LP) siding, had

Small homes on one of the city's most unique streets, SE Pershing.

developed mold and was removed and replaced—a common occurrence in the city during the early 2000s.

Continue walking north on 16th. North of SE Rhine Street is the oldest section of Brooklyn, part of the first subdivision in 1870 that ran north to Division. At 3415 and 3411 are two Queen Annes built in 1905. At 3404 is an 1890 foursquare, plain and solid. It shares a picturesquely decaying wall with its neighbor. At 3384 is an 1891 Queen Anne with a unique diagonal second-story porch. Its original roofline was shaped like a witch's hat.

13 From 16th, turn left onto SE Pershing Street. This narrow street of early Brooklyn homes easily takes you back a half-century or more, depending on what is parked along it. The four tiny houses on the right, from 1912, occupy lots of less than 1600 square feet each, far less than the interior of most new homes. They lack a parking strip and yard but have plenty of charm and give the block a feeling akin to an old East Coast village.

At 1516 is the 1883 Adam Hemmrich farmhouse, the oldest house in Brooklyn. Hemmrich was a German immigrant who harvested and hauled lumber, which he stored in the barn behind the home. As you approach SE 14th

An aerial view of the Ross Island Bridge, circa 1926. The Poulsen and Inman homes are visible on either side of Powell Boulevard. Note the quiet stretch of roadway now occupied by McLoughlin Boulevard. Photo courtesy of the Oregon Historical Society.

Avenue, on the left is an old barn. It belongs to the 1913 house to the west, originally owned by the Mantia family. In the barn they stored produce from their extensive gardens. Sawdust was stuffed in the barn walls to insulate the produce from heat.

From Pershing, turn left on 14th and then right on SE Haig Street. The home at 1324, from 1911, has some delicate porch columns—unusual for a Craftsman bungalow. At 1183 is the 1899 Queen Anne home of Daniel Sherrett, most likely the namesake of Portland's quirky Sherrett Square in Sellwood.

14 From Haig, turn right onto Milwaukie. Here is a cluster of old commercial buildings from the streetcar days, with a combination bookstore–coffee shop to put your feet up in and rest a while.

Cross Milwaukie at the crosswalk at Pershing, toward Brooklyn Park, site of an 1887 school. Just to the right of the park is a path. Take it one block to its end at SE 11th Avenue. Go right on 11th and then left onto SE Franklin Street. Homes here, such as 1025 and 1015, date from 1906 or so.

Follow Franklin to the walk's starting point.

To get a closer look at a historic home usually glimpsed only from the Ross Island Bridge or McLoughlin at 50 miles per hour, walk to Franklin's end at McLoughlin. A sidewalk to the right curves around in half a block to the Johan Poulsen home, a nine-bedroom 1891 Queen Anne mansion built for one of the owners of the Inman-Poulsen sawmill. Though Poulsen never lived in the home, its position on the bluff was designed to allow him to look down at his riverside mill (at the foot of SE Clinton Street). Poulsen's partner, Robert D. Inman, built a near-identical home across SE Powell Boulevard at 6th Avenue and Woodward Street, which was torn down in 1958 for a parking lot. Soon after building this home, Poulsen built another on NE Hassalo Street, on the site of the Red Lion Hotel at the Convention Center.

SOUTH PORTLAND TO SOUTH WATERFRONT PARK LOOP

DISTANCE 3.25 miles

STARTING POINT SW Kelly Avenue and Curry Street

GETTING THERE AND PARKING From downtown Portland, travel south on Naito Parkway beyond SW Columbia Street. Just after passing SW Sheridan Street, you will travel over Interstate 405. Once over the freeway, look for a sign for Highways 26 and 43, Ross Island Bridge and Lake Oswego, exiting to the right. Take this two-lane exit. Get in the right lane and follow the sign that reads "Macadam/Lake Oswego next right." This puts you on SW Kelly Avenue. Drive three blocks to the starting point. Park south of SW Curry Street, where there are no restrictions.

TriMet: Take bus 43 (Taylors Ferry Road), bus 35 (Macadam), or bus 36 (South Shore), which all stop within a block of the starting point.

RESTROOMS AND DRINKING FOUNTAINS Restrooms are at Lair Hill Park, Duniway Park, and South Waterfront Park (just south of SW Montgomery Street, along River Drive). Drinking fountains are at Lair Hill Park, Duniway Park, SW 3rd Avenue and Clay Street, and RiverPlace.

FOOD AND DRINK Ross Island Grocery and Café, 3336 SW Corbett Avenue, is located near the beginning of the walk. RiverPlace, which falls midway through the walk, offers cafés, restaurants, pizza joints, and coffee houses. Old Lair Hill Market Café, at 2823 SW 1st Avenue, is a good place to stop near the end of the walk; it is open weekdays.

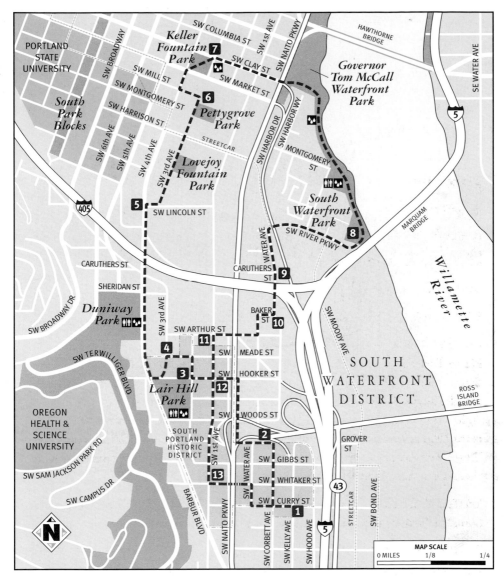

SW COLUMBIA ST
SW 1ST AVE
SW NAITO PKWY
HAWTHORNE
BRIDGE
SE WATER AVE

PORTLAND
STATE
UNIVERSITY

Keller
Fountain
Park **7**
SW CLAY ST

SW BROADWAY
SW MILL ST
SW MONTGOMERY ST
SW MARKET ST

South
Park
Blocks

SW HARRISON ST
6
Pettygrove
Park
SW HARBOR DR
SW HARBOR WY

Governor
Tom McCall
Waterfront
Park

STREETCAR
SW MONTGOMERY ST

SW 6th AVE
SW 5th AVE
SW 4th AVE
SW 3rd AVE

Lovejoy
Fountain
Park

I-5

I-405
5
SW LINCOLN ST

South
Waterfront
Park
8
SW RIVER PKWY

MARQUAM
BRIDGE

Willamette
River

CARUTHERS ST
WATER AVE
CARUTHERS ST **9**

SHERIDAN ST
SW 3rd AVE

Duniway
Park

BAKER ST **10**

SW MOODY AVE

SOUTH
WATERFRONT
DISTRICT

ROSS
ISLAND
BRIDGE

SW BROADWAY DR
SW TERWILLIGER BLVD

SW ARTHUR ST
4 **11**
SW MEADE ST
3 SW HOOKER ST
12

Lair Hill
Park

OREGON
HEALTH &
SCIENCE
UNIVERSITY

SW SAM JACKSON PARK RD
SW CAMPUS DR

SOUTH
PORTLAND
HISTORIC
DISTRICT

SW WOODS ST

2
SW 1ST AVE
SW WATER AVE
SW GIBBS ST
SW WHITAKER ST
SW CURRY ST **1**

13

GROVER ST
43
STREETCAR
SW BOND AVE

N

SW NAITO PKWY
BARBUR BLVD
SW CORBETT AVE
SW KELLY AVE
SW HOOD AVE
I-5

MAP SCALE
0 MILES   1/8   1/4

WALK 11. *South Portland to South
Waterfront Park Loop*

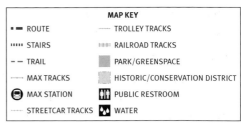

MAP KEY

▪·▪ ROUTE
⋯⋯ TROLLEY TRACKS
⁙ STAIRS
⊬⊬ RAILROAD TRACKS
– – TRAIL
PARK/GREENSPACE
MAX TRACKS
HISTORIC/CONSERVATION DISTRICT
🚈 MAX STATION
🚻 PUBLIC RESTROOM
STREETCAR TRACKS
WATER

BEST TIMES TO VISIT   The area is best visited during the week. On weekends the fountains and walkways in downtown's South Auditorium Urban Renewal Area are largely vacant, and the fascinating Great Northwest Bookstore (3314 SW 1st Avenue) is closed. However, on warm-weather weekends, South Waterfront Park is a delight, with a lively sidewalk restaurant scene and good people-watching.

ACCESSIBILITY   This walk, while among my favorites, was challenging to construct because this once-cohesive grid of pedestrian-oriented streets has been overlaid with a spaghetti-like mess of curving bridge ramps, freeways, and elevated thoroughfares. The route entails subgrade road crossings, an elevated pedestrian walkway, a stroll under a freeway, an unimproved roadway, a few stretches along busy roads, and an optional unregulated pedestrian crossing of SW Naito Parkway. There is one steep, block-long stretch at **10**. Options for circumventing stairs and unregulated pedestrian crossings are given.

THIS WALK BEGINS AND ENDS in the South Portland Historic District. The homes and businesses here, built between the 1880s and the 1920s, were once central to the lives of Italian and Jewish immigrants. North of this district, the walk explores an experiment from the 1960s called the South Auditorium Urban Renewal Area, which razed the northern half of South Portland's immigrant neighborhood. The southern half of the walk offers blocks of restored nineteenth-century homes; the northern half, historic fountains, great city views, and a beautiful stroll along South Waterfront Park, one of the city's newest parks.

   In the 1970s, Corbett and Lair Hill (subneighborhoods of what is now called South Portland) was the area to get your hash pipe and other countercultural sundries. Absentee owners, vacant buildings, and student renters occupied a dying neighborhood that one hundred years before had boomed as one of Portland's first suburbs.

   From 1860 to 1880, Portland's population grew from eight hundred to seventeen thousand, all on the west side (East Portland was a separate town). South Portland was a relatively easy place to develop, being a broad bench between the Willamette and the West Hills. (Its limits were Harrison on the north, the Park Blocks on the west, Bancroft on the south, and the Willamette on the east.) In the 1870s the first homes were built in the new neighborhood. Houses were generally in various Victorian styles, most from pattern books, and were home to workers at nearby docks, warehouses, and riverside industries. In Lair Hill, blocks of these homes are extant, the oldest from 1876. Development

Crowded conditions in South Portland brought comfort to some immigrants, and a reason to leave for others.

was spurred by the city's first horse-drawn streetcar, which began operating in 1886.

In the 1890s the great wave of European immigration began washing over America, and eastern European Jews and Italians from southern Italy began to move into South Portland. In the first decades of the twentieth century the neighborhood was poor but thriving, and like most immigrant neighborhoods, its streets were alive with peddlers, children, and wares spilling out from storefronts. Five synagogues, several churches, three bakeries, a theater, a kosher butcher shop, Italian grocers, and Chinese laundries, where workers ironed clothes on the sidewalk—all were within an easy walk of most homes.

The 1920s brought the beginning of the end of this pedestrian culture. Immigrants moved on to newer, more upscale, or less dense neighborhoods, and some of the neighborhood's vitality went with them. In 1926 the Ross Island Bridge was built. At first it did not impinge on city streets, but in 1935 the bridge approaches were expanded, and Barbur Boulevard became a major automobile thoroughfare. In 1943 Front Avenue (now Naito Parkway) was widened and turned into an early-day freeway, splitting the neighborhood in two. Soon after, the Ross Island Bridge approaches were enlarged again.

The 1950s saw homeowners leaving for the suburbs and outlying neighborhoods, and South Portland's decline seemed irreversible. Interstate 405 and Interstate 5 were built in the 1960s, eating up more neighborhood streets. Change, however, came that same decade as students at Portland State College (now Portland State University), the University of Oregon Medical Center (now Oregon Health and Science University), and Lewis and Clark College moved in, attracted by cheap rentals. It wasn't long before these newly educated boomers recognized the area for its potential. By the 1970s, neighborhood activism had led to a resurgent pride. In 1980 a large area south of SW Arthur Street was designated the South Portland Historic District by the National Register of Historic Places. Increasingly, investors returned, old homes were renovated, and by 2006, a small Lair Hill bungalow cost half a million dollars.

1 In the block where this walk begins, bounded by SW Curry Street, SW Kelly Avenue, SW Whitaker Street, and SW Hood Avenue, was the first log cabin in the neighborhood, built in 1842 by a sailor on Captain John H. Couch's ship *Maryland.* The sailor himself became a river captain and built his home on this rise overlooking the Willamette, at the foot of Ross Island. Indian trails went east from this location to Mount Hood, with the shallow Ross Island bar allowing people to walk across the river during low water.

In the northeast corner of Kelly and Curry is the 1890 home of Milton W. Smith. Unlike most homes in the neighborhood, this one was architect-designed, by Whidden and Lewis, who a few years later designed City Hall. It is one of the city's first Colonial Revival homes.

Walk one block west on Curry, and turn right onto SW Corbett Avenue, a street of old Queen Annes, one of the best of which is at the corner, 3434 Corbett, with a fine old southern magnolia complementing the style beautifully. It was built in 1885.

Cross Whitaker, where you can grab a cup of coffee at the 1908 Ross Island Grocery.

Cross SW Gibbs Street, whose airspace has been claimed by the Portland aerial tram. Contentious as its construction was, the tram is a marvel and a fun ride. Plans are to build a pedestrian walkway along the Gibbs alignment to connect this neighborhood to the South Waterfront district, where the tram terminates. Look west to the Peter O. Kohler Pavilion at Oregon Health and Science University (OHSU), built in 2006. The tram ends at its ninth floor, where in an open-air patio you can enjoy some of the best views in town.

At Gibbs, cross to the west side of Corbett to avoid a dangerous crossing.

At 3204 is an Italianate home from 1876 that once enjoyed a serene perch here. No longer. Next to it, Corbett is rudely interrupted by ramps of the Ross Island Bridge that are too dangerous for a pedestrian crossing.

2 Turn left off Corbett onto SW Grover Street, which runs adjacent to the bridge ramps. Midway through the block, look right to the 1912 Failing School, which sits marooned by transit corridors, cut off from the neighborhood it once served. Ninety percent of Failing's students were children of immigrants. The name honors Josiah Failing, a driving force in creating public schools for all of Portland's children. I wonder if school leaders of today would have the guts to give that name to a school, no matter whom it was honoring.

Ahead is SW Naito Parkway. Take the stairs that lead up to it. (To avoid the stairs, continue on the sidewalk that runs under Naito. It emerges on SW 1st Avenue. Turn right and rejoin the walk near **3**.) From the top of the stairs, turn right, cross a ramp at a crosswalk, and turn right to follow the sidewalk along Naito. It's a bit unpleasant, but the view is nice, and it provides a good feel for how Naito bisects South Portland.

Before President Dwight Eisenhower promulgated a national system of interstate highways in the 1950s, Front Avenue had been widened in 1943 to become part of the West Coast interstate system. In Portland, Interstate Avenue, the Steel Bridge, Front Avenue, and Barbur Boulevard were part of the system. Widening Front and closing its access to intersecting streets intentionally changed its nature from a street used both for local and through-traffic into a road used primarily to route traffic from outlying areas into the city and beyond.

It was a new concept in the 1940s, one which soon evolved into the modern interstate highway system.

At Naito and SW Hooker Street, turn right to get to the ramp leading up to a pedestrian walkway. The building in the northeast corner is the Helen Kelly-Manley Center, built in 1912 as a community center for Italian Americans. The ramp begins adjacent to the Failing School. The school was decommissioned in 1958 and became part of Portland Community College in 1969. Since the mid 1990s it has been home to the National College of Natural Medicine (formerly the National College of Naturopathic Medicine). Founded in 1956, it is the oldest of the nation's accredited naturopathic medical schools. It also offers a master's degree in Oriental medicine.

Climb the ramp. It provides great views of OHSU, the campus perched on the wooded hillside, and the recipient of many National Institutes of Health research grants. The contrast is striking between its gleaming new towers and the National College of Natural Medicine's recycled building. Visible on the hillside campus is another pedestrian conveyance: a blue aerial walkway, an eighth of a mile long, that spans a forested canyon between medical buildings.

After coming off the ramp (or walking north on 1st if you skipped the stairs in the prior section), walk west on Hooker to SW 2nd Avenue. In the southwest corner is the 1921 South Portland Library, a Carnegie library built in the Mediterranean style in Lair Hill Park. It operated as a library until 1954. In front is a spectacular purple beech.

While not on the route, Lair Hill Park and its buildings are worth a look. In the 1870s this parkland was the estate of Mr. and Mrs. Charles E. Smith. She was an amateur horticulturist who reputedly planted the trees in the park. Their large home later became the first County Hospital. It was torn down in 1923 and replaced by an extant building on the OHSU campus. At the southeast corner of the park is the Multnomah County Hospital Nurses Quarters, from 1918, and across from it, at the northeast corner of 2nd and SW Woods Street, is Neighborhood House, designed in 1910 by A. E. Doyle as a settlement home for Jewish and Italian immigrants. Inside were a clinic, dispensary, pool, and classrooms, with classes ranging from English to sewing to swimming.

3 From Hooker, turn right on 2nd. On the right, at 2826 and 2822, are two Stick-style homes from 1892 and 1882, respectively. Walk to the intersection of 2nd and SW Meade Street. Congregation Kesser Israel, an Orthodox synagogue, stood in the southeast corner here until 2006.

The intriguing history of Jews in South Portland is well documented in *The Jews of Oregon* by Steven Lowenstein. German Jews arrived in Portland in the

1850s, coming west as peddlers who supplied settlers and miners. Peddling was common for Jews in Europe, where they were not permitted to obtain licenses for permanent stores. In America, without this impediment, and with a background in merchandising, they became retail merchants. By the 1880s, mansions along the Park Blocks housed German Jewish families, who settled close to Temple Beth Israel, then at 12th and Main. Nob Hill also was home to many German Jewish families, who were generally more secular than Jews of eastern Europe. There was no Jewish enclave in Portland at that time.

In 1881 events began in Russia that would change the face of South Portland. In that year, the Russian czar died, and the new czar implemented anti-Semitic policies. Compounding this hardship, many Jewish peddlers found markets for their wares drying up as mass-produced goods made their way gradually into eastern Europe via new rail lines. A mass exodus began. Between 1881 and 1910, 1.5 million Jews emigrated from eastern Europe to the United States. Overcrowding in New York slums created fear of an anti-Semitic backlash and anti-immigrant legislation, so in 1901 the Industrial Removal Office (IRO) was formed to relocate unemployed Jews from New York to communities across the nation. Ben Selling (father of Rae Selling Berry of the Berry Botanic Garden) was Portland's IRO agent. He helped hundreds of Jews settle in South Portland, an affordable location near places of employment. Immigrants worked as tailors, upholsterers, seamstresses, varnishers, secondhand dealers, grocers, and small manufacturers of hats, mattresses, and umbrellas.

As the neighborhood evolved into a Jewish and Italian enclave, buildings evolved too. The building at 2nd and Meade was built in 1900 as Immanuel Baptist. In 1912 the Baptists sold the building, and it became Kesser Israel, also known as the Meade Street Shul. In December 2006, Kesser Israel became the last of the original synagogue buildings to close when it moved to temporary quarters while a new synagogue was built further out in Southwest Portland, where most of its members live. The move was precipitated so that members could continue to make shomer Shabbat observance (walking, not driving, to the synagogue on the Sabbath). The building was sold to the Church of All Nations for $515,000.

Don't miss the exuberantly arty 1886 Corkish Apartments at the northeast corner of Meade and 2nd. John Corkish built them as family residences for working-class immigrants. Corkish came to the Northwest from the Isle of Man to work as an agent for an oil company, but moved on to start two large corporations, Puget Sound Pipe and Goldendale Milling. Since South Portland had access to a streetcar as early as 1886, multifamily homes are common, as they are in many city neighborhoods served by a streetcar. This building is nicer than most, with its stained glass, corbeled caps on the chimneys (in which the upper termination of the chimney projects outward in one or more courses), carved wood panels, and ornamental brackets.

You may want to wander down 2nd, past the Corkish. At 2726 and 2724 2nd are two homes once occupied by the Zidell family. They were built, respectively, in 1880 and 1908. In 1915, Sam Zidell arrived in this country from eastern Europe and soon opened Zidell Machinery and Supply, selling to the city's factories. Today the Zidell Companies manufacture barges and welding fittings, the last of the riverside industries along SW Moody Avenue, in the area being rebuilt by OHSU and others.

Back at the corner of 2nd and Meade, walk west on Meade. Just beyond where the road turns to gravel are some small cottages from the 1890s. This section is especially nice, as it retains a bit of the feel of properties built along Marquam Gulch when it was still a natural gulch running through South Portland. Many Italian immigrants settled along the gulch, from SW Broadway Drive downstream to a section of SW Sheridan Street near SW Water Avenue (seen later in the walk). Most of their homes are gone, lost to freeway and urban renewal. Typical was Nat Costanzo, who lived on Broadway Drive; he made a living pouring concrete, and like many Italians, he built a bread oven in his backyard.

4 On Meade a concrete sidewalk curves up the hill on the left. Take it, and you'll end up on SW Hooker Street, next to Lair Hill Park, with more great views of the modern university buildings towering over nineteenth-century homes, and the forest buffering the eras. The park is named for William Lair Hill, who bought this land in 1868.

Turn right on Hooker and walk uphill to Barbur Boulevard. Cross it at the light and turn north. In 1868 Joseph Gaston followed an Indian trail into the Tualatin Valley and turned it into the Oregon Central Railroad line to bring the valley's agricultural products to city docks. In 1935 the line was abandoned and Barbur Boulevard was built along its alignment.

Walk north on Barbur past the Metro Family YMCA. The green field and track adjacent to it sit on landfill that has smothered a creek canyon. In 1868, Gaston's rail line ran over the gulch here along a high wooden trestle, and the creek below was tapped as part of the city's water supply. By the 1890s the gulch had become the city dump, with Italian immigrants living along its flanks. The dump was an eyesore and a dangerous playground for children, so in 1918 the city filled it part way, creating Duniway Park, named for Abigail Scott Duniway, an Oregon publisher, writer, and leader in women's right to vote. It was filled further in the 1960s with spoils from the construction of Interstate 405. If

Marquam Gulch, circa 1920, looking northwest toward Portland Heights. Fill had already begun. Note the wooden sidewalk leading downhill, at the left side of the photo. Photo courtesy of the City of Portland Archives.

you look over at Barbur's east side, you can see the fill slope. Above the park, the canyon's natural beauty makes for great hiking. The Marquam Trail to the west leads up to Council Crest, the highest point in the city at 1073 feet. The Duniway Park track itself is historic. Laid in 1995, it was the first of its kind, its surface made from twenty thousand athletic shoe soles donated by Nike.

North of the park the walk enters the South Auditorium Urban Renewal Area. Cross SW Sheridan Street, SW Caruthers Street, and Interstate 405, which circles the city's core. Planning for this freeway began in the late 1950s; by 1966, homes had been razed, earth had been excavated to form the trench, and this section through South Portland was complete.

In the distance to the right is the Marquam Bridge, which the route will pass under. By this point in the route, Barbur has changed names and is now SW 4th Avenue.

5 From 4th, turn right on SW Lincoln Street, walking down its north side. Just past the first building on the left, the Parkside Center, turn left onto a paved promenade between the buildings and have a seat on the bench to read about the background of this district.

Besides the assaults on this neighborhood by the auto, two other elements contributed to the area's decline: in the 1920s, as immigrants prospered, many moved out of South Portland into newer neighborhoods. Italians settled in Southeast, where lower density meant they could garden on vacant lots. Jews moved to Irvington, Nob Hill, and Laurelhurst. Then, in the 1930s, the Depression meant that little was invested in real property anywhere in the nation.

After the Depression, dilapidated housing stocks were a national issue. Franklin Roosevelt, in his second inaugural address in 1937, noted that "one-third of the nation is ill-housed, ill-fed, and ill-clothed," and he challenged the United States to do better. Not until after World War II, however, was action possible. The Housing Act of 1949 was Congress's first attempt to improve housing. It helped cities address economic disinvestment by providing federal funds for infrastructure, public spaces, and renovation or construction of buildings to meet housing and social needs, and to increase tax bases.

In this environment the South Auditorium Urban Renewal Area was born. In 1958 it was voted in, and notices of condemnation and eviction were sent to the twenty-three hundred residents from Front Avenue (Naito Parkway) to 4th Avenue and from Market Street to Arthur Street, along with a brochure: "Let's perk up Portland with urban renewal." By 1963 fifty-four blocks had been bulldozed. The goal was to replace single-family homes and mom-and-pop businesses with a "streets in the sky" utopia of modern housing, meant to attract middle-class residents back to the city center. Some of these buildings will be seen shortly.

Walk north on the pedestrian promenade that used to be SW 3rd Avenue. The first park encountered is Lovejoy Fountain Park, one of three parks in the South Auditorium Urban Renewal Area designed by famed landscape architect Lawrence Halprin and his associates between 1965 and 1970; the other two are Pettygrove Park and Keller Fountain Park. Halprin felt that people were losing a sense of place, owing to the vast destruction of what had been developed slowly over generations, and he designed the three parks to evoke places of nature. The Lovejoy, with its stark angles and plateaus, is meant to suggest the erosional forms of the high desert. Halprin's wife, Anna, is a choreographer, and the fountains reflect her influence. In this case, the stagelike stepping "stones" across the water invite theatrics, dance, or impromptu poetry reading. He wanted his fountains to say "come in" rather than "keep out," which today seems like a sine qua non for a public park. At the time it was a revelation.

In 2005 the Lovejoy was described as the least maintained of Halprin's Portland parks, but appreciation for it and its sister parks seems to be grow-

The Portland Center Apartments (now the Harrison condominiums) replaced a neighborhood of single-family homes in the city's first urban renewal project.

ing. Randy Gragg, the *Oregonian*'s former architecture critic, calls the Portland parks "the most well preserved sequence of parks in the U.S." designed by Halprin, and Gragg notes that "the three plazas—Lovejoy, Pettygrove and Keller Fountain—now stand with Pietro Belluschi's Commonwealth Building

163

and Alvar Aalto's Mount Angel Abbey Library as Oregon's most internationally significant works of architecture."

Other Halprin fountains across the United States have fallen into disfavor, most notably Denver's Skyline Park, an austere sculptural landscape seen as a dated eyesore and demolished in 2003. One familiar Halprin park to Northwesterners is Freeway Park in Seattle, which reconnected a neighborhood severed by Interstate 5. Halprin also designed the Franklin Delano Roosevelt Memorial in Washington, D.C., and the Lucasfilm campus at the Presidio in San Francisco.

The tower to the north of Lovejoy Fountain Park was designed in 1965 by Skidmore, Owings, and Merrill (SOM), a Chicago-based architecture firm that had a Portland office at that time and built several downtown office buildings. SOM was a leader in the International style of architecture and designed many buildings in the South Auditorium Urban Renewal Area. Other buildings it designed from that era are the John Hancock Center (1969) and Sears Tower (1973) in Chicago. The tower is one of three that were persuasively named Portland Center Apartments. In 2007 the 537 apartments in the three towers were converted into the Harrison condominiums.

Stay on the promenade. The area seems to be in transition, but after forty years the "Portland Center" appellation seems more appropriate than it perhaps initially was, with the South Waterfront district coming on line, and the streetcar running through the South Auditorium Urban Renewal Area to connect it with busy Portland State University and the rest of downtown.

Continue along the pedestrian promenade to Pettygrove Park. Its green hummocks are a welcome relief from the warren of right angles and plate glass that the promenade traverses. They are meant to evoke mountain meadows and meandering streams.

The elegant black glass building on the park's north side was built in 1971. In 2006 it won Leadership in Energy and Environmental Design (LEED) Gold certification for its retrofits to conserve energy and water, and for purchases that encourage sustainable practices.

6 From the promenade, turn left at a large yellow sculpture. Here, at 3rd and SW Mill Street, stood one of the synagogues of South Portland: Talmud Torah. Walk toward SW 4th Avenue. Ahead is the 1894 Saint Michael's Church, spiritual home to the Italians of South Portland.

From Mill, turn right on 4th. In 1866 the massive stone wall across the street was built at the site of the first Saint Mary's Academy. The rock was ballast in an English ship then loading in the Portland Harbor. The old school was torn down in 1970 and a new one built one block west. It is the oldest continually operating high school in Oregon.

Walk north on 4th and enter Keller Fountain Park. Of Halprin's three parks, this is the easiest to love. Its inspiration, mountain cataracts, is splendidly recreated in a concrete sculpture, with pines, rushing water, cliffs, and ledges. When the city hired Halprin's firm for this park, it envisioned a utilitarian vehicle turnaround, a place where patrons of the Civic Auditorium (now Keller Auditorium) could be dropped off. Halprin had other ideas. His firm designed a park that is people-centric rather than automobile-centric, an idea received with "winces" (as reported by the *Oregonian*) from city officials in February 1968. By September 1968, sentiments had evolved, and Mayor Terry Schrunk and his commissioners were delighted that the park had been designed "with people in mind, rather than the vehicle"—a change of heart that is a testament to the power of an elegant idea. At the opening of the park, hundreds of Portlanders turned out to splash and hang out on the ledges, to the surprise of the dignitaries lined up to make congratulatory speeches. Halprin himself jumped in the water, raising eyebrows and causing some conservative Portlanders to take pen to paper and complain to the *Oregonian* about "hippies [now] having a place to bathe" in the "giant wading pool." Note the stagelike squares over the water at the base of the falls, inviting acts of civic theater. Without Halprin's fountains, Portland's collection of people-oriented fountains may not be as evolved; Pioneer Courthouse Square may never have happened, nor Salmon Street Springs or Jamison Square.

Exit the park at its northeast corner, 3rd and SW Clay Street. Cross 3rd at the Keller Auditorium, built in 1916 and rebuilt in 1967.

7 From 3rd, turn right on Clay, and walk three blocks to SW Naito Parkway. Cross to a sidewalk entering Governor Tom McCall Waterfront Park, located where a highway ran from 1940 to 1974. In 1984 the park was named for McCall, whose achievements protecting our state's natural assets contributed to the progressive legacy we Oregonians are so proud of. The Hawthorne Bridge is ahead. The Marquam Bridge is the next bridge upstream from the Hawthorne. Head toward the river and turn right to walk in front of the riverside shops at RiverPlace. In 1979 the Portland Development Commission (PDC) acquired the 73 acres of waterfront land between the Hawthorne and Marquam Bridges. The land was undeveloped at the time, as earlier industrial uses had moved on, except for Pacific Power and Light, which agreed to move its steam plant then operating along the river. The first phase of RiverPlace, including shops, restaurants, and a hotel, was completed in 1985.

In the floods of February 1996, the walkway here was under water.

8 Keep to the river, but don't miss the beautiful gardens at the foot of SW Montgomery Street. The riverside walkway ends at more beautifully landscaped ground under the Marquam Bridge. This rehabilitated area is a wonder to behold if you've been in town a while; a former industrial area, it had languished as a tarp-covered eyesore as pollution problems were addressed.

From under the Marquam Bridge, turn right, cross some grass, and emerge onto SW River Parkway (in front of the Residence Inn.) To avoid the grass, turn inland, away from the river just north of the bridge on a sidewalk that leads to River Parkway.

Cross SW Moody Avenue at the light and continue on River Parkway. The trolley tracks should be on the right. Cross SW Harbor Drive at the light, and walk a few steps along SW Harrison Street before turning onto a sidewalk that takes you to a dead end of SW Water Avenue, in front of the International School. Belgian block pavers cover the road here, and rail tracks are visible from the area's industrial days.

From Water's dead end, walk south on Water to SW Caruthers Street.

9 As you cross Caruthers, look to the right at two cottages—fragments of the neighborhood once here. The current owner told me that both homes, built in 1896, had Italian owners who inscribed their names in the sidewalk and left another bit of living history in the yard, where, according to the owner, "oregano is growing everywhere."

Walk under the freeway. As you cross SW Sheridan Street, on the right is a Greyhound garage from 1931. In mid 2007 this was slated to be torn down, with Portland General Electric to build its Marquam substation here.

10 From Water, turn right onto SW Baker Street, an unimproved stretch of road that leads uphill for one block to the return of Water Avenue, as its alignment jogs. Turn left onto Water and walk by some very old cottages. The house at 2624 dates from 1876, the home at 2623 from 1892, and the home at 2637 from 1888. At Water and SW Arthur Street, turn around to see the topography created by the creek that once ran down from the hills and drained into the Willamette. Homes on this block of Water sat on the creek's southern flank. (To keep to accessible sidewalks, don't turn off Water onto Baker; stay straight on Water as it turns into SW Corbett Avenue, and turn right on Arthur.)

From Water, turn right onto Arthur and pass an 1887 cottage. This antique bit of street ends with the new Arthur: four speeding lanes of traffic, surrounded by new buildings. A slightly alarming underpass, complete with New

York City–style subway tiles, lets a pedestrian cross Arthur underground. The skanky subterranean passage symbolizes where pedestrians stood during the 1960s. Don't take the passage. Instead, from the top of the stairs leading to it, walk west on the north side of Arthur. Carefully cross an entrance ramp to Naito Parkway, walk under Naito, and come to the intersection of Arthur and SW 1st Avenue.

A century earlier, you would be standing in the commercial core of South Portland, bounded by 1st, Naito, Arthur, and Sheridan. Within steps were Cottrell's drugstore, Harper's deli, Mosler's bakery, Korsun's market, and Colistro and Halprin's grocery. Colistro was a southern Italian, Halprin a Russian Jew.

11 From Arthur, reenter the South Portland Historic District by turning left onto 1st Avenue, a totally delightful street, especially after that bit of urban orienteering. Many businesses once lined this street, taking advantage of the city's first horse-drawn trolley. The line was electrified in 1889 and ran south to Fulton Park.

On 1st, at 2737, is the 1894 boyhood home of Earl Riley, Portland mayor from 1940 to 1948. In his last year in office, Riley was ambiguously described by the Office of War Information as "America's most typical mayor." His home was originally a few blocks south on 1st; it moved here in 1979.

Across the street, 2732 was an investment property built in 1884 by attorney Philip Marquam, thirty-three years after he first homesteaded in Portland. His many real estate investments led to his being called "the greatest landowner in Multnomah County." Marquam Hill, where OHSU sits, is land he once owned, as was the Fulton District and parts of what is now Riverview Cemetery. He also owned the house at 2740.

Before you cross SW Meade Street, look right; the second house from the corner, at 116, is the original South Portland Library from 1913. When the new library, seen earlier in the walk, opened in 1921, children of the neighborhood carried armfuls of books up Meade in a procession headed by the American flag, a copy of the Constitution, and a picture of George Washington.

The closeness of the immigrant community here was not just created by ethnic ties; the house at 2803 SW 1st sits on a 1200-square-foot lot, within arm's reach of its neighbors.

Cross Meade. The Italianate home at 2806 was built by Peter Taylor in 1882. A Scottish immigrant, Taylor founded Willamette Iron Works in 1865, manufacturing city fire hydrants among other things. He later sold his business to W. W. Corbett. The home at 2818 was built in 1888 by two Swiss immigrants, the Haehlen brothers, who ran the Knickerbocker Coffee and Oyster House on Washington Street. Based on the look of the house, they were successful, but I wouldn't place money on that combination of fare today.

At 2823 is a 1910 Classical Revival home, with the Lair Hill Market Café on the ground floor. The Weinstein family operated this grocery for years; they lived upstairs with their five daughters. One daughter, Esther, married Albert Schulhaus, a Holocaust survivor, and they took over the store and lived upstairs.

The contrast between the historic nature of this street and the urban renewal area is striking. If original plans had come to pass, the Lair Hill area south of Arthur would have looked much different. By the 1960s, as noted earlier, Lair Hill was on the ropes. The City of Portland believed it should be cleared and rebuilt with low-density apartments or large apartments for the elderly or Portland State students. In 1968 the clearance project was scheduled. The plan would have included leveling all buildings in a twenty-block area from Arthur to Curry and from Barbur to Corbett. However, residents and other community activists, including a young lawyer named Neil Goldschmidt, spoke out against the project (which, fortunately, was not the city's first priority due to the costs involved), and it did not go forward. In fact in 1977 the city council, convinced that the architecture and the community were historically significant to the people of Oregon, designated the Lair Hill neighborhood one of the first historic conservation districts in Portland.

12 On 1st, cross SW Hooker Street, continuing south past a block owned by Walsh Construction. A plaque explains the unusual portal by artist Keith Jellum. Cross SW Porter Street. Buildings on this block have housed for years some of the world's most effective humanitarians at Mercy Corps; in 2007, with 150 employees in six buildings, it purchased the Skidmore Fountain Building in Portland's Old Town, with plans to renovate it and move in 2009. The brick building at 3015 dates from 1978; it owes some of its style to its neighbor at 3025, a 1916 streetcar-era commercial building.

At the southwest corner of 1st and SW Woods Street is an 1890 Queen Anne apartment building. The National Register application for the district calls this "one of the outstanding structures in the neighborhood."

(If you want to avoid the grade-level Naito Parkway crossing at the end of the walk, turn left at the sidewalk leading downhill at SW Grover Street. Follow it to the pedestrian underpass of Naito seen earlier. Once through, turn right on SW Water Avenue, a street of beautiful pre-1900 homes. On Water, walk three blocks south to SW Curry Street. Turn left and walk two blocks to the starting point.)

If you remain on 1st, cross Grover. At 3215 a small vernacular cottage from 1889 has held onto its sloping green lawn, giving it a semirural quality that evokes the time when even urban homes had enough yard for a cow and chickens.

Cross SW Gibbs Street, where an 1890 Gothic Revival church sits at the southeast corner. Originally the Fourth Presbyterian Church, it later housed various congregations, including the New Age Church of the Divine Man, and today hosts the Great Northwest Bookstore, a fine place to breathe in the dusty past and find connections to the present. It is open weekdays only.

This block is home to more beautifully restored bungalows, Queen Annes, and Italianate homes from the 1880s to 1906.

13 From 1st, turn left on SW Whitaker Street, which offers more stunning Queen Annes, and a modern queen whose austere lines echo the earlier style. This home, at 21 Whitaker, was co-winner of a 2004 Living Smart competition for homes built on narrow infill lots; it measures just 16 feet wide. House plans are available for free from Portland's Bureau of Development Services at www. livingsmartpdx.com.

The Stick-style home at 14 features Eastlake detailing and was built in 1892 by Robert Foulkes, an emigrant from Wales, for his son Edward. Robert was a compositor for the *Oregonian*. When Henry Pittock, Robert's boss, was planning a new mansion in 1913, he hired Edward Foulkes to design it. It is now one of the most magnificent elements in the Portland Parks and Recreation system.

Carefully cross Naito Parkway. A median is the only pedestrian amenity, but the sight distance is good here. Take the stairs down to the continuation of Whitaker. Walk one block, turn right on Water, and in one block left on Curry, to return to the starting point.

WALK 12

GOOSE HOLLOW TO KING'S HILL LOOP

DISTANCE   About 2 miles, plus optional detours

STARTING POINT   SW 18th Avenue and Jefferson Street

GETTING THERE AND PARKING   From downtown Portland, drive west on SW Jefferson Street. Park on Jefferson east of SW 18th Avenue or on nearby streets. Note that the only daylight hours when parking is unrestricted in this neighborhood are on Saturdays and Sundays prior to 1:00 p.m. Other than that, parking is limited to two hours or less.

TriMet: This walk starts adjacent to a MAX stop. Take the MAX Red or Blue Line to the Goose Hollow/SW Jefferson Street stop near SW 18th and Jefferson, the starting point of the walk.

RESTROOMS AND DRINKING FOUNTAINS   There are no public restrooms on this route. However, restrooms for patrons are inside Fehrenbacher Hof Coffee House (1225 SW 19th Avenue, about one block off the route), Zupan's Market (2340 W Burnside Street), and McDonald's (1831 W Burnside, near the end of the route). Drinking fountains are at SW 18th Avenue and Jefferson Street, 18th and Salmon Street, and 18th and Morrison Street.

FOOD AND DRINK   In addition to options under "Restrooms and Drinking Fountains," NW 23rd Avenue, north of W Burnside Street (just off the route), is a restaurant row, with many great venues in old buildings.

BEST TIMES TO VISIT   Many homes on the walk are listed on the National Register of Historic Places. A listing brings with it tax advantages and an obligation to open the home to the public once per year. You may want to time your walk to coincide with the dates of an open house in King's Hill. For a calendar

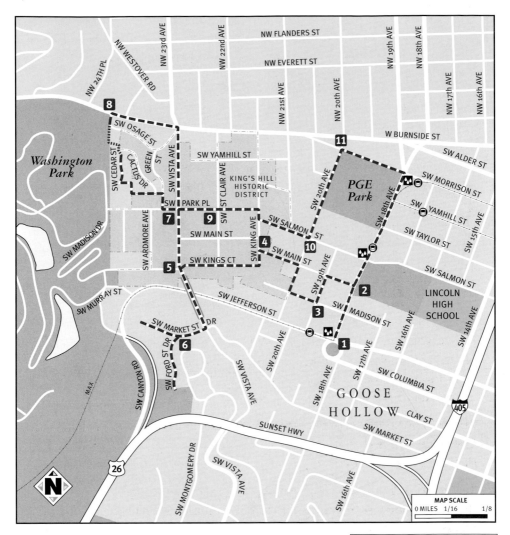

WALK 12. *Goose Hollow to King's Hill Loop*

MAP KEY

- ▬ ▬ ROUTE
- ׀׀׀׀׀ STAIRS
- ‒ ‒ TRAIL
- ······ MAX TRACKS
- Ⓣ MAX STATION
- ‒‒‒‒ STREETCAR TRACKS
- ······· TROLLEY TRACKS
- ┼┼┼┼ RAILROAD TRACKS
- ▨ PARK/GREENSPACE
- ▦ HISTORIC/CONSERVATION DISTRICT
- 🚻 PUBLIC RESTROOM
- 🌊 WATER

MAP SCALE
0 MILES   1/16   1/8

of upcoming openings, visit the Oregon Parks and Recreation Department Heritage Programs Web page, egov.oregon.gov/OPRD/HCD.

ACCESSIBILITY This walk climbs steeply uphill on city sidewalks and streets. There are stairs at **7**; directions in the text provide an alternate route that avoids them. The elevation is 110 feet at the start and about 300 feet near **8**.

THIS WALK BEGINS in Goose Hollow, home in the 1850s to a community of geese-herding women whose husbands left Oregon virtually denuded of men when they rushed to the California gold fields. It climbs out of the hollow into King's Hill, an area of mansions from the late nineteenth century. It is a short walk, but the area is so densely packed with architectural treasures and offers enough places to stop and eat that a morning could easily be made of it. Some streets not on the route are worth a look as well, especially SW Main Street between King and Vista Avenues, SW Saint Clair Avenue, and streets off SW Park Place above Vista.

For a longer walk, combine this route with Walk 13, which starts nearby at SW 18th Avenue and Morrison Street.

1 From the MAX stop, cross SW Jefferson Street at the light. Once across, enjoy one of Portland's signature attractions, a cold draught of mountain water from an ever-bubbling water fountain. This is not one of the original twenty Benson Bubblers from 1912 (gifts from timber baron Simon Benson to provide an alternative to saloons—at the time the only place to quickly quench one's thirst), but it follows the tradition. As of September 2005, the city maintains 129 drinking fountains, most of them ever-flowing bubblers (except late at night, when timers shut them off).

From Jefferson, walk north on SW 18th Avenue. Along both sides of the street are sidewalk etchings about local history. The one at 18th and Jefferson is a tribute to Goose Hollow's beloved Bud Clark, mayor of Portland from 1984 to 1992, and owner of the Goose Hollow Inn at SW 19th Avenue and Jefferson.

On the right at 18th and SW Main Street is Lincoln High School's athletic field, once the site of an orchard belonging to Jacob Kamm, whose adjacent mansion was moved when the school was built in the early 1950s. (The home, from 1871, is near the walk's starting point, at 1425 SW 20th Avenue.) Lincoln's excellent track and field, renovated in 2003, receives near constant use. Grant and Benson High Schools also play their home games here. The track is made of recycled tennis shoes, and the field turf consists of 4-inch-long "grass" blades in a bed of rubber pellets that are periodically raked to restore their fluff. George Osgood of Lincoln's Booster Club remembers when games on the old, overused natural turf field were played in stinky, fertilizer-laden muck.

Portland is among the last large American cities where most middle-class parents send their kids to public schools. Lincoln is one of eleven public high schools in town, and with students' SAT scores comparable to those from expensive private schools, Lincoln attracts families from the nearby well-to-do neighborhoods. Matt Groening, creator of the animated series *The Simpsons*, is a Lincoln alumnus, as is Fred Child, host of American Public Media's *Performance Today*. In 2006, three out of sixteen Rhodes Scholarship finalists in a seven-state region came from Lincoln.

The foundation of the multi-unit apartment at the southwest corner of 18th and Main is composed of granite, a stone not found in these parts.

2 From 18th, turn left on Main to begin climbing out of Goose Hollow, passing two small Queen Anne homes with foundations also made of granite. Since owners of these small dwellings would not have imported rock for the construction, the stone's provenance is likely ballast, used to balance the loads on oceangoing ships. Once in the Portland harbor, the ballast was no longer needed and so was offloaded and used for buildings and landscaping. Much of it was used to fill Couch Lake in the 1880s (see Walk 14).

From Main, turn left onto SW 19th Avenue. The empty city block uphill from 19th and Main is owned by the Multnomah Athletic Club, one of the city's oldest private clubs. (More on it later.) Walk along 19th to SW Madison Street. For coffee or sweets, continue half a block on 19th to the Fehrenbacher Hof, a perfect coffee house—good food and drink, no loud music, and two floors filled with chairs and worktables that invite you to stay.

3 From 19th and Madison, head west (uphill) on Madison. This block rewards a walker with six intact vintage homes on one side and a ghostly staircase to nowhere on the other. The home at 1906 is an intriguing mix of styles: Queen Anne with Eastlake detailing, Arts and Crafts half-timbering, and with a bungalow shed dormer on the roof. Uphill from it, two sets of mirror-image twin houses belonged to folks in the middle rung of the socioeconomic ladder—not as working class as Goose Hollow houses, but not as tony as the houses just a block or so further up the hill. These homes, at 1914, 1916, 1924, and 1926, were built around 1888 as rentals owned by the Haseltine family, who lived around the corner at 1129 SW 20th Avenue in a home built in 1889.

From Madison, turn right on 20th and pass the Haseltine house. In one block are two new apartment buildings erected in this neighborhood on the sites of grand homes. In the parlance of the National Register of Historic Places, such buildings are "noncontributing." Well put, I'd say.

From 20th, turn left onto SW Main Street and keep climbing. The slopes here, their wilderness tamed beyond recognition, are foothills to the Tualatin Mountains, a 30-mile chain that runs southeast to northwest, with peaks up to 1600 feet. Most Portlanders don't call this chain the Tualatin Mountains; they are known as the West Hills. At 2030 Main, the street returns to the nineteenth century; this is the oldest home in the neighborhood, and with it you begin a passage through some of the city's most densely packed grandeur. The home was built in 1882 in the Italianate style by F. R. Chown, founder of the still-existing, family-run Chown Hardware.

4 From Main, turn left onto SW King Avenue, a street lined with one grand home after another, and named for Amos Nahum King, whose donation land claim encompassed this area. Most of the homes here are on the National Register of Historic Places and date from around 1890 to 1914. A Colonial Revival at 1131 King has the symmetry native to that style; designed in 1891 by Whidden and Lewis, it features prominent quoins and Tuscan columns.

At 1150 King is a 1914 Colonial Revival with a large façade dormer centered over a balustraded entrance portico, again with Tuscan columns.

King Avenue bends onto SW King's Court, a former dirt path along the canyon wall. No front yards means that pedestrians have unfettered views of some very fine architecture. The first encountered, at 1151, is an enormous 1904 Arts and Crafts home. The home at 2178 was built by Robert Livingstone, head of the Scottish American Investment Company, the company that successfully developed the Willamette Heights subdivision adjacent to the 1905 Lewis and Clark Exposition. The home at 2190, from 1904, is built in the Shingle style, but this one pairs that plain aesthetic with a formal Palladian window.

Giant timber bamboo sways over the street at 2229, the 1910 home of Erskine Wood. Born in 1879, he was the son of Charles Erskine Scott (C. E. S.) Wood, the famous lawyer, poet, and satirist whose charm and intellect allowed him to flourish in society while seriously overstepping its boundaries. As a soldier, C. E. S. Wood had been present in 1879 when Chief Joseph surrendered to the U.S. Army. It was he who recorded Joseph's statement, "I will fight no more forever." C. E. S. Wood later worked to bring Joseph and his tribe back to the Northwest after their forced relocation to Indian Territory (Oklahoma), and he sent Erskine to live with Joseph during the summers of 1892 and 1893. Of this

On SW King's Court. Photo by Zeb Andrews.

idyllic time, Erskine Wood wrote, "[Another boy] and I had to take care of the pony herd. Almost every day we would ride bareback out into the hills, find the herd, drive them to water in the Nespelem River and then turn our own horses loose and catch new ones for the camp." Erskine Wood lived until 1983, after practicing law into his nineties.

Next door to Erskine Wood's home is the Portland Garden Club, once the site of Erskine's childhood home, owned by C. E. S. and his wife, Nanny Wood, an accomplished gardener. Horticultural expertise is on display in the expertly trained wisteria and espaliered climbing hydrangea and euonymus. Don't miss the splendid katsura tree at the corner of King's Court and SW Vista Avenue. (More on the Woods later.)

5 King's Court emerges onto Vista at the edge of the Vista Avenue Bridge. For a walk into the wilder fringes of Goose Hollow, turn left onto the stairs that lead to a concrete bench built into the bridge, and then onto the bridge proper, which carries you over the canyon of Tanner Creek and offers views of downtown Portland and Cascade foothills and volcanoes.

At the end of the bridge, carefully cross Vista, where traffic is fast as cars fly down the hill from Portland Heights. Turn right onto SW Market Street Drive, which curves along the forested canyon wall.

6 From Market, take the first left onto SW Ford Street Drive, one of the few unpaved streets left in this part of town. This gravel road may be a vestigial bit of Vista, which used to be called Ford Street. Only one home occupies Ford Street Drive, which also serves as both a backdoor entrance to a grand home uphill, on SW Prospect Drive, and to a public structure that sits above the west entrance to the Vista Ridge Tunnels, through which the Sunset Highway passes. Ford Street Drive is noteworthy in that down the slope you can see an earlier version of Canyon Road (Jefferson Street), now abandoned, adjacent to the current roadbed. This road was a much improved version of the first single-track path through the canyon, which had challenged farmers in the 1850s as they brought their produce to riverside docks. With time, this improved roadbed also became obsolete as more fill was brought into the canyon to raise and broaden the road. Prior to the tunnels' construction in 1969 and 1970, Jefferson Street/Canyon Road was the only route to the Sunset Highway from downtown.

After exploring Ford Street Drive, come back out on Market Street Drive and meander down to its dead end in one block. The old home at the end, circa 1890, faces the canyon and harks back to another era, in which the clatter of farmer's wagons might still be imagined if you have headphones to drown out the modern cacophony.

From Market, return to Vista, and turn left to walk back across the bridge. From the west side of the bridge you can see the MAX line disappearing into a tunnel in the basalt, from which it emerges, 3 miles from here, on the other side of the West Hills. Also visible is an 1894 reservoir in Washington Park that, despite its antiquated open-air design, still holds drinking water from the Bull Run watershed east of the city.

Once off the bridge, continue to walk north on Vista. At 1132 is the front view of the Portland Garden Club headquarters, a John Storrs design from the 1950s in the Northwest Regional style. In 1888, C. E. S. and Nanny Wood bought the property at Ford (Vista) and King's Court. C. E. S. ordered 250 feet of Japanese quince from New York for a hedge that still lines the property, although it is mostly grown over with holly. The couple had moved to Portland in 1884 after a happy time at Fort Vancouver, and C. E. S. began a law practice. Shortly after moving, they were invited to a society ball at the Failing mansion at King Avenue and Main Street. They did not have money for a carriage, so C. E. S. placed a wooden box atop Erskine's sled, lined it with Alaskan furs, and hauled Nanny to the party. Being a resourceful one herself, Nanny wasn't deterred by her lack of a fine dress: she made one out of muslin curtains.

Their happy years eroded with C. E. S. Wood's serial affairs. In 1904 Nanny returned from Germany where she'd spent two years nursing Erskine through tuberculosis at a sanatorium. C. E. S. picked them up at Union Station, and he and his wife happily chatted while he loosened the reins and let the horse find his way home. Instead of stopping at home, however, the horse stopped at the mansion of Helen Ladd Corbett. In addition to his affairs, Wood's radical politics raised eyebrows, ultimately causing him to leave socially conservative Portland. He spoke against slavery to the Daughters of the American Revolution; supported antiwar protestor Dr. Marie Esqui when she was charged with sedition; defended Emma Goldman, a proponent of birth control and women's suffrage; and defended Margaret Sanger when she was arrested in Portland on obscenity charges for having written a book on family planning.

In 1918, the sixty-six-year-old Wood left Portland and spent the rest of his life in California with Sara Bard Field, a national speaker on women's suffrage whom he had met in 1910. He died in 1944 at ninety-two, having spent the last three decades with Field.

Nanny Wood also planted the beech north of the house and the stunning sycamore on the north edge of the garden. The hedge hides other horticultural treasures, but the block-wide gardens do have regular hours for visitors. Because the club keeps its door locked, it's best to call 503-222-2845 to let them know you'd like to stop by.

More grand homes line up along Vista. At 1135 is another Colonial Revival by Whidden and Lewis, built circa 1899. The home at 1111 is worth a look for its lovely arches on the glassed-in front porch; I like the slightly impudent look of the eyebrow window above the porch. When this house was built for Hardy Wortman, a department store magnate (Olds, Wortman and King), it looked at Saint Helens Hall, an Episcopal school for girls once located on the site of the Vista Saint Clair apartment tower. The block continues with more large homes built from the late 1890s to 1910.

7 From Vista, cross SW Park Place at the light and turn left. Walk a bit uphill to an elaborately columned 1907 mansion at 2329 Park Place; it lost its splendid views when the ten-story Park Vista Apartments went up. The King's Hill Nomination to the National Register of Historic Places sums up the awkward scene here today: "The high rise apartment buildings [in King's Hill] are noncompatible both in scale and style with a majority of buildings within the district."

From Park Place, turn right on SW Green Avenue, named for the Henry Green family, who in 1879 bought the hillside in front of you. Their estate, Cedar Hill, was reportedly home to rollicking parties. The Greens were grandparents of John Reed, the American Communist who wrote *Ten Days that*

The old and stately alongside the new and incompatible, on King's Hill. Photo by Zeb Andrews.

Shook the World. They made their fortune by founding the Portland Gas Light Company, which imported coal from Vancouver Island and used it to produce gas at the foot of NW Davis Street.

From Green, turn left onto SW Cedar Street (the leftmost left off Green), a twisty street that used to be the Greens' driveway, now home to a chaotic, crowded, but somehow intriguing mess of dwellings that reminds me of the aftermath of a debris-filled wave sweeping up a steep beach. (This steep street ends at a staircase. To avoid it, stay on Green, follow it to the corner of Burnside and Vista, and rejoin the route there.)

Follow Cedar's turns past the backyards of Park Place mansions and upward to a cul-de-sac, which is about where the Greens' home used to be situated. Here, a set of stairs will lead you down to SW Cactus Drive, which has its own cul-de-sac. Cactus was likely named in reference to the several hothouses the Greens had on the hill here. To the east is the back side of a familiar Northwest Portland landmark, the 1929 Envoy Apartments. The grocer Fred Meyer lived here, in the penthouse apartment. In 2003 the Envoy was converted to condominiums.

The Cactus cul-de-sac also has a staircase, to the right of 2362. Take these stairs down a short two flights, and then walk west along a one-story apartment house on a sidewalk that suddenly drops you into Washington Park, near the original 1871 entrance. In the park, walk a few steps to the right and take a concrete staircase of thirty-five steps down to a path. Once on the path, look left; the level grassy spot on the hill here was the site of seal and waterfowl ponds from the first location of the zoo. Animals were scattered about this hillside, with most in cages just east of present-day Wright Avenue. (This was before the zoo moved to its next location at and in the vicinity of today's Japanese Garden.)

8 From the park path, walk straight to the corner of Burnside and SW Osage Street. Here you stand near what Harvey Scott described in 1890 as the mouth of a "stony canyon whose natural roughness has been aggravated by gravel diggers. Out of this rises, or did rise King's Creek, a stream of most delicious water which has now been consigned to more than Tartarean gloom in a sewer." That description sent me to the dictionary; *Tartarean* refers to Tartarus, a sunless abyss below Hades where Zeus imprisoned the Titans.

Burnside was cleared by Francis Pettygrove in 1845 and was an extension of Washington Street. During Portland's earliest years it was the main road west (before Canyon Road) and was also called the Tuality Road because it led to the Tuality Plains (now known as the Tualatin Plains). Because it stayed higher on the hills than Canyon Road, which traversed a mucky ravine, it was preferred until Canyon Road was planked in 1851.

From Osage, turn right onto Burnside. Zupan's Market, a local grocery store, is a good place for a snack.

From Burnside, turn right onto Vista. At 733 Vista is the home of architect Emil Schacht, who designed many of the homes of Willamette Heights.

The many upscale apartment buildings in the next block, most from the prosperous late 1920s, were built to take advantage of a streetcar that ran along Burnside. Especially nice is the Rena Villa, a Moorish-style three-story building at 815, from 1930. The Vista Avenue Apartments are located across the street, where a coast redwood guards a private sidewalk leading into the beautiful grounds. These garden apartments were designed by Pietro Belluschi. Each unit has hardwood floors and a fireplace, plus a private entrance and garage. Built in 1941, the apartments inhabit the site of a home and barn built in 1873 by Arthur Johnson, whose gentleman's farm ran from here south to King's Court. Johnson had made his money operating a slaughterhouse alongside a small stream at today's NW 23rd Avenue and Flanders Street. The old redwoods were likely planted by the Johnson family, and one notable aspect of Belluschi's work was how he fit the architecture into the existing landscape. The Vista Avenue Apartments are the only example of the Half-Modern (or Transitional) style of architecture in King's Hill.

Turn left on Park Place, a steep downhill. At Park and SW Saint Clair Avenue, the apartment tower in the northeast corner mitigates its architectural hubris with a spectacular cherry blossom display in late March.

9 Cross Saint Clair. The next two blocks were once part of the Theodore B. Wilcox estate. On the left, at 2185, is the Oregon Society of Artists, at the site of the Wilcox formal gardens. Founded in the old Portland Art Museum in 1926, the society built this structure in 1954, much of it with donated labor and expertise. Classes are offered, and the gallery is open to the public for a few hours every day but Monday.

On the right, at 2164, is what architect William J. Hawkins III calls "surely one of the most handsome entrances in the city," with its truly magnificent domed canopy of wrought iron and glass. I quite agree. This house was built around 1901.

Across from it, at the corner of King Avenue and Park Place (931 King), is Wilcox's 1893 home. As a teller at the Ladd and Tilton Bank, Wilcox caught the eye of the boss; he became William Sargent Ladd's protégé and was later hired to manage Ladd's Albina Flour Mills. Wilcox became president of the mill upon Ladd's death in 1893, and was also a director of the bank. As president of Portland Chamber, Wilcox had his hands on just about every commercial enterprise of his day, from dredging the Columbia to developing diverse interests such as neighborhoods (Rose City Park), the city's water supply, and the Lewis and Clark Exposition. He left this house in 1919, as the neighborhood was changing, and moved onto an enormous estate in the West Hills. This house was later used as a school for Russian children and housed the Portland School of Music. Whidden and Lewis designed it, in a bit of a departure from their signature Colonial Revival style. The home has a sandstone first floor, typical of the rusticated stonework of the Richardsonian Romanesque style popularized in the 1880s.

Near the corner of King and Park are two historic homes that merit a side trip: at 806 King, about two blocks to the left, is the 1900 home of Edward King, Amos's youngest son, and the last surviving home of the Amos Nahum King family. At 916 King is a home, circa 1895, owned by two sisters who were granddaughters of both Captain John H. Couch (more on him in Walks 13 and 14) and Captain George Flanders. Between these two homes is, surprisingly, a 1950s-era motel, the Washington Park Inn.

Cross King (at this intersection, Park turns into SW Salmon Street) to the unusual brick wall surrounding the Town Club, a club for women founded in

1928. Despite its private nature, the club is generous with views into its garden, which was originally the sunken garden of the Wilcox estate.

Barbara Bartlett Hartwell, a member of the National Society of the Colonial Dames, described garden walls in Portland at the turn of the century: "Fences were few, and always low enough to look over. It was undemocratic, in fact downright English, to conceal one's green lawn and monkey puzzle tree from the gaze of the passerby." This wall probably received a nod of approval from her. The clubhouse at 2115 Salmon was built in 1930 to resemble an Italian villa; especially wonderful to behold are the crocheted curtains visible in every window.

At Salmon and SW 21st Avenue, the barrel vault of the Multnomah Athletic Club (MAC) looms. Founded in 1891 as the Multnomah Amateur Athletic Club, it later dropped the Amateur. Today, MAC members compete internationally in events ranging from synchronized swimming to tennis, karate, and squash, but it is also a social club, a crucial element in the portfolio of many Portlanders.

10 Cross SW 20th Avenue and turn left on it. Ahead in the distance is the Byzantine dome of Temple Beth Israel and the volcanic dome of Mount Saint Helens. Walk down 20th to steps where you can look into the stadium. In 1893, the Multnomah Club began leasing the lowland here, calling it Multnomah Field; it was used for baseball, football, track and field events, bicycle races, cricket, and as a venue for visiting dignitaries. The adjoining stadium, designed by A. E. Doyle, was built in 1925. Originally called Multnomah Stadium because it was owned by the Multnomah Club, it was renamed Civic Stadium when the city purchased it in 1966. In 2001 it received another new moniker, PGE Park, when Portland General Electric bought the naming rights during a renovation.

Walk along the stadium toward Burnside. At SW Yamhill Street is the site of Amos King's first home, a log cabin he and his wife, Melinda, built in 1852 in which four of their children were born. As their fortunes quickly grew, the Kings built a larger home in 1856, adjacent to the cabin, at 20th and SW Morrison Street, a site now occupied by a U.S. Bank. King had cleared some of the dense fir forest and grew prize-winning potatoes here. He lived here until his death in 1901 and was fondly remembered for his pride in King's Hill. Even in his old age, he was seen with shovel or broom in hand, cleaning up after city work crews or sweeping debris out of the gutters.

11 From 20th, turn right on Morrison. Walk along the front of PGE Park, and then turn right again at SW 18th Avenue to walk along the park's east side,

From what is now PGE Park: looking uphill at King's Hill, date unknown, but probably circa 1890. The photo's caption reads, "2nd fence up became SW Salmon. 3rd to left is SW Main. Fence on top now SW 20th." Photo courtesy of the Oregon Historical Society.

where generously spaced ironwork allows for streetside viewing of the games below. Original plans for the stadium called for a complete horseshoe shape, with grandstands on both the 20th and 18th Avenue sides. But the grandstand along 18th was never built, and after a streetside wall was removed in 2001, the space became a boon for those without the money for a ticket.

The field sits well below the street grade in a hollow formed by Tanner Creek. Because of the access to water and hemlock (the bark of which contains hide-curing tannins), in the 1840s the stadium was the site of a tannery, a valuable franchise in frontier days, when buckskin was often the most durable, and sometimes only, clothing available. Amos King bought the tannery in 1849 and ran it for a dozen years before he began making more money by subdividing his land and selling lots to the city's wealthiest residents. When Multnomah Stadium was built, the tannery vats were left in place—a treasure for future archeologists to unearth; and the creek was buried in a vast culvert 50 feet below third base.

While the hills were valuable real estate, the creek hollow, a deep lowland ravine at the base of King's Hill, was never home to millionaires. As late as 1890 it was filled with the shacks of Chinese farmers, who gardened on the frequently flooded but verdant slopes. In *Sprigs of Rosemary*, Barbara Bartlett Hartwell recalled the beauty of the produce grown here and at other sites such as Guilds Lake, where Portland's Chinese community lived:

> The Chinese pervaded Portland. They washed its laundry, raised its vegetables, trotted from door to door . . . carrying bamboo baskets balanced on a pole filled with the most exquisitely pearly green vegetables crawling with bacteria, having been fertilized in the immemorial Chinese fashion, the way of the Middle East, Mexico. The Chinese put earthen pots at intervals down their vegetable rows, and when the pleas of Portland's Dr. Giesy for their removal fell on deaf ears, he took to shooting at the pots from his buggy. The Chinese surrendered to direct action.

As you look down into the stadium from 18th, you may see a few of its more unusual employees: a colony of a dozen or so feral cats, maintained for their rat-catching acumen. Their benefits consist of all the vermin they can eat, plus some chow donated each month by the Oregon Humane Society when they tire of *Rattus rattus*. Just as the stadium was retrofitted with ramps in 2001 to comply with the Americans with Disabilities Act (ADA), older kitties use a ramp to help them negotiate the feeding and water station. Cheers to PGE Park for its use of a nontoxic means to control pests.

Continue on 18th and cross Salmon. The Zion Lutheran Church at the corner was designed in 1950 by Pietro Belluschi in the Northwest Regional style.

Continue along 18th back to the starting point.

WALK 13

NOB HILL LOOP

DISTANCE   2.6 miles

STARTING POINT   Civic Plaza: SW 18th Avenue and Morrison Street

GETTING THERE AND PARKING   From downtown Portland, drive west on SW Morrison Street toward SW 18th Avenue. Park at a five-hour meter on 14th, 15th, or 16th Avenues. Parking is free on Sundays.

TriMet: This walk starts at a MAX stop. Westbound, get off the MAX at the PGE Park stop at SW 18th and Morrison. Eastbound, get off at the PGE Park stop at SW 17th and Yamhill, and walk one block north to the starting point. Alternatively, from downtown Portland take bus 15 (NW 23rd Avenue), bus 51 (Vista), or bus 20 (Burnside/Stark) to a stop near 18th and Morrison.

RESTROOMS AND DRINKING FOUNTAINS   Restrooms for customers are in McDonald's (18th and W Burnside) and at restaurants and coffee shops along NW 18th, 21st, and 23rd Avenues. Couch Park (NW Hoyt Street and 19th Avenue) has public restrooms open year-round. Find drinking fountains at SW 18th and Morrison Street, NW 18th and Couch Street, and NW 20th and Hoyt (in Couch Park).

FOOD AND DRINK   The walk crosses NW 21st and 23rd Avenues, both of which are dense with restaurants, coffee houses, and bars.

BEST TIMES TO VISIT   Any time!

ACCESSIBILITY   This walk is on city sidewalks and is virtually flat, with about 50 feet of elevation gain.

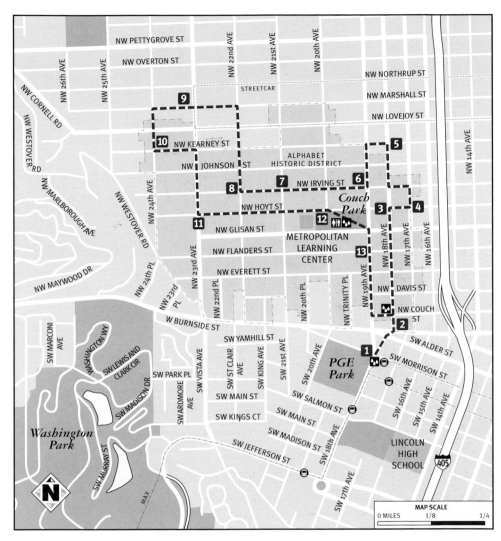

NW PETTYGROVE ST
NW OVERTON ST
NW NORTHRUP ST
STREETCAR
NW MARSHALL ST
NW LOVEJOY ST

NW 26th AVE
NW 25th AVE
NW 22nd AVE
NW 21st AVE
NW 20th AVE
NW 14th AVE

NW CORNELL RD
NW WESTOVER RD

9

10 NW KEARNEY ST

5

NW JOHNSON ST
ALPHABET HISTORIC DISTRICT

NW MARLBOROUGH AVE
NW WESTOVER RD

NW 24th AVE

8   **7** NW IRVING ST   **6**

NW HOYT ST
Couch Park
3   **4**

11

NW GLISAN ST
12 👫💧

NW 24th PL

NW 23rd AVE

NW FLANDERS ST
METROPOLITAN LEARNING CENTER
13

NW 18th AVE
NW 17th AVE
NW 16th AVE

NW MAYWOOD DR

NW EVERETT ST

NW 22nd AVE
NW 20th PL
NW TRINITY PL
NW 19th AVE
NW DAVIS ST

NW 23rd PL

NW COUCH ST
💧

2

SW MARCONI AVE
WASHINGTON WY
SW LEWIS AND CLARK CIR

W BURNSIDE ST

SW ALDER ST

SW YAMHILL ST

SW 20th AVE
SW 21st AVE
SW KING AVE
SW VISTA AVE
SW ST CLAIR AVE

SW PARK PL
SW ARDMORE AVE

1 👫💧
SW MORRISON ST
PGE Park

SW 16th AVE
SW 15th AVE
SW 14th AVE

SW MADISON DR

SW MAIN ST
SW SALMON ST

SW KINGS CT
SW MAIN ST

Washington Park

SW MURRAY ST

SW MADISON ST
LINCOLN HIGH SCHOOL

SW JEFFERSON ST

SW 18th AVE
SW 17th AVE

405

🧭 N

MAX

MAP SCALE
0 MILES   1/8   1/4

WALK 13. *Nob Hill Loop*

MAP KEY
▪━ ROUTE
⁞⁞⁞⁞ STAIRS
– – TRAIL
⋯ MAX TRACKS
🔵 MAX STATION
⋯ STREETCAR TRACKS
⋯ TROLLEY TRACKS
⊞⊞ RAILROAD TRACKS
▨ PARK/GREENSPACE
▨ HISTORIC/CONSERVATION DISTRICT
👫 PUBLIC RESTROOM
💧 WATER

THIS CITY WALK IS STEEPED in Portland history that begins with Captain John H. Couch, whose vote of confidence was vital in making Portland, and not Oregon City, the state's most populous town. Couch was a thirty-four-year-old sea captain in 1845 when he speculated on a land claim just north of the Portland town site. After spending time in Oregon City, then the primary settlement along the Willamette River, he came to believe that its prosperous days were numbered because the river downstream of Oregon City presented too many obstacles to navigation.

Couch pronounced Portland to be the "head of navigation" and through his integrity, experience, and personality pulled others along to this same conclusion. In the late 1840s and early 1850s, he sailed ships between Portland and San Francisco, a profitable venture given that gold miners in the Sierra were an insatiable market for just about everything. In 1852 Couch sent for his wife and daughters, and they settled in a lakeside cabin in the woods near the site of today's Union Station, where Couch was said to shoot ducks from his front porch.

By 1860 the burgeoning waterfront forced the Couches to move, and a wealthy residential district grew along 4th and 5th Avenues (in what is now Northwest Portland). When business began encroaching on those streets, families moved further up the hill; it was then that Couch subdivided his land claim in the area of this walk. Along 19th between Everett and Johnson Streets, he gave a double block to each of his four daughters and one to his brother-in-law, Captain George Flanders. They all, except one daughter, built homes there between 1881 and 1885, which became the core of Nob Hill. As early as the 1880s, investors began to build luxury rental properties in the neighborhood. Then, as Portland's growth exploded following the 1905 Lewis and Clark Exposition, the neighborhood began to add more multifamily units—townhomes and apartments—for middle-income individuals, a trend that eventually pushed out the first families.

During World War II, with 125,000 people—most of them newcomers—working in the wartime Kaiser shipyards, Nob Hill was densely occupied, with large mansions divided into rental units. Neighborhood decline came during the postwar infatuation with the automobile and suburbia. In this era, many grand homes from the late nineteenth century were destroyed.

After two decades of decline, in 1967 the area was classified as "depressed" by the City of Portland. By the 1970s, however, neighborhood activism awakened, and the district became attractive to investors, young families, and preservationists. This interest has continued to the present, with owner-occupied homes running upwards of $1 million (though monthly rentals in the old apartment houses can still be had for as little as $500).

Among this walk's many architectural treasures is the city's largest concentration of upper-class, early-twentieth-century apartment buildings, many of them stunningly beautiful, especially to modern eyes grown used to structures for which beauty is not in the budget. The grand homes, houses of worship, and apartment buildings seen along this walk tell the tale of Portland's progress better than words.

For a longer walk, combine this route with Walk 12.

1 Start at Civic Plaza, a triangular park at the westbound PGE Park MAX stop. Take a few moments to read the thought-provoking essay on the stainless steel art installation. TriMet invites you to ascend one of the podiums here if you feel an urge to orate.

Head north on SW 18th Avenue. At 18th and SW Alder Street, cross to another triangle, this one between 18th, 19th, and Alder. This is Firefighters Park, a memorial to Chief David Campbell, who died fighting a fire in 1911. Today a Willamette River fire boat is named for him, and each year on June 26, firefighters hold a service here.

Cross Alder, turn right on W Burnside Street, and walk half a block to 18th, which has made a slight jog. Cross Burnside at the lighted pedestrian crossing. The street alignment change is due to a decision made by Captain Couch. As a seafaring man who made use of the North Star, he aligned streets north of Burnside with true north when he platted them in 1865. The streets south of Burnside, platted in 1845, were aligned with magnetic north. The angle formed between magnetic north and true north is the declination, which changes over time, but in Portland in 1845 it was about 20 degrees east of true north. Hence, between the river and NW 23rd Avenue, you'll find odd triangle lots and a slight jog to some of the numbered streets as they cross Burnside and adjust for the declination.

2 From Burnside, head north on 18th into the Alphabet Historic District, an area on the National Register of Historic Places. Captain Couch didn't bother with the politically charged process of naming streets in his claim, instead simply giving them letters of the alphabet. In 1891 each street was given a name, starting with Ankeny and running north to Yeon. There is no X or Z. The historic district runs from Burnside to Marshall and from 16th to 24th.

At 18th and NW Couch Street stand the Tudor Arms Condominiums, built in 1915 as luxury apartments toward the end of the building boom that followed the Lewis and Clark Exposition. The style is Jacobethan, with a high contrast between the dark red brick and the white-glazed terra-cotta decorative

The Lawn Apartments, one of the earliest investment properties in Nob Hill, from 1884.

elements such as quoins and finials. Across 18th is Saint Mary's Cathedral of the Immaculate Conception, built in the Italian Renaissance style in 1925. It was designed by Joseph Jacobberger.

At 133 18th is one of the earliest investment properties in the area, the Stick-style 1883 Lawn Apartments, built by George Williams, a conservative lawyer who became a U.S. senator, U.S. attorney general, and Portland mayor. His 1881 mansion, similar in style, was adjacent to the south, and was replaced by the Tudor Arms.

Continue on 18th and cross NW Davis Street. Along 18th from Davis to NW Everett Street is a classic, hand-carved basalt wall now outlining something it's much too good for: a parking lot. The wall was built to surround the Knapp mansion, eighteen exuberantly ornate rooms constructed in 1882 for $80,000. It had been described as the most perfect example of a Victorian house design west of the Mississippi. In 1950 the cathedral bought the house; in the postwar focus on the suburban good life, a campaign to restore this urban treasure failed. It was demolished in 1951, and salvageable parts were sold at auction.

At 221 to 225 18th is an 1884 Italianate duplex, with two-story polygonal bay windows, a feature common to that style. At Everett, on the left is the 1909 First Church of Christ, Scientist, a Roman-style building with a central crowned dome flanked by two barrel-vault wings. At 325, in an otherwise unremarkable building, is a mysterious and splendid bit of stained glass above the door, reading "The Chetopa Annex" in Art Deco script.

Cross NW Flanders Street, named for George Flanders. On the right, at 410, is the Wickersham, a 1910 streetcar-era apartment (now condos). It dates from the boom that followed the Lewis and Clark Exposition, when the city grew from 90,000 in 1900 to 207,000 in 1910. Even at that time, many block-size estates, some only twenty years old, were demolished to make room for apartments such as this one.

Across from the Wickersham, at 415, an 1890 Queen Anne home sits unmolested by the vagaries of the neighborhood's fortunes. At 425 is the superbly ornate Italianate Elliston Apartments, built in 1889 as the home of Colonel Henry Dosch, a board member of the Lewis and Clark Exposition. He was a boot merchant with a side interest in horticulture, serving on the state's Horticultural Commission. In 2006 the building became part of the Portland International Youth Hostel.

Come to NW Glisan Street. In the northwest corner, at 1805 Glisan, is an Arts and Crafts home built in 1896 by Christian Landenberger, a leader in the city's German community. The home has the style's characteristic blend of building materials: stone foundations with a mix of clapboard and shingle siding.

Stay on 18th. At 513 18th is one of the oldest homes in the neighborhood, an 1880 shiplap cottage that predates even the mansion era. The garage with living space above, added much later, is a harmonious complement to the home, something that cannot often be said for residential additions.

Come to NW Hoyt Street. The church at the northwest corner of this intersection (607 18th) was built in 1915 as the First Norway and Danish Methodist Episcopal Church, one of several local institutions that served an immigrant Scandinavian community here. It was designed in the twentieth-century Gothic Revival style.

3 From 18th, turn right on Hoyt. On Hoyt between 18th and 17th Avenues are a wonderful group of Queen Anne homes, with fishscale shingles, narrow casement windows, lattice, and spindlework. Around 1890 this area was attractive to workers in town because of its extensive streetcar system. With the increasing demand for housing, Hermann Trenkmann, a machinist and toolmaker, built eight frame houses here as rentals. Two of them, 1716 and 1704, have transom windows that show a three-digit address, a relic from Portland's early days. The new address, in porcelain tile, has a story to tell.

City work crew, and supervisor, installing address tiles in 1932. The old address is still in place above the front door. Photo courtesy of the City of Portland Archives.

By 1930 Portland's address system was a mess. Separate towns such as Sellwood, Linnton, East Portland, and Albina had been annexed over the prior fifty years. In additions (subdivisions) such as Laurelhurst and Rose City Park, streets were named by developers with no master naming plan guiding them. The result was a mishmash of street numbers and names, with twelve 1st Streets and other duplicates. In 1920 the *Oregonian* plaintively noted, "Three business firms on 6th Street carry the number '147' over their doors." After years of fielding complaints, in 1931 the city arrived at the plan in use today. Portland was divided into five sections, duplicate street names were eliminated, and a unified numbering system was created that used a hundred numbers to the block rather than twenty. Burnside Street, the Willamette River, and Williams Avenue became baselines. (Prior to that, the east side had used Patton Avenue [Interstate], and the west side had used Hood Street for their east and west baselines, and Ankeny Street had been the divider between north and south.) The geographic locators in each address (NE, NW, SE, SW, and N) were, on the advice of the postmaster, embedded between the house number and the street, to avoid being dropped off by hasty letter writers. Streets ran east to west; avenues ran north to south. Even numbers were for the south and east sides of streets, odd numbers for the north and west sides. The result is that an address, such as 1563 NW Davis Street, contains several locational clues: it lies north of

Burnside and fifteen blocks west of the Willamette, and the building is on the north side of a road that runs east to west.

A contract to manufacture porcelain address tiles was awarded to Gladding, McBean, a tile manufacturer in Lincoln, California (whose red ceramic tiles today cover most of the buildings on the Stanford University campus). For $20,000, it manufactured 396,000 tiles. These were installed in a Depression-era work relief project in which crews of three to five men walked city streets, pushing carts filled with number tiles that they installed on all homes and businesses. At night, after the men had installed one hundred to two hundred addresses, carts were stowed in the nearest firehouse. It took twenty-two months to install tiles at 93,596 locations. With 30,000 surplus digits, new homes in subsequent years were given the tiles, until they ran out. Originals can be found at architectural salvage stores. Replicas made by a Portland pottery shop are available at Rejuvenation, Winks, and Pratt and Larson, three stores that are themselves Portland originals.

4 From Hoyt, turn left on NW 17th Avenue, where an old and flaky madrona leans over the walk, and left again on NW Irving Street. In this block is another cluster of magnificent Queen Anne rentals, built by investor Daniel Campbell in 1893. Resembling a block in Greenwich Village, this is the city's only collection of brick townhomes. They run from 1705 to 1719 Irving. Though clearly a family, each with a similar two-story bay, ornamentation is varied: clustered columns at the porches, window pediments, leaded glass transom windows, and decorative sandstone work in the gable ends. In 2005, owners of the homes replaced an aging sidewalk with a handsome brick walkway, which the construction foreman told me cost $1 per brick. (Though not on the route, the townhomes continue along NW 17th Street.)

Continue walking west on Irving. Just west of the Campbell townhomes is another set of historic townhomes. These were built in 1884 as an investment by the Couch family. The success of these early tract homes, as well as the Trenkmann and Campbell rentals, proved that a market existed for middle- and upper-income people to live in multifamily housing. More soon came.

At the end of the block, turn right and you're on 18th again. The building in the northwest corner of 18th and Irving was built in 1929 as the Associated Oil Building, an early gasoline service station. In one block, at the northwest corner of 18th and NW Johnson Street, is an 1892 Colonial Revival by Whidden and Lewis, architects known locally for their many grand homes in this style. A signature element is the two-story rounded bay windows, whose circular shape is

The Campbell townhomes, investment properties from 1893. Photo by Zeb Andrews.

mimicked by the curved front porch. This same rounded bay is incorporated in City Hall, which Whidden and Lewis designed three years later. This house was built for Winslow Ayer, a lumberman and library and art museum patron who very likely planted the English walnut in the front yard.

While on 18th, cross Johnson. At 825 18th is Havurah Shalom, a Reconstructionist Jewish community. Unlike Orthodox and Conservative Judaism, Reconstructionism does not view inherited Jewish law as binding, but as a source of guidance. It also differs from Reform Judaism, which emphasizes the autonomy of the individual; instead, Reconstructionism emphasizes religious community and blending traditional ritual with new observances relevant to life today.

5 From 18th, turn left onto NW Kearney Street and then left in one block onto NW 19th Avenue, one of the two streets Captain Couch platted out for estate-size properties. At the northwest corner of 19th and Kearney is a Mission-style office building, the Cambridge. It was erected in 1931 as the Lovejoy Exchange Building, past the era when new single-family residences were being built here.

At 829 19th is a home from the grand era, another Whidden and Lewis from 1895, though a modern front entrance mars its front. At 811 is the second mansion for Winslow Ayer, designed twelve years after the first, again by Whidden and Lewis, this time in the regal Jacobethan style, although the pediment over the front door is pure Colonial Revival. The asphalt front yard is not original.

Cross Johnson. At 732 is the Koehler House, another Colonial Revival by Whidden and Lewis, from 1905. In the 1920s a postwar boom brought more apartment buildings, and folks in these large mansions continued their exodus out of the area, into Dunthorpe, King's Heights, Green Hills, or Portland Heights. One such apartment is the elegant Olympic, built during the last gasp of the 1920s, with cast-stone details and flourishes that seem a bit poignant considering the somber decade that followed its construction. Note the Etruscan urns, tile accents, and Moorish curves. The designer, who was not an architect, was Elmer Feig, who designed twenty-one apartment buildings in the neighborhood, and eighty-one in the city, many of them ornamented with exotic motifs.

At the southeast corner of 19th and Irving is First Immanuel Lutheran Church. When built in 1905, it had already been serving a congregation of immigrant Lutheran Swedes for twenty-five years. Built of stucco in the Gothic Revival style, its striking stained glass windows are worth a walk around the building.

6 From 19th, turn right on Irving. This block is a wonderful grab bag of 1920s apartment buildings. The entire block on the right was the estate of Rodney Glisan in the 1880s. At 1929 is the Mayfair, with Art Deco elements like chevrons and elaborate floral cast-stone medallions. Across from this late-1920s beauty is the modern Addison. Next to the Mayfair are twin Mission-style apartments (1943 and 1953) from 1929, designed by Elmer Feig. Across from them are the plain Greenway Apartments, built in 1926, whose designer took Mission simplicity to its extreme. As the route approaches NW 20th Avenue you encounter the staggered brick wall of the Zenabe Court Apartments. Though the walk continues straight on Irving, walk a few feet down 20th to the fabulous entrance of Zenabe Court, with its Spanish Colonial Revival arches, Deco tile work, mature palm trees, and, in the foyer, cool basketweave tile floor. It is another 1929 design by Feig.

Cross 20th. The block in front of you has it all: old luxury apartments, single-family homes of various vintages, and another Swedish landmark, the lovely Linnea Hall. First, on the left, are the Alhambra Condominiums built in 1926 as luxury apartments. Beyond them are three single-family homes built before the 1920s apartment boom: 2036 is a 1907 Craftsman, 2039 is a 1916 Colonial Revival with operable shutters, and 2046 is a large 1897 Arts and Crafts. The Irving Court garden apartments across the street came later, in 1948, as the neighborhood was changing. At 2066 is Linnea Hall, built in 1910. Its cornerstone says "Svenska-sällskapet [Swedish Society], 1888–1910." It was organized in 1888 as Svenska Broderna (The Swedish Brothers) but opened membership to both sexes later. Wooden pilasters with Corinthian capitals define a recessed entry. Above it, two stained glass windows flank a painted wood carving of the Swedish national emblem. The society was integral to Portland Swedes from the 1880s to 1930s. At picnics, parties, and meetings, only Swedish was spoken, only Swedish food was prepared, and Swedish folk traditions were observed. Membership began declining in the 1930s as Swedes assimilated, and by 1946 there were only 125 members. In 1979 the hall was sold.

Across from Linnea Hall is the oldest home on the block, an 1886 Queen Anne. When later owners moved from Nob Hill into Dunthorpe, they took the house's architectural details with them. A subsequent owner went down to Dunthorpe, took photos of the details, and recreated them, bringing this house back to some of its original beauty.

7 At the intersection of Irving and NW 21st Avenue you can see the hills of King's Heights, a neighborhood that was new in the 1910s, where many families moved as this neighborhood changed character. In the 1920s, as Nob Hill's population swelled with apartment dwellers, 21st became a street of neighborhood services, and it still has a bit of a locals-only feel, as nearby NW 23rd Avenue serves as flypaper for most tourists. Plenty of good restaurants and shops invite you to linger here.

Cross 21st, and Irving's architectural attractions continue, with well-kept single-family homes and old apartment houses. On the right at 2127 is the Irving, a wonderfully antique building that looks like it would be at home along the coast of South Carolina. Built in 1907 as apartments, it was featured in Gus Van Sant's 1989 film *Drugstore Cowboy*. It's a quirky mix of styles, with its mansard roof, bungalow-like porch columns, and Queen Anne oval cutouts on the railing. Building codes and the average person's height have both changed over the last century, shown by the extra horizontal bars installed above the original, and very low, railings.

8 From Irving, turn right on NW 22nd Avenue. At 726 is what has been called the most ornate Queen Anne in Portland. Built in 1890 with stained glass doors, it still sports its original address. Other classic features are its hipped roof with intersecting pedimented gables, and carved floral-patterned panels. This house was built by Nathan Loeb, a merchant from Germany and a founding member of Temple Beth Israel, seen later in the walk.

Cross NW Johnson Street. At NW Kearney Street's southwest corner is an 1898 shiplap fourplex, probably home to young doctors at Good Samaritan Hospital when it was built by the Amos King (of King's Hill) family as an investment.

Stay on 22nd, crossing Kearney and NW Lovejoy Street, to reach the Legacy Good Samaritan Hospital and Medical Center, founded by Episcopal Bishop B. Wistar Morris.

When Good Samaritan opened its doors in 1875, it already had competition: Saint Vincent's had opened two months before a bit further up the hill. Despite the sudden availability of hospital beds, Portlanders took a while to warm to the idea of leaving home when sick to be tended by strangers, and in the first few years the hospital's finances were uncertain. Compounding Good Samaritan's problem was the fact that its location was in a field of "brush and briar" far from town. Bishop Morris, who chose the spot, was criticized for the hospital's inaccessibility, and not just by ordinary citizens. In an effort to recruit patients, doctors in the early years would pick up a sick person at his home and deliver him to the hospital—a trip whose last several hundred yards were a slog through "ruts of unknown depths and plowed land," and reportedly accompanied by much cursing. The hospital actually closed in 1878 for a year, while it worked to improve the roads to its doors. After reopening in 1879, business accelerated, and by 1883 the hospital orphanage closed in order to free up space for more beds. In 1884 the City of Portland paid Good Samaritan fifty cents per day for indigent patients, whose rehabilitation was likely aided by the pastoral scene of the hospital's three resident cows grazing in the field next to the building.

Today, all trace of those early years is gone; the buildings are spare and virtually featureless in their clean modern lines.

From 22nd, turn left at NW Marshall Street. Follow the sidewalk that runs in front of the Theodore B. Wilcox Memorial Hospital, from 1921, a maternity hospital endowed by the heirs of the same Wilcox whose residence is featured in Walk 12. Look up to see sweet cast-stone decorations of a mother cuddling her baby. The sidewalk leads into the Healing Garden, part of the hospital's innovative horticultural therapy program to nurture the spirit as well as the body. Walk through it to stairs at its northwest corner that lead to NW 23rd Avenue. The red brick Northrup Building, on the corner of NW Northrup Street and 23rd, was built in 1936 as a residence building for student nurses. (To avoid the stairs, retrace your steps out of the Healing Garden to 22nd, and follow city sidewalks to 23rd and Marshall.)

9 Cross 23rd at the painted crosswalk to Marshall, and walk west on Marshall, a street of century-old homes with plenty of details to admire. The generous, curved porch at 2324 was probably built to maximize views of the Cascade Mountains now blocked by the hospital's buildings.

Walk one block on Marshall, then turn left on NW 24th Avenue. Approaching Lovejoy, note the garden to the left; it's one of my favorites in town. Especially nice is the shock of climbing hydrangea erupting wildly above a garden gate, an espaliered group of variegated euonymus on a fence, and the nontraditional foundation plantings.

On 24th, cross Lovejoy, and the homes get bigger. The house at 927 dates from 1892. At 24th and Kearney, the Alano Club of Portland inhabits a colonnaded mansion that was donated to the club in the 1960s by Cora Kline. Inside is the largest recovery support center in Oregon, home to programs such as Alcoholics Anonymous, Debtors Anonymous, Workaholics Anonymous, and many others. More than one hundred meetings are held here each week.

10 From 24th, turn left on Kearney, another block of nice old duplexes and homes, all vintage 1890 to 1910. After one block, turn right onto 23rd, formerly a street of neighborhood businesses, now a destination shopping experience (as retail marketers say). Despite its preciousness, 23rd is fun, with plenty of shops to lure you into spending your money, and good restaurants. While the architecture is not usually what gets noticed on 23rd, it is a significant part of the ambience, as many stores and restaurants are built into old homes and businesses.

At the southeast corner of 23rd and Kearney is a 1911 building built as the Nob Hill Theater, a nickelodeon. In the 1870s a brickyard operated at 23rd and Johnson. Beginning in the 1990s the northwest corner was home to Music Millennium, a Portland institution since 1969, and one of the last surviving independent music stores in the country. In-store concerts featured performers such as Cyndi Lauper and Gillian Welch. The store on 23rd closed in 2007 as the music industry changed and rents rose. At 706 is Rich's Cigar Shop, one of three locations of a store that has seen the turn of two centuries. Until 1950, a streetcar line ran along this street, and its steel rails still make an occasional appearance in potholes.

11 From 23rd, turn left onto NW Hoyt Street at the five-story Campbell Hotel, built in 1912. Hoyt has more to admire. At 2234 is a cool, old Queen Anne cottage; and the 1911 Casa Linda at 2226 looks like an elderly aunt of the modern condominiums at 2222. I especially enjoy the house at the northwest corner of 22nd and Hoyt, which has unabashedly maximized its prime location with tiers of additions that climb far higher than any respectable Craftsman should really go.

Cross NW 22nd Avenue. The landscaping award of the walk goes to Patricia Court, a 1930 set of sixteen townhomes surrounding a miniature forest at 2182. The licorice fern making its home in the weeping brick of the courtyard wall is just one of many exquisite touches. Further on, at 2134, is a home built as an investment by Amos King: the 1885 Italianate Joseph Bergman house. It was built closer to the river and in the early 1900s was sawed in half, moved to this site, and reassembled.

At NW 21st Avenue, another eating and shopping opportunity presents itself. Continue on Hoyt into the heart of the Couch family history. The building at 2061 that sits sideways and back from the road dates from 1884 and was a schoolhouse. Rather than send their children off to city schools, the extended Couch family had them walk to this family school, built right on the Couch properties.

On the right, the large red brick building is the 1915 Couch School, a Portland public school built on the site of Henry Hewett's and Levi White's mansions. Since 1971, Couch School has been known as the Metropolitan Learning Center, an alternative K–12 public school with an emphasis on experiential learning and expeditions à la Outward Bound.

\ Before you enter the park east of the school, take time to study the stone and slate mansion at NW 20th Avenue and Hoyt. It was built in the massive Richardsonian Romanesque style by Dr. Kenneth MacKenzie and his artist wife, Cora, in 1892. Typical of the style is the recessed entry porch with rounded arches. The stag head on the south side is part of the MacKenzie family crest. MacKenzie was a founding faculty member in 1887 of the University of Oregon Medical School (now Oregon Health and Science University), which in its early years was located in an abandoned grocery building at 23rd and Lovejoy. After Dr. MacKenzie's death in 1920, this house became a speakeasy and boarding house, and was purchased in 1971 by the Episcopal Church as William Temple House, a center for counseling and social assistance.

12 From Hoyt, turn right on 20th to enter Couch Park. Take the sidewalk into the park and follow it along the play structure. The large, old trees date from the days when women in lace and long white gloves strolled the grounds of the Clementine Couch Lewis home that occupied this land. The house was located in about the center of the block bounded by 20th Avenue, 19th Avenue, Glisan Street, and Hoyt Street. Take the right fork where the paved path splits at a tubular sculpture. Come out of the park at Glisan and 19th.

At Glisan, turn right on 19th to walk by Temple Beth Israel, built in 1928 at the estate of Captain George Flanders. The Byzantine-style temple is considered to be a masterpiece of lead architect Herman Brookman. The exterior is Mankato stone (a limestone from Minnesota), Willamina brick from Oregon's Coast Range, Ohio sandstone, and terra-cotta ornamentation such as pilasters, spandrels, and moldings. On the south side, a covered entry has a vaulted roof supported by six sandstone columns. The main entrance stairs, on the west side, are Norwegian granite. The vestibule's pilasters are topped by lions. The mature trees of the Flanders estate (which occupied the entire block), combined with the building's grandeur, make this one of the most beautiful blocks in the city.

13 Cross NW Flanders and Everett Streets. On the right is Trinity Episcopal Cathedral, the oldest Episcopal parish in the state. This church building was built in 1905 in the twentieth-century Gothic Revival style, with a square bell tower, crenellated parapet, and wall buttresses. Church doors are the traditional Episcopal red, a color that most likely symbolizes sanctuary. In early times, it was understood that soldiers could not pursue an enemy beyond a church's red door. Another theory relates to Passover. Just as the Angel of Death would not enter homes with the blood of a lamb smeared on the door's lintel and posts, the red symbolizes the blood of Jesus Christ (to Christians, the Lamb of God). Before the

The Irving, built in 1907, one of many apartment buildings constructed after the 1905 Lewis and Clark Exposition, when Portland's population experienced a large growth spurt. Photo by Zeb Andrews.

church was built, this was the site of the Bishop Scott Academy. The land was given to the Episcopal Church (which operated the school) by Captain Flanders and Caroline Couch and the cornerstone was laid in 1870. Harvey Scott wrote, "The grounds at that time were away out in the woods in the western part of the city, and it required great faith in the development of the country and the town to establish a school at that time and place."

On 19th, continue south. Ahead is the Civic, a condominium tower built in 2007 on the site of the Civic Apartments (named for Civic Stadium, now PGE Park). On that site long ago was the North Pacific Industrial Exposition Building, built in 1888 and once one of the city's most notable buildings, where machinery was exhibited and public events and concerts held.

From 19th, turn left on Couch and pass an 1885 home at 1824. Walk one block on Couch, and turn right on 18th to retrace your steps to the starting point.

WALK 14

PEARL DISTRICT TO SLABTOWN LOOP

DISTANCE 3.3 miles

STARTING POINT Union Station: 800 NW 6th Avenue

GETTING THERE AND PARKING From downtown Portland, drive north on Broadway. Turn right onto NW Irving Street and left onto NW 6th Avenue. Drive along the front of Union Station and continue past it on NW Station Way under the elevated approach to the Broadway Bridge. On the left, between Lovejoy Court and Marshall Street, is Station Place Garage, a Smart Park, which offers the cheapest hourly rates among parking garages in the area. Note that there is no free parking in the Pearl District except at meters on Sundays.

TriMet: Take bus 9 (Powell), bus 17 (NW 21st Avenue/Saint Helens Road), or bus 77 (Broadway/Halsey) to stops near Union Station. Alternatively, take the MAX Blue Line to the Old Town/Chinatown stop at NW 1st and Davis. Walk west on Davis five blocks to NW 6th, and north on 6th six blocks to Union Station. (Note: The MAX Green Line along NW 5th and 6th Avenues opens in late 2009, with a stop adjacent to Union Station.)

RESTROOMS AND DRINKING FOUNTAINS Restrooms are inside Union Station and in coffee shops, stores, and restaurants along the route (for customers). Drinking fountains are at NW 6th Avenue and Hoyt Street, NW Broadway and Glisan Street, and in Jamison Square.

FOOD AND DRINK Options at Union Station include a snack shop and Wilf's Restaurant and Bar. Pearl Bakery is located midway through the walk at NW 9th Avenue and Davis Street, and there are scores of other options in the Pearl District.

WALK 14. *Pearl District to Slabtown Loop*

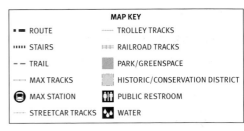

MAP KEY

- ▪▬ ROUTE
- ┄┄┄┄ TROLLEY TRACKS
- ▪▪▪▪▪ STAIRS
- ╪╪╪ RAILROAD TRACKS
- ▬ ▬ TRAIL
- PARK/GREENSPACE
- ┄┄┄ MAX TRACKS
- HISTORIC/CONSERVATION DISTRICT
- Ⓔ MAX STATION
- ❖ PUBLIC RESTROOM
- ┄┄┄ STREETCAR TRACKS
- WATER

Labels on map: NW THOMPSON ST, N THOMPSON ST, N TILLAMOOK ST, NW FRONT AVE, NW VAUGHN ST, NW UPSHUR ST, N WHEELER AVE, N INTERSTATE AVE, N DIXON ST, NW THURMAN ST, NW SAVIER ST, Willamette River, NW QUIMBY ST, NW PETTYGROVE ST, NW OVERTON ST, NW NAITO PKWY, FREMONT BRIDGE, N RIVER ST, BROADWAY BRIDGE, STATION WAY, Tanner Springs Park, NW NORTHRUP ST, NW MARSHALL ST, NW LOVEJOY ST, NW KEARNEY ST, NW JOHNSON ST, NW IRVING ST, Jamison Square, UNION STATION, NW BROADWAY, STEEL BRIDGE, Couch Park, NW 17th AVE, NW 16th AVE, NW FLANDERS ST, NW EVERETT ST, NW HOYT ST, NW GLISAN ST, North Park Blocks, NW 4th AVE, NW 3rd AVE, NW 2nd AVE, NW 1st AVE, NW 13th AVE, NW 12th AVE, NW 9th AVE, NW PARK AVE, NW DAVIS ST, NW COUCH ST, W BURNSIDE ST, Waterfront Park, NW 20th AVE, NW 19th AVE, NW 18th AVE, NW 14th AVE, NW 13th AVE HISTORIC DISTRICT, STREETCAR, NW 11th AVE, NW 10th AVE, SW ALDER ST, SW MORRISON ST, MAX, SW 12th AVE, SW WASHINGTON ST, SW 6th AVE, SW 5th AVE, MAP SCALE, 0 MILES 1/8 1/4

BEST TIMES TO VISIT Combine this walk with dinner at one of the Pearl's many great restaurants, where options range from an Italian trattoria straight off of the Via degli Equi in Rome to upscale Peruvian cuisine.

ACCESSIBILITY This walk follows city streets and sidewalks with little elevation gain. Where stairs are encountered, elevators are available.

THIS WALK FOLLOWS the streets and railroad spur lines of Portland's railroad heyday, from the 1880s to the 1920s. Renamed the Pearl District in the 1990s, this functionally obsolete rail and warehouse district was reborn as a neighborhood of condominiums, art galleries, restaurants, and shops. The area, which was once known as the North End, has now come full circle: before the warehouses and rail lines, it was residential. Captain John H. Couch, who claimed this land in 1845, first lived at the site of Union Station, and in the 1860s built a larger home at today's NW 4th Avenue and Hoyt Street.

During the 1870s, as industry expanded, the wealthy moved away from the river and into Nob Hill (west of 18th Avenue and north of Burnside Street). The area between 10th and 16th Avenues became a working-class neighborhood of European immigrants employed by waterfront warehouses and mills.

More change soon came. By 1882, with rail lines creating a shipping hub in Portland, the Northern Pacific Terminal Company was formed to provide terminal facilities such as depots, freight houses, yards, and dock warehouses for the various railroads entering the city. Within three years the company controlled thirty-nine blocks in today's Pearl District. Union Station went up in 1896, handling both freight and passenger traffic, and soon after, spur lines began to branch from it. A spur line allowed freight cars to pull up to docks of warehouses not directly adjacent to the main terminal.

By the late 1890s the North End's days as a residential district were numbered. In 1904, houses along 13th Avenue came down and warehouses went up when the roadway became a rail spur from Johnson Street to Glisan Street. (This is now the NW 13th Avenue Historic District.) In 1907, with a spur line coming to 15th Avenue, the western end of the working-class neighborhood effectively disappeared; it moved west, up to the boundary of Nob Hill, and then ballooned northward, with working-class homes north of Lovejoy Street, from the industrial area west to about 27th Avenue, an area known then as Slabtown.

In the 1920s, trucks began to supersede trains for moving freight, and the warehouse district began severing its ties to the railroads. By the 1950s, follow-

Today's Pearl District as it appeared in 1939, when it was occupied by rail yards and warehouses. Union Station is at the top right corner, with NW Broadway running, elevated, alongside it up to the Broadway Bridge. The Lovejoy viaduct, demolished in 1999, runs off the bridge in a westerly direction over the rail yards. The street coming off it to the south is NW 10th Avenue. The two long, low buildings along NW 11th Avenue near the bottom center of the photo were the North Bank Station, and today are beautiful townhomes, seen midway through the walk. The Ecotrust building at NW 9th and Irving is the building near the center of the photo with "Central Truck Terminal and Freight" printed on the side. Photo courtesy of the City of Portland Archives.

ing the Depression and World War II, the inner Northwest Portland industrial district seriously declined as factories and warehouses moved away from the central city to areas where one-story facilities reflected the latest in materials handling, and where trucks had wide open spaces to maneuver. Spur lines were no longer needed. In 1970 the Hoyt rail yards stopped handling freight.

During the 1970s, Portland was a much different town than it is today. In 1972 one government report classed all of Northwest Portland (except Willamette Heights) as blighted, and the industrial district, though still home to many businesses, quietly decayed. Change came, slowly, with Powell's Books opening in 1971 and a few artists such as Tad Savinar renting loft space in vacant warehouses. By the mid 1980s, when the area was known as the Northwest Triangle (bounded by Interstate 405, Burnside, and the river), it began to audibly hum again, this time with the buzz of art galleries and investors. First

Thursday, a monthly evening of gallery openings, was born. In 1990, growth exploded when Burlington Northern Railroad sold 50 acres to developers. The first loft apartments appeared in the mid 1990s, with a 750-square-foot condo costing less than $100,000. A decade later, condominium conversions of old warehouses and construction of new condominiums in the former rail yards continued at a pace that left longtime Portlanders scratching their heads as they walked through the Pearl District, trying to remember what used to be.

Freight trains continued to run on NW 12th and 13th Avenues even as the area gentrified, bringing grain to the Blitz-Weinhard Brewery and bone chips and animal parts to the Wilbur-Ellis feed plant at NW 12th and Marshall. The last train pulled away from the brewery in 1999, and the brewery closed soon after. The last train on NW 13th ran in 2003, delivering its final load to Wilbur-Ellis before the company moved to North Portland.

1 The walk starts at Union Station, built in 1896. It is a civic jewel, with corridors that take you back a century, a classic marble-lined concourse, and a restaurant your grandparents would recognize for its midcentury gentility. The brick and stucco station building, designed in the Italian Renaissance style, manages to be both friendly and impressive, with striped window awnings and decorative wrought-iron scrollwork. I especially like the detail that hints of the pride Americans once felt in their train system: winged train wheels above the second-story windows. The neon "go by train" sign on the station's clock tower was added in 1948; it went dark in 1971 and was restored in 1985.

Walk inside, where travertine and marble floors are waxed to a shine, and marble walls reflect vintage neon signs to "baggage," "newsstand," and "telephones." The city leases office space on the third floor, which is worth a walk up the steps. Follow the restrooms sign and then the sign to the "south stairway." Wood flooring, transom windows, original doors, lights, wainscoting, glass exit signs, and that indefinable old-building smell take you back a century or so. Low-tech, old-fashioned occupations such as architecture and legal investigations are plied here, just as you'd hope, although "The College Lady," who undoubtedly counsels panicked twenty-first-century parents, adds a contemporary touch.

Come out of the station and turn left onto the sidewalk.

2 If you're an aficionado of views, check out the relatively new vantage point just past the south end of the station: a pedestrian bridge over the train tracks. It leads to the Station Place Apartments on NW Naito Parkway. From the top of the bridge, look down at what used to be Couch Lake. Fifteen feet deep and about twenty-two city blocks in size, it was one of several swampy bottomland lakes alongside the Willamette. In the 1880s when the Northern Pacific Terminal Company bought the land, it began filling the lake with ballast from incoming ships and sand from the riverbed. Couch Lake was gone by the time Union Station opened in 1896.

Retrace your steps off the bridge and walk south on NW 6th Avenue, away from the station. From 2007 to 2008, the Portland Mall rehabilitation project brought life back to a previously uninviting stretch of roadway.

3 From 6th, turn right on NW Glisan Street. Cross Broadway. On the right is the 1916 Federal Building. At NW 8th Avenue (the east side of the Park Blocks) is the vacant, ancient Harlow Block, once the Park Hotel. It was built in 1882 by Captain John Harlow on the site of his former home. He achieved a bit of infamy for importing carp to Oregon in 1880, with the aim of raising them to sell to restaurants. His carp farm consisted of ponds adjacent to the Sandy River. When the river flooded one spring, it inundated his ponds, liberating thousands of fish to explore their new home in the Northwest. Harlow stocked either this same pond or another with trout, hence the name of the town at the mouth of the Sandy River: Troutdale.

Turn left into the park adjacent to 8th and enter the North Park Blocks, seven contiguous blocks north of SW Ankeny Street that were dedicated to the city in 1869 by Captain Couch. Original plans were for a park running north to the river, but Tanner Creek and the swampy ground prevented that. Today the blocks are lined with a mix of old buildings and new condominiums, accented by century-old elms.

Cross NW Everett Street. On the left is the elaborate Italian Renaissance–style U.S. Customs House. From 1901 to 1968 it was the city's branch of the U.S. Customs Service. Across from it is the Portland Dog Bowl, a canine water fountain in a stone "kitchen floor" created by William Wegman. He reportedly toyed with making the fountain a toilet—the source, he says, of his own famous dogs' daily water. The result is just as realistic.

4 From the North Park Blocks, turn right onto NW Couch Street. At NW 10th Avenue and Couch, the route encounters Powell's City of Books, a multistory, block-size bookstore that has swallowed years out of the lives of many Portlanders. After working one summer with his son, Michael, at Michael's bookstore near the University of Chicago, Walter Powell came back to Portland

The Armory with the Henry behind it, a condominium tower built on the site of the Blitz-Weinhard Brewery. This photo was taken during the Armory renovation. Workers removed the all-white paint job; it came readily off of the basalt base but not off of the brick upper section, as seen here. Ultimately the bricks were repainted, but in red, not white. Photo by Zeb Andrews.

and opened his own shop, buying used books and selling them at a former car dealership at 10th and Burnside. Michael joined his dad in 1979. Powell's is now the world's largest independent bookseller.

From Couch, turn right onto 10th. The 1891 National Guard Armory building is on the left. Its medieval bluster, complete with turrets, crenellated roof, and gunslots, was meant to be imposing in an era of class conflict, during which militias were trained to respond to local riots over bread shortages, labor conditions, or racial conflict (such as the riots that took place during the 1880s against the Chinese in Seattle). No shots ever rang out from the Armory, and by 1928 it was an anachronism. It was reborn as an event space for dog shows, circuses, and boxing events, until the late 1960s when the neighboring Blitz-Weinhard Brewery used it for storage. After the brewery left town, the Armory was renovated, its all-white paint job blasted away to reveal the gorgeous basalt block; it reopened in 2006 as the new home to Portland Center Stage.

At 312 10th is the 1910 Portland Buddhist Church, built on the site of an earlier residence. In the early 1900s, Portland's Japanese community, numbering about fifteen hundred, was centered in Northwest Portland. This building, the first Buddhist church in Oregon, was home to worship, socials, a hostel for students and laborers, and, on the third floor, the minister's residence. In 1965 a new church was built at SW 34th Avenue, and this was converted to office space.

North of the Portland Buddhist Church, in a small plaza, are some of the columns that supported the Lovejoy viaduct. Built in 1927, the viaduct extended from NW 14th Avenue and Lovejoy Street, over the rail yards, and on up to the elevation of the Broadway Bridge—an unsubtle symbol of the emerging ascendance of automotive traffic over the rail lines. Greek immigrant Tom Stefopoulos painted murals on the columns between 1948 and 1952, during slow spells while he worked as a watchman at the rail yards. The viaduct, which cast a shadow over the land below, came down when condominiums started going up.

Still on 10th, cross NW Flanders Street. The Gregory, on the left, only looks like an Art Deco jewel from the 1920s; it was actually built in 2000. Inside are 133 residences. As you cross Glisan and Hoyt, you are entering what used to be rail yards, with virtually all the buildings in the next few blocks built after the 1990s, when Burlington Northern Railroad sold its acreage to a developer.

At NW Irving Street, one block to the right is the Ecotrust building (721 NW 9th Avenue), which is worth a visit. The building started life as the McCraken warehouse and was used by storage and distributing companies. It was home to Rapid Transfer and Storage until 1997, when Ecotrust bought the building and began a green renovation. Today the Jean Vollum Natural Capital Center, the building's more formal name, is a marketplace for the ideas and products of the conservation economy. The public is welcome inside during weekday business hours. I recommend a trip up the stairs (in the steel towers on the outside of the building) to the third-floor rooftop balcony, where views are incredible. The steel towers date from the renovation; they are tied to interior posts and beams and provide the structural and seismic reinforcement needed to bring the building up to modern codes.

5 From 10th, turn left at NW Johnson Street, crossing over what used to be rail tracks, and walk through Jamison Square, a park opened in 2002. On hot summer days it holds the city's densest concentration of toddlers, who thrash around in the pool formed by waterfalls emerging from the rocky steps. The tiki totem poles on the west side were designed by Kenny Scharf to cover the catenary poles that supply electricity to the streetcar line. The park is named for William Jamison, one of the first art gallery owners in the district; he is credited for initiating the Pearl District's First Thursday gallery walks.

Exit Jamison Square on its west side, and turn left (south) on NW 11th Avenue.

At Irving, here a grassy arcade, walk on 11th between the 200-foot-long Pearl Townhomes, built in a former rail station. In 1905, James J. Hill's Portland and Seattle Railway promised faster access to the East Coast than the Union Pacific, at the time run by E. H. Harriman. Harriman didn't believe in friendly competition, so he blocked Hill's railway from access to Union Station. Hill, not to be thwarted, surreptitiously bought land along Hoyt and converted the rail yard freight house you see here, at 11th and Hoyt, into the North Bank Station. Passenger trains for Chicago left from here, as did a line to Astoria, where passengers could disembark and then board a luxury steamer to San Francisco. Trains ran from this station until 1931.

6 From 11th, turn right on NW Hoyt Street. Just past NW 12th Avenue you enter the NW 13th Avenue Historic District, with classic warehouses from the early twentieth century. Historic features include water towers, original painted advertising signs, loading docks, and brick masonry construction (left exposed or covered with plaster). Many share a classically derived tripartite design with a cornice at the top, a midsection, and a ground floor. Some buildings have strong belt courses separating the sections; in others, the fenestration (design of windows) defines the sections.

At the southeast corner of Hoyt and 13th is the Modern Confectionery Building, one of the earliest warehouses in the historic district. When it opened in 1904, twenty women worked here making candy for the local market. Sales grew and the company became one of the largest candy manufacturers on the West Coast. According to one manager, sales growth was aided by the Eighteenth Amendment: "Prohibition helps the candy business more than anything. Men who drink do not care for candy. Men who do not drink have a sweet tooth." In 1936 the company went out of business.

At the northeast corner is the Prael, Hegele Building from 1906, a good example of the tripartite design, with the top having a corbeled cornice. Prael, Hegele distributed crockery and glassware. Later, from the 1920s to the 1980s, the building was a transfer and storage facility.

7 From Hoyt, turn left onto 13th. This street runs along the backside of the warehouse buildings, with their loading docks open to the rail spur line that ran here until 2003. As part of the historic district guidelines, docks must be preserved, and new docks are encouraged. Docks are wood or concrete, projecting into the street, with canopies above and rollup doors.

Cross NW Glisan Street. On the right is the red brick Dale Building at 411. In 1862, pioneers Robert and Eliza Dale built a cottage at this site, reportedly with the help of local Native Americans. Mrs. Dale later sold the house, and it was torn down in 1915 to build this warehouse.

At the northwest corner of 13th and NW Flanders Street is the 1910 Armour meatpacking plant. Armour was one of several Midwestern meatpacking companies to make Portland their West Coast hub. (Kenton was a meatpacking company town created by Swift and Company; see Walk 1.)

In the southwest corner of the same intersection is the 1939 Meier Building designed by Richard Sundeleaf. In it the L. K. Liggett Company wholesaled drugs, after buying up scores of local drugstores in the Northwest and California and selling them under the Rexall name.

8   From 13th, turn right onto Flanders and walk one block west to NW 14th Avenue. At the southwest corner of Flanders and 14th is a former Meier and Frank warehouse, out of which mattresses, recliners, and area rugs were shipped. Unlike 13th and 15th Avenues, 14th had no rail spur on it; it was reserved instead for horse traffic.

Turn right onto 14th. At 14th and NW Glisan Street is a filling station from 1940. At 14th and NW Irving Street is the Irving Street Lofts, a 1924 building that housed pharmaceutical wholesalers from 1925 to 1981. In the northeast corner of the same intersection, the Crane Building, rehabbed in 2006, was built in 1910 by the Chicago-based Crane Company, as a branch house carrying plumbing supplies for West Coast markets.

At NW Johnson Street in the southeast corner is the Wool Growers Building, a wood-frame brick building from 1905. Each floor is delineated by a corbeled belt course. For its first thirty years, it housed a furniture wholesaler. In 1936 the Pacific Wool Growers, a trade group dedicated to stimulating the national market for West Coast wool, bought the building. Wool was delivered via the 13th Avenue rail spur, and piles of wool were graded on the top floor. The trade group operated until 1973. Across 14th at 1410 Johnson is the American Chicle Company, which in 1914 invented Chiclets, the first candy-coated gum. Chicle is a product of the sapodilla tree and was the source of modern chewing gum.

9   From 14th, cross NW Lovejoy Street and turn left onto it. This was where the Lovejoy viaduct began climbing to the Broadway Bridge. Though it was a familiar site to longtime Portlanders, now that it is gone it's hard to imagine that it ever existed here.

On the left is the seven-story Marshall-Wells building, a historic warehouse converted into 164 lofts in 2001. In 1914 the warehouse was one of Portland's early reinforced concrete structures. It was originally four stories high, with the last three stories added in 1915. The Marshall-Wells Hardware Company was a wholesaler of hardware, mining, and railroad supplies. In 1959 it was bought by Coast-to-Coast Hardware.

While on Lovejoy, cross 15th. Old rail spur lines are visible here in the pavement. Walk under the elevated Interstate 405, where 100,000 cars a day pass overhead.

As you come out from under the freeway ramps, you leave the tony Pearl District for the humbler vibe of Slabtown, a name from Portland's past that didn't stand the test of time. From the 1880s onward, Slabtown was a neighborhood of the industrial lower class. Immigrant Irish, Croatians, Russians, Germans, and Poles came to work in sawmills and other lumber-related businesses, such as a planing mill and a door manufacturer, as well as at Willamette Iron and Steel, and Portland Iron Works, which made metal architectural fixtures. Cigars, carriages, sheet metal, and sewer pipes were also manufactured here, as were coffins, at the Oregon Casket Company on NW 21st Avenue.

Slabtown had two centers: one from NW Raleigh to NW Thurman Street between 21st and 27th Avenues, and another north of NW Overton Street and east of 20th. Workers lived in cottages, several of which will be passed on the walk. Slabtown was a bit of a rough-and-ready place. One former resident recalled a high school classmate in the 1930s telling him that if it weren't for the guys from Slabtown, Lincoln High wouldn't have had any athletes. The area thrived until the 1950s, when industry and parking lots for Consolidated Freightways (now Con-way Freight) began swallowing up homes. In 2007, in a nice bit of historical loop-closing, Con-way began plans to redevelop these lots into housing.

As for Slabtown's name, during the first decades of the 1900s, many Portland homes had cordwood dumped in their parking strips, to be seasoned and hauled into basements to fuel wood-burning furnaces. In Slabtown, mill workers had a cheaper fuel source dumped in their front yards: slabs from nearby mills. Slabs were pieces of wood, with bark intact, left over after the four sides were shaved from a log.

At NW 16th Avenue and Lovejoy is a sign, "Slabtown," for a bar—the only overt indication of that era.

10 From Lovejoy, turn right on NW 17th Avenue. Cross NW Marshall Street, a very cool intersection, with a 1918 ivy-covered former home (the newer garage entrance occupies what used to be the front porch and doorway) and a 1911 apartment house at the northeast corner.

Keep walking north on 17th, which from NW Overton Street north has lost any trace of history, with cement block buildings that I suspect will not delight twenty-second-century walkers in the same way we enjoy the old brick warehouses. The view from 17th and NW Raleigh Street, next to the gargantuan concrete piers that support Interstate 405 far above, gives a walker an ant's perspective of life.

11 From 17th, turn left onto NW Thurman Street. Walk one block. At the northwest corner of NW 18th Avenue and Thurman, Norm Thompson sold the Oregon mystique. Here was the flagship store until 2005, when the company moved to Hillsboro and was purchased.

12 From Thurman, turn left onto NW 19th Avenue, where Saint Patrick Catholic Church stands, its dignity unbowed by the proximity of freeway ramps. In 1889 the Irish community constructed Saint Patrick's. It has twenty-two Povey windows in its Italian Renaissance façade. The rectory is next door. After World War II, as the neighborhood lost housing to industry, parishioners fled. The adjacent school closed in 1957. Today it is hard to imagine crowds of schoolchildren playing in a schoolyard or parents walking to church with their large families—there's not a house within sight.

Past Saint Patrick's, continue walking south on 19th. Cross NW Quimby Street. The two-story home on 19th at 1435 dates from 1904.

Cross NW Pettygrove Street. At the intersection is a store from 1884, with living quarters above. This type of live/work space, popular again today, was common before cars. Each day neighborhood folks could send a child over to pick up the milk, eggs, or produce needed for the day. Next to it were homes of some store customers: at 1327 and 1323 are two well-preserved shiplap cottages from 1884.

13 From 19th, turn left on NW Overton Street. At 1828 and 1822 are two of the oldest homes I know of in town, both from 1875, built when only about ten thousand people lived in Portland. At that time the rail yards were still a lake, and the likely employment for residents of these homes was the Weidler Sawmill, constructed in 1870 at the foot of Savier Street.

Continue on Overton, crossing under Interstate 405.

14 From Overton, turn right onto NW 14th Avenue. In one block, turn left on NW Northrup Street, walking down its south side. On the right is the BridgePort

Brewing Company, Portland's first microbrewery of the current era, brewing beer in a formerly vine-covered hemp rope factory since 1984. After decades of chewing away at the building's mortar, the exuberant Virginia creeper that cloaked the building from curb to roof came down in 2007.

On Northrup alongside BridgePort, look down at the purple glass squares in the sidewalk. Based on the color, these sidewalk lights, or vault lights, probably date from the 1910s. They were originally clear; manganese added to the glass slowly turns purple after years of exposure to ultraviolet light. The underside of the glass is prism shaped to better distribute light to basement areas below. Such lights were first used on ships in the 1840s as deck lights, and then were adapted for city use. By the 1930s, with the prevalence of electric lights, they became obsolete. Over the years many have been paved over.

15 From Northrup, turn right on NW 13th Avenue. The new pavement at your feet went down in 2005, the last downtown street to be paved. On this side of BridgePort the creeper was cut, and its immense stump paved over when BridgePort poured its new dock in 2006. The trunk once supported a vine that completely engulfed the iron catwalk over 13th at the third floor. The catwalk led to the Cronin Block, a brick warehouse in the block to the east. That warehouse was torn down in 2005 and replaced by a fifteen-story condominium tower; the lower part of the tower uses the Cronin Block bricks in its façade, and in 2007, when construction was complete, the catwalk was reinstalled—no longer functional, but most definitely historic.

From 13th, turn left on NW Marshall Street. Belgian block pavers made of basalt cover the street here.

16 At Marshall and NW 11th Avenue, enter Tanner Springs Park, installed in 2005. The park is experimental: it is designed to replicate, in the heart of a densely populated area, the natural cleansing action of a wetland. This is the middle of three water-themed city greenspaces between 10th and 11th meant to evoke the lost Tanner Creek, which sprang from the West Hills and drained into the now-filled wetland of Couch Lake. The big "if" in the park's success is the Pearl District's pet population. Too many piles and puddles will destroy the wetland's ability to filter pollutants, and algae will take over. On one warm summer day, the water was clear and beautiful, and the park's serenity, enjoyed by just three people, was a marked contrast to the rowdy preschool scene at Jamison Square. At the east end, railroad ties—part of this site's past—are reborn as art. Painted art glass blocks within the ties represent lost wildlife.

Virginia creeper, old wood, and brick team up for timeless beauty on this old factory building, since 1984 the home of the BridgePort Brewing Company. Photo by Zeb Andrews.

After exploring the park, return to Marshall and walk east. Turn right at NW 9th Avenue and left at NW Lovejoy Street. Here, one sidewalk climbs to the Broadway Bridge; the other stays on ground level. Take the latter one block to NW Station Way and the starting point at Union Station.

8/18/09
Phyllis

GARDEN HOME TO RALEIGH HILLS LOOP

DISTANCE   About 6 miles

STARTING POINT   Garden Home Recreation Center: 7475 SW Oleson Road

GETTING THERE AND PARKING   From downtown Portland, drive west on Highway 26. Get off at the Sylvan exit and drive south on SW Scholls Ferry Road toward Raleigh Hills. Just prior to the intersection with Beaverton-Hillsdale Highway (Highway 10), Scholls Ferry becomes commercial. Watch for the left turn lane; it appears prior to the stoplight for Beaverton-Hillsdale Highway. The road you want is marked "Progress/Scholls 210." Turn left onto this road and cross Beaverton-Hillsdale Highway onto SW Oleson Road. Follow Oleson 1.4 miles to the Garden Home Recreation Center, located on the right. Park in the parking lot.

TriMet: Take bus 45 (Garden Home) to the stop at SW Oleson and Garden Home Road, just south of the starting point. Or take bus 54 (Beaverton-Hillsdale) to the stop at SW 99th Avenue and Beaverton-Hillsdale Highway, and begin the route at **9**.

RESTROOMS AND DRINKING FOUNTAINS   Restrooms are inside the Garden Home Recreation Center and at Vista Brook Park (along the Fanno Creek Greenway Trail, an ADA-compliant portable toilet). Drinking fountains are inside the Garden Home Recreation Center and at McMillan Park (SW Chestnut Place) and Vista Brook Park.

FOOD AND DRINK   A variety of semi-fast food options are located in the triangle between Allen Boulevard, 92nd Avenue, and Scholls Ferry Road. At the walk's turnaround point is McCormick's Fish House and Bar (9945 SW Beaverton-Hillsdale Highway, Beaverton; 503-643-1322), a local landmark. A bowl of

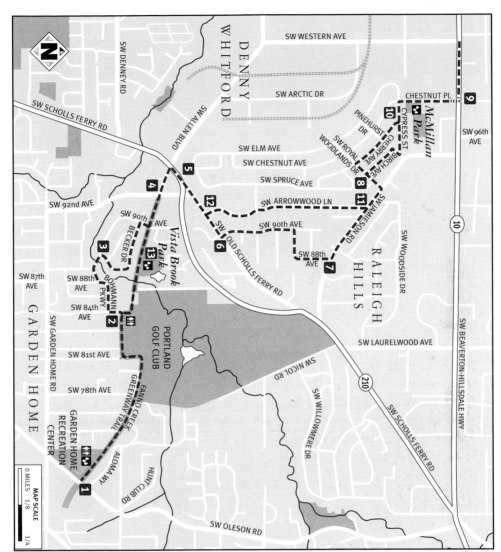

SW WESTERN AVE

DENNY WHITFORD

SW ARCTIC DR

CHESTNUT PL

McMillan Park

SW 96th AVE

SW SCHOLLS FERRY RD

PINEHURST DR

SW ELM AVE

SW CHESTNUT AVE

SW ROYAL WOODLANDS DR

CYPRESS ST

CHERRY AVE

BIRCH AVE

SW DENNEY RD

SW ALLEN BLVD

SW SPRUCE AVE

SW ARROWWOOD LN

SW JAMIESON RD

RALEIGH HILLS

SW 92nd AVE

SW 90th AVE

BECKER DR

Vista Brook Park

SW OLD SCHOLLS FERRY RD

SW 90th AVE

SW 88th AVE

SW WOODSIDE DR

SW 87th AVE

SW 88th AVE

BOHMANN PKWY

SW 84th AVE

PORTLAND GOLF CLUB

SW LAURELWOOD AVE

GARDEN HOME

SW GARDEN HOME RD

SW 81st AVE

SW NICOL RD

FANNO CREEK GREENWAY TRAIL

ALOMA WY

SW 78th AVE

GARDEN HOME RECREATION CENTER

HUNT CLUB RD

SW WILLOWMERE DR

SW SCHOLLS FERRY RD

SW BEAVERTON-HILLSDALE HWY

SW OLESON RD

MAP SCALE
0 MILES 1/8
1/4

WALK 15. *Garden Home to*
Raleigh Hills Loop

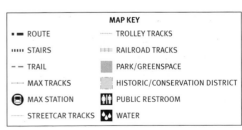

MAP KEY

▬ ▬ ROUTE	⋯⋯ TROLLEY TRACKS
⋯⋯⋯ STAIRS	⊞⊞⊞ RAILROAD TRACKS
– – TRAIL	▨ PARK/GREENSPACE
—⊢— MAX TRACKS	▨ HISTORIC/CONSERVATION DISTRICT
⊜ MAX STATION	🚻 PUBLIC RESTROOM
—‖— STREETCAR TRACKS	♥ WATER

clam chowder and salad of greens make a perfect destination for this suburban walk.

BEST TIMES TO VISIT   Any time!

ACCESSIBILITY   The route is on paved paths, city sidewalks, and streets, some of which are fairly busy and have no sidewalks and narrow shoulders. Where sidewalks are missing, a less traveled alternate route is given. Elevations range from 200 feet at **2** to 330 feet between **6** and **7**.

THIS WALK COMBINES a stroll along an old rail line, quiet streets with plenty of beautiful midcentury homes, and a short section along one of the metro area's busy arterials. The last is noisy but surprisingly intriguing. The hubbub is more than offset by a visit to one of the Northwest's signature restaurants, and the satisfied feeling of being on foot in an area where most people are trapped inside cars.

1 The Garden Home Recreation Center, where this walk begins, was built in 1912 as the Garden Home School. The gym was a 1930s addition, a work relief project. It and other additions remain, but the original building was torn down in 1967, and in 1982 the school closed. The center is run by the Tualatin Hills Park and Recreation District.

Begin at the paved walking path along the northern edge of the center's grounds. This path runs west for 1.2 miles, following the alignment of the Oregon Electric Railway. Trains ran from 1908 to the 1930s. In 1922, at the railway's peak, sixty-five trains left Portland each day; twenty were commuter trains that stopped in Garden Home, while others went further, to Forest Grove, Salem, Albany, and Eugene. After passenger service ended around 1933, the tracks were used for a time by steam trains to haul freight and logs.

The old railway segment is now part of the Fanno Creek Greenway Trail, a 15-mile trail that when complete will run from Willamette Park on the Willamette River to Fanno Creek's confluence with the Tualatin River in Durham, Oregon, a tiny town between Tigard and Tualatin.

The trail here passes through a forest of fir and cedar. On the right a phalanx of apartment buildings occupies ground that from the 1920s to 1990 was a 36-acre estate, Garden Home Farm, developed by Aaron Frank. He was the son of Sigmund Frank, and a third generation of the family that founded the Meier and Frank department store. The land north of the Garden Home Farm was the Portland Hunt Club from about 1906 through 1930. From it, equestrian-minded Portlanders galloped the fields and lanes of Garden Home. (The club's stone entrance markers are still visible at SW Hunt Club Road, off Oleson, just north of this route.)

Frank's manor house, designed by Herman Brookman, can be seen from the trail at the point where the chain-link fence makes a right-angle turn. It is a one-story shingled home with a sign in front. It sits on SW Aloma Way, named for Frank's most prized horse. He owned show horses for a time until they were killed, some in a fire and some in a train accident.

(A related site in Southwest Portland is Fir Acres, an estate owned by Aaron's brother Lloyd. It has become Lewis and Clark College.)

At the point where the chain link ends and a black fence begins is SW 78th Avenue, formerly Firlock Lane. Here was Firlock Station, where Frank's horses mounted a ramp to rail cars that took them to shows nationwide.

The Franks, who were by far the wealthiest people in Garden Home, left some lasting memories. Melvin David Replogle's father's property bordered the Frank estate, on the other side of the tracks, at about 78th. In Virginia Mapes's *Garden Home: The Way It Was*, Replogle remembers a birthday party at the estate: "Mr. Frank had chartered an airplane to drop by small parachutes, gifts for the kids. It was Dick Frank's birthday. One parachute landed off the grounds and fell into [my] eager clutches." He ripped it open and found a fine pocket-knife, which his father made him return. Replogle also remembered the time when Amelia Earhart visited and performed aerial acrobatics above the estate. Aaron Frank died in 1968.

At the black fence, the trail begins to border the southern edge of the Portland Golf Club, founded in 1913. Membership at this private club is by invitation only. "During the Depression years," recalled Melvin David Replogle, "the lucky kids got jobs weeding the lawns of the Frank Estate. The rest of us toughed it out caddying at the Portland Golf Club. Those of us who caddied soon had a liberal education. Older men, often drunk, were not too tolerant of kids. Fights were common."

On the left are the streets of Garden Home. There is no fence at 81st and 82nd to separate the trail from its neighbors, and the absence makes for a much more enjoyable experience than the walk beside the cagelike black fences adjacent the golf club.

2 From the Fanno Creek Greenway Trail, turn left onto SW 84th Avenue, where the post-and-beam homes date from the late 1960s, the work of Oregon builder Robert Rummer. Most of his homes sold in the $20,000 to $30,000 range. These streets, the Vista Brook neighborhood, contain the largest concentration of Rummer homes in the Northwest. (See Walk 16 for more on the elements of Rummer homes.)

From 84th, turn right on SW Bohmann Parkway. Cross SW Cecilia Terrace, a remarkable street of mid 1960s homes so low slung that they appear shocking to an eye grown used to two-story entrance arches and other elements of today's enormous homes. More Rummers, these from 1966, reside on the 8500 block of Bohmann.

At SW 86th Avenue, stay on Bohmann. Beyond 86th are homes from the late 1950s, such as 8680 (1959) and 8685 (1957), a decade when Portlanders began fleeing close-in neighborhoods for a more suburban setting.

Cross Fanno Creek, a year-round stream formed from seven creeks originating in the West Hills, with a 32-square-mile watershed.

3 From Bohmann, turn right onto SW Becker Drive. Homes in this neighborhood, in unincorporated Washington County, have a Portland address, a Tigard zip code, and children who go to Beaverton schools. The houses date from the early to late 1960s. Vista Brook Pool is private, primarily for neighborhood residents.

At 8866 Becker is a large dawn redwood (*Metasequoia glyptostroboides*), one of the few deciduous conifers. A dinosaur cruising down this suburban street would recognize this tree, as it has inhabited the earth for fifty million years. Dawn redwoods were found in the fossil record and thought to be extinct until stands were found growing in China in 1941.

From Becker, turn right on SW 90th Avenue. After half a block, turn left onto the Fanno Creek Greenway Trail. In Garden Home's earlier rural days, many residents owned horses. Pat Tiedeman was a little girl living near the train tracks here. A favorite pastime for Pat and her friends was to put on cowgirl hats, pack some toy guns, hop on their horses, and chase the train, pretending to be Wild West train robbers. I wonder what Homeland Security would do with such a child today.

The trail is lined with Himalayan blackberry, a nonnative, extremely invasive plant whose days in Oregon may be numbered. A blackberry killer known as blackberry leaf rust fungus has made its way into the state from California. The disease, which occurs naturally in Africa and Europe, has been used as a biological control in Chile, Australia, and New Zealand for decades. It is not clear how it immigrated to the United States or what impact it will have on this Oregon interloper.

A car on Scholls Ferry Road across from the Portland Golf Club, 1931. Photo courtesy of the City of Beaverton.

4 At SW 92nd Avenue the trail ends. Cross 92nd at the marked crosswalk to SW Allen Boulevard and walk one block on Allen. In the triangle surrounded by Allen, Scholls Ferry, and 92nd are various lunch options: Mexican food, burgers, Chinese food, pizza. The intersection of Allen and Scholls Ferry was named Whitford, a station on the Oregon Electric Railway line.

From Allen, cross Scholls Ferry Road at the light, and then turn right to walk briefly on the sidewalk that runs on its west side. An old market road turned state highway, Scholls Ferry runs northeast from Scholls, Oregon (where in the 1850s a ferry crossed the Tualatin River), and ends at its intersection with Highway 26 atop Sylvan Hill in Portland.

5 From Scholls Ferry Road, keep left at SW Old Scholls Ferry Road, an earlier road alignment. There is no sidewalk here, and cars use this as a cut-through, so walk with care, facing traffic as you climb the one big hill on this walk.

(To avoid walking on busy roads without sidewalks, turn left off Scholls Ferry onto SW Elm Avenue, then right onto SW Chestnut Lane and right onto SW Spruce Avenue. Follow Spruce all the way to SW Royal Woodlands Drive, turn left, and then turn right onto SW Birch Avenue to rejoin the walk at **8**.)

A 1960s ranch in a parklike setting.

6   From Old Scholls Ferry, turn left onto SW 90th Avenue, which offers views to the north and some very nice ranches, many built around 1960. The home at 6110 is especially noteworthy, with a beautifully landscaped 16,000-square-foot lot. I'm a fan of unfenced yards, and the 1957 home at 5975 is a good example, looking like it is set in a park rather than inside a box, as fences often suggest.

From 90th, turn right onto SW Laurel Leaf Terrace, and follow it as it curves left, becoming SW 88th Avenue. The Colonial Revival ranches here date from the early 1960s.

7   From 88th, turn left onto SW Jamieson Road, an old rail alignment. Walk 0.3 mile along its shoulder, facing traffic, and then turn left onto SW Royal Woodlands Drive. This is the Raleigh West neighborhood; you've left unincorporated Washington County for the higher taxes of Beaverton proper.

8   From Royal Woodlands, turn right onto SW Birch Avenue, a street of smaller lots and homes from the early 1960s. From Birch, turn right onto SW Pinehurst Drive, and then immediately left onto SW Cypress Street.

From Cypress, turn right onto SW Chestnut Place. Here is McMillan Park. A creek runs beyond the tennis courts; two old weeping willows near it make for a nice picnic spot. Chestnut climbs away from the creek, and at 4800 sits a bungalow built in 1920, when its hilly location looked over farms and small forest parcels. Beyond it are houses from the days immediately following World War II, tucked into the cul-de-sac.

Keep walking to Chestnut's cul-de-sac, where a wooded path takes you instantly to another landscape: the fast-moving scene along Beaverton-Hillsdale Highway.

9 Across the highway is McCormick's Fish House and Bar. In the late 1970s, Bill McCormick and Doug Schmick turned an old steakhouse into an urban dining experience in the suburbs. Since then they've established more than fifty restaurants and catering operations throughout the United States, starting in the early 1970s when McCormick bought one of Portland's signature restaurants, Jake's Famous Crawfish on SW Stark Street and 12th Avenue. The food and service are always excellent.

To cross the highway safely, walk west to SW Western Avenue a few blocks away. Shops along the way make walking this busy road bearable.

After lunch retrace your steps back to Chestnut. From it, turn left onto Cypress.

10 From Cypress, turn right onto SW Cherry Avenue, a street with nice old flowering cherries in some of the parking strips. Follow Cherry to Royal Woodlands, turn left, and in two blocks turn right onto Jamieson, crossing to its east side to walk against traffic.

(To walk on quieter streets with less traffic, pass Royal Woodlands, staying on Cherry until it turns onto Spruce; turn right on Spruce and follow it to its intersection with Chestnut and Elm. Turn left there and walk to Scholls Ferry, rejoining the route between **12** and **13**.)

11 From Jamieson, turn right onto SW Arrowwood Lane, probably the most beautiful street of the walk, with ranches on 20,000-square-foot lots. They date from the mid 1950s.

Beyond the peak of the hill, as the road begins to slope down again, is the grandmother of all the homes on the street, a 1929 Cape Cod on a 54,000-square-foot lot, looking beautiful on its perch near the top of the hill.

Sculptural plant forms suit the plain elegance of this 1950s ranch on SW Arrowwood Lane

12 From Arrowwood, turn right onto Old Scholls Ferry, again walking against traffic. Turn right on Scholls Ferry, and walk to the light at Allen. Cross Scholls Ferry here, walk one block east on Allen to 92nd, cross it, and turn right to rejoin the Fanno Creek Greenway Trail.

13 Walk back on the trail, which soon passes 4-acre Vista Brook Park. The park's pond is part of a marshy area of creeks, springs, swamps, and ponds extending along Fanno Creek, including the Oregon Episcopal School Marsh east of SW Nicol Road.

The large building behind the gate on the right side of the trail at about 86th is a sewage facility. Next to it, a home occupies a large and lovely lot that extends from 86th to 84th along the trail.

Cross Fanno Creek on a bridge; from it is a nice vantage point to view the hillside just climbed. Continue on the trail to the starting point.

The Fanno Creek Greenway Trail.

WALK 16

BEAVERTON LOOP

DISTANCE   6.25 miles

STARTING POINT   Beaverton Central MAX station: north of SW Canyon Road near the junction of Hall Boulevard and Watson Avenue

GETTING THERE AND PARKING   Beaverton is about 7 miles from Portland. From downtown Portland, drive west on Highway 26. Pass the exit for the Oregon Zoo and watch for signs for Canyon Road. Take the exit for Canyon Road (also known as Highway 8) and Beaverton. After entering Beaverton and passing under Highway 217, turn right on SW Hall Boulevard, and left on SW Westgate Drive. Do not park in lots adjacent to the MAX but on Westgate Drive, a street north of the station between Hall and Cedar Hills Boulevards, and walk south to the station from there.

TriMet: Take the MAX Blue Line to the Beaverton Central station (not to the Beaverton Transit Center, which is the next station east).

RESTROOMS AND DRINKING FOUNTAINS   A portable toilet is at the northwest corner of Shiffler Park (SW Erickson Avenue and 10th Street), just west of the route midway through the walk. Restrooms are also found at City Park (SW

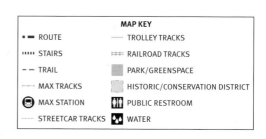

MAP KEY

▪ ▬ ROUTE	⋯⋯ TROLLEY TRACKS
ⅠⅠⅠⅠⅠ STAIRS	⊬⊬⊬ RAILROAD TRACKS
‒ ‒ TRAIL	▢ PARK/GREENSPACE
⸺ MAX TRACKS	▨ HISTORIC/CONSERVATION DISTRICT
Ⓔ MAX STATION	🚻 PUBLIC RESTROOM
⋯⋯ STREETCAR TRACKS	💧 WATER

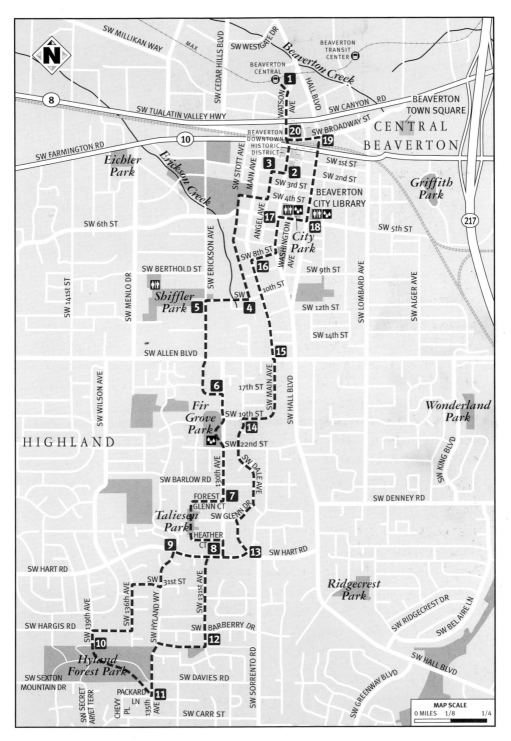

WALK 1. *Beaverton Loop*

5th Street and Watson Avenue) and inside the Beaverton City Library (SW 5th Street and Hall Boulevard) during library hours. There are drinking fountains at the Fir Grove Park playground (SW 22nd Street and 130th Avenue), City Park, and the Beaverton City Library.

FOOD AND DRINK There are coffee shops and restaurants at the Round, a mixed-use development at the Beaverton Central station, and downtown Beaverton offers choices ranging from donuts to steakhouses to Asian restaurants. Nearby SW Hall Boulevard, SW Cedar Hills Boulevard, and Beaverton Town Square (between Highways 8 and 10, directly west of Highway 217) offer post-walk options, including locally owned ethnic restaurants as well as chain eateries.

BEST TIMES TO VISIT Don't miss the Beaverton Farmers Market, the largest agriculture-only farmers market in the Northwest, open summer and fall, Saturdays and Wednesdays, at SW Hall Boulevard between 3rd and 5th Streets. Visit www.beavertonfarmersmarket.com for hours and annual open and close dates.

Across the street from the market is the Beaverton City Library, a great place to relax after a long walk. Visit the second-floor periodicals room overlooking a historic sycamore tree. Call 503-644-2197 for hours.

ACCESSIBILITY This walk follows city sidewalks except for routes through several parks, where trails can be avoided as described in the text. The only inaccessible portion is Hyland Forest Park **10** and **11**). The walk climbs from north to south, with elevations from 170 feet at the start to 350 feet in Hyland Forest Park, the turnaround point.

BEAVERTON, an agricultural community turned suburb that is now a major employer in its own right, lies within Washington County's Tualatin Valley, once home to the Kalapuya Indians. Early encounters with trappers and traders from the 1780s onward brought smallpox and death; with later incursions by European Americans, diseases wiped out most of the remaining indigenous peoples. One branch of the Kalapuyas was the Atfalatis, which early whites translated as "Tuality." Their center was in the area around Beaverton and Fanno Creeks—modern-day Beaverton. They called the place Chakeipi, meaning "place of the beaver." Soldiers in the British army noted that the Tualatin Valley consisted of water connected by swamps; the lakes were caused by the beavers' damming of the valley's many streams. Early settlers, arriving when the beaver had

been virtually trapped out by the Hudson's Bay Company, built their first dwellings atop the beaver dams and called the area along Beaver and Fanno Creeks
"Beaver Dam," which eventually led to the name Beaverton.

Isabelle Watts Strong, as an elderly woman, recalled Beaverton of the 1860s,
as quoted in Virginia Mapes's *Chakeipi:*

> The land was an overflowed beaver swamp so the homesteaders settled
> around it on more raised portions. They could not drain it as it covered
> miles and miles through the valley. I can hear those frogs yet, armies and
> armies of them. Finally rich men came who knew the untold wealth of
> beaver dam land. [Through ditching and draining] a real garden of Eden
> was converted from our frog ponds. The drained land was leaf mold eight
> to ten feet deep. In the summer, farmers could run the handle of their hoes
> down through the light, flour-like mulching and not touch bottom.

Hall Boulevard, encountered near the end of the walk, is named after the
Beaverton area's first land claimant, Lawrence Hall, who built a grist (flour) mill
in the 1840s to support the burgeoning farm population. He was the first to
begin draining the beaver dam land for cultivation. Beaverton farmers connected
to Portland in 1850 via the Plank Road (now Canyon Road), which provided
a reliable, if still arduous, conduit to bring their products to market. By 1868,
trains connected Tualatin Valley farmers to the rest of the world, and Beaverton
was platted out around the new rail terminal.

By the 1930s, Beaverton-area farmers were famous for celery, horseradish, and
onions. Beaverton remained small and agriculture based until the early 1950s,
when its population was just twenty-five hundred. In the decades following
World War II, however, subdivisions were built to house baby boomers and
their parents. The city is now home to seventy-six thousand people and is more
ethnically diverse than Portland, with a population that is 10 percent Asian and
11 percent Hispanic according to the 2000 Census. Today, agriculture thrives
primarily in the farther reaches of Washington County.

1 The Beaverton Central station lies in the fertile Beaverton Creek floodplain.
Beaverton and Fanno Creeks are subtributaries of the 83-mile-long Tualatin
River, which rises in the Coast Range west of Forest Grove and loops lazily
through its 712-square-mile watershed before flowing into the Willamette River
at Willamette Park in West Linn. Here on Beaverton Creek in the 1920s, the
newly widowed Rose Biggi began growing horseradish on her 14-acre vegetable
farm. The pungent root became her fortune. With earnings from selling ground

The Beaverton Central MAX station sits on what was once "beaver dam land," where horseradish, onions, and other produce were grown.

Rural Beaverton, date unknown. The white building is the railroad depot, at about today's SW Watson Avenue and Farmington Road. Photo courtesy of the Washington County Historical Society.

horseradish root to Portland grocers, she built the Beaverton Horseradish Factory, which later became Beaverton Foods, today the largest specialty condiment manufacturer in the United States. In 2001 the company moved from its original location on SW Cedar Hills Boulevard to Hillsboro.

From the station, walk east a bit to SW Watson Avenue and turn right. Cross SW Canyon Road, which from this point west is known as the Tualatin Valley (TV) Highway. Canyon is one of those zooming arterials for which Beaverton is often deplored, but in 1930 when it was first paved, children roller-skated on it. Louise Merlo recalled in Virginia Mapes's *Chakeipi*, "My sister and I had gotten roller skates for Christmas. We'd go up and back, clear to Saint Mary's. We hardly ever met a car."

After crossing Canyon, cross SW Broadway Street, the heart of old Beaverton; you'll walk along it later. Here is the Beaverton Downtown Historic District, included on the National Register of Historic Places for its cohesive, original layout of road and rail lines, and intact buildings.

After Broadway, cross the railroad tracks that were so instrumental to the success of Washington County farmers. Just beyond the tracks, cross SW Farmington Road, named for an old community on the Tualatin River about 9 miles southwest of Beaverton. East of here, the road is known as the Beaverton-Hillsdale Highway, which follows another old railway alignment into Portland. (In Portland, SW Barbur Boulevard was part of the route.) In this congested area, be thankful you're not a driver. Take a minute to look around at the many old buildings lining the rail tracks.

At the southeast corner of Farmington and Watson is a Spanish Colonial Revival building from 1923, built as the Bank of Beaverton, which didn't out-last the Depression. It reopened under another name and was a U.S. National Bank until 1964. Across from it in the southwest corner is the Cady Building, built by Fred Cady, whose father came to Beaverton at age sixty-nine in 1892 and promptly became the first mayor when the town incorporated in 1893. This 1914 building was the birthplace of the Beaverton Library in 1925 and home to dentists and other professionals, including an earlier bank. It was the first brick building in Beaverton.

The historic storefronts on Farmington deserve a bit of a detour if you're so inclined. The route, however, remains on Watson.

2 From Watson, turn right onto SW 2nd Street, the southern end of the historic district. At the northeast corner of 2nd and SW Angel Avenue is a splendid Oregon white oak; you'll see many of these native trees along the route. In 1826, Scottish botanist and plant explorer David Douglas noted that the low hills of western Oregon were covered in these oaks. They can live up to five hundred years, and their leaves have a high protein content. In 1880, during a hard winter, Willamette Valley settlers saved their cattle by feeding them white oak twigs and leaves. Native Americans cooked and dried the acorns as a meal for eating, and also used the meal to mend cracks in clay pots.

3 From 2nd, turn left onto Angel. Walk two blocks to SW 4th Street. At the northwest corner of Angel and 4th is a very old, multitrunked Ponderosa pine; after Douglas fir, this pine is the second most common tree in Oregon, though its range is predominately east of the Cascade crest.

From Angel, turn right on 4th, which dead-ends at a bike path. On the right is the Beaverton Swim Center. Go left on the path and walk along the Beaverton High School athletic fields. The path offers views to the left of pre-suburban Beaverton. Especially nice is a 1920 home at 12870 SW 6th Street. The Beaverton Lodge is on the right at SW 9th Street, which is unmarked.

4 From the bike path, turn right at the next street, SW 10th Street. In half a block you'll cross Erickson Creek, a Beaverton Creek tributary that rises from springs in the hills a few blocks south of here. After it joins Beaverton Creek, the water runs northwest to join Rock Creek south of Orenco, before ultimately flowing into the Tualatin River.

On 10th, walk by a community garden. The street ends at Shiffler Park.

5 From 10th, turn left on SW Erickson Avenue, named for Otto Erickson, who brought the first auto dealership to town in 1915. Unassembled Fords were delivered from Michigan to his Beaverton Garage, where the cars were assembled and sold. Erickson later became mayor of Beaverton. In 1923 his stepson, Guy Carr, took over the family business, and Carr Auto Group exists today.

On Erickson, walk south 0.2 mile, and cross SW Allen Boulevard. South of Allen, Erickson winds through a pretty set of garden townhomes from the late 1960s, and then curves left, turning into SW 17th Street.

6 From 17th, turn right on SW 130th Avenue. Walk along the east side of the street, as the sidewalk on the west side appears to be private (although this side is the only accessible way into the north end of Fir Grove Park, the next stop on the walk). Soon you'll see forested Fir Grove Park on the west side of 130th. Cross back over to walk along the park, and then enter the park at an asphalt path across from 6450 130th. The 4.7-acre park is a dense fir forest with an open, lacy understory of Oregon grape and vine maple. It's great when a place name reflects current reality instead of paved-over history, and Fir Grove Park is such a place. Walk along the path. As it forks, keep left and take the path that leads into a playground.

From the playground, exit the park onto 130th, and continue south a few blocks. The street, now climbing toward Sexton Mountain, is lined with small ranches from the late 1960s and early 1970s.

7 From 130th, turn right onto SW Forest Glenn Court, the northernmost of three cul-de-sacs in a subdivision laid out by Robert Rummer in 1966. Rummer homes (the first of which on this route can be seen at 13055 Forest Glenn Court) are now prized for their spare midcentury lines; Rummer built in several areas of Beaverton. The homes' design was inspired by homes built by Joseph Eichler, a commercial home builder who built thousands of houses in California from 1949 to 1967. Eichler created architect-designed homes using high-quality materials at an affordable price (less than $10,000 in the 1950s). In the 1960s Rummer essentially brought the look to the Northwest. Other Rummer homes on this street are at 13070, 13125, and 13120.

The signature element of the modestly sized Eichler and Rummer homes is walls of glass that create an illusion of space. These walls are made possible by post-and-beam construction. Instead of wood studs placed 2 feet apart to create a load-bearing wall, as in traditional home construction, posts are spaced 3 to 6 feet apart, with beams placed on them. The roof load is concentrated on the beams rather than continuously on the walls, allowing for floor-to-ceiling expanses of glass. Low-pitched or flat roofs with deep eaves create a long horizontal orientation. Other common elements include blank front façades, a kitchen open to the family room, wood siding, radiant-heated concrete floors, and an interior courtyard. Later Eichler homes were built around an atrium, and Rummer, with his first homes coming near the end of Eichler's innovations, adopted this feature. Other features are double-A roofs that give a cathedral effect to the interior, and a split plan, with the master bedroom and study on one side of the living space, and other bedrooms on the other.

The Rummers were built as affordable homes. Some have been kept up in the original style, while others have been drastically altered. Increasingly, these homes are being restored and enhanced by buyers who appreciate anew the 1960s aesthetics.

At the cul-de-sac on Forest Glenn Court, take the paved path next to the Rummer home at 13170. Follow the path to an open, grassy space. (The next section is not accessible; to stay on the paved path, from the grassy space, head straight on the asphalt toward some homes. They are located on the middle of

A Rummer home at the edge of Taliesen Park.

Rummer's three cul-de-sacs: SW Glenn Court. Turn left into Glenn Court, and then turn right on 130th to rejoin the walk at **8**.) Head into this lawn area toward a magical 1.6-acre remnant of a fir forest. This is Taliesen Park; it was donated to the city by Rummer. Once in the trees, turn left onto a dirt path that runs south. At the next grassy space, walk into it a bit to see the floor-to-ceiling glass walls along the back of a beautiful Rummer home. Continue walking on the forest path to an asphalt path; turn left and follow it to the third of Rummer's cul-de-sacs, SW Heather Court, where you can see the front of this same home. Next to it is a Rummer with a double-A frame roof with a center greenhouse courtyard. A few other well-loved Rummers on this street are at 13120 and 13220.

8 From Heather Court, turn right onto 130th and then right again onto SW Hart Road, a pleasant, woodsy street with more Rummer homes to look at. Cross Hart at the crosswalk at 13125 and continue walking west.

9 (From here the route leads to an inaccessible area, Hyland Forest Park, but I recommend walking the streets between Hart Road and the park because they are the most beautiful of the walk. If you decide to walk up to the park entrance at

SW 139th Avenue and Hargis Road but wish to avoid the park, simply backtrack to this point and walk east on Hart to **13** to rejoin the route.)

From Hart, turn left onto SW Hyland Way, a street of upscale 1970s ranches. Turn right on SW 31st Street and then left on SW 136th Avenue. The sidewalk ends, but the streets are quiet and shady as they climb steeply up Sexton Mountain, named for Edward Sexton, who settled here in 1853. From 136th, turn right on Hargis, a gorgeous wooded street with a variety of early 1960s architecture set against the backdrop of Hyland Forest Park. From Hargis, turn left onto 139th.

10 Enter Hyland Forest Park at the dead end of 139th. The park's 20 acres of woods are laced with trails; rather than follow minute directions that will keep your head in the book, let yourself wander.

The route resumes along SW 135th Avenue, so as long as you keep generally to the southeast you'll get there. If you want to explore further up the slopes of the mountain, keep due south while in the park. You'll then end up in a 1990s-era subdivision, and can follow the map to rejoin the walk.

11 Come out of the park along 135th. Walk north on this street and turn right at SW Rock Cress Court, where homes date from the 1980s. Take the paved path for pedestrians and bikes next to 13415. This straight path would have a nicer feel if it weren't so oppressively fenced. A tiny tributary of Fanno Creek runs behind the fence on the right.

12 The bike path breaks for a street, SW 131st Avenue; turn left here. This street dead-ends at a magnificent giant sequoia and a pretty bike path sheltered by the arching limbs of hazelnut trees.

The bike path ends at SW Hart Road. Turn right on Hart and cross it at 13125 to walk on its north side.

13 Hart leads to a traffic circle. From here, turn left on SW Sorrento Road, and then right on SW Glenn Drive, a street of more beautiful old Oregon white oaks. Turn left at SW Dale Avenue, and walk along this quiet, tidy street for several blocks, passing the intersection of Hill and Dale. At SW 20th Court, look right to a beautiful cul-de-sac with a forest backdrop.

14 From Dale, turn right onto SW 19th Street. Walk to its dead end, where you'll encounter another bike path. Carefully enter it and turn left. After a curve, a beautiful marsh opens up, a part of Erickson Creek that was saved from the parking lot that was poured around it. This marsh and pond are remnants of the type of land early settlers encountered, land that was later tiled (drained) to make it farmable.

At the marsh and parking lot, look left to the unmarked SW Main Avenue, where the bike path ends. Follow Main north past some old homes. The Beaverton Resource Center, which houses various community functions, is on the right. Before it was the Resource Center, this was the Beaverton Library, housed ignominiously in an old grocery store. Keep this building in mind, as the route soon encounters the 2000 Beaverton City Library—a vast improvement.

15 Still on Main, cross SW Allen Boulevard at the light to enter the Central Beaverton neighborhood, where homes' ages run the gamut from the 1910s to the 2000s. The house at 5795 Main is from 1948, 5705 is from 1918, 5495 is from 1950, 5490 is from 1961, and 5455 is from 1930.

16 From Main, turn right on SW 8th Street. A cow, chickens, and a kitchen garden likely shared the land with a tiny cottage from 1910 at 12770 8th, in what was once rural Oregon.

At the intersection of 8th and SW Watson Avenue is a 1922 bungalow with a cute little shed dormer. Across from it is Memorial Park, a good place to sit. Take your pick of one of eleven picnic tables in this small park that honors war heroes and victims.

From the park, walk north on Watson.

17 From Watson, cross SW 5th Street to enter City Park, built in the late 1990s during a bout of urban renewal. A fountain filled with kids in the summer, nice lawns, restrooms, and a snack kiosk make it a great place to people-watch.

Walk east through the park to SW Hall Boulevard. The Beaverton City Library, opened in 2000, anchors the south end of downtown, at 5th and Hall. Across from it, on Hall, the Beaverton Farmers Market occupies the parking lot between 5th and 3rd.

The library is a beauty, worth a visit inside. It was designed by Thomas Hacker and Associates of Portland, a firm responsible for just about every new library within the Multnomah County Library system, from Hollywood to Midland to Hillsdale, plus renovations at other branches. On the second floor, sixteen graceful "trees" made of glue-laminated beams support the clear vertical grain fir ceiling, an effect inspired by the historic American sycamore in the library's front lawn. Clerestory windows let in such abundant natural light that lamps seem superfluous even on a cloudy day. On a gray October day, while I was enthusing about the beauty, one friendly librarian toned me down a bit by advising me to come back on a sunny afternoon between 4:00 and 6:00 p.m. or so and see how nice it is to work with the sun glaring through the windows. "It's so bad that we all wear sunglasses," she said. "And do you see that recycling bin over there? I put it on my desk and hide behind it so I can see my computer screen." Even with refuse bins on the desks, it's still a vast improvement over the grocery store library it replaced.

Before you leave the library, note the ceramic wall in the foyer. Each of the 455 tiles weighs 10 pounds. The installation is the work of Jun Kaneko.

18 From the library at Hall and 5th, walk north on Hall. At SW 2nd Street is a coffee shop in an old gas station.

19 From Hall, turn left on SW Broadway Street. In the northeast corner is the Beaverton Bakery, in business under various names since 1925 when it first began turning white flour and sugar into treats. It is housed in an 1887 home built by the town's first doctor, Francis Marion Robinson. In 1893 Robinson had a pharmacy built next to his home. The bakery also uses the 1925 Beaver Theatre next door, where traveling stage shows once played.

The Fisher Building, 12440 to 12580 Broadway, was built in 1916. Designed for stores on the main level and professional offices above, it is dilapidated but has great bones: three gabled porch stoops, nine storefronts with transom windows (now covered), and an elegant brick façade. Across from it is the Rossi Building from 1926. Its east side is decorated with cute beavers and their sticks in bas-relief.

20 From Broadway, turn right on Watson to return to the starting point.

8/3/11 PR

WALK 17

FOREST GROVE LOOP

DISTANCE 4.1 miles

STARTING POINT Old College Hall at Pacific University, on College Way just north of Pacific Avenue

GETTING THERE AND PARKING Forest Grove is about 23 miles west of Portland. From downtown Portland, drive west on Highway 8, Canyon Road, which becomes the Tualatin Valley (TV) Highway in Beaverton. Follow the TV Highway through Hillsboro and Cornelius before entering Forest Grove, where it becomes Pacific Avenue. From the intersection of Highway 47, drive 1 mile on Pacific to Cedar Street, the east edge of the Pacific University campus. Either park on Cedar or drive to streets along the west edge of campus and park along 22nd Avenue, between A and Main Streets, where up to four hours are allowed; or on A Street north of 21st Avenue.

TriMet: Bus 57 (TV Highway/Forest Grove) runs every fifteen minutes from the Beaverton Transit Center, which is on the MAX Blue and Red Line. Get off the bus at Pacific Avenue and Council Street/College Way. Walk half a block north on College Way to the starting point.

RESTROOMS AND DRINKING FOUNTAINS Restrooms can be found at the Pacific University Library (just inside the doors), in Rogers Park (an ADA-compliant portable toilet), and at coffee shops and restaurants in downtown Forest Grove (for customers). Drinking fountains are inside the Pacific University Library, 2020 Main Street, and at Rogers Park.

FOOD AND DRINK Restaurants are centered on Main Street between Pacific and 21st Avenues, and on 21st Avenue in the blocks west of College Way.

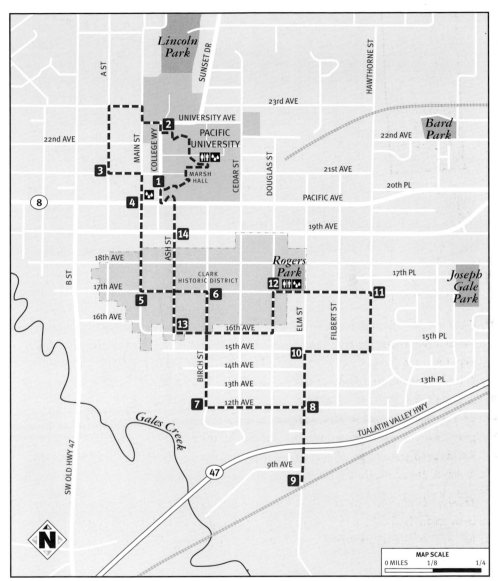

Lincoln
Park

A ST

SUNSET DR

HAWTHORNE ST

23rd AVE

22nd AVE

MAIN ST

COLLEGE WY

2

UNIVERSITY AVE

**PACIFIC
UNIVERSITY**

22nd AVE

Bard
Park

3

1

MARSH
HALL

CEDAR ST

DOUGLAS ST

21st AVE

20th PL

8

4

PACIFIC AVE

19th AVE

14

ASH ST

18th AVE

B ST

17th AVE

16th AVE

CLARK
HISTORIC DISTRICT

Rogers
Park

12

17th PL

Joseph
Gale
Park

5

6

11

13

ELM ST

FILBERT ST

15th PL

16th AVE

15th AVE

14th AVE

13th AVE

BIRCH ST

10

13th PL

7

12th AVE

8

TUALATIN VALLEY HWY

Gales Creek

SW OLD HWY 47

47

9th AVE

9

N

MAP SCALE
0 MILES   1/8   1/4

WALK 17. *Forest Grove Loop*

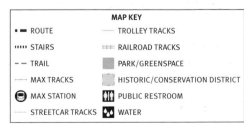

MAP KEY

- ▪▪ ROUTE
- ⁞⁞⁞⁞ STAIRS
- – – TRAIL
- ⸱⸱⸱ MAX TRACKS
- 🚇 MAX STATION
- ⸱⸱⸱ STREETCAR TRACKS

- ⸱⸱⸱⸱⸱ TROLLEY TRACKS
- ╫╫ RAILROAD TRACKS
- ▓ PARK/GREENSPACE
- ░ HISTORIC/CONSERVATION DISTRICT
- 🚻 PUBLIC RESTROOM
- 💧 WATER

BEST TIMES TO VISIT Complement a trip to Forest Grove with a visit to nearby wine country. Contact the Convention and Visitors Bureau of Washington County at 503-644-5555 or www.countrysideofportland.org/visitors/wine-home.php for a list and map of county wineries.

To combine the walk with a tour at the SakéOne saké brewery, call 503-357-7056. It is on the route at **9**.

Old College Hall at Pacific University is open the first Wednesday of each month for afternoon tours.

For more details on this historic town, contact Friends of Historic Forest Grove at 503-992-1280 or www.historicforestgrove.org.

ACCESSIBILITY This walk is quite flat, with only 30 feet of elevation change, on sidewalks and streets. It is of normal accessibility, except for a crossing of Highway 47, where traffic passes at 55 miles per hour and there are no pedestrian amenities. Sight distance is good; but this crossing should be undertaken only if you feel confident of your ability to assess oncoming traffic and quickly cross a four-lane highway. To avoid this stretch, follow directions given in the text.

THE WALK STARTS at Pacific University, the school to which Forest Grove owes its existence. In 1842 in Glencoe, a small settlement north of present-day Forest Grove, a school for Native American children was founded by Reverend Harvey Clark and his wife, Emeline. Within a few years the Clarks moved, taking a donation land claim in what is now Forest Grove. They built a log cabin on it, and Harvey Clark became the pastor of the First Congregational Church, housed in another log cabin located on what is now the university campus.

Soon after, in 1846, Tabitha Brown arrived in Oregon. She and Harvey Clark pooled their humanitarian interests: she wanted to create an orphanage for the many children whose parents had died while making the overland trek to Oregon; he wanted to establish another school. Together they founded the Orphan Asylum in 1847. Its pupil base quickly broadened to include children left behind during the California gold rush of 1848 and 1849.

In 1848 Reverend George Atkinson, also with education on his mind, joined forces with Clark and Brown "to found an Academy which should grow into a College" in the New England model. And so, in 1849, the Orphan Asylum became the Tualatin Academy. A few years later it did grow into a college, and in 1854 was renamed Tualatin Academy and Pacific University. In 1915 the academy (a high school) closed and Pacific University stood alone.

1 Begin at Old College Hall, the cream-colored wooden Classical Revival building bordering College Way. Built in 1851 for the Tualatin Academy, it is reputedly the oldest building in continuous educational use in the Northwest. It was the first frame building erected on the Tualatin Plains, built at a time when log cabins were the best most people could do. It has been moved three times, the last in the early 2000s to make way for the new campus library.

From the campus side of Old College Hall, look right to the brick Carnegie Hall, built in 1912. It is a relatively rare breed: one of only about one hundred Carnegie libraries built for college rather than for municipal use. It was retired in 1967 when the Harvey Scott Memorial Library was built (itself superseded in 2005).

From Carnegie Hall walk diagonally toward the great brick building, Marsh Hall, the original site of Old College Hall. It is located at the intersection of three donation land claims. Along the way, look left to see a petrified stump sitting in the grass. It marks the site of the log cabin Harvey Clark built as a school and church. This area of lawn was once a graveyard. Clark himself was buried here, but in the 1870s the bodies in the graveyard were exhumed and moved to Mountain View Cemetery.

Marsh Hall was designed by Whidden and Lewis in 1895, about the same time they designed Portland's City Hall. It was named for Pacific's first president, the Reverend Sidney Marsh, who served from 1854 to 1879. It burned in 1975, and the inside was completely rebuilt within the shell. The exterior stonework is from a quarry in Gaston, which also furnished the stone for downtown Portland's Pioneer Courthouse. Inside are administrative offices and functions.

From in front of Marsh Hall, continue on the diagonal sidewalk and then turn right to walk on Marsh's north side, following the sidewalk that runs east. Behind Marsh are beautiful old oaks. On the left is the Pacific University Library, built in 2005.

Walk the sidewalk along the library, and then turn left to enter it at its east doors. Inside is a collection of art ranging from woodblock prints to sculpture to illuminated texts. The cathedral-like building was designed by Fletcher Farr Ayotte of Portland. It displaced not only Old College Hall but also many old Oregon white oaks. The felled trees were turned into organically shaped chairs and tables set in conversation areas around the library. Go upstairs to the mezzanine beyond a wall of multicolored cast glass to a spectacular reading area. A wall of clear glass practically brings the century-old oak grove outside into the

The Pacific University campus, circa 1900. Marsh Hall is on the left; Old College Hall sits behind it. The building on the right has since been demolished. Note the absence of trees on what is today a deeply shaded campus. Photo courtesy of the Pacific University Archives.

building. The cast glass is by Walter Gordinier, a Portland artist and Pacific alumnus. Libraries like this make certain sorts of hearts skip a beat.

Exit the library not by the doors you entered but by the west doors. Ahead is Trombley Square, the center of the campus. On its west side sits Scott Hall, named for Harvey Scott, the first graduate of Pacific University in 1863. After fighting Indians during the winter of 1855 to 1856, Scott trekked on foot from his family's home on Puget Sound to Forest Grove to get an education. He later went on to a forty-year run as editor of the *Oregonian*. Scott Hall was the library from 1967 to 2005.

The north edge of the square borders a roadway lined with birches. For years this was the official entrance to the campus, but many of the birches were lost in the 1962 Columbus Day storm. Also nearby are trees of epic proportions—giant sequoias planted in the 1880s. You'll see sequoias scattered around Forest Grove; their planting is attributed to John Porter, a nurseryman who first brought the seeds up from the tree's native California.

From the square, walk north. On the right is Washburne Hall, built in 1964 as the University Center, where students get mail, food, books, and other vital elements of college life. Walk along its west side. North of Washburne is a depression with a sand volleyball pit in it. This was the site of two former gymnasiums built in 1895 and 1910.

From Washburne, veer into the lawn in front of McCormick Hall, built in 1924 as a men's residence hall. During World War II it was referred to as The Hall of Vanishing Men; by 1944 only fourteen men were left on campus.

The buildings all around are residence halls. Walk west to College Way. Ahead is Knight Hall, an 1879 Queen Anne built for President Marsh's family but not finished until after his death. His wife and children lived there for years afterward.

2 From the west side of McCormick Hall, turn right on College Way, left on University Avenue, right on Main Street, left on 23rd Avenue, and finally left on A Street. The homes at 2250 and 2240 A Street are both old, with well-integrated two-story additions. The home at 2240 dates from 1905 and was designed in the Greek Revival style.

At 2125 is the 1895 Harry Crosley house, a splendid Queen Anne with lots of Stick-style detail and great landscaping. Next to it at 2117 is the Blank House, a stagecoach stop on the stage that ran from Tillamook to Portland beginning in 1870. Built in 1859, it is one of four remaining structures in town from the 1850s. Note the second story; the house is just one room deep.

3 From A, turn left onto 21st Avenue, where shops invite browsing, and from 21st, turn right onto Main Street. Walk down the east side of Main for the best views of the old brick buildings on the street's west side. All date from the early 1890s, when the city formed a "Fire Control District" downtown; its goal was to convert all wood-frame buildings to brick after fires had destroyed many such buildings downtown. This block of intact brick buildings, most of them restored, dates from that decade. At 2036 is the nicely restored Ingalls Porter building from 1891. At 2020 is Woods and Caples, a dry goods and general merchandise store built in 1893; the large bay windows on the second floor give it a bit of a residential look, charming on a commercial building.

Don't miss the pedal-operated water fountain midway down the block's west side; the water sounds as if it's being drawn up from a well beneath your feet. It was made by Murdock Manufacturing, which still manufactures water fountains at its Cincinnati plant, run by the fifth generation of the Murdock family.

The east side of the block is a different story. Undeveloped for years, it was the town square, along the lines of a New England small town. The land was owned by the Congregational Church until 1912, when the church sold it to raise funds. Buildings on the east side, then, date from after that period. Most notable is the Holbrook Masonic Lodge at 2019, built in 1925.

4 On Main, come to Pacific Avenue. In the northwest corner is the First National Bank of Oregon; it was built around 1910 and lasted until 1937. In the southeast corner is an intriguing brick building. Built in 1898, it replaced a wood-frame livery building from the 1880s. Extensive renovations that changed its character led to it being denied status on the National Register of Historic Places, but it is still attractive.

On Main, cross 19th Avenue. Midway down the block the route enters the Clark Historic District, created in 2002. The area is named after Harvey and Emeline Clark, who donated the land to the Tualatin Academy in 1849, intending for the school to use the property as an endowment. Clark platted the land into 1-acre lots, and the school sold the lots as needed to raise funds. The plat was named Forest Grove in 1851. In this beautiful district are homes built for owners across the occupational and economic strata of Forest Grove life, with most built between the 1850s and 1950s. Look for old farmhouses; many of them have been added on to over the years as family fortunes improved.

Come to 18th Avenue. At 2011 18th (a few steps east of Main) is the circa-1865 Smith-Schofield House, a bit of an odd take on the Second Empire style; it's the only remaining example of this style in Forest Grove.

Back on Main at 18th is the Central School. A school has operated at this location since 1855, with a new school replacing the original in 1885. Later, in 1911, the city's first high school seniors graduated from here; and in 1915, with the new public high school in place, the Tualatin Academy closed. In 1930 the 1885 building was demolished and the current building erected. The school was filled with children until the 1993 Spring Break Quake, an earthquake centered in Scotts Mills that measured 5.6 on the Richter scale. After the quake the building was no longer deemed safe for students; it was renovated and turned into district offices.

Across the street are homes that date from the 1880s onward. Continue south on Main. At the northeast corner of 17th Avenue and Main is a 1905 house with an intriguing convex jerkinhead roof (a roof with a sloping end truncating a gable). It was reputedly condemned in 1977 but has been restored.

5 From Main, turn left onto 17th, where a huge plane tree dominates one corner. This block is a lovely mix of homes to enjoy.

At 2126 17th is an 1872 farmhouse built by Thomas and Mary Ann Roe. They came to Forest Grove to educate their sons at Pacific University, and pur-

A farmhouse-style home under some of the many oaks in the Clark Historic District.

chased 500 acres of land near town to raise hay, horses, and cattle. One of their children, Charles, was an undertaker; in 1897 he built the house west of his parents' home, at 2120 17th.

6 From 17th, come to Birch Street. At the southeast corner of 17th and Birch (1653 Birch) is the Rasmussen-Price House. Jenny Rasmussen, once upon a time, fell in love with a young Pacific University math teacher who boarded at her parent's house. They got married, and her father built them this house in 1905.

Before turning right on Birch, don't miss the home at 2220 17th, a very inventive renovation. Now head south on Birch. In the northwest corner of Birch and 16th Avenue is the 1859 Hines House, the oldest in the historic district. Thomas and Mary Hines were among the earliest settlers in the Tualatin Valley, arriving in 1848. Thomas left for the gold rush but came back. In 1858 he bought 420 acres in Forest Grove and built this house so that his children could live in town, a not-uncommon situation. The house was moved from 12th Avenue in the 1880s. Thomas and Mary lived here until around 1900.

Streets here are wonderfully peaceful, a pleasant change from more bustling Portland neighborhoods. The Oregon white oaks are thick and form canopies over individual houses and entire streets. (See Walk 16 for information on this native tree.) The house at 1503 is unusual for the neighborhood, a 1939 Art Moderne with clean horizontal lines.

Continue south on Birch. At 1306 the sidewalk ends, but the streets are quiet enough for safe walking. At 13th's dead end is a wonderful view of the flood-plain of Gales Creek, a mile or so above its confluence with the Tualatin, the meandering river for which the vast fertile valley between the Coast Range and the Tualatin Mountains is named. Gales Creek rises in the Coast Range directly to the west. Its tributary, Clear Creek, supplies about half of Forest Grove's water, with the rest coming from the Scoggins Reservoir (also known as Hagg Lake) and Barney Reservoir.

7 From Birch, turn left onto 12th Avenue, once the south edge of town. At 2206 is a large Craftsman. When it was built in 1916, its owners enjoyed a 180-degree view of the valley below it, before newer subdivisions went in and the new route for Highway 47 carved through the once-quiet bottomland. This area overlooking the farmlands is called Knob Hill.

At 2225 12th is a Queen Anne mansion built in 1888 by a wealthy Portlander, A. I. Macrum, who commuted to Forest Grove by train. In the 1890s two passenger trains and one freight train ran daily from Forest Grove to Portland. During World War I this home was used as a hospital. It is oriented to the east, its former front yard now occupied by a much newer home.

8 On 12th, come to Elm Street. To visit the SakéOne sakéry and the old Carnation settlement, turn right on Elm. (If you want to avoid walking across Highway 47, turn left on Elm and rejoin the walk at Elm and 15th, **10**.) Walk two blocks and carefully cross Highway 47.

9 Come to SakéOne at 820 Elm. It was founded by Grif Frost in 1992 in part-nership with Momokawa Brewing of Japan, a saké producer since 1856. Saké, or rice wine, has been around for sixty-eight hundred years and is made from four ingredients: excellent water, rice, yeast, and an enzyme-producing mold called *koji-an*. Saké is like beer, best drunk when fresh, and unlike wine, it has no sulfites. After aging three to six months, it has a 21 percent alcohol content but is diluted with water to finish at 15 percent. According to Frost, who left SakéOne in 2001 but remains a saké guru, one out of every three glasses of wine lifted in the world is saké. The company started as an importer and soon became a brewer, adopting the name SakéOne in 1998. There are only a handful of sakéries in the United States, and SakéOne is the only one that is American owned.

The area beyond SakéOne looks barren, but it has a rich past. The rail tracks here were the first laid in the valley, part of a line started by Joseph Gaston in 1868 that brought Tualatin Valley products to Portland docks. The railroad wanted a Forest Grove station, but residents did not want to spend $30,000 to help finance it, so a station was located here at about 9th and Elm, south of the town site. Soon after, commerce surrounded the depot: a post office, general store, lumberyards, and a hotel. In 1902 Pacific Coast Condensed Milk Company of Kent, Washington, opened a milk condensery at the depot and began producing Carnation Condensed Milk, giving the area the name Carnation. From here, Carnation products were shipped across the United States. A streetcar carried passengers from downtown Forest Grove along Elm Street to the depot.

Carnation's prosperity was short lived, however. In 1908 the Oregon Electric Railway began service from Portland to Forest Grove. Its depot was at 19th and Ash, a more central location, and commerce around the Carnation depot dropped off steeply. In 1912 the Southern Pacific ran a line south and east with a station at 19th and Main, also in downtown Forest Grove. In 1929 the condensery was shut down, and Carnation became a footnote in Forest Grove's history.

From SakéOne, carefully recross Highway 47 and walk north on Elm for 0.3 mile. At Elm and 15th in the southeast corner is a plaque stating that Pacific University was founded here in 1842. According to Mary Jo Morelli, a Forest Grove historian who leads historic walking tours, the site is where Harvey Clark built his own home, a log cabin. The cabin built for his school was on today's campus. Across the street at 1504 Elm is the 1890 Barnes home, a Queen Anne with a tower typical of that style.

10 From Elm, turn right on 15th; walk two blocks, and then turn left on Hawthorne Street. This area of newer homes is less remarkable but still peaceful and pleasant. The payoff comes at 1651 Hawthorne, an 1878 Italianate home owned by Alanson Hinman, an Oregon Trail pioneer and Tualatin Academy trustee. It has not one but five giant sequoias towering over it. These giants, planted in the 1880s, are virtual infants compared to the oldest-known specimen, which has been growing in California for thirty-two hundred years.

11 From Hawthorne, turn left on 17th Avenue. In one block, on the left at 2606 17th, is another very old home, the James D. Robb House built in 1875. Robb was a principal of Tualatin Academy and superintendent of Washington County Schools. The home later belonged to suffragist Samantha Coleman.

Walk one more block to Elm. On the right is Rogers Park. George Rogers was a dentist and collector of fine porcelain (he is not the George Rogers of the eponymous park in Lake Oswego, seen in Walk 18); Adeline Fiske Rogers was a philanthropist. When they moved to Oregon in 1888, they were quite wealthy and in 1890 built a large Italianate home in the middle of this block, in a grove of mature Oregon white oaks. Kids played on the grounds and it became an unofficial park.

George died in 1900, and Adeline lived in the house until 1922. The Rogers home sat vacant until the 1930s, when new owners deconstructed it and used the materials in a new home on C Street. During World War II, a trailer park was erected in the Rogers block to house migrant workers who filled the void created when agricultural workers went to work in Portland shipyards or fight in the war. By 1950 the last trailer was hauled off, and soon the block was purchased by the city as a park.

The grove of white oaks is of ornithological interest: it is home to one of the country's two northernmost colonies of acorn woodpeckers (*Melanerpes formicivorus*). The other colony is in the Columbia Gorge. According to the Tualatin Riverkeepers, this little redhead is easy to spot, being a late riser who can still be found working at midday. Look for a woodpecker with a red cap, black back and tail, white sides and rump, and white spots on the undersides of its wings.

12 From 17th, turn left onto Douglas Street. Walk one block, passing tiny farmhouses at 1629 and 1623, and one at 1617 that dates from 1890.

From Douglas, turn right onto 16th Avenue, a gorgeous street. Follow 16th three blocks to Ash Street.

13 From 16th, turn right onto Ash. On the corner, at 1603, is a nice bungalow in a grove of oaks. Note the house at 1622; Les AuCoin lived here during the 1970s after his election to the U.S. House of Representatives.

At 1636 is a vernacular farmhouse from 1892 with a great purple beech in the side yard. At the southeast corner of 17th and Ash is a farmhouse with its many later additions clearly visible. The home at 1724 is a well-blended mix of styles: a Queen Anne with Stick-style details and Craftsman porch.

14 At Ash and 19th Avenue is the site of the 1908 depot for the Oregon Electric Railway. (Part of its line can be seen on Walk 15.)

Cross Pacific Avenue and walk into the campus. The building to the left is the Tabitha Brown Hall, home of the art department. Like the building on the right, Warner Hall, it is a World War II salvage item, moved here after the war from Camp Adair, an infantry training camp near Corvallis. In 1950, both buildings were sided with bricks.

The labyrinth and Old College Hall at Pacific University.

Between Brown and Warner Halls is a large rock, a memorial dedicated in 1949 to the pioneer women of the Oregon Country. Compared to all the statues honoring men in the world, this chunk of raw, common rock honoring women of such immense bravery and endurance is either a masterful bit of understatement, a sign of a less prosperous era, or a mark of how little women's contributions were valued. A more thoughtful tribute to pioneer women is the statue in Vancouver's Esther Short Park (seen in Walk 20).

From the rock, turn and walk along Carnegie Hall, and then turn left in front of it. Ahead is a peaceful spot, a labyrinth and garden dedicated to Faith Gabelnick, a Pacific University president. Walking a labyrinth has become, in the last few decades, a practice used to reduce stress, provide reflection, or replenish energy. Labyrinths differ from mazes in that with a labyrinth the path is clearly seen to the walker, and there is only one path to the center, with no false dead ends. In the Middle Ages, when the Crusades made a pilgrimage to Jerusalem a dangerous proposition, labyrinths in cathedrals enabled pilgrims to symbolically enact the journey.

The labyrinth is adjacent to Old College Hall, and here the walk ends.

WALK 18

LAKE OSWEGO LOOP

DISTANCE   5.3 miles

STARTING POINT   George Rogers Park, along the Willamette River at Oswego Creek, next to the stone furnace stack

GETTING THERE AND PARKING   Lake Oswego is about 8 miles from Portland. From downtown Portland, drive south on Macadam Avenue (Highway 43) along the Willamette River. Once beyond the Sellwood Bridge turnoff, the road is wooded for about 3 miles until it runs into Lake Oswego, where it is called State Street. On State Street, turn left at the fifth stoplight, Wilbur Street. (Caution: On the right, this street is labeled Middlecrest Road.) Drive to Wilbur's end at Furnace Street. Turn right on Furnace and drive to the parking lot at George Rogers Park. From there, walk to the starting point.

Alternatively, take the Willamette Shore Trolley from Portland (a forty-minute ride), which arrives in Lake Oswego at State Street and A Avenue. To get to the starting point, walk down State Street to Wilbur, and follow the directions above. For fare information and dates and hours of operation, visit trainweb.org/oerhs or call 503-697-7436.

TriMet: Take bus 35 (Macadam) or bus 36 (South Shore) to the stop at State Street and Wilbur Street. Walk east on Wilbur to Furnace, turn right, and walk south into the park and to the starting point.

RESTROOMS AND DRINKING FOUNTAINS   Restrooms and drinking fountains are at George Rogers Park (on the river side of the stone furnace stack), Lake Oswego Public Library (4th Street and D Avenue, during library hours), and Millennium Plaza Park. The many restaurants and coffee shops along the route have facilities for customers.

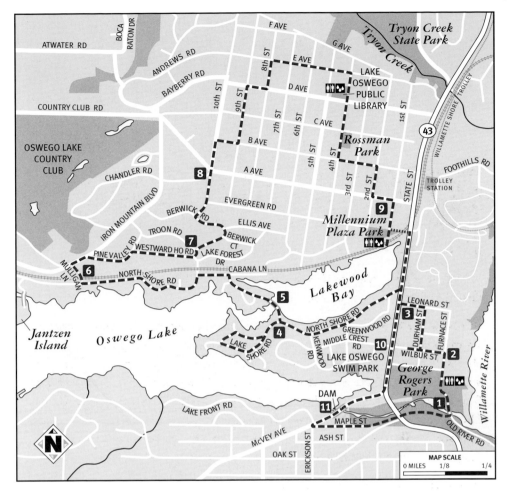

WALK 18. *Lake Oswego Loop*

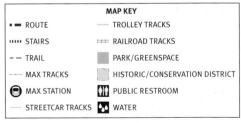

MAP KEY

- ■■ ROUTE
- ⋯⋯ STAIRS
- – – TRAIL
- ⋯⋯ MAX TRACKS
- 🚏 MAX STATION
- ⋯⋯ STREETCAR TRACKS
- ⋯⋯ TROLLEY TRACKS
- ╠═╣ RAILROAD TRACKS
- ▉ PARK/GREENSPACE
- ▉ HISTORIC/CONSERVATION DISTRICT
- 🚻 PUBLIC RESTROOM
- 💧 WATER

FOOD AND DRINK   Near the start of the walk are various options at State and Leonard Streets. More restaurants cluster near the end of the walk, in an area centered on A Avenue and 1st and State Streets.

BEST TIMES TO VISIT   Lake Oswego Farmers Market is held in Millennium Plaza Park, 1st Street and Evergreen Road, on Saturdays from May through October; see www.ci.oswego.or.us/farmersmarket for more information. Many other events and concerts are held at Millennium Plaza Park as well; see www.ci.oswego.or.us/parksrec.

ACCESSIBILITY   Elevations range from 10 feet at the mouth of Oswego Creek near the start of the walk to 230 feet in the First Addition neighborhood (**8** to **9**). Some streets have no sidewalks, and extra care is needed on them. A forest trail at **11** can be avoided by following directions at **10**.

LAKE OSWEGO is one of the state's wealthiest towns. Spending a day here— walking the lakeside neighborhoods hidden under tall firs, and then doing a bit of shopping and eating—feels like a mini-vacation.

The city was born as Oswego in 1850, platted out by Albert Durham, who held a donation land claim. His claim included Oswego Creek, a creek that dropped 100 feet in 0.3 mile, making it a good mill site. At that time the creek and the lake it drained went by the name Sucker. Durham named his claim Oswego after his New York home town, and built the first dam on the lake, raising its level to generate power for his creekside sawmill, box shuck, and flour mill, thereby initiating Lake Oswego's first land-use dispute; he was sued by farmers at the west end of the lake for flooding their fields. The site of this first dam is seen later on the walk. Durham did well with his mill and invested his profits in riverboats. He built a large home at the top of the bluff overlooking the Willamette (at today's Church and Furnace Streets), with a fine view of ship traffic. In 1864 Durham's sawmill was bought by John Trullinger, who began milling wood for Portland sidewalks, and Durham moved to the eponymous area near Tigard.

After Durham left, the town began to thrive by extracting another resource. A low-grade ore had been discovered at what is now the Oswego Lake Country Club along Iron Mountain Boulevard. In the early 1860s, Portland financiers looking for a local source of iron tested the ore; on finding it good, they formed the Oregon Iron Company in 1865 with the hope of making Oswego the "Pittsburgh of the West." The first charcoal iron smelter, whose furnace is the starting point of the walk, went into production in 1867. Within a decade the company encountered problems as Scottish pig iron could be had for less cost. In 1877 Oregon Iron was sold at auction, and the old furnace was already considered primitive. The successor company, Oregon Iron and Steel, built a new, larger iron smelter on today's Oswego Pointe site starting in 1883; later, in 1888, the company built a pipe foundry to provide pipe for Portland's Bull Run water system, then in the early stages of planning.

From the 1860s to the 1890s the timber around Sucker Lake was felled and burned for charcoal to fire the furnace, leaving the lake perimeter a mess of stumps. Up until 1900, the lake had no value to Oregon Iron and Steel except as a source of power.

At its iron-age peak in 1890, Oswego was booming, with three areas of settlement: Old Town, First Addition (then called New Town), and South Town. All are on the route. The boom didn't last. In 1894 the smelter ceased operations, since iron from the East Coast could be shipped to the Northwest more cheaply than it could be produced here.

Up until then the lake had been unappreciated and unused except by local children. In 1900 the Nelson family began getting requests from fishermen to use the boats its children had brought to the lake. The enterprising Nelsons began a boat rental business. Soon Portlanders discovered the pleasures of a Sunday outing to Sucker Lake to go fishing, picnicking, and swimming.

A light went on in the corporate brain of Oregon Iron and Steel. Around 1905 it began a 13,000-acre facelift of its scrubby hillside and stump-rimmed lake. The company raised the lake level with a new dam to submerge the stumps and create more high-value lake frontage, and sold large tracts to developers. In 1912 Oregon Iron and Steel petitioned the U.S. Geographic Board to change the lake's name to the more enticing Oswego Lake. Paul Murphy, later known as Mr. Oswego, had developed Laurelhurst in 1909, and in 1912 purchased large tracts of land in Oswego from the Ladd Estate Company, which had acquired control when Oregon Iron and Steel defaulted on loans owed to Ladd banking interests.

In keeping with the residential park style then in vogue, Murphy platted out a country club, the center of a "country club district." Like Laurelhurst, streets curved with the topography, and restrictions were set in place against commercial venues and nonwhite residents. Murphy encouraged noted architects to design homes in romantic styles such as Arts and Crafts, Tudor, and English Cottage. In 1914 the rail line to Portland was electrified, turning Oswego into a streetcar suburb, a place where you could "live where you play." Development boomed from that point on; in 1920 sixty-four trains each day made it easy for Oswego residents to work in Portland and live in a parklike setting. Construction of new homes continued even during the Depression. In 1960 Oswego merged with Lake Grove, a community at the west end of the lake, and took the name Lake Oswego.

In 2006, Lake Oswego had thirty-six thousand residents.

1 Begin the walk at the archway in George Rogers Park. In front of you is a 13,000-pound salamander, a term for a mass of solid iron that accumulates at the bottom of blast furnaces when molten metal escapes through the hearth. Its name derives from the mythical salamander, a creature that makes its homes in fires. Salamanders had to be removed from the furnace when their growing size began to impede air flow.

On the left is the blast furnace stack from 1867, built of basalt hewn from the site. To produce a ton of iron, 166 bushels of charcoal, 4970 pounds of ore, and 884 pounds of limestone were poured into the stack. It was called a 10-ton stack because it could produce 10 tons of iron in one day. In 1878, in an attempt to make the furnace more economically viable, 10 feet were added to the top; the cruder rockwork was completed by a less skilled craftsman than the earlier work.

The furnace stack's arch influenced the design of the arbor at the park's entrance as well as the barbecue picnic ovens, each a miniature furnace stack made from iron slag recovered from the area. Slag is a term for impurities of iron ore that are separated out from the molten metal. It has commercial purposes, from road-surfacing to railroad track ballast to fertilizer.

From the salamander, walk uphill to a "do not enter" sign at the north end of the parking lot, and on to Furnace Street. This is Old Town, the first area of settlement in Oswego, platted by John Trullinger in 1867 as he anticipated an influx of residents to work at the new blast furnace. Street names are either self-explanatory (Furnace) or in honor of the owners or operators of the Oregon Iron Company. At the intersection of Furnace and Ladd Street, the town site's first school was built in the early 1850s. Furnace was once the most socially desirable street in town, with its bluff-top location along the Willamette.

2 From Furnace, turn left on Wilbur Street. Cross Durham Street, the main street of early-day Oswego, and the early town's social delineator (east of Durham were homes of merchants and professionals, west were homes of laborers). In the northwest corner is the 1929 home of George Rogers. It was designed in an unusual combination of Mediterranean and Arts and Crafts styles by Van Evera Bailey, later one of the creators of the Northwest Regional style. The driveway

The iron furnace chimney as it appeared around 1908, two decades after the smelter ceased operations, in an area that is now George Rogers Park. The streets of Old Town are visible in the background. Oswego Creek is on the left. Note the covered bridge over the creek. Photo courtesy of the Lake Oswego Public Library.

bricks and lower half were salvaged from the 1888 furnace plant. Rogers, born Jorge Rodrigues on Portugal's Madeira Island, was devoted to rehabilitating the old furnace property along Oswego Creek. He died in 1961, and the park's name honors his efforts.

At 40 Wilbur is a tiny 1900 cottage. Earlier worker homes, built in the 1860s and 1870s, once lined Wilbur but are gone now. By the time this cottage was built, the iron industry had left town.

Backtrack to the corner of Wilbur and Durham Streets and turn left (north) on Durham. At Church Street is the 1890 Odd Fellows Hall, a center of early Oswego life; people rowed across the Willamette from Oak Grove and traversed muddy roads on Monday nights for meetings. It operated until 1975, when membership was low enough that the building was sold. In 1990 the hall was restored and is now apartments.

Walk two blocks further on Durham Street and turn left on Leonard Street, where the Old Town neighborhood ends.

A workman's cottage in Lake Oswego's Old Town neighborhood.

3 From Leonard, turn right on State Street. On the right are some chain restaurants and coffee shops, their usual gaudy signs toned down to a tasteful Lake Oswego level. Walk a few steps north on State Street to North Shore Road.

Cross State Street at the stoplight to follow North Shore and enter the Lakewood area. At this point North Shore is misnamed, as it runs along the water's south shore, but it will soon cross the lake and run along the correct side. North Shore has no sidewalk but can be safely walked if you pay attention, face traffic, and don't get too caught up ogling the views.

The body of water on the right was originally a swamp called the Duck Pond. It was separate from the main lake and was mined for its clay from the 1880s to 1925. The clay was used in the making of molds for pipe at the foundry. In the 1920s the Ladd Estate Company was selling Oswego lots as fast as it could plat out the land. To capitalize on the demand, the company dug a channel in 1928 between the Duck Pond and the main lake, thereby flooding the pond, erasing its ugly potholes and swampy smells, and instantly creating hundreds more lakefront lots on the renamed Lakewood Bay. In late 2006 in a periodic lowering of the lake so homeowners can perform maintenance on docks, Lakewood Bay looked like a mucky swamp again, with virtually all the water drained away.

The homes along the bay are generally older than they appear; the house at 179 dates from 1955, and 201, 207, and 217 date from 1954. The house across the street at 364 is older, from 1930.

At about Kenwood Road, leave the Pleistocene-era flood deposits of the Missoula Floods to walk on basalt laid down fourteen million years ago.

4 From North Shore Road, turn left onto Lake Shore Road, which leads to a peninsula jutting into the main lake. Where Lake Shore forks, stay right. The homes on this valuable peninsula fit together like pieces of a jigsaw puzzle and are a mix of ages and styles: from elegant, smaller, older homes to newer, larger homes that maximize every inch of airspace their lot lines allow, in what I call the "because I can" effect. Meander down the lovely dead ends of North Point, West Point, and South View Roads before completing the Lake Shore loop.

As you rejoin North Shore, turn left onto it, and then stop on the small causeway that separates Oswego Lake from Lakewood Bay. Here is the channel dug in 1928 to flood the Duck Pond. Views are wonderful from this vantage point.

The lake is a natural body of water enhanced in size by a manmade dam. After the first dam in 1850, subsequent dams raised the level higher. One other factor came into play to increase the lake's size. In the 1860s the Tualatin River Navigation and Manufacturing Company began working to craft a continuous waterway from the farms of the Tualatin Valley to Portland docks. Though it seems hard to believe, steamboats once plied the shallow and winding Tualatin as far west as Forest Grove. Until rail lines went in, the river was a viable transportation option at a time when roads were difficult to build and nearly impossible to maintain. In 1872 Chinese laborers hand-dug a canal through the basalt from the Tualatin River to the west end of Sucker Lake. This new source of

Homes along Oswego Lake.

water from the Tualatin combined with a new, higher dam raised the lake level significantly, increasing it from 2.75 to 3.5 miles in circumference.

The original lake bed is an ancient channel of the Tualatin River. By the time of the Missoula Floods, the Tualatin had moved south to its present location, and the floodwaters scoured out and deepened the old channel. When the flood retreated, the water was impounded in the depression now known as Oswego Lake. The maximum depth of the lake is 55 feet.

The lake is a private waterway managed by the Lake Oswego Corporation (also known as the Lake Corp), formed in 1941 to control the lake and protect the interests of lakefront property owners. Not only is the lake's shoreline off limits to anyone not owning shares in the corporation; the water itself is too, except for two public swimming areas.

Originally pure, Oswego Lake has suffered the effects of intense urbanization. Six hundred and ninety-four homes ring it, and its watershed captures pollutants that contribute to an algae problem so severe that the lake has at times been closed to swimmers. Hypolimnetic aeration, alum injection, aquatic weed harvesting, dredging, and surface debris skimming are means used to reduce algae-feeding nutrients and debris. The Tualatin had been blamed as the source of the excess nutrients; however, in 2006, even after the canal from the river had been closed for several years, algae problems continued. The 2006 lake drawdown was the first in which the Tualatin was not used to refill the lake, in hopes that rain and runoff from the lake's own, much smaller watershed would bring in fewer nutrients.

5 Come off the causeway and continue walking along North Shore. Just past the bridge on the left is an outcropping of native basalt.

At a T intersection with Berwick Road, turn left to stay on North Shore and walk by some of the most expensive real estate in Oregon. Homes vary from grand to surprisingly humble, with some retaining the charming feel of a summer cabin. Even with its algae problems, the lake is stunningly beautiful, as is the light it reflects; and the homes on the rocky shore tuck themselves into the woods in a generally understated way.

After 1308, views to the lake open up at the Forest Hills Easement, a swimming and picnicking area and boat dock for residents whose non-lakeside properties afford them the right to use the lake. The pleasant sight of the lifeguard station, swimming area, and sandbox is a bit unsettling when seen through a locked chain-link fence topped with barbed wire.

Continue on to the first road on the right, the unmarked Mulligan Lane. It is across from an impressive stone home at 1650. This home was built in 2000 on the site of the Charles Ertz house, a Tudor home the Ladd Estate Company used as its architectural showplace to entice new residents. It was torn down.

From North Shore, the route turns right at Mulligan, but you may want to continue to the end of North Shore, where you can see Jantzen Island at 1850. It was purchased during the Depression by Carl Jantzen of Jantzen Knitting Mills (the swimwear company). He built a medieval-themed home there.

6 From North Shore, turn right on Mulligan Lane. The parking lot on the left is an overflow lot for the Oswego Lake Country Club, just across Iron Mountain Boulevard.

From Mulligan, turn right on Iron Mountain, part of a system of scenic boulevards around the lake designed in 1913 and completed in the 1930s. Take the first right, at Pine Valley Road, a street of lakeside views and houses built in the Colonial and Northwest Regional styles.

From Pine Valley, turn right at Westward Ho Road. Here, at 1136 (from 1934) and 1139 (from 1932), are homes that illustrate the picturesque style that Paul Murphy and the Ladd Estate Company envisioned for the hills above the lake. Builders were encouraged to build homes in styles that incorporate natural elements to make a home a seamless, though highly refined, extension of its surroundings.

7 From Westward Ho, turn left at Berwick Road. Stay left as Berwick crosses Ellis Avenue. Here the route climbs the lower flanks of Iron Mountain, a 500-foot-high basalt peak. The basalt was laid down in a series of flows that originated in eastern Oregon. Between flows, vegetation grew in pockets and pools. As plants decomposed, the bogs turned to mulch and were compressed by subsequent basalt flows into hematite, creating beds of ore.

The homes at 162 and 184 Berwick are more examples of the picturesque style.

At a triangular patch, turn right off of Berwick onto 10th Street. At Chandler Road, keep right on 10th. On the left is the Oswego Heritage House, built in 1928 by Murphy and his partner as their office, located at the main entrance to the country club district.

8 Still on 10th, cross A Avenue at the stop sign. Ore was carried by rail down from Iron Mountain in a 2.6-mile line, following the approximate alignment of A Avenue. This is the First Addition neighborhood, called New Town when it was established in 1888. Oregon Iron and Steel platted it to provide housing to workers at its new iron smelter, located on the river due east of here. First Addition sits on flood deposits, whose more gentle topography permits a gridlike pattern to the streets in the neighborhood.

You may want to skip the directions below and let your instincts lead you through the peaceful and scenic streets of this neighborhood; if so, simply rejoin the walk at A Avenue and 1st Street (**9**).

From 10th, turn right on B Avenue, and then left on 9th Street. A 1920 Craftsman with a Prairie porch sits at 544 9th. From 9th, turn right on D Avenue, and left on 8th Street. Many small homes in this neighborhood have been torn down, with new homes built on their lots.

In 1867, two decades before First Addition was platted, charcoal pits pocked the Oswego landscape. To make the iron, trees were cut and burned in the pits to make charcoal. The process took weeks, with the potential to completely burn up a sixty-cord load of timber if you weren't vigilant or didn't know what you were doing. Charcoal burners were recruited from Ohio, and they taught locals the fine art. When it was first platted, 8th Street had pits along it.

From 8th, turn right on E Avenue. A few blocks north, behind G Avenue, is Tryon Creek, a year-round creek that flows from the Multnomah neighborhood of Portland into the Willamette at Lake Oswego.

From E, turn right on 4th Street. At the northeast corner is a home from the earliest days of New Town, the 1892 John F. Conway house. At the southeast corner is a home built in 1885, predating the neighborhood plat.

From 4th, turn left on B Avenue, where the commercial area begins, offering eating and shopping options. At the southeast corner of B and 2nd Street is a 1907 home. The hall on the second floor was used for community square dances.

From B, turn right on 2nd. Then turn left on A Avenue.

9 From A, turn right on 1st Street. On the left is Lakeview Village, a collection of shops and restaurants that opened in 2003. At the end of 1st is Millennium Plaza Park, scene of concerts and the Lake Oswego Farmers Market.

When you are ready to leave the park, take the stairs from the courtyard between the shops of Lakeview Village; they lead to State Street. (To avoid the stairs, retrace the route to A Avenue, turn right, and from A, turn right onto State Street to rejoin the walk.) Turn right. Just over the train tracks is a small park next to the Lakeshore Inn. Sixty-five-thousand-dollar bronze cattails are a visual deterrent to would-be waders.

Walk south along State Street past the Lake Twin Cinema, designed in 1940 by Richard Sundeleaf, who designed many Oswego homes. Boats could moor behind it while their owners took in a movie and dinner at a lakeside restaurant. At Middlecrest Road is the 1928 Oswego School. It closed in 1978 and has been reborn as the Lakewood Center for the Arts.

10 (This section of the walk contains an unregulated crossing, a busy road, and a rocky forest trail. To avoid these, return to the start by turning left onto Wilbur Street [across from Middlecrest] and then right onto Furnace Street, which leads to the starting point.)

For a view of the dam and creek that have been so vital to the city's history, continue south on State Street. Turn right at McVey Avenue, the next light after the Lakewood Center. Walk a short way to the Lake Oswego Corporation office. Just beyond it is a bridge. On the north side the concrete dam is visible; carefully cross McVey, and on the south side you can see the basalt ledges cut by Oswego Creek. This is where in 1850 Albert Durham built his mill and wooden dam. Water coming off the dam turned a 36-inch-diameter wheel to power the mill. The last wooden dam was built in 1909 for Oregon Iron and Steel; in 1921 a concrete dam was poured that further raised the level of the lake, drowning out the last of the lakeside stumps that remained from the age of the iron smelters.

11 From the bridge, walk on the south side of McVey; there is no shoulder, and traffic is fast, so use caution. Turn left at the first street, Maple. This is the South Town area, platted in 1883 as a neighborhood for workers at the iron smelter. Maple shows few signs of those early days. Follow it to its dead end, where a narrow path leads into the woods; this is part of George Rogers Park.

Follow the path along Oswego Creek. Ivy needs to be removed from this lovely forest, but despite its intrusion, the area is special. Along the way, a jumble of car-size boulders sprout caps of licorice ferns like green punk haircuts; the trail passes under the beautiful concrete arches of Highway 43, built when the road was part of the Three Nation Highway, running from Canada to Mexico; and the creek is visible to the left through dark trunks of Douglas fir. During the smelter era, a 900-foot-long flume carried logs from the dam to a landing along the Willamette River.

Follow the trail to the footbridge over the creek, and turn left to return to the parking lot.

Explore further by turning right at the footbridge and walking along the extremely scenic paved path that follows the Willamette. This is the historic River Road that led to West Linn prior to the construction of Highway 43.

Back in George Rogers Park, don't miss the river beach at the mouth of Oswego Creek, a great place to cool your toes. Until the riverboat era ended in the 1920s, this sandy beach was the point of embarkation for Oswego residents and goods. Downstream is a 1910 railroad bridge operated by Union Pacific.

The furnace stack from 1867, once used to smelt iron ore, inspired the twenty-first century design of picnic grills in George Rogers Park.

WALK 19

OREGON CITY LOOP

DISTANCE About 4 miles

STARTING POINT McLoughlin House: 713 Center Street

GETTING THERE AND PARKING Oregon City is about 12 miles south of Portland along the Willamette River. From downtown Portland, drive south on Highway 99E (McLoughlin Boulevard). After passing under Interstate 205, follow signs for downtown Oregon City. Turn left at a stoplight onto 10th Street. Follow 10th as it climbs the bluff and becomes Singer Hill Road. At the top of the bluff, you're on 7th Street. Drive one block east on 7th, turn left, and park near the McLoughlin House, at the corner of 7th and Center Street. On weekdays parking is restricted to two hours unless you park a few blocks east of the McLoughlin House, where parking is unrestricted.

TriMet: Take bus 33 (McLoughlin) to the stop at 5th Street and Washington Street in Oregon City. Walk two blocks north on Washington to 7th Street, and one block west on 7th to Center Street.

RESTROOMS AND DRINKING FOUNTAINS A public restroom is inside Barclay House (next to the McLoughlin House), at Willamette Falls Locks (on the outside of the lock master's office), at Richard Bloom Sr. Tot Park (6th Street and Jefferson Street), and at coffee shops and restaurants off Main Street and along 7th (for customers). Drinking fountains are outside the McLoughlin House, outside the courthouse at Main and 8th Street, at the top of the Oregon City Municipal Elevator, at 7th and Van Buren, and at 7th and John Quincy Adams.

FOOD AND DRINK Find food and drink midway through the route at the Carnegie Center (606 John Adams Street) and at restaurants along 7th Street.

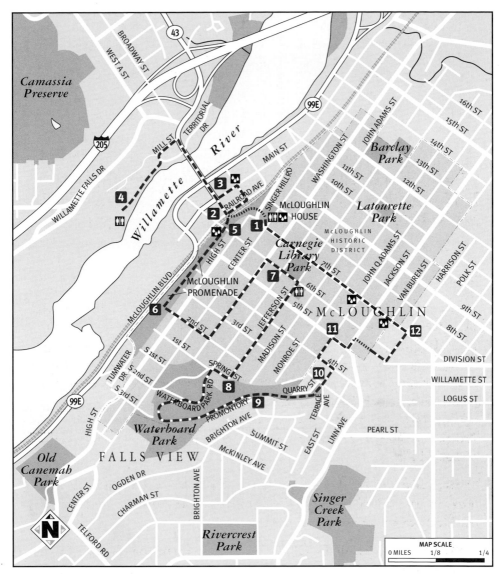

WALK 18. *Oregon City Loop*

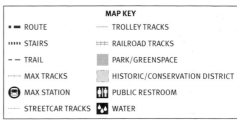

MAP KEY

- ■·■ ROUTE
- ⋯ STAIRS
- – – TRAIL
- ⎯ MAX TRACKS
- Ⓔ MAX STATION
- ⋯ STREETCAR TRACKS

- ⋯ TROLLEY TRACKS
- ⊢⊣ RAILROAD TRACKS
- ▓ PARK/GREENSPACE
- ░ HISTORIC/CONSERVATION DISTRICT
- 🚻 PUBLIC RESTROOM
- ♦♦ WATER

BEST TIMES TO VISIT   It's easy to spend a day in this riverside town, where change seems to take a slower pace than in Portland. Historic homes and museums along the route are staffed by knowledgeable docents and packed with fascinating artifacts. An hour's stop at one or more is a perfect complement to a stroll through the city's historic streets. All the attractions listed here are on the route except for the End of the Oregon Trail Interpretive Center (about ten blocks north of the route) and the Museum of the Oregon Territory (two blocks south of the route). Call for hours and prices; some venues are closed seasonally and on certain days of the week, and admission to one museum may get you into some others.

The McLoughlin House, where this walk begins, is part of the National Park System. For information on house tours, call the Fort Vancouver National Historic Site at 360-696-7655, extension 10. Admission is free.

The Oregon City Municipal Elevator at 7th Street and Railroad Avenue is open each day of the week. Admission is free.

The Stevens-Crawford Heritage House at 603 6th Street is open for tours. Call 503-655-2866 for hours and admission.

Lock Fest at the Willamette Falls Locks is held annually and is the only time the locks are in operation. See www.willamettefalls.org for details.

The Carnegie Center, a historic library building that now houses a gallery, art school, and coffee shop, is at 606 John Adams Street. Call 503-723-9661 for hours.

The Museum of the Oregon Territory at 211 Tumwater Drive offers the best view of Willamette Falls. Call 503-655-5574 for hours.

The End of the Oregon Trail Interpretive Center, 1726 Washington Street, was built in 1995 at the site of Abernethy Green, the actual end point of the trail. Call 503-657-9336 for hours.

ACCESSIBILITY   This walk has about 400 feet of elevation gain, and much of the route covers inaccessible terrain. Avoid various inaccessible portions between **1** and **5** by proceeding from the McLoughlin House at **1** to the McLoughlin Promenade running south from 7th Avenue and exploring the flat, gridlike streets of the McLoughlin Historic District. The walk is also not accessible by ADA standards between **8** and **12**, where it traverses trails and staircases. To stay on city sidewalks, from **8**, use the map to return to 7th Street, at about

John Quincy Adams Street, and follow 7th west to the starting point. In addition to these impediments, curb cuts are lacking at many intersections.

CAUTION One section of the walk through wooded Waterboard Park is isolated. Use your judgment about walking alone in wooded areas. During autumn an abandoned asphalt road here is slick with leaves, which hide the road's many pits and fallen rocks. Use caution.

OREGON CITY'S LARGEST natural attraction is 40-foot-high Willamette Falls, the living remnant of millions of years of carving action in the Columbia River Basalts that flowed over two-thirds of Oregon. With the cascades of the Columbia silenced at the bottom of dam-made lakes, viewing the still-wild Willamette Falls is a real treat.

The land east of the falls is a geologic staircase. The first, or river, level is where European settlement began. It consists of alluvium from Quaternary floods and, nearer the falls, the bedrock of Columbia River Basalt. This level lies within the floodplain of the Willamette. A 100-foot-high cliff separates this terrace from the McLoughlin Historic District, a level field of basalt mantled on its north and east sides by the Troutdale Formation, a sedimentary layer laid down by river flooding three to four million years ago; it is this layer that causes homeowners heartache, as heavy rains can cause it to slide down into the canyons that carve through it. This level of town then steps upward to a vast flow of the Boring Lavas, volcanic outcrops from two million years ago that pepper the east side of the Willamette River all the way to Mount Hood. This area is characterized by vast plains of lava and outcrops such as Rocky Butte, Mount Tabor, and Mount Scott.

Bring binoculars; this walk presents several superb viewpoints of Willamette Falls, the surrounding mountains, and downtown Portland.

1 This walk begins at the house of John McLoughlin, often called the "Father of Oregon." A Canadian employed by the British Hudson's Bay Company (HBC), McLoughlin aided early settlers coming to the Oregon Country (today's Oregon, Washington, Idaho, and parts of Montana, Wyoming, and British Columbia). He came to the Oregon Territory in 1824 as the chief factor (agent) of the HBC's Columbia Department, which controlled the fur trade in British-controlled lands in North America. For the headquarters, HBC decided upon Belle Vue

Point along the Columbia River, renaming it Fort Vancouver—now Vancouver, Washington. (See Walk 20 for more on McLoughlin.)

In 1818 the United States and Great Britain had agreed to a ten-year joint occupation of the Oregon Country. Toward the end of the ten years, the HBC established trading sites as far south as possible to secure a good position for the coming boundary negotiations. To that end, McLoughlin established a settlement at the falls of the Willamette River in 1829.

In the early 1840s more and more American settlers began to straggle over the mountains to the Willamette Valley. McLoughlin, in part to stave off attacks on his well-provisioned fort, gave the exhausted and often desperate men and women aid and supplied them with goods on credit. Despite having encouraged the newcomers to settle south of the Columbia River, thereby preserving British claims to lands to the north, he was severely reprimanded by his superiors for giving aid to these settlers, whose presence hindered British claims. His reply:

But what else could I do as a man having a spark of humanity in my nature? I did not invite the Americans to come. To be frank, I greatly regretted their coming, but they did come, covered with the dust of travel, worn out by fatigue, hardships and dangers incident to a very long and perilous journey. . . . The Bible tells me that if my enemy is hungry, I must feed him, if naked, I must clothe him, but these destitute men and helpless women and children were not my enemies, and I am sure that God does not want me to do more for my enemies than these.

In a last-gasp effort to secure the area south of the Columbia for England, McLoughlin had the site at Willamette Falls platted in 1842 and named it Oregon City. However, the area was by then de facto American, and in 1845 Oregon City was voted by settlers to be the seat of the Oregon Territory's first provisional government. McLoughlin, by this time forced to retire for mucking up the British claim to the land, joined the crowd. In 1845 he paid the HBC $20,000 for the Oregon City claim and built his retirement home there. By 1846 seventy homes had been built, five hundred people lived in Oregon City (more than in Portland at the time), and the United States–Canada border had been set at its present location along the forty-ninth parallel. McLoughlin became an American citizen in 1851, partly to ward off claims that a citizen of the Crown could not own property in an American territory. He died in 1857 in Oregon City, after donating much of his land to public use, churches, and industry.

McLoughlin's house, one of the oldest in the state, was built in 1846 in the Georgian style. It originally sat at 3rd and Main, on the lower level of town, but was hauled up Singer Hill Road in 1909 to escape industrialization. A tour of the interior, led by a lively and informative guide, is well worth the time. Next door is the 1849 Barclay House, home to the town doctor, who would jump on his pony night or day to attend the sick of Oregon City. This house was also moved from its original location on the first level.

After looking over these historic homes, walk into the backyard of the McLoughlin House. Here lie the remains of John and Marguerite (here spelled Margaret) McLoughlin as well as a cannon whose 1789 date of manufacture is inscribed on its side. Originally mounted on an HBC ship that likely carried furs from Northwest forests to English markets, the cannon was on its retirement voyage from Fort Vancouver to Oregon City in 1847 when the boat foundered at Clackamas Rapids (at the confluence of the Clackamas and Willamette). It rested at the bottom of the Willamette until the 1930s when dredging brought it to the surface. Its maker's initials, E. B., have survived the centuries.

From the cannon, walk past a fountain in the yard and toward a tunnel leading under Singer Hill Road. Walk through the tunnel to a graceful Depression-era staircase leading down to the river level. Before Euro-American settlement, a path here was used by Native Americans. At the top of the steps, Singer Creek emerges from a culvert, flows under the steps, and then emerges to cascade down the bluff over wide concrete terraces that create a minimalist rendition of the original falls. The creek's name came from the Singer Flour Mill, which it powered in the 1880s and 1890s. Along the way, stop to enjoy the harmony created by the fern-draped basalt cliffs, hand-hewn basalt walls, and curving staircase.

2 Near the bottom of the stairs is the rail line that entered Oregon City in 1868. Continuing down the steps, enter a tunnel. At the bottom of the steps, turn right and pass under the train tracks. Once out of the tunnel, turn right onto Railroad Avenue.

Railroad is busy during the week, with commuters using it to access Singer Hill Road, so use caution. Walk one block on Railroad and turn left on 8th Street. Ahead on the right is Henry Weinhard's 1895 Beer Hall, a saloon and distribution center for his Portland-made beer. Though the façade on Main is much changed, a bit of the cast-iron columns framing the entrance are still visible.

At the intersection of 8th and Main is the Art Deco Clackamas County Courthouse from 1935, partly built with work relief funds. Cross Main to the drinking fountain at the courthouse. Here is a good vantage point to see the bluff face with the cascading Singer Creek.

From 8th and Main, walk south on Main (or for a food break, continue along 8th to McLoughlin Boulevard, turn right, and find McMenamins Oregon City pub at 9th Street). At 707 Main is the 1907 Masonic Building, an odd jumble of architectural styles. It was home to the first Masonic lodge west of the Mississippi, and was founded in 1848 in a log cabin adjacent to Willamette Falls.

3 From Main, turn right onto 7th to cross the Willamette River on the Oregon City–West Linn Bridge. In 1922, at the opening of the bridge, a "wedding of two cities" was celebrated as Ella Parker from West Linn married Louis Hartke from Oregon City in the center of the span. The bridge's arch design is similar to the well-known Yaquina Bay Bridge; both were designed by Conde McCullough, a state bridge engineer who designed many of the bridges along the Oregon Coast. This bridge replaced one built in 1888.

At the West Linn end, cross to the south side of the bridge carefully; there are no pedestrian markings or traffic control features. Once off the bridge, immediately turn left at a sign for the Willamette Falls Locks National Historic Site, at Mill Street. Stay straight on Mill at Territorial Drive. Walk past a truck parking lot. A sign for West Linn Paper Company directs you to a pedestrian walkway leading downhill to the river. The walkway and steps soon hug basalt cliffs pockmarked with vesicles, tiny holes formed by the releasing of gasses trapped in the molten basalt as it cooled. Just before a decrepit but beautiful old yellow building (built in 1922 as the paper company headquarters), turn left, take steps down to a lawn, and walk to the locks. An interpretative display is on the right a ways down.

4 Before railroads, rivers were the best avenues to transport cargo, people, and products. At the falls of the Willamette, everyone and their goods disembarked for a portage. In 1868 the rail line went in, lifting some traffic off the river, but its freight rates were high, and the Willamette was still a viable transportation option. To make the river more easily navigable and more competitive with the railroad, the locks were built in 1873 by a private firm. A lock on a river raises or lowers boats between stretches of water of different levels, such as at a waterfall or rapids. Eventually other rail lines went in, and rail freight rates declined, making river transport relatively obsolete. The age of semitrailers and freeways further usurped the river's role. In 1974, when traffic through the locks had subsided to a trickle, the locks were placed on the National Register of Historic Places.

Willamette Falls, looking southeast from the west shore, 1867. Note Moore's Island in the foreground, today home to West Linn Paper. The narrow slot to the west became the locks. The small
city of Canemah is beyond the falls. Photo courtesy of the Oregon Historical Society.

Today they open rarely and during the annual Lock Fest. During that festival,
the museum (in the original lock master's office) is open. The locks themselves
are rather unprepossessing, narrow slots running alongside the West Linn Paper
factory, invisible until you're practically atop them. But a closer look inside the
lock chambers reveals the artistry of enormous, hand-cut basalt blocks lining the
channel. The blocks, from the preconcrete era, have remained watertight since
they were installed.

The paper mill sits on Moore's Island, adjacent to the site of Linn City,
founded here along the west bank of the river in 1842 by Robert Moore. In
1846, owners of a tavern, chair manufacturer, cabinet shop, gunsmith, and
wagon shop eked out a living. All buildings were washed away by the river in
1861, and Linn City was not rebuilt.

After looking at the locks, retrace your steps to the Oregon City side of the
bridge. Ahead is the space-age-style Oregon City Municipal Elevator. Once off
the bridge at the intersection of 7th and Main, walk east on 7th to the tunnel
under the railroad tracks; it leads to the elevator, one of only four municipal elevators in the world. This free elevator is the latest conveyance up the 100-foot-
high bluff. At one time, four staircases climbed the bluff. The first elevator was
installed in 1915; it was powered by water, and the local water board fielded

complaints from annoyed residents who lost pressure each time someone took a ride. In 1924 that elevator was converted to electricity, and in 1955 the current elevator began operating.

5 Take the elevator to the second level of town. Outside the elevator, a glassed-in observatory provides a panorama of the river scene below. Come out of the elevator building, turn right, and walk south along the McLoughlin Promenade, built on land deeded to the city by John McLoughlin in 1847.

Just after the first cross street (6th) is the home of Linn and Erma Jones. He was an Oregon state senator and Oregon City mayor. This 1913 bungalow is classic in its use of deep eaves, natural stone, and cedar shakes. Just north of 5th Street are two homes belonging to a prominent Oregon City family, the Latourettes. First is a 1904 foursquare, and to the south of it is one of the last grand Queen Anne homes on the bluff, the Charles Latourette home, built in 1880 by the cofounder of the Bank of Oregon City.

Below is the Blue Heron Paper Company. Since the 1830s its location has been the site of flour mills, sawmills, woolen mills, and paper mills that have gradually swallowed up the earliest homes and businesses in town. In the tall shed with the heron on it, trailers are upended and their cargo of wood chips dumped onto the floor to be sucked out and piled in the holding pens below the bluff. Half of the mill's raw material comes from newsprint, magazines, and other paper that it recycles into various grades of newsprint, specialty papers, and bag paper for the fast food industry.

At 406 McLoughlin Promenade is a Queen Anne cottage built in 1877 by carpenter G. R. H. Miller, who built the first steps up the bluff in 1867. At 306 is another such cottage, from 1880, richly detailed with its patterned shingles and ornamental bracket in the gable end. In the 1890s tailor Pieter MacIntire lived here and commuted to his job in the woolen mills below via the steps Mr. Miller had built. Before sitting at his machine, he would pass the old McLoughlin house at 3rd and Main, directly below. By the 1890s McLoughlin's house had been turned into the Phoenix Hotel, a home for unsavory sorts. (For an accessible route off the promenade, leave it just past 4th Street [a three-story yellow brick apartment building is on the left]. Veer off the promenade onto an asphalt path that leads to 3rd Street. Turn left on 3rd, then left on Washington Street to rejoin the route.)

South of 3rd, the promenade runs along a lush lawn punctuated with large outcrops of basalt that make a perfect place to play king of the hill. For a good view of the falls, walk to a point below the second set of power lines, or to the grassy knoll just beyond them. On the west side of the river, perched in the riv-

Willamette Falls as seen from the McLoughlin Promenade in Oregon City. The concrete lip around the top of the falls is a dam. It has raised the upstream river level by 14 feet to increase the water pressure at turbines at a riverside electric plant. The flat concrete structure in the falls' horseshoe is a fish ladder.

erbed, rests an abandoned concrete building. Logs were rafted into this building, where immense stone wheels stripped the bark off and pulverized the trees into pulp for the paper mill. No longer in operation since pulp began being used in the 1950s, this building and surrounding complex evoke raw, nineteenth-century-style industry, when there were no green, manicured campuses or company-paid health care. Perched on Roman-arched foundations set in the riverbed, the mill on the west bank is straight out of Dickens—effluent issuing from below, steam puffing from various stacks, and sulfurous scents rising on the updrafts.

Prior to Euro-American settlement, Willamette Falls was a focal point for fishing and trade among Clowwewalla, Cashhooks, and Mollala Indians. In the first decades of the 1800s, white fur traders brought disease, decimating the native population. By the time of white settlement, about 650 Clowwewalla and Cashhooks remained. They were later relocated to the Grand Ronde reservation.

Upstream of the falls on the east bank is Canemah, a National Historic District. Its name means "canoe place," the upstream endpoint for the falls portage for both Native Americans and early settlers. Canemah is well worth a look after the walk.

(Though not on the route, the promenade continues a bit more; two blocks beyond it is the excellent Museum of the Oregon Territory, which provides great views and interpretations of the sites below it.)

6 Exit the promenade by crossing over the grassy lawn to 2nd Street. (It is aligned with the second power lines.) Walk east on 2nd. After passing through the McLoughlin Historic District, the walk will climb to the top of the forested bluff ahead.

From 2nd, turn left on Washington Street and walk four blocks to 6th Street. (For a food break, walk one more block north on Washington; along 7th are restaurants.)

At 6th and Washington is the 1908 Stevens-Crawford Heritage House, a museum that is well worth an hour-long visit. Mertie Crawford, a thirty-something spinster, moved here with her parents in 1908 from the rapidly industrializing Main Street on the first level. Told by her doctor that she was too fragile to marry, Mertie proceeded to live sixty-one more active years in this house. As a child of pioneers, she was aware of her heritage as a daughter of Oregon and kept everything, from her babyhood rocking horse to her mother's corset bag (where a woman stored her corset at night, of course), a hand-operated washing machine, and medicine and spice bottles. With no children to ding up the fir woodwork, and every room furnished with the Crawfords' possessions, the house is a remarkable stock piece of early-twentieth-century life. The best part is the intact kitchen with its original fir cabinetry and wood cookstove. Linoleum counters that Mertie ordered in the 1950s look as though they were just installed. When she died in 1969, Mertie left $800,000 in an endowment to defray college costs for Clackamas County high school seniors.

From Washington, turn right on 6th. Next to the Stevens-Crawford House, at 6th and John Adams Street, is the Ermatinger House, built in 1845. In it, Asa Lovejoy and Francis Pettygrove flipped a coin to decide the name of Oregon's largest city: heads was Portland, tails was Boston. The house has been moved from its original location on the river level.

Kitty-corner from it is the Atkinson Memorial Church, designed by Portland architect Willard Tobey in 1925, at the midpoint of his fifty-year career. Inspired by medieval English churches, its poured-cement and sand-coated exterior were unusual then, and its windows are treasures from Portland's famous Povey Brothers Art Glass Works, which operated from 1888 to 1929. Now Unitarian, it was originally the First Congregational Church.

The Carnegie Center, a former Carnegie library, in the foreground with the Atkinson Memorial Church beyond.

In the northeast corner of 6th and John Adams is the Carnegie Center, a Carnegie library built in 1913. The library sits on a city block set aside in 1850 by McLoughlin as a public park. Inside is a wonderful art gallery and coffee shop, a nice place to soak in the friendly ambience of Oregon City.

7 From the Carnegie Library Park, walk east on 6th to Jefferson. At 610 Jefferson (directly east of the Carnegie Center) is the 1913 Andresen house, a foursquare with an unusual elliptical porch roof, projecting wall dormer, and a faint nod to Japan with its flaring roofline and pagoda-like roof brackets. Andresen was a mayor and jewelry store owner.

From 6th, turn right onto Jefferson, a street of large and small architectural treasures. At 514 is a rare Gothic Revival cottage from 1891. Across from it is the only intact surviving carriage house in town, which belongs to the 1895 Judge Thomas Ryan House (715 5th Street).

Walk further on Jefferson to 5th. At the southeast corner (802 5th) is an 1893 Queen Anne owned by Emma McDonald. Shiplap siding, steep gables, and a bullseye window are part of its charm.

Cross 5th Street. At 415 Jefferson is one of the few Colonial Revival houses in the city. Built around 1874, it has narrow windows and a balustraded balcony above a lovely porch. The much newer homes on either side tell of an earlier version of today's infill issue, where spacious yards become too valuable to grow only grass and trees. Across from it at 410 is another, later Colonial Revival, built around 1913, a time when the style had gotten bigger. Its two-tiered entry and side porch are supported by stout Tuscan columns.

Still on Jefferson, cross 4th Street. The home at 308 Jefferson was built in 1881 and is surrounded by old plantings that give it the air of a secret garden. It was the childhood home of William Howell, who was the head of the city water works at the turn of the last century, and who in adulthood built the next house, a bungalow at 306, in 1913.

Cross 3rd Street. The 1893 cottage at 221 Jefferson is a scaled-down Italianate with tall, narrow windows and a truncated hipped roof. The home at 204 is an 1898 Queen Anne built by Frank and Annie Busch, founders of Busch Furniture Company, with spindlework fans, patterned shingles in the gables, and a porch with a spindlework frieze. Tucked into the near-end of the street, at 121, is a 1900 bungalow with a wraparound porch that would be a great place to listen to the birdsong coming out of the forested bluff.

8 From Jefferson's seeming dead end at the foot of the bluff, turn right on Spring Street. Walk one block and turn left on John Adams, keeping left where the road forks. Follow the street to the unmarked entry to Waterboard Park, where it begins to climb into a forest. The road is closed to automobiles, as the unmitigated effects of landslides have made it impassable. Sans traffic, moss, cracks, and refrigerator-size boulders are reclaiming it.

Ivy is pestilent, but even it can't tarnish the calm beauty here as the road climbs 200 feet up the bluff to the third level of Oregon City. Near the top is the scarp of a landslide, a beautiful outcrop of columnar basalt formed by the cooling of a lava flow, much as mud cracks into jointed sections as it dries.

9 At the top of the bluff you emerge at a road, Promontory Avenue. From the walled overlook are spectacular views of downtown Portland, looking like the Emerald City in a sea of green trees, and east side volcanic buttes.

From the wall, stay straight, walking along the top of the cliff. Pass a barrier into a lawn-covered greenspace, a right-of-way. Follow the dirt path through the grass and enjoy the view through trees that have been liberated from ivy. The trail passes a street, then is paved with asphalt as it drops downhill to its end at the intersection of 3rd Street, Quarry Street, and Terrace Avenue.

10 At this intersection, turn left onto Terrace. In one block come to the intersection of 4th Street and Jackson. Turn left on 4th, which claims to be a dead end. As a pedestrian, never trust the automobile-centric dead-end sign. In this case not only is there a path at the street's end, but it's paved. Take the path, which drops you downhill to the corner of 5th and John Quincy Adams Street.

11 Cross 5th and turn right to walk on the sidewalk on 5th leading uphill. Walk one block, and then turn left onto Jackson. Walk another block, crossing over the steep banks carved into the land by a seasonal stream. At about 6th, on the right is a staircase too long and steep to resist, though at this point in the walk you may disagree. Take the stairs, and don't forget to look at the vista behind you as you climb. At the top, a pair of giant sequoias overwhelm a tiny home. This pocket of the city has some of the verdant lushness of Appalachian hollers.

From the top of the stairs, walk one block to Harrison Street, and turn left.

12 From Harrison, turn left onto 7th Street. This downhill stretch gives great views, all the way to the radio towers of Portland's Council Crest. Along the way is a fine parade of old homes, and after about Jackson, options for food and drink. Tiles embedded in the sidewalk tell the ages of the adjacent buildings. Quiz yourself before you look, to see how close you can get.

At 1210 and 1204 are two Stick-style homes. Don't miss, at 914, the exuberant patterned shinglework of the 1890 home of Mrs. Mindwell Church (a name straight from the heart of an optimistic mother). Mrs. Church was the first female deputy sheriff of Clackamas County. At 624 is the 1923 Oregon City Fire Station, in the Mission style, with a jazzy neon sign, corbeled center gable, and front porch with original bronze lanterns.

At Center Street, turn right to return to the McLoughlin House.

WALK 20

VANCOUVER LOOP

DISTANCE   About 5 miles

STARTING POINT   The parking lot adjacent to the Hudson's Bay Company (HBC) fort at the Fort Vancouver National Historic Site

GETTING THERE AND PARKING   From Portland, drive north on Interstate 5. Cross the Interstate Bridge over the Columbia River into Washington. Take the Mill Plain Boulevard exit (Exit 1C). Turn right (heading east) at the light, onto Mill Plain Boulevard. From Mill Plain, turn south at the first stoplight onto Fort Vancouver Way. At the traffic circle, go straight to drive on the road marked "U.S. Army, Vancouver Barracks, Est. 1849." Fort Vancouver Way ends at 5th Street. Turn left onto 5th, drive about 0.1 mile, and turn right into the parking lot adjacent to the fort.

TriMet: Take the MAX Yellow Line to Delta Park or take bus 6 (Martin Luther King Jr. Boulevard) to its terminus at Jantzen Beach. From either Delta Park or Jantzen Beach, take a C-TRAN bus 4 (Fourth Plain) to Vancouver. Get off at Broadway Street and Evergreen Boulevard. Either walk the route starting from this point **9**, walk from here to the start at **1**, or transfer to bus 32 (Evergreen/Andresen) and disembark at Officers Row **16** and then walk to the start. Call C-Tran at 503-283-8054 or visit www.c-tran.com for assistance and fare information.

RESTROOMS AND DRINKING FOUNTAINS   Restrooms are adjacent to the Fort Vancouver Visitor Center (E Evergreen Boulevard), in Esther Short Park, and at restaurants and coffee shops in downtown Vancouver and Uptown Village (for customers). Drinking fountains are at the Fort Vancouver Visitor Center, 9th Street and Broadway, and Esther Short Park.

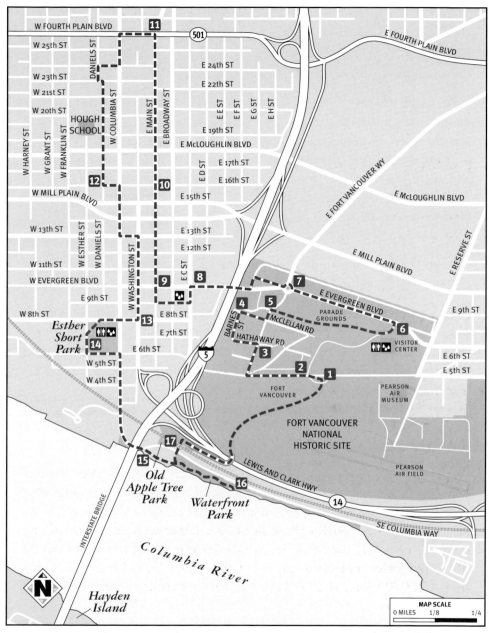

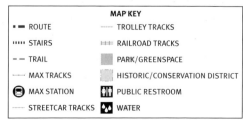

WALK 20. *Vancouver Loop*

MAP KEY

- ▪━ ROUTE
- ⋯⋯ STAIRS
- ─ ─ TRAIL
- ─── MAX TRACKS
- 🚇 MAX STATION
- ⋯⋯⋯ STREETCAR TRACKS
- ⋯⋯ TROLLEY TRACKS
- ╫╫╫ RAILROAD TRACKS
- ░ PARK/GREENSPACE
- ░ HISTORIC/CONSERVATION DISTRICT
- 🚻 PUBLIC RESTROOM
- 🚰 WATER

FOOD AND DRINK   Many restaurants and coffee shops are located in downtown Vancouver and Uptown Village, between **8** and **11**, and between **13** and **14**. Near the end of the walk, two restaurants with outdoor seating areas overlook the Columbia River, just east of the Interstate Bridge.

BEST TIMES TO VISIT   Fort Vancouver offers many annual events and ongoing programs, such as living history demonstrations. See nps.gov/fova for current information. A small fee is charged for entrance within the fort's palisades; other sites are free. Marshall House tours and exhibits are open weekdays and selected weekends. Call 360-693-3103 for hours and other information. Pearson Air Museum, part of the Fort Vancouver Historic Reserve, is adjacent to the route. See www.pearsonairmuseum.org for hours.

The Vancouver Farmers Market runs March through October on Saturdays and Sundays, with more than two hundred vendors, along the west edge of Esther Short Park.

The Clark County Historical Museum, along the route, is open Tuesday through Saturday. See www.cchmuseum.org for current hours and other details.

The Uptown Village Street Festival takes place each August along Main Street. See www.uptownvillage.com for dates.

ACCESSIBILITY   This walk is relatively flat, with about 100 feet of elevation gain from the Columbia River to the route's highest elevation, 130 feet, at Fourth Plain Boulevard and Main Street. The route is accessible, on paths, sidewalks, and quiet streets.

YOU CAN EASILY spend a day on this city walk. Vancouver is a treasure for urban explorers, though it is often overlooked by Portlanders, blessed as we are with our own set of civic riches. From Columbia River beaches to Uptown Village, a 23rd Avenue–like bit of cityscape, Vancouver surprises with its variety, historic sites, and beauty. Bring a Frisbee and a picnic lunch, and spend the day in one of the city's great public spaces: Fort Vancouver's grassy parade grounds, the fountain at downtown's Esther Short Park, or a Columbia River beach.

1 This walk begins at the spot where Vancouver itself began: the Hudson's Bay Company fort.

In 1825 John McLoughlin, the chief factor (agent) of the HBC's Columbia Department, was instrumental in bringing the company to Vancouver to set up a Northwest fur-trading outpost. The powerful HBC, founded in 1670, controlled the lucrative fur trade throughout British-controlled North America. From Vancouver, McLoughlin presided over a de facto government, ranging from Russian Alaska to Spanish California. His word was law for fur trappers, trade ships, and laborers at the company's wharves, smithies, orchards, and fields.

When in 1829 McLoughlin realized that the local Indians were no threat, he moved the fort from its first location (on the bluff a mile east of today's fort site) to this site in order to be closer to river and commerce routes, and for better access to the fertile floodplain. After epidemics in the 1830s virtually wiped out the indigenous population, the only real threat came from the possibility that the Americans who began trickling into the Oregon Country in the early 1840s would plunder the fort for supplies. McLoughlin eliminated that threat by selling goods on credit to the starved and strapped immigrants, later earning the sobriquet "Father of Oregon." His charitable actions did not endear him to his superiors, however, who correctly saw American settlement as a threat to the British claim on the Oregon Territory. (See Walk 19 for information on McLoughlin's life after he left Fort Vancouver in 1845 and moved to Oregon City.)

By the late 1840s, the fur trade was in decline, and American settlers were pouring into the land south of the Columbia River. With the long-disputed international boundary resolved to its current location in 1846, the British HBC found itself located deep inside American territory. In 1849 the U.S. Army settled in just yards away from the old fort. In 1860 the HBC left Vancouver forever, moving all of its Northwest operations to Fort Victoria on Vancouver Island, British Columbia. Today the HBC is the oldest commercial operation in North America. Its headquarters are in Toronto, and it operates more than five hundred retail stores under various names.

From the parking lot, walk into the fort's garden. The Pacific Northwest is renowned for its agricultural fecundity, and the farming started here: Fort Vancouver is the oldest large-scale farm in the region. The agricultural reach of the fort extended 30 miles along the Columbia River and 10 miles inland, with 1400 acres of cultivated fields, 7 acres of formal gardens, thousands of acres of pastureland, and a 5-acre orchard. The HBC chose Vancouver, with its stairstep series of open, fertile plains separated by tracts of forest, largely because of its

Looking west from the fort's gardens. In the foreground is cardoon, an artichoke-like plant common in nineteenth-century gardens. Beyond is the bastion at the corner of the fort. Below the bastion is a tent sheltering an archeological dig. To the right of it is one of the trees of the recreated orchard that John McLoughlin tended here. Beyond are the towers of the Interstate Bridge over the Columbia River.

potential to lessen the fort's dependency on supply ships. Food grown here fed employees at the fort, crews of trading ships, and later, starving Oregon Trail immigrants. During the HBC era, the plains were given such names as the Fort Plain, the Mill Plain, and the Fourth Plain. These names persist.

The garden was reborn in 1984 through the efforts of the aptly named Bill Green. Volunteers will happily stop weeding and watering to answer questions. Plants in the garden are typical heirloom varieties from the 1820s. Crops are used in the fort's living history program or are donated. The gravelly soil consists of glacial flood deposits laid down during the Missoula Floods.

An orchard to the west of the garden re-creates McLoughlin's orchards. Beyond it is the location of the Company Village, home to the fort's multicultural labor force, including a large contingent of Hawaiians. It has been referred to historically as Kanaka Village (the Hawaiian word *kanaka* means "people").

From the garden, enter the fort itself. The original fort burned in 1860. The orchard and any remaining traces of the fort were wiped off the plain during World War I, when at this site the army built the world's largest spruce lumber mill, with wood used to construct airplanes.

Archeological excavations of the fort began in the 1940s. Today, eleven of twenty-three buildings within the palisades have been reconstructed and are open for exploring. Protective asphalt pads mark locations of building sites that have not yet been excavated. In time it is hoped that all the original fort buildings will be excavated, documented, and reconstructed. Inside the fort are interpretive displays and knowledgeable guides.

2 When you're ready to leave the fort, head back through the gardens to 5th Street. Turn left onto 5th, and walk to Fort Vancouver Way to enter Vancouver Barracks, an army installation of elegant wood-frame and brick buildings. At the northwest corner of 5th and Fort Vancouver Way is a horse stable.

From 5th, turn right onto Fort Vancouver Way. From the 1850s, Fort Vancouver was an outpost of civility and beauty in a rugged land, a place where officers could hunt, fish, ride, and even golf, and return to a dinner served on fine china. Its many century-old buildings, sheltered in old groves of Oregon white oak, reflect its glory days. At one time the fort encompassed the area from the Columbia River up to Fourth Plain Boulevard. Its influence waned during World War II, when Fort Lewis, Washington, superseded it. In the 1980s the army began its gradual release of fort property as surplus. By 2008 all of the West Barracks property (on the west side of Fort Vancouver Way) had been deeded to the City of Vancouver. The Vancouver National Historic Reserve Trust, formed in 1998, works to preserve the buildings and historic sites at both the HBC fort and the U.S. Army installations.

3 From Fort Vancouver Way, turn left on Hathaway Road. In the northeast corner is the beautiful Auditorium building. Walk west on Hathaway, passing wood-frame artillery barracks from the early 1900s on the right, and on the left, brick duplexes built in 1936 for noncommissioned officers. Don't miss the interpretative signage along the sidewalks. In the city's long-term plan, Hathaway will connect via a pedestrian bridge across Interstate 5 to downtown Vancouver, and buildings in the barracks area will be renovated for a variety of uses, from education and the arts to restaurants and hotels.

From Hathaway, turn right on Barnes Street and walk by the Red Cross Service Club, built in 1919 as a convalescent home for soldiers. Since its restoration in the early 2000s, it has been used as a reception hall. On the left is the imposing Barnes Hospital building. The hospital went up in 1904 with open porches to provide light and fresh air to patients. In the 1930s the porches were enclosed in glass. The hospital closed in the 1940s, and the new Barnes Hospital was built on what is now the Veteran's Administration complex on Fourth Plain

Boulevard. Across from the hospital building are infantry barracks from 1887, the oldest building at Vancouver Barracks.

4 From Barnes, turn right at McClellan Road and pass the 1907 hospital steward's home.

From McClellan, turn left at Fort Vancouver Way. On the left is the Howard House, built in 1879. It was named for Oliver Otis Howard, the commander to whom Chief Joseph of the Nez Perce made his famous speech in 1877, surrendering his claim to his people's homeland in northeast Oregon. After the Civil War, Howard had been an outspoken and much-criticized advocate for the suffrage and education of freed slaves. He cofounded Howard University as an all-black college in Washington, D.C.

5 From Fort Vancouver Way, at Anderson Street, take the long sidewalk that runs on the north side of a row of wood-frame barracks from 1904. Note the beautiful stone foundations, deep porches, and many windows in these Craftsman buildings.

The sidewalk along the barracks ends, but continue walking east on a broad lawn. You're on the military parade ground here, so chin up, shoulders back. Picnic tables, old oaks and firs, and wide swaths of well-tended lawn make this a perfect spot to soak up the fort's beauty.

Walk toward a 1960s building, the Fort Vancouver Visitor Center. Inside you can look over rare HBC artifacts, watch a movie about the site, and get questions answered by informative staff or volunteers.

6 From the front of the visitor center, take a pedestrian crosswalk across Evergreen Boulevard to the sidewalk running along Officers Row, a lineup of restored Queen Anne homes beautifully sheltered by trees planted by the U.S. Army. The homes continue to the east, but the route walks west from here along the parklike row. The first officers' homes, log cabins, were built along Officers Row in the 1850s. All but one have been replaced.

By the 1970s the homes were in disrepair, and in 1981 were listed by the federal government as surplus to be sold at public auction. A group of citizen activists stopped the process, and in 1984 Officers Row was deeded to the City of Vancouver. Renovations began in 1987. The Vancouver National Historic Reserve Trust manages the homes for the city, which rents them out either as residences or to private businesses.

The first home encountered that is open to the public is the Marshall House, built in 1886 as the commanding officer's quarters, replacing the less impressive

Fort Vancouver, around the mid 1850s, looking east. Officers Row is on the terrace in the middle left; the HBC fort, with its palisades, is on the right, and the Columbia River is on the far right. Photo courtesy of the University of Washington Libraries, Special Collections.

Howard House. Go in for a look at the period furnishings and a tour. The home was named to honor George Marshall. As commander, with the rank of brigadier general of the Fifth Infantry Brigade, Marshall was stationed at Fort Vancouver from 1936 to 1938, where he received visits from President Franklin Roosevelt. In 1938 Marshall was called back to Washington to be Roosevelt's army chief of staff. During World War II he authored the central strategy for Allied operations in Europe, selected Dwight Eisenhower as supreme commander in Europe, and designed Operation Overlord, the invasion of Normandy. He was named secretary of state in 1947; his Marshall Plan provided the blueprint of American aid for rebuilding war-devastated European economies. For it he received the Nobel Peace Prize in 1953, becoming the only career soldier to have received that award. Marshall's days at Fort Vancouver, where he also supervised the Civilian Conservation Corps, were "a pleasant dream," he later wrote.

Further west on Officers Row is the Grant House. It was the original commanding officer's quarters when built in 1850 as a log cabin and is the oldest surviving building on the reserve. By the 1880s it was an officer's club. Later, the logs were covered by milled siding. Ulysses S. Grant, for whom it is named, was stationed at Fort Vancouver from 1852 to 1854, but he did not live in this house. It was named to honor his service in the Civil War and as president. Don't miss the petroglyphs on the grounds.

7 Keep straight at a traffic circle at Fort Vancouver Way and follow the row of houses to its end. At the end of Officers Row, turn left at a sidewalk, and then turn right to walk along Evergreen Boulevard. Here, at the west edge of Fort Vancouver, a town was platted out in 1845; it was called Vancouver City.

Cross over Interstate 5, which cut its swath through town in 1955. Look over your shoulder for good views of the Barnes Hospital. When Interstate 5 was built, a western addition had to be moved and tacked on to the south end of this building, destroying its symmetry.

Over the bridge, at 411 Evergreen, is the 1907 Craftsman home of John P. Kiggins. He was a Vancouver mayor and theater owner, whose theater the walk will soon pass. This house enjoyed a quiet view when it was built on high ground overlooking the river.

On the right is a smokestack labeled "Academy." Here is the brick House of Providence, built in 1873. It was designed by the indomitable Mother Joseph of the Sisters of Charity. Born Esther Pariseau in Quebec in 1823, she was trained in carpentry by her father, who predicted on the day he brought twenty-year-old Esther to the convent that she would become a mother superior. She was not only the building's architect (as she was of the first Saint Vincent's Hospital in Portland) but also its chief contractor, at times demanding that shoddy brickwork be torn out and relaid. The House of Providence was an orphanage, school, hospital, and convent.

Upon Mother Joseph's death at the House of Providence in 1902, after sixty years of service to the poor, a fellow sister said, "She had the characteristics of genius: incessant works, immense sacrifices, great undertakings, and she never counted the cost to self." Her statue is one of one hundred (two for each state) in the National Statuary Hall in the United States Capitol; she shares the honor with Marcus Whitman. John McLoughlin represents Oregon in the hall, along with Jason Lee. In 1953 the American Institute of Architects declared Mother Joseph "the first architect of the Pacific Northwest."

8 From Evergreen, turn left at C Street, walk half a block, and turn right into the city's Sculpture Garden. Walk west through the garden to Broadway and 9th. Walk west on 9th, and turn right onto Main Street. At the southwest corner of Main and Evergreen is the magnificent 1911 Elks Building, with elements of Mission and Italian Renaissance styles. At the northeast corner is the Mediterranean-style Vancouver Savings and Loan, built in 1920. Next to it is the Jerusalem Café, a great place for lunch.

The House of Providence, designed and built by Mother Joseph in 1873. In 1966 the Sisters of Providence sold the building to the Hidden family (of the Hidden Brick Company), whose bricks had been used to build it nine decades earlier.

9 From Evergreen and Main, walk north on Main, which was once a dirt road leading to the HBC's northern farms. At 1011 Main is the 1930s Art Deco Kiggins Theatre, built by John P. Kiggins.

At 13th Street, in the northwest corner, is the Lowell M. Hidden House. It was built in 1884, thirteen years after he founded the Hidden Brick Company, reportedly at the urging of Mother Joseph, who needed bricks for her academy and orphanage. The Hidden yard provided bricks for Mother Joseph's other projects, many downtown buildings, and homes seen later in the walk. Hidden built this house next to his original log cabin, which sat at 14th and the west side of Main. Behind the house is a brick barn that once held four Percheron horses, a large breed whose size was needed to pull the heavy brick wagons. The barn is visible if you walk half a block west on 13th, an interesting block that is worth a look; alternatively, you can see the front of the barn by walking on Mill Plain Boulevard half a block west of Main.

On Main, cross Mill Plain. The eponymous grist mill was located a few miles east of the fort.

In this block are three one-story buildings, rather plain except for the exuberant brickwork, an extravagance made possible perhaps by the buildings' proximity to the Hidden brickyard at 15th and Main. For more than fifty years, bricks were manufactured here, the site of a clay deposit 6 feet deep that ran northwest to 27th Street and Kauffman Avenue, where the brickyard moved in 1929.

At 16th Street and Main is the Clark County Historical Museum. On the parapet, the building's original purpose is revealed: "Vancouver Public Library." It was built in 1909 and funded by Andrew Carnegie's foundation. The massive limbs of a vintage 1915 American elm in the front yard are kept aloft by steel supports. In front of the building is a rock with a hole in it, reputedly a test hole blasted into the rock by engineers planning the Grand Coulee Dam. The museum is well worth a visit.

10 From 16th, continue walking north on Main, a commercial area that boomed around 1910 when a trolley line ran up Main to 33rd Street. At McLoughlin Boulevard is Compass Church, with more beautiful brickwork. Here, Main becomes a classic Main Street straight out of *It's a Wonderful Life*. Called Uptown Village, this stretch is lined with antique stores, clothing shops, and cafés in original streetcar-era buildings.

Just before Fourth Plain Boulevard (which would be 26th if it were a numbered street) is Hi-School Hardware. This was the site of the original Hi-School Pharmacy (1925), which grew into a chain of Northwest pharmacies, some of which were bought out by Walgreens in 2003. Its name came from Vancouver High School, which was across Main Street at the time.

11 From Main, turn left at Fourth Plain. Orchards, Washington, just east of Interstate 205, was called Fourth Plain until 1904. Walk one block and turn left on Columbia Street.

On Columbia, walk two blocks and turn right onto 24th Street. This is the Hough (pronounced "howk") neighborhood, with the city's largest concentration of Craftsman bungalows. Its quiet, scenic streets make for pleasant strolling. Patrick Hough was an Irishman who came to Vancouver to teach in the 1880s.

From 24th, turn left onto Daniels Street. At 23rd, jog left to stay on Daniels. At 19th Street, on the right is land mined by the Hiddens for its clay. When the clay was gone, they sold the land to the city, and Hough School was built on the site. It is brick.

12 From Daniels, turn left on 16th Street, walk one block, and turn right onto Columbia Street. From Columbia, turn left at 13th Street and then right at Washington Street. In the northeast corner of 13th and Washington is Foster Hidden's house. The son of Lowell Hidden, Foster built this Colonial Revival home next to his dad's in 1913.

Kitty-corner from Foster's home is Saint James Catholic Church, established in 1838 at Fort Vancouver as the Mission of Quebec. The current church building was built in 1884 as the Cathedral for the Diocese of Nisqually. When the diocesan offices were moved to Seattle in 1905, the cathedral was demoted to church status, but its soaring brick Gothicism still impresses.

At Washington and 11th Street is the gorgeous Art Deco Vancouver Telephone Exchange, built in 1934 with nice terra-cotta accents. A copper and bronze elliptical canopy covers the entry, where the original bell logo remains visible. From this point, there are more restaurants and cafés to visit.

13 From Washington, turn right on 8th Street. At Columbia, come to Esther Short Park. Amos and Esther Short jumped the claim of Henry Williamson, who had left his land to pursue gold in California. After resisting harassment, including having their crops dug up and being forced onto a boat and hauled away to Linnton, Oregon, Amos and Esther and their ten children prevailed, in part perhaps because Amos had become a probate judge, a court that later ruled favorably on his claim. Amos died in 1852 at the mouth of the Columbia River on a trading expedition, without having finalized his claim. Not to be deterred, and despite her cloudy title, Esther gave this public plaza to the city in 1853, in a winning bit of gamesmanship. She also donated riverfront acreage for a public wharf, the beginnings of the Port of Vancouver. Not until fifty years later was the land's title settled.

Midway along the north edge of the park, at 8th, is *Pioneer Mother Memorial*, carved in 1928 by Avard Fairbanks. The bronze sculpture was cast in Florence, Italy, while Fairbanks was studying there under a Guggenheim Fellowship. It is a tender piece, the woman's strong hands guiding a daughter who is helping her mother by comforting a younger sibling. Fairbanks has three statues in the National Statuary Hall.

Walk west on 8th along the north edge of the park and turn left onto Esther Street. All around the park is evidence of urban renewal: shops, condominiums, and the combined Vancouver Convention Center and Hilton Hotel on the park's south side. The Vancouver Farmers Market has operated here since 1990.

14 From Esther, turn left onto 6th Street at the 1867 Slocum House. This Italianate home was moved here in 1966 from a few blocks south. In the park's southeast corner is Propstra Square, with a carillon, otherwise known as a glockenspiel ("player of bells"). Bronze salmon thrust themselves out of the tower, and water flowing around blocks of columnar basalt makes this a pleasant spot to sit and cool your toes. The square was funded by George Propstra, who founded the Burgerville restaurant chain in Vancouver in 1961.

From 6th, turn right onto Columbia Street and walk along the gleaming Vancouver Convention Center and Hilton Hotel. Just past the railroad underpass is a bike path you could take for a scenic detour up to the Interstate Bridge across the Columbia River. Staying on Columbia, follow the sidewalk to the river's edge. Here Esther Short donated more land for a ferry landing, and then built a restaurant and hotel next to it.

Walk under the bridge. Just to the east is a public fishing pier, with great river and bridge views. When it was opened in 1917, the Interstate Bridge was called the Pacific Highway Bridge and was the long-sought link across the Columbia. At that time the northbound span stood alone and did not have the hump in the center. The southbound span was built in 1958, three years after Interstate 5 came through Vancouver. The center portion of the 1917 bridge was raised at that time to match the shape of the new bridge, a configuration that allowed most ships to pass under it. By the early 2000s the bridge was inadequate, creating daily bottlenecks during rush hour.

The bridge crosses the main channel of the Columbia to Oregon's Hayden Island. This island had many names before eventually being renamed for Guy and Mary Jane Hayden, who lived there in the 1850s. (Mary Jane used her skill with a gun to keep filching soldiers and Indians from her island orchard.) Lewis and Clark called it Image Canoe Island because a large canoe carved with images of men and animals emerged from behind it as they approached. However, Lieutenant William Broughton had already named it in 1792 after his ship's botanist, Menzies, on the same trip in which he named Vancouver after his commander.

15 From the riverfront under the bridge, walk along the Columbia on a public walkway that borders the patios of two riverside restaurants. Just past the restaurants, look left. Across Columbia Way is a tunnel through the railroad embankment. This leads to a 40-foot-wide, earth-covered land bridge over Highway 14 that rejoins two historic but long-separated areas of Fort Vancouver: the river, with its docks, shops, and forges; and the Fort Plain, where people lived and farmed. The bridge, completed in 2008, is part of the Confluence Project, seven sites within the Columbia River Basin that mark important confluences of rivers and ecosystems and Native and European cultures, as well as aspects of the Lewis and Clark Expedition.

Before heading to the land bridge, consider walking a bit further along the river. East of the restaurants the land is managed by the National Park Service. This area was once home to the HBC's wharf, tannery, and boat-building operation. If you stay along the river, follow the shaded walkway eastward past several interpretive displays and small parking areas.

16 At the last parking area, a ramp leads down the embankment to a beautiful log-strewn beach. From the beach, retrace your steps to the tunnel.

17 The tunnel leads to the oldest apple tree in the Northwest, which began its life as a seedling tended by John McLoughlin in the 1820s. Follow signs to the starting point of this walk.

Uptown Village in Vancouver.

ACKNOWLEDGMENTS

As in *Portland Hill Walks*, many people shared their civic enthusiasm with me as I wrote this book. First are the local activists and archivists: Polina Olsen and Stephen Leflar of South Portland. Polina's two books of South Portland history are gems, the sort of homage to a place that every neighborhood should receive. Stephen, thank you for sharing so generously your trove of South Portland history. Thanks, too, to Carol Alhadeff of Jantzen's archives; Claire Kellogg of Lake Oswego; Covington Vego of Oregon City; Jim Heuer and Robert Mercer of Irvington, whose knowledge of that neighborhood is encyclopedic; Mike Ryerson of Northwest Portland; Don Porth of the Historic Belmont Firehouse and Safety Learning Center; Linda Nettekoven of the Hosford-Abernethy Neighborhood Association, who seems to know everything about Southeast Portland; Jim Gersbach of Kaiser Permanente; and Lenny Anderson, whose enthusiasm for Swan Island is contagious. Thank you to Kathy T. Orton of Brooklyn, whose walking tour booklet provided invaluable information; David Porter, executive director of the End of the Oregon Trail Interpretive Center; and Nancy Davidson Shaw, who gave me the inside view of her father's Kerns' business.

Thank you to friends and readers who have walked the routes in this book and given them the tweaks they needed, especially Larry and Liz Volchuk, with whom I shared a totally delightful day in Hollywood; Kristin Beiers Jones, who convinced her family of six to walk around Irvington; Judy Blankenship, whose eye as a writer and photographer helped me fine-tune the walks; John Johnston and Maria Menor, who shared with me their enthusiasm and thoughtful critiques; and Zeb Andrews, whose photos deserve a book of their own.

Brian Johnson at the City of Portland Archives helped me again find historic photos that bring the stories alive; his welcoming attitude and belief that the city's records belong to all of us made me feel as if I were poking around in my own attic, not an august civic repository. Winnifred Herrschaft at the Washington County Historical Society and Museum plied me with photos until I found the one I wanted. Rich Cassidy, senior planner with the City of Portland's Transportation Options, who shares my enthusiasm for city neighborhoods, let me lead walks in his popular walk series. The staff and volunteers at the Oregon Historical Society were generous with their time and knowledge. Christina Robertson-Gardiner at the City of Oregon City helped me find my way around the city's historic districts. Blair Fitzgibbon of Portland Public Schools always provided the information I sought about old school buildings. Denyse McGriff at the Portland Development Commission never made me wait when I hankered for facts. And Neal Van Horn, also of the PDC, shared the commission's drafty loft full of news clippings with me one wonderful day.

I am so very grateful to William Willingham, who graciously read the entire manuscript, and to those who read individual chapters. Among them are Lawrence Fellows of Kenton; Alex Toth, Linda Saari, and Elias Gilman of Pacific University, who provided much assistance regarding Forest Grove; and both Greg Shine, chief ranger and historian at the Fort Vancouver National Historic Site and Vancouver National Historic Reserve, and Mary Grgich, who set me straight on the fascinating but complicated history of Fort Vancouver.

Readers who have offered great suggestions on how to improve my walking books include Martha Gies and Marsha Weber. Thank you! My books are a collaboration between me and other Portlanders, and I appreciate suggestions on how to make them more usable.

I am fortunate to be published by Timber Press, a company located in the city where I live. From conceptual brainstorming to editing, marketing, and publicity events, I have enjoyed the entire publishing process. Thanks especially to editorial director Eve Goodman, editor Mindy Fitch, publicity manager Lake Boggan, and production director Darcel Warren, as well as Lisa Brower, of Seattle, who created the wonderful maps for the book.

Finally, thank you to the Regional Arts and Culture Council (RACC) for again funding my work through its grants for artists.

GLOSSARY OF ARCHITECTURAL TERMS

ARCADE

A passage or walkway covered by a series of arches supported on piers or columns. A blind arcade is a row of arches applied to a wall as a decorative element.

ART DECO

A style derived from the 1925 Exposition Internationales des Arts Décoratifs et Industriels Modernes held in Paris in which designs were to respond to the aesthetics of the machine age. Characterized by stylized sculptural ornament and geometric ornament in low relief, including chevrons, zigzags, fluting, sunbursts, and horizontal and vertical banding. Popular from the 1920s to early 1930s.

ART MODERNE

A successor style to Art Deco characterized by a smooth wall surface, usually stucco; flat roof, usually with coping at the roofline; horizontal grooves or lines in walls and horizontal balustrade to give a horizontal emphasis; and a façade that is usually asymmetrical. One or more corners may be curved; windows frequently are continuous around corners.

ARTS AND CRAFTS

A style popular in Oregon from 1900 to 1920 that derives from an interest in handcrafted (or apparently so) construction and decoration. Elements include steeply pitched gabled roofs, asymmetry, large chimneys, small-paned windows, and frequently a combination of local materials: stone, wood with stucco, or half-timbering in the Tudor style.

BALUSTRADE

A handrail supported by balusters (small posts that support the upper rail of a railing).

BARGEBOARD

Also called vergeboard, a board, often decorated or jigsaw cut, that acts as trim and is attached to the overhanging eaves of a gable roof. Common in Gothic Revival and Craftsman homes.

BUNGALOW

A popular form from 1905 to 1925. A rectangular single-story home with a low-pitched roof, overhanging eaves, and often large porches.

BYZANTINE

A revival style of the late 1800s and early 1900s, seen most often in religious and public buildings. Characterized by round arches, vaults, domes, brick and stucco surfaces, symbolic ornamentation, and decorative mosaics.

CLASSICAL REVIVAL

A style referencing ancient Greece and Rome. Characteristics are bilateral symmetry, porches supported by columns, a complete entablature with cornice, frieze, and architrave; pilasters at the building's corners, and a low-pitched gable roof.

COLONIAL REVIVAL

A revival style that followed the 1876 Philadelphia Centennial Exposition, which stirred new interest in colonial architecture. Elements include an accentuated front door, normally with a pediment; doors with fanlights or sidelights; corner pilasters; and often side porches. There is frequently a symmetrical façade (more traditional), though asymmetrical styles with superimposed colonial details are common as well. This style is often intermarried with Queen Anne elements.

COPING

A finishing or protective course or cap to an exterior masonry wall.

CORBEL

A bracket composed of a single projecting block, or of several graduated projecting courses of masonry, providing a ledge that sometimes supports a load but is sometimes solely for decorative effect.

CORNICE

The prominent, continuous, horizontally projecting feature on a wall; or, in classical architecture, the upper element of an entablature, which is the entire area between the columns and the eaves.

CRAFTSMAN

A style that originated in California and became dominant among American homes from about 1905 to the early 1920s. Elements include a low-pitched, usually gabled roof with wide, unenclosed eave overhang; roof rafters, usually exposed with decorative (false) braces under the gables; and porches, either full or partial width, often with tapered square columns or pedestals that extend to ground level without breaking at the porch floor. Columns are either wood, stone, shingles, brick, river rock, or stucco, with the materials often occurring in combination.

DUTCH COLONIAL

A style from the Colonial Revival era characterized by a side-gabled, gambrel roof (originally designed to increase both roof span and usable space) and often a full-width shed dormer.

EASTLAKE

Also called gingerbread, an overlay of ornament often found on Stick and Queen Anne structures built from the 1870s to 1890s. Elements include rows of spindles and knobs, incised wood ornamentation, circular perforations and cutouts, sunbursts, and curved brackets. Such detailing is common on porches, gable ends, or a frieze suspended from a porch ceiling. Named after Charles Eastlake, an English furniture designer who advocated similar design elements.

EGYPTIAN REVIVAL

A rare style usually found on commercial buildings (especially mortuaries), with Egyptian decorative motifs such as the feroher, or winged disc, as well as sarcophagus elements.

ENGLISH COTTAGE

A romantic style that was popular after World War I. It is essentially Tudor, but often with rolled eaves and other picturesque elements such as curving sidewalks, embedded stones in brickwork, and leaded glass windows.

FARMHOUSE

A simple, side-gabled, one-story home, often two rooms wide and one room deep, frequently enlarged over time. A British folk form.

FOURSQUARE

A subtype of the Prairie style popular between 1905 and 1915. This was the earliest Prairie form developed and the most common vernacular version, spread nationwide by pattern books and magazines. Characterized by a simple square or rectangular plan, low-pitched hipped roof, and symmetrical façade. The entrance may be centered or off-centered. Hipped dormers and full-width front porches are common.

GABLED ROOF

A roof consisting of two sloping planes supported at their ends by a triangular extension of two walls. These walls are sometimes called the gables or the gable ends. In gabled roofs, the junction of roof and wall occurs not in a single plane (as in hipped roofs) but at varying levels and angles.

GAMBREL ROOF

A subtype of gabled roofs, with dual pitches on each side, with the lower pitch steeper than the upper. A defining characteristic of the Dutch Colonial style.

GEORGIAN

One of the antecedents of the Colonial Revival style. A Georgian house is usually a simple one- or two-story box, two rooms deep, with doors and windows in strict symmetry.

GOTHIC REVIVAL

A style characterized by a steeply pitched roof, usually with steep cross gables, and windows commonly extending into the gables, often with a pointed-arch (Gothic) shape. Commonly applied to churches starting in the 1850s, harkening back to medieval Gothic cathedrals.

GREEK REVIVAL

A style characterized by prominent classical columns, often used across the full width of the home, or to the full height of a two-story home.

HALF-MODERN

Also called Transitional, a simplified style based loosely on Tudor but with a lower roof pitch and the elimination of traditional detailing. Used from the 1930s to the early 1950s.

HALF-TIMBERING

A term originally applied to late medieval architecture in which heavy timber framework is exposed with spaces in between filled with wattle and daub, plaster, or brickwork. In the Stick, Queen Anne, and Tudor styles, half-timbering is a nonstructural surface decoration, often called false half-timbering.

HIPPED ROOF

A roof having four equally sloped sides. In hipped roof construction, the roof meets all four walls in a single horizontal plane.

INTERNATIONAL

First appearing in the 1920s, a machine age style that turned its back on historic precedents. Features a flat roof, no ornamentation, geometric layout, and corner and ribbon windows set flush with the wall surface. Use of modern building materials such as aluminum and tinted glass.

ITALIANATE

A style characterized by a low-pitched roof with deep eaves supported by decorative brackets, and tall, narrow windows, commonly arched or curved above. Began in England along with Gothic Revival as part of the Picturesque movement. Popularized by pattern books.

ITALIAN RENAISSANCE

The details of this style are more historically accurate than those of the earlier Italianate style. The roof is low pitched or sometimes flat, often covered with ceramic tiles. Eaves are boxed, frequently with decorative brackets beneath. There are often arches above doors, first-floor windows, and porches. First-floor windows are often full length, while upper-story windows are smaller and less elaborate. Entrance areas are frequently recessed with small classical columns or pilasters. Decorative details include quoins, roofline balustrades, pedimented windows, and belt courses. Walls are stucco or masonry.

JACOBETHAN

A coined term denoting a combination of elements from the Tudor eras: Elizabethan (Elizabeth I, 1558 to 1603) and Jacobean (James I, 1603 to 1625), with elaborate façade details and parapeted gables.

MANSARD ROOF

A subtype of hipped roofs, this roof has two pitches on all four sides, with the upper slope flat or nearly so, and the lower slope nearly vertical, often concave in profile, and with dormer windows. Popularized by architect François Mansart in the 1600s during a time when houses were taxed by the number of floors below the roof. By placing dormer windows in the roof, occupants could enjoy an extra, tax-free floor. A revival of mansard roofs in the United States in the mid 1800s was part of the so-called Second Empire style (referring to the Second Empire in France, 1852 to 1870).

MEDITERRANEAN

Also called Mediterranean Revival, a style based on vernacular stucco buildings in villages along the Mediterranean Sea. Similar to the Spanish Colonial Revival style. Popular from 1910 to the 1930s.

MISSION

A style inspired by the Spanish missions of California and popular from the 1890s to about 1920. Characterized by a mission-shaped dormer or roof parapet, commonly with a red tile roof; widely overhanging eaves with exposed rafters; and a porch roof supported by large square piers, often arched above. Walls are usually smooth stucco. Some homes have visor roofs—narrow, tiled roof segments cantilevered out from the wall.

NORMAN COTTAGE

A picturesque style based on Norman farmhouses; often asymmetrical with a tower housing the main doorway.

NORTHWEST REGIONAL

Elements include a broad gabled or hipped roof with deep eaves, and generous use of glass and natural wood siding. Board and batten siding is common. Like the International style, this style features an open floor plan and lack of historic decoration, but it also uses native materials, in the home as well as in the hardscape and landscape.

PARAPET

A wall that extends above the roofline.

PEDIMENT

A low, triangular gable in classical architecture; or an imitation of this, used as ornamentation above windows or doors, common in the Colonial Revival style.

PILASTER

A rectangular column or shallow pier projecting from a wall, often to the sides of a door, or at corners in classically derived styles.

PORTE COCHERE

Literally means "carriage door." A covered structure extending from the entrance of a building to shelter passengers getting in or out of a vehicle.

PRAIRIE

A style that originated in Chicago in 1893 with Frank Lloyd Wright's Winslow House. Elements include a low-pitched roof, usually hipped, with widely over-hanging, enclosed eaves; usually two stories; façade detail emphasizing horizontal lines often with rows of windows; and often massive square porch supports.

QUEEN ANNE

An eclectic Victorian-era style with multitextured (varied shinglework) walls; asymmetrical façades with towers, bays, overhangs, and wall projections; and steeply pitched roofs. Some Queen Anne homes have spindlework decorative elements (Eastlake detailing); others use classical elements such as round porch columns and dentil moldings. The name is a misnomer: Queen Anne ruled from 1702 to 1714, and this style borrows from earlier styles of the Elizabethan and Jacobean eras.

QUOINS

Cornerstones of a building rising the entire height of a wall and distinguished from the main construction material by size, texture, or conspicuous joining.

RANCH

A form that originated in the 1930s in California, based loosely on Spanish Colonial Revival structures, with influences from the Craftsman and Prairie styles. The dominant American form from the end of World War II to the 1970s. One-story homes with very low-pitched roofs and broad, rambling façades. Many ranches eschew detailing, but decorative detailing based on colonial precedents is common.

RICHARDSONIAN ROMANESQUE

A style named after American architect Henry Hobson Richardson. Characterized by a massive quality; round-topped arches over windows, porch supports, or entrance; and often polychrome (multicolored) masonry, usually with rough-faced stonework. Towers are common, often with conical roofs.

ROMANESQUE

A style characterized by a massive quality, thick walls, round arches, and decorative arcading. In contrast with both Roman and Gothic architecture in which the load-bearing structural members are, or appear to be, columns, pilasters, and arches, Romanesque architecture relies upon its walls. Arcading is the most significant decorative feature.

SECOND EMPIRE

A style characterized by a mansard roof with dormer windows on a steep lower slope. Another common element is a decorative cornice with brackets.

SHINGLE

A style in which homes are asymmetrical, often complex shapes including cross gables, towers, half towers, or even partial bulges, with tower roofs often blending into the main volume of the house. The home's shape is enclosed within a smooth, unornamented shingle exterior, without corner boards.

SPANDREL

The space between an arch and the rectangle that encloses it. In a multistory building, it is used for the space between the top of a window or opening and the sill of the window in the story above. The term is used primarily when there is a sculpted panel or other decorative element in this space.

SPANISH COLONIAL REVIVAL

A popular style from the end of World War I to about 1940. Characterized by a low-pitched, typically gabled tile roof with little eave overhang; asymmetrical, round-arched windows and door openings, typically with one or more prominent arches at doors or principal windows; and often wrought-iron balconettes. Details are borrowed from historical Spanish architecture, which includes Moorish, Byzantine, Gothic, and Renaissance elements. Related to the Mission style.

STICK

A style superseded by the Queen Anne movement. Rather than doors and windows being primary decorative elements as in classical architecture, wall surfaces are ornamented with patterns of horizontal, vertical, and diagonal boards. Roofs often feature decorative trusses at the gable ends, with overhanging eaves. Meant to evoke the structural members of medieval half-timbered homes.

TUDOR

Common elements of this style include steeply pitched, front-facing gabled roofs; decorative half-timbering; tall, narrow windows, usually in multiple groups; and massive chimneys, often crowned with decorative chimney pots. Stucco and brick cladding predominate.

VERNACULAR

A term used to describe the traditional building style of a period or place, especially in reference to homes, barns, silos, fences, mills, and factories. Refers to use of traditional materials and methods by carpenters who learned not through formal education but through training and observation.

BIBLIOGRAPHY

Abbott, Carl. 1985. *Portland: Gateway to the Northwest.* Northridge, California: Windsor.

Abbott, Carl. 2001. *Greater Portland: Urban Life and Landscape in the Pacific Northwest.* Philadelphia: University of Pennsylvania.

Barthlow, Joe. 2006. Rummer Homes. http://www.portlandmodern.com/rummer/index.html.

Beaverton, City of. 1968. *Beaverton: 75 Years of Progress.*

Beelart, Joe. 2005. Casting pool waits for water to fill it. *Oregonian*, August 25.

Beeson, M. H., et al. 1991. *Geologic Map of the Portland Quadrangle, Multnomah and Washington Counties, Oregon, and Clark County, Washington.* Portland: Oregon Department of Geology and Mineral Industries.

Blankenship, Judy. 2003. *Intersections: TriMet Interstate MAX Light Rail Community History Project.* Portland: TriMet.

Brenneman, Kristina. 2003. Pearl in a word: Boomtown. *Portland Tribune*, September 12.

Buan, Carolyn M. 1995. *A Changing Mission: The Story of a Pioneer Church.* Forest Grove, Oregon: United Church of Christ.

Buan, Carolyn M. 1999. *This Far-Off Sunset Land: A Pictorial History of Washington County, Oregon.* Virginia Beach, Virginia: Donning Company.

Clark, Rosalind. 1983. *Oregon Style: Architecture from 1840 to the 1950s.* Portland: Professional Book Center.

Corning, Howard McKinley. 1947. *Willamette Landings: Ghost Towns of the River.* Portland: Binfords and Mort, Oregon Historical Society.

Deane, Early. 1968. Landscape architect helps Portland rediscover human being. *Oregonian*, September 25.

Dirr, Michael A. 1998. *Manual of Woody Landscape Plants: Their Identification, Ornamental Characteristics, Culture, Propagation, and Uses.* 5th edition. Champaign, Illinois: Stipes.

Ditto, Jerry, and Lanning Stern. 1995. *Eichler Homes: Design for Living.* San Francisco: Chronicle Books.

Dublin, William Brooks. 1982. *Trail's End: Oregon City, Where the Past Meets the Present.* Saint Louis: Warren H. Green.

Dunham, Elisabeth. 2000. California dreamin'. *Oregonian*, November 30.

Episcopal Church. 2006. Why is the church door red? http://www.episcopal-life.org/26727_62882_ENG_HTM.htm.

Forest Grove, City of. 2001. *Clark Historic District, National Register of Historic Places Continuation Sheet.* http://www.ci.forest-grove.or.us/NewSite/Landmarksboard/documents/ClarkDistrictContext.pdf.

Friends of Trees. 2006. Northeast Ainsworth Linear Arboretum. http://www.friendsoftrees.org/tree_resources/arboretum.php.

Frost, Grif. 2007. Is saké the wine of the future? http://www.wineloverspage.com/reports/sake.phtml.

Fulton, Ann. 2002. *Iron, Wood and Water: An Illustrated History of Lake Oswego.* San Antonio, Texas: Lammert Publications.

Gilford, Steve. 1998. Search for the source of the Permanente. *The Permanente Journal.* xnet.kp.org/permanentejournal/sum98pj/moment.html.

Gilman, Elias. 2006. Carnation, Oregon. Unpublished paper. Forest Grove: Pacific University.

Gragg, Randy. 2000. Diamond in the rough: With seismic reinforcement and luxury suites, PGE Park takes shape. *Oregonian*, December 28.

Gragg, Randy. 2003. Urban plazas that set Portland's modern landscape. *Oregonian*, June 29.

Gragg, Randy. 2005. Tanner Springs Park, Portland's newest, comes with instructions. *Oregonian*, July 31.

Gragg, Randy. 2006. Recycling the Armory. *Oregonian*, September 24.

Hamburger, Robert. 1988. *Two Rooms: The Life of Charles Erskine Scott Wood.* Lincoln: University of Nebraska.

Hartwell, Barbara Bartlett. 1975. *Sprigs of Rosemary.* Portland: National Society of the Colonial Dames.

Hawkins, William J., III, and William F. Willingham. 1999. *Classic Houses of Portland, Oregon, 1850–1950.* Portland: Timber Press.

Heinz, Spencer. 2006. Westmoreland Park has its pond back. *Oregonian*, October 12.

Heritage Investment Corporation. 1986. *Northwest Thirteenth Avenue Historic District National Register Nomination.*

Hirsch, Alison. 2005. *The Fate of Lawrence Halprin's Public Spaces: Three Case Studies.* Master's thesis, University of Pennsylvania.

Houck, Michael C., and M. J. Cody, eds. 2000. *Wild in the City: A Guide to Portland's Natural Areas.* Portland: Oregon Historical Society.

Irvington Community Association. 2007. History of the Irvington neighborhood. http://www.ica.org.

Jantzen Apparel, LLC. 2006. *A Brief History of Jantzen.* Typescript.

Jaquiss, Nigel. 2005. Lake O-be-gone. *Willamette Week*, April 27.

Jensen, Edward, and Charles Ross. *Trees to Know in Oregon.* 1994. Corvallis: Oregon State University Extension Service, Oregon Department of Forestry.

Jollota, Pat. 2004. *Images of America: Downtown Vancouver.* Charleston, South Carolina: Arcadia.

Klooster, Karl T. 1987. *Round the Roses: Portland Past Perspectives.* Portland: Karl T. Klooster.

LaBarre, Mary. 1975. *Through Brush and Briar: The First 100 Years . . . Good Samaritan Hospital and Medical Center.* Portland: Good Samaritan Hospital.

Labbe, John T. 1980. *Fares, Please: Those Portland Trolley Years.* Caldwell, Idaho: Caxton.

Lake Oswego Corporation. 2006. Watershed information. http://lakecorp.com/watershed.php.

Lake Oswego Public Library. 1976. *In Their Own Words: A Collection of Reminiscences of Early Oswego, Oregon.*

Lednicer, Lisa Grace. 2006. Lake Oswego delays action on fertilizers. *Oregonian*, October 13.

Leflar, Stephen. 2005. A history of South Portland. *Southwest Neighborhood News*, September. http://swni.org/newsletter_archives/newsletter_archives_2005.

Leon, Philip W. 2003. *Nanny Wood: From Washington Belle to Portland's Grande Dame.* Bowie, Maryland: Heritage Books.

Leonard, Rita. 2006. Brooklyn tours and touts its storied history. *The Bee*, September.

Lowenstein, Steven. 1987. *The Jews of Oregon: 1850–1950*. Portland: Jewish Historical Society.

MacColl, E. Kimbark. 1976. *The Shaping of a City: Business and Politics in Portland, Oregon, 1885 to 1915*. Portland: Georgian Press.

MacColl, E. Kimbark. 1979. *The Growth of a City: Power and Politics in Portland, Oregon, 1915 to 1950*. Portland: Georgian Press.

MacColl, E. Kimbark. 1988. *Merchants, Money, and Power: The Portland Establishment, 1843 to 1913*. Portland: Georgian Press.

Macky, Ian. 2004. Vault lights. http://www.glassian.org/prism/vault/index.html.

Maddux, Percy. 1952. *City on the Willamette: The Story of Portland, Oregon*. Portland: Binfords and Mort.

Mapes, Virginia, ed. 1980. *Garden Home: The Way It Was*. Beaverton School District.

Mapes, Virginia. 1993. *Chakeipi "The Place of the Beaver": The History of Beaverton, Oregon*. City of Beaverton.

Marlitt, Richard. 1978. *Nineteenth Street*. Portland: Oregon Historical Society.

McAlester, Virginia, and Lee McAlester. 1984. *A Field Guide to American Houses*. New York: Knopf.

McArthur, Lewis A. 2003. *Oregon Geographic Names*. Portland: Oregon Historical Society.

McCarthy, Nancy. 2007. Despite changes, Sullivan's Gulch retains pioneer spirit. http://www.sullivansgulch.org.

Miranda, Gary, and Rick Read. 2000. *Splendid Audacity: The Story of Pacific University*. Seattle: Documentary Books.

Mitchoff, Alta. 1997. *History of the Kenton Neighborhood*. Portland: Kenton Neighborhood Association.

Moerman, Daniel E. 1998. *Native American Ethnobotany*. Portland: Timber Press.

Morelli, Mary Jo. 2006. Tabitha Moffat Brown: A pilgrim in the wide world. *Washington County Historian* (Spring/Summer).

Murphy, Paul C. 1916. *Laurelhurst and Its Park.* Portland: Laurelhurst Company.

National Association for Olmsted Parks. 2006. Olmsted: His essential theory. http://www.olmsted.org/index.php?tg=articles&idx=More&topics=46&article=63.

National Register of Historic Places, National Park Service. 2007. Portland Buddhist Church. http://www.nps.gov/history/nr/feature/asia/2004/portland.htm.

Norman, James B., Jr. 1991. *Portland's Architectural Heritage: National Register Properties of the Portland Metropolitan Area.* Portland: Oregon Historical Society.

Oelheim, Phoebe. 2002. Artist Edward Quigley's romantic vision of the West. http://www.ochcom.org/quigley.

Olsen, Polina. 2004. *A Walking Tour of Historic Jewish Portland.* Portland: Smart Talk Publications.

Olsen, Polina. 2006. *The Immigrants' Children: Jewish and Italian Memories of Old South Portland.* Portland: Smart Talk Publications.

Oregon City, City of. 1982. *McLoughlin District Neighborhood Walking Tour.*

Oregon City, City of. 2007. Historic context statement. http://www.orcity.org/community-develop/planning/historical_context.htm.

Oregon Historical Society. 2007. Glossary of architectural terms. http://www.ohs.org/education/oregonhistory/narratives/subtopic.cfm?subtopic_ID=504.

Orton, Kathy T. 1998. *Brooklyn Historical Tour.* Portland: Brooklyn Action Corps.

Patten, Carolyn. 2006. Mediterranean masterpiece. *Oregonian,* January 22.

Piedmont Neighborhood Association. 1991. *Walking Tour of Historic Piedmont.*

Plotnik, Arthur. 2000. *Urban Tree Book: An Uncommon Field Guide for City and Town.* New York: Three Rivers Press.

Portland Bureau of Planning. 1977. *Corbett, Terwilliger, and Lair Hill Policy Plan.*

Portland Bureau of Planning. 1987. *Northwest Thirteenth Avenue Historic District, National Register of Historic Places Registration Form.*

Portland Bureau of Planning. 1988. *Ladd's Addition Historic District, National Register of Historic Places Registration Form.*

Portland Bureau of Planning. 1989. *East Portland Grand Avenue Historic District, National Register of Historic Places Registration Form.*

Portland Bureau of Planning. 1989. *Portland, Oregon's Eastside Historic and Architectural Resources, 1850–1938.*

Portland Bureau of Planning. 1991. *Brooklyn Neighborhood Plan.*

Portland Bureau of Planning. 1991. *Buckman Neighborhood Plan.*

Portland Bureau of Planning. 1993. *Concordia Neighborhood Plan.*

Portland Bureau of Planning. 1993. *Piedmont Historic Design Zone/Neighborhood Conservation District.*

Portland Bureau of Planning. 1997. *South Portland Historic District, National Register of Historic Places Registration Form.*

Portland Bureau of Planning. 1999. *Historic Alphabet District, National Register of Historic Places Registration Form.*

Portland Bureau of Planning. 2000. *Historic Alphabet District, Community Design Guidelines Addendum.*

Portland Bureau of Planning. 2000. *Historic Alphabet District, National Register Nomination.*

Portland Bureau of Planning. 2001. *Kenton Commercial Historic District, National Register of Historic Places Registration Form.*

Portland Bureau of Planning. 2001. *King's Hill Historic District Guidelines.*

Portland Bureau of Planning. 2003, 2005. *Northwest District Plan, Appendix A: Northwest District History.*

Portland City Council. 1996. *Northwest Thirteenth Avenue Historic District, Design Guidelines.*

Portland Historical Landmarks Commission. 1978. *King's Hill: A Report to the Historical Landmarks Commission.*

Portland Historical Landmarks Commission. 1979. *Inventory of Historic Landmarks and Districts.*

Portland Historical Landmarks Commission, Portland Bureau of Planning. 1978. *Potential Historic Conservation Districts: An Inventory of Historic Resources.*

Portland Parks and Recreation. 1978. *TimeImage: Neighborhood History Project.*

Portland Parks and Recreation. 2005. Peninsula Park Community Center. http://www.portlandonline.com/parks/finder/index.cfm?action=ViewPark&Property ID=1124&c=38308.

Portland Parks and Recreation. 2006. Eastbank Esplanade. http://www.port-landonline.com/parks/finder/index.cfm?action=ViewPark&PropertyID=105&c=38308.

Portland Parks and Recreation. 2006. Portland historical timeline. http://www.portlandonline.com/auditor/index.cfm?&c=cheai.

Portland, City of. 1984. *Historic Resource Inventory: Selected Properties.*

Price, Larry, ed. 1987. *Portland's Changing Landscape.* Portland State University Department of Geology and Association of American Geographers.

Pulse. 2005. The last train. *The Pulse: Bi-Monthly Beat of the Pearl District* (August/September): 13.

Reynolds, Phyllis C., and Elizabeth Dimon. 1993. *Trees of Greater Portland.* Portland: Timber Press.

Ritz, Richard Ellison. 2002. *Architects of Oregon: A Biographical Dictionary of Architects Deceased—19th and 20th Centuries.* Portland: Lair Hill.

Roos, Roy E. 1997. *The History and Development of Portland's Irvington Neighborhood.* Portland: Roy E. Roos.

Rose City Park Neighborhood Association. 1997. *Rose City Park History Book.* Portland.

Ryerson, Mike, and Tim Hills. 2006. *Twenty-third Avenue History Tour.* Portland: *Northwest Examiner*, McMenamins Pubs.

Sanderson, William. 1968. Landscaper jolts planners. *Oregonian*, February 25.

Scott, Harvey, ed. 1890. *History of Portland, Oregon: With Illustrations and Biographical Sketches of Prominent Citizens and Pioneers.* Syracuse, New York: D. Mason.

Smith, Nadine. 1985. *Downtown Beaverton Historic District, National Register of Historic Places Registration Form.*

Snyder, Eugene. 1970. *Early Portland: Stumptown Triumphant.* Portland: Binfords and Mort.

Snyder, Eugene. 1979. *Portland Names and Neighborhoods: Their Historic Origins.* Portland: Binford and Mort.

Snyder, Eugene. 1991. *Portland Potpourri: Art, Fountains, and Old Friends.* Portland: Binford and Mort.

Sullivan's Gulch Neighborhood Association. 2007. Sullivan's Gulch history. http://www.sullivansgulch.org/AboutUs/history.htm.

Tannler, Nancy. 2005. Preserving artful architecture. *The Southeast Examiner*, December 8.

Tims, Dana. 2006. Drawdown under way to lower Oswego Lake. *Oregonian*, October 30.

Toll, William. 1982. *The Making of an Ethnic Middle Class: Portland Jewry over Four Generations.* Albany, New York: State University of New York.

TriMet. 2006. Art on Interstate MAX Yellow Line. http://www.trimet.org/publicart/yellowlineart.htm.

Tualatin Riverkeepers. 2002. *Exploring the Tualatin River Basin: A Nature and Recreation Guide.* Corvallis: Oregon State University.

U.S. Department of Housing and Urban Development. 2007. City of Portland honored for Rosemont redevelopment. http://www.hud.gov/local/or/news/2004-09-14.cfm.

Van Arsdol, Ted. 1986. *Vancouver on the Columbia: An Illustrated History.* Northridge, California: Windsor.

Van Arsdol, Ted. 1991. *Northwest Bastion: The U.S. Army Barracks at Vancouver, 1849–1916.* Vancouver, Washington: Heritage Trust of Clark County.

Vancouver, City of. 2005. *The City of Vancouver's Heritage Trees.* Urban Forestry Commission.

Vancouver National Historic Reserve. 2006. *Vancouver National Historic Reserve Long Range Plan.* https://cms.pwr.nps.gov/fova/parkmgmt/upload/longrangeplan.pdf.

Vaughan, Thomas, and George A. McMath. 1967. *A Century of Portland Architecture, Portland, Oregon.* Portland: Oregon Historical Society.

Von Hagen, Bettina, et al. 2003. *Rebuilt Green: The Natural Capital Center and the Transformative Power of Building.* Portland: Ecotrust.

Wollner, Craig, et al. 2001. A brief history of urban renewal in Portland, Oregon. http://pdc.us/pdf/about/urban_renewal_history.pdf.

Wood, Erskine. 1978. *Life of Charles Erskine Scott Wood: A Renaissance Man.* Portland: Erskine Wood.

Wortman, Sharon Wood, and Ed Wortman. 2006. *The Portland Bridge Book.* Portland: Urban Adventure Press.

Zisman, Karen, et al. 1989. *East Portland Historic District, Nomination to the National Register of Historic Places.* Prepared for the Central Eastside Industrial Council and Hawthorne Boulevard Business Association.

INDEX

acorn woodpecker, 246

address system, 55, 189–191

adidas Village, 27, 39–40

aerial tram. *See* Portland aerial tram

agriculture, Pacific Northwest, 279–280, 289

Ainsworth Linear Arboretum, 45–46

Alameda Ridge, 76

Alano Club, 196

Alberta Art Hop, 42

Alberta Park, 46–47

Alberta Street (NE), 47–50

Alberta Street Fair, 42

Albertina Kerr Nursery Home, 95

Alphabet Historic District, 187–199

Anna Lewis Mann Old People's Home, 110

Arbor Lodge (neighborhood), 21–22, 35–36

Architectural Heritage Center, 108, 132

Armory, 206

Atfalati Indians, 226

Atkinson, George, 238

Bailey, Van Evera, 252

ballast stone, 164, 173

Banfield Freeway. *See* Interstate 84

Barbur Boulevard, 156–157, 160

Barnes Hospital, 281

Beaumont (neighborhood), 79–80

Beaverton, 224–235

Beaverton Bakery, 235

Beaverton City Library, 226, 234–235

Beaverton Creek, 226–227

Beaverton Downtown Historic District, 229

Beaverton Farmers Market, 226

Beaverton Foods, 228–229

Belluschi, Pietro, 67, 118, 163, 179, 183

Belmont Street (SE), 98, 107–108

Belmont Street Fair, 98

Bennes, John, 57, 62, 67, 81, 83

Benson Bubblers, 172

Benson Polytechnic High School, 95

Bess Kaiser Medical Center, 36, 39

Biggi, Rose, 227

Binford Garden Townhomes, 74, 75

Bitar, Robert and Mabel, 108

blackberry, Himalayan, 218

Blitz-Weinhard Brewery, 204, 206

Blue Heron Paper Company, 270

Boring Lava, 265

Bosco, Jerry, 107–108, 132

BridgePort Brewing Company, 211–213

Broadway (NE), 69

Broadway Bridge, 54, 203, 207

Brooklyn (neighborhood), 140–144, 148–151

Brooklyn Action Corps, 143

Brooklyn Park, 150

Brookman, Herman, 105, 108, 198, 217

Brown, Tabitha, 238

Buckman (neighborhood), 84–90, 95–97, 123–124, 126–139

Buckman Arts Magnet Elementary School, 86, 90

Buckman Community Association, 90

Buckman School. *See* Buckman Arts Magnet Elementary School

Bureau of Environmental Services, 22, 24

Burnside Bridge, 130, 138

Burnside Skatepark, 138

Burnside Street, 139, 179, 187, 190

Campbell, David, 187

Campbell townhomes, 191–192

Canemah (district), 269, 271–272

Canyon Road, 176, 227, 229

Carnation, Oregon, 245

Carnegie, Andrew, 33

Carnegie libraries, 33, 158, 239, 272, 286

carp, 205

cast stone, 18–19, 116

cats, feral, 183

Central Eastside Urban Renewal Area, 126–139

charcoal making, 251–258

Child, Fred, 173

Cistus Nursery, 58

City Beautiful movement, 30

City Life homes, 148–149

City Park, Beaverton, 234

City Repair, 35

Civic Auditorium. *See* Keller Auditorium

Clark, Bud, 172

Clark, Emeline, 238, 242

Clark, Harvey, 238–239, 242, 245

Clark County Historical Museum, 278, 286

Clark Historic District, 242–244, 246

Clear Creek, 244

clinker bricks, 60, 109, 122

Clinton Street (SE), 120

Coca-Cola syrup plant, 95

Coe, Henry Waldo, 76, 103

Colonel Summers Park, 87

Colonial Heights (neighborhood), 119

Columbia Park, 22

Community Cycling Center, 48

community gardens, 39, 51, 87

Concordia (neighborhood), 44–46

Concordia University, 45–46

Confluence Project, 288–289

Corbett (neighborhood). *See* South Portland

Couch, John H., 186–187, 193, 202, 205

Couch Lake, 173, 205, 212

Couch Park, 198

Couch School, 197

Crystal Springs Creek, 147

dams, Oswego Lake, 250–251, 255, 259

Davidson Baking Company, 92–93

da Vinci Arts Middle School, 86, 95

Dawson, O. B., 33

deed restrictions, 54–55, 57, 118
Delahunt, Marcus, 57, 68
Division Street (SE), 119–120
Doernbecher, Frank, 62
Doernbecher Furniture Factory, 62
Donald E. Long Center, 82
Doyle, A. E., 108, 158, 181
Duniway Park, 160–161
Durham, Albert, 250, 259

East Portland, 66, 86–87, 101, 115,
    128–139, 154, 190
East Portland Grand Avenue Historic
    District, 129–134
Eastbank Esplanade. See Vera Katz
    Eastbank Esplanade
Ecotrust Building. See Jean Vollum
    Natural Capital Center
Eichler, Joseph, 231
18th Avenue Peace House, 67–68
End of the Oregon Trail Interpretive
    Center, 264
Erickson, Otto, 230
Erickson Creek, 230, 233–234
Ermatinger House, 272
Ertz, Charles, 90–91, 257
Esplanade. See Vera Katz Eastbank
    Esplanade
Esther Short Park, 278, 287–288

Failing School, 157–158
Fairbanks, Avard, 287
Fanno Creek Greenway Trail, 216,
    218, 223
farmers market. See Beaverton
    Farmers Market, Hollywood
    Farmers Market, Interstate
    Farmers Market, Lake Oswego
    Farmers Market, Vancouver
    Farmers Market
Farmington Road, 229
Feig, Elmer, 93, 193–194
Fernhaven Court, 103
Fernhill Park, 44, 51
ferry landings, 114, 130, 137, 219,
    288
Fir Grove Park, 230–231
fire stations, 20, 62–63, 76–77,
    98–99, 107, 135, 275
First Addition, 258–259
Fletcher Farr Ayotte, 239
Forest Grove, 236–247
Fort Vancouver National Historic
    Site, 278–284
Frank, Aaron, 216–217
Frazer Detention Home, 82
Frazer Park, 72, 82
Freightliner, 24–26
Fremont Street (NE), 79
Friends of Historic Forest Grove, 238
Friends of Trees, 45
Front Avenue. See Naito Parkway
Frost, Grif, 244
fur trade, 265, 271, 279

Gales Creek, 244
Gardenburger, 122–123
Garden Home (neighborhood),
    216–218
Garden Home Farm, 216–217
Garden Home Recreation Center,
    216
Garden of Wonders, 117
Gaston, Joseph, 160, 245
George Rogers Park, 252–253, 260,
    261
Girls Polytechnic High School, 95

Goldschmidt, Neil, 120, 168

Good Samaritan Hospital. *See* Legacy Good Samaritan Hospital and Medical Center

Goose Hollow (neighborhood), 170–173, 175–176, 181–183

Governor Tom McCall Waterfront Park, 138, 165

Gragg, Randy, 163–164

Grand Avenue (SE), 130–132, 134

Grant, Ulysses S., 283

Grant House, 283

Grant Park (neighborhood), 62–63, 80

Gravelly Hill. *See* Alameda Ridge

Green, Henry, 177–178

Groening, Matt, 173

Guilds Lake, 23

Hall, Lawrence, 227

Halprin, Anna, 162

Halprin, Lawrence, 162–165

Harlow, John, 205

Harriman, E. H., 208

Hartwell, Barbara Bartlett, 181, 183

Havurah Shalom, 193

Hawkins, William J., 180

Hawley, Willard, 67

Hawthorne, James C., 124

Hawthorne Boulevard (SE), 119, 122, 124

Hawthorne Bridge, 116, 130, 135, 165

Hayden Island, 288

Hazel Fern Farm, 101

Hefty, Henry, 66

Helen Kelly-Manley Center, 158

Heuer, Jim, 61, 65

Hidden Brick Company, 285–286

Highway 43, 260

Hill, James J., 208

Hines, Thomas and Mary, 243

Hi-School Pharmacy, 286

Historic Belmont Firehouse, 98–100, 107

Hockenberry, Raymond, 61–62

Hogan, Sean, 58

Hollywood (neighborhood), 80–82

Hollywood Farmers Market, 72

Hollywood Theatre, 81, 83

horse rings, 55

Hosford-Abernethy (neighborhood), 112–122

Hosford Middle School, 121

Hough (neighborhood), 286

House of Providence, 284–285

Howard, Oliver Otis, 282

Hudson's Bay Company, 265–267, 279–280, 283, 289

Humboldt (neighborhood), 32–34

Hyland Forest Park, 233

Independent Order of Odd Fellows, 133

Inman Poulsen sawmill, 143, 151

International Rose Test Garden, 32

Interstate Avenue (N), 36, 157

Interstate Bridge, 288

Interstate Corridor Urban Renewal Area, 19, 36

Interstate Farmers Market, 30

Interstate 5, 18, 35, 136–137, 156, 281, 284, 288

Interstate 84, 64–65, 92, 100

Interstate 405, 156, 160–161, 210

iron curb bands, 55

Iron Mountain, 250, 257–258

iron ore mining and smelting, 250–253, 261
Irving, Elizabeth, 54–55, 58
Irving, William, 54
Irvington (neighborhood), 52–62, 66–69
Irvington Club, 61
Irvington Community Association, 67
Irvington firehouse, 62–63
Irvington Racetrack, 58
Irvington School, 58
Italian immigration, 117, 155, 160, 162, 166

Jacobberger, Joseph, 33, 61, 62, 133
Jamison Square, 207
Jantzen, Carl, 91, 257
Jantzen Apparel, 90–91, 97
Jantzen Beach, 91
Jean Vollum Natural Capital Center, 203, 207
Jefferson Dancers, 32
Jefferson High School, 32
Jewish immigration, 155–156, 158–159
Joan of Arc statue, 103
Johnson, Arthur, 179
Joseph (Chief), 174, 282

Kaiser, Bess, 36, 39
Kaiser, Henry J., 36
Kaiser Permanente, 36
Kaiser Town Hall, 36
Kalapuya Indians, 226
Katz, Vera, 136
KBOO, 139
Keller Auditorium, 165
Keller Fountain Park, 165

Kennedy Community Garden, 51
Kennedy School, 44, 50–51
Kenton (neighborhood), 14–21
Kenton Commercial Historic District, 19–20
Kerns (neighborhood), 86, 90–95
Kesser Israel, 158–159
King, Amos Nahum, 174, 181
King's Hill Historic District, 170–172, 174–181
Knapp mansion, 188

labyrinth, 247
Ladd, William Sargent, 101, 115
Ladd Estate Company, 101–102, 251, 255, 257
Ladd's Addition, 112–119
Ladd's Circle, 116, 188
Lair Hill (neighborhood). See South Portland
Lair Hill Park, 158, 160
Lake Grove. See Lake Oswego
Lake Oswego, 248–261
Lake Oswego Corporation, 256–257, 259
Lake Oswego Farmers Market, 250
Lakewood Bay, 255
land bridge, 288–289
Last Thursday on Alberta, 42, 49
Laurelhurst (neighborhood), 98–106, 108–111
Laurelhurst Club, 104
Laurelhurst Park, 104–105, 109
Lawrence, Ellis, 30, 60–61, 68, 109, 128
Legacy Good Samaritan Hospital and Medical Center, 195–196

Lewis and Clark Exposition, 30, 34, 68, 72, 115, 174, 180, 186–187, 189

licorice fern, 56

Lincoln High School, 172–173

Linn City, Oregon, 269

Linnea Hall, 194

Lipman-Wolfe, 129–130

Little Chapel of the Chimes, 33

Living Smart homes, 169

Llewellyn, Henderson, 146

Lloyd, Ralph, 65

Lloyd District, 65–66

Lone Fir Cemetery, 96

Lovejoy columns, 207

Lovejoy Fountain Park, 162–164

Lovejoy viaduct, 203, 207, 209

Lowenstein, Steven, 158

Lytle mansion, 66–67

Madison South (neighborhood), 72, 74–76

Madrona Park, 39

Mapes, Virginia, 217, 227, 229

Marquam, Philip, 167

Marquam Gulch, 160–161, 166

Marshall, George, 283

Marshall House, 278, 282–283

MAX light-rail, 100, 120

McCarthy Park, 25

McCormick, Bill, 221

McLoughlin, John, 265–267, 279

McLoughlin Historic District, 265–267, 270–275

McLoughlin House, 264–265, 267, 270

McLoughlin Promenade, 270–272

meatpacking industry, 17–20, 209

Mercer, Robert, 61, 65

Mercy Corps, 168

Metanoia Peace Community, 67–68

Metro, 96

Metropolitan Learning Center, 197

Meyer, Fred, 80–81, 178

Miller Paint, 130

Milligan, Ben, 107–108, 132

Milwaukie Avenue (SE), 114, 142, 147

Minnesota Freeway. See Interstate 5

Mische, Emanuel T., 32, 104, 116

Missoula Floods, 34, 64, 74, 78, 143, 256, 280

Mock, Henry, 21

Mock, John, 22

Mocks Bottom, 21–24

Mocks Crest, 21–22

Moe, Maria, 75–76

Monroe High School, 95

Moore's Island, 269

Mooshe, 68

Morelli, Mary Jo, 245

Morrison Bridge, 101, 106, 116, 130, 137–138

Mother Joseph, 284–285

Mount Hood Freeway, 120–121

Multnomah Athletic Club, 173, 181

Multnomah Stadium. See PGE Park

Municipal Terminal 2, 137

Murphy, Paul, 109, 251

Museum of the Oregon Territory, 264, 272

Music Millennium, 197

myrtle, California, 117

myrtle, Oregon, 117

Naito Parkway (SW), 156–158

Naramore, Floyd, 50

National College of Natural
   Medicine, 158
National Statuary Hall, 284, 287
Nityananda Institute, 110
Nob Hill (neighborhood), 184–199
Normandale Park, 73
North Bank Station, 203, 208
North Park Blocks, 205
North Portland Library, 33
Northwest 13th Avenue Historic
   District, 208–209
npGREENWAY, 16, 25

Oaks Bottom Wildlife Refuge,
   145–146
Officers Row, 282–284
Old College Hall, 238–240, 247
Old Town, 252–254
Olmsted, Frederick Law, 101, 104
Olmsted Brothers, 101, 104
Oregon City, 262–275
Oregon City Municipal Elevator, 264,
   269–270
Oregon City–West Linn Bridge, 268
Oregon Electric Railway, 216, 219,
   245–246
Oregon Health and Science
   University, 157–158, 167
Oregon Insane Hospital, 124
Oregon Iron Company, 250–251
Oregon Iron and Steel, 251, 258–259
Oregon Society of Artists, 180
Oswego. See Lake Oswego
Oswego Creek, 250, 253, 260
Oswego Lake, 250–251, 255–257,
   259
Overlook (neighborhood), 36–41
Overlook House, 38
Overlook Park, 36–38

Pacific University, 238–241,
   246–247
Pauling, Linus, 89
Pearl Townhomes 203, 208,
Pearson Air Museum, 278
Peck, Grace Olivier, 120–121
Peninsula Park, 30–32
permeable pavements, 26–27, 147
Pettygrove Park, 164
PGE Park, 181–183
Piccolo Park, 120
Piedmont (neighborhood), 30–32,
   34–35
Piedmont Conservation District,
   33–35
Pipes, Wade, 57
Plank Road. See Canyon Road
Plummer, Oakes, 56
Plummer maples, 56
Portland aerial tram, 157
Portland Buddhist Church, 206–207
Portland Community College
   Cascade Campus, 32
Portland Country Club and Livestock
   Association, 74
Portland Department of
   Transportation, 23
Portland Development Commission,
   19, 35, 130, 132, 134, 165
Portland Garden Club, 175–177
Portland Golf Club, 217
Portland Hunt Club, 216–217
Portland Memorial, 146–147
Portland Public Schools enrollment,
   72–73
Portland Shipyard, 23
Portland Union Stockyards, 17, 20
Port of Portland, 22, 23, 25, 38, 137
Poulsen mansion, 150–151

Povey, John, 56
Povey Brothers Art Glass Works, 56,
    107, 147, 211, 272
Powell, Michael, 205–206
Powell, Walter, 205–206
Powell's City of Books, 203,
    205–206
produce markets, 133, 135
Propstra Square, 288

Quigley murals, 58
Quonset hut, 48–49

rail lines, 17, 64, 73, 100–101, 117,
    130, 142, 160, 202, 216, 219,
    227–229, 244–245, 251–252,
    267–268
rail spur lines, 202–203, 208–210
rail yards, 37–38, 47, 142–143,
    202–204, 207–208, 211
Raleigh Hills (neighborhood),
    220–222
REACH Community Development,
    89
redlining, 47, 57–58
redwood, dawn, 218
residential park neighborhoods, 100,
    251, 257–258
Richmond (neighborhood), 122
Riley, Earl, 167
RiverPlace, 165
River Renaissance, 16
River Road, 260
rivers as transportation routes, 186,
    250, 255, 260, 268
Rogers, George (Jorge Rodrigues),
    252–253
Rogers Park, 245–246
Roos, Roy, 55

Rose City Cemetery, 79
Rose City Golf Course, 74–75
Rose City Park (neighborhood),
    70–79, 82
Rose City Park Club, 76
Rosemont Court, 35
Roseway (neighborhood), 75–76
Ross Island, 143, 146, 156
Ross Island Bridge, 143, 150–151,
    156
Rummer homes, 217–218, 231–232

Sacred Heart Parish, 143–144
Saint Helens Hall, 177
Saint James Catholic Church, 287
Saint Mary's Academy, 164–165
Saint Patrick Catholic Church, 211
Saint Philip Neri Catholic Church,
    117–120
Saint Stanislaus Church, 36
SakéOne, 238, 244
Sanderson, Parker, 58
Sandy Boulevard, 76–77, 81
Save Our Elms, 115
Scandinavian immigrants, 189, 194
Schacht, Emil, 67, 179
Schmick, Doug, 221
Scholls Ferry Road, 219
Scott, Harvey, 240
Sellwood (neighborhood). See
    Sellwood-Moreland (neighbor-
    hood)
Sellwood-Moreland (neighborhood),
    144–148
sequoia, giant, 240, 245
sewage treatment, 27, 137
Sexton Mountain, 231, 233
shipbuilding, 23, 87, 186
Short, Amos, 287

Short, Esther, 287–288
Singer Creek, 267
Skidmore, Owings, and Merrill, 164
Slabtown, 210–211
South Auditorium Urban Renewal
    Area, 154, 161–165
Southeast Asian Vicariate, 78
South Portland, 152–169
South Portland Historic District,
    152–160, 167–169
South Waterfront (neighborhood),
    164
South Waterfront Park, 154, 166
Spring Break Quake, 242
Star of Oregon, 23
Steel Bridge, 130, 157
Stephens, James, 96, 114–115, 125,
    128–129
Stevens-Crawford Heritage House,
    264, 272
Storrs, John, 176
streetcar lines, 47, 119, 120, 124,
    167, 194
Strong, Isabelle Watts, 227
Sucker Creek. *See* Oswego Creek
Sucker Lake. *See* Oswego Lake
Sullivan, Timothy, 64
Sullivan's Gulch (neighborhood),
    63–66
Sullivan's Gulch Neighborhood
    Association, 63, 66
Sullivan's Gulch Trail, 64
Sundeleaf, Richard, 33, 90–91, 209,
    259
Sunnyside (neighborhood), 106–108,
    122–123
Swan Island, 14–15, 22–27
Swan Island Airport, 23
Swan Island Industrial Park, 23–24

Swan Island Lagoon, 22, 24
Swan Island Pump Station, 27
Swift and Company, 17

Taliesen Park, 232
Tanner Creek, 175–176, 182, 212
Tanner Springs Park, 212
Temple Beth Israel, 108, 159, 195,
    198
Tenino sandstone, 123, 132
Thomas Hacker and Associates, 234
Tibbetts, Gideon, 142
Tobey, Willard, 123, 272
Town Club, 181
tram. *See* Portland aerial tram
Trenkmann townhomes, 189
Trinity Episcopal Cathedral,
    198–199
Troutdale, 205
Troutdale Formation, 265
Troy Laundry, 128
Tualatin Mountains. *See* West Hills
Tualatin River, 227, 244, 255–256
Tualatin Valley agriculture, 227, 228,
    245, 255
Tualatin Valley Highway, 229
21st Avenue (NW), 194–195
23rd Avenue (NW), 196–197

Union Station, 55, 186, 202–205,
    208
University of Portland, 22, 40
University Park (neighborhood), 22
Uptown Village, 278, 286
urban renewal area. *See* Central
    Eastside Urban Renewal Area,
    Interstate Corridor Urban Renewal
    Area, South Auditorium Urban
    Renewal Area

Vancouver, 276–289

Vancouver Barracks, 281–282

Vancouver Farmers Market, 278, 287

Vancouver National Historic Reserve Trust, 281–282

Vancouver Sculpture Garden, 284

Vanport, 20, 47, 57

vault lights, 130, 212

Vera Katz Eastbank Esplanade, 135–138

Vernon (neighborhood), 46–49

Vietnamese immigration, 74

Villa Saint Rose. See Rosemont Court

Vista Brook Park, 222

Volunteers of America, 129–133

Washington High School, 89–90

Washington Park, 176, 178–179

Waterboard Park, 265, 274

Waterfront Park. See Governor Tom McCall Waterfront Park

Waud Bluff Trail, 16, 22, 24

Wegman, William, 205

Wenner, Paul, 122

West Hills, 174

Westmoreland (neighborhood). See Sellwood-Moreland (neighborhood)

Westmoreland Park, 147

Whidden and Lewis, 66–67, 156, 174, 177, 180, 191–193

Whitehouse, Morris, 119

white oak, Oregon, 22, 229

Wilcox, Theodore B., 72, 180–181, 196

Willamette Falls, 265–266, 269–272

Willamette Falls Locks, 264, 268–269

Willamette Greenway Trail, 25–27

Willamette River seawall, 136, 138

Willamette Shore Trolley, 248

William Temple House, 198

Willingham, William, 11

wineries of Washington County, 238

Winterhaven School, 148

Wood, Charles Erskine Scott, 174–177

Wood, Erskine, 174–175

Wood, Nanny, 175–177

Woodmen of the World, 133

Works Progress Administration art, 58

world's fair. See Lewis and Clark Exposition

World War II, population growth following, 87, 186

WPA art. See Works Progress Administration art

Zehntbauer, Roy and John, 91

Zell, Adelle, 89

Zidell, Sam, 160

ABOUT THE AUTHOR

Infected with the acquisitive fever of the 1980s, Laura O. Foster earned a finance degree and became a banker. In an Evan-Picone suit and tidy pumps, she loaned money to manufacturers of bolts and screws, woven labels, and architectural millwork. Her clients' entrepreneurial spirit soon overwhelmed her desire to have a personal secretary and corner office, so she quit banking to study ornamental horticulture. That rudderless foray into a life of backbreaking work resulted in a good knowledge of the Latin names of street trees and not much else. But after moving to Portland in 1989, Foster abandoned her suits and gardening gloves for a topic of inexhaustible charm and interest: Portland itself, with its geologic stories, hidden staircases, four-mountain vistas, and thriving streetcar neighborhoods. With a city so rich in natural beauty, history, and architectural treasures, she feels as if her books write themselves.